INTRODUCTION TO THE SEMITIC LANGUAGES

Gotthelf Bergsträsser

GOTTHELF BERGSTRÄSSER

INTRODUCTION TO THE SEMITIC LANGUAGES

Text Specimens
and Grammatical Sketches

Translated with Notes and Bibliography
and an Appendix on the Scripts
by Peter T. Daniels

WINONA LAKE, INDIANA
EISENBRAUNS

This translation of *Einführung in die semitischen Sprachen* produced with the permission of Max Hueber Verlag, Ismaning/München, © 1928 Max Hueber Verlag München, 3rd printing, 1977.

Library of Congress Cataloging in Publication Data

Bergsträsser, Gotthelf, 1886-1933.
Introduction to the Semitic Languages.
1. Semitic languages. I. Daniels, Peter T. II. Title.
PJ3021.B413 1982 492 82-11588
ISBN 0-931464-10-2 (paper)
ISBN 0-931464-17-x (cloth)

to H. Ritter
in true friendship

G.B.

in memory of my grandmother
Bessie Wiener (1891-1979)

P.T.D.

Contents

§ 4 Aramaic

§ 5 South Arabic — Ethiopic

List of Tables

Analytic Table of Contents

Translator's Preface

Gotthelf Bergsträsser (1886-1933) was one of the great Semitic linguists and philologists. This small volume encapsulates his learning, and every page yields concise statements of remarkable insight. He intended the book for elementary classes in Semitic linguistics, but only one familiar with the material can begin to appreciate the achievement in these brief chapters.

A translation seemed called for for several reasons: It is generally agreed that Bergsträsser's *Einführung* has not been superseded, and is unlikely to be. In more than half a century, no similar work has appeared, either a chrestomathy or a succinct characterization of each of the major Semitic languages, that can be used in an introductory class in Semitic linguistics. The historical approach, moreover, contrasts nicely with the descriptive orientation of □1.11 but, in America at least, the decline of foreign language teaching (or, rather, learning) means that the book is inaccessible to most of the undergraduates, seminarians, and beginning graduate students who would benefit from it most; an English version seemed imperative. The specialist, too, may find it convenient to refer to this volume.

Bergsträsser supplied no bibliography. This lacuna has been filled with lists of books and articles that should be helpful to the student beginning the study of Semitic linguistics; it is meant to include all the standard reference grammars, and the more important articles on individual topics. References to the bibliography entries throughout the notes are by classification number preceded by the box □.

Section numbering and titles have been supplied, to facilitate reference and comparison; the bibliography entries are keyed to the same numbering system.

Where possible, the original orthography of the text specimens has been provided, in order to offer some familiarity with and practice in reading Semitic texts in their ordinary guise. An appendix on the scripts is therefore added. For convenience, abbreviated paradigms from the literary languages are included.

The notes are intended to supplement or clarify Bergsträsser's remarks; nothing in the text besides typographical errors has been intentionally altered without notice. The text specimens have occasionally been rerendered in the light of newer scholarship; but whenever an option seemed possible, Bergsträsser's interpretation, of course, has been followed. The author's notes are numbered serially through a chapter, the translator's are signified by letters. All editorial materials are found in the left margin (or column) of the page.

The question naturally arose whether to include samples and discussion of the great Semitic literary language discovered after the book was written, Ugaritic. It was, happily, decided in advance, since the vowels of that language are only partially transmitted and Bergsträsser treats only fully vocalized dialects. Ugaritic, as well as the other unvocalized dialects (Phoenician, Epigraphic South Arabic) and the problematic Amorite and Eblite, however, are included in the notes and bibliography.

It is a great pleasure to acknowledge the assistance of my teachers at the University of Chicago, who have read and commented on the appropriate chapters: Gene B. Gragg (chapters 1, 2, and 5), who is in no small part responsible for this project, whose enthusiasm for it was most encouraging, and who has also made numerous improvements in the clarity of the whole book; I. J. Gelb (chapter 1); Erica Reiner (chapter 2); Dennis G. Pardee (chapter 3); Stephen A. Kaufman (now at Hebrew Union, Cincinnati, chapter 4); and Carolyn G. Killean (chapter 6). My colleague Dr. Robert D. Hoberman (now at Stony Brook) has done the same for Chapter 4/2/2, and reviewed the Modern Hebrew specimen. Professors Fazlur Rahman and Walter Farber (Chicago), Johannes Renger (Berlin), and Richard Steiner (Yeshiva), and Dr. Wilfred van Soldt (Amsterdam) have also contributed useful suggestions. Dr. Jeremy Black is responsible for countless stylistic felicities; he also took on the responsibility of bringing the Akkadian transcriptions and transliterations into line with modern practice, and he drew the cuneiform signs for the first part of Table 12 and prepared the list of values in its second part. Professor Dietz Otto Edzard, of Bergsträsser's own University of Munich, was kind enough to advise me, during his stay at the Oriental Institute, on numerous matters of German style as well as on the content of the book. Professor Anton Spitaler, Professor Emeritus at Munich, has graciously communicated the alterations presented during the author's classroom lectures in 1929, as well as certain corrections of his own; they have been incorporated silently. I am particularly pleased to be able to point out this link with the author himself; I am most grateful to all these scholars for the numerous improvements they have introduced into my translation and annotations. I now understand writers' frequent claims that their books would have been better if they had followed more of the advice they solicited — that is certainly true in this case.

Especial thanks go, too, to the staff of Eisenbrauns, named in the Colophon, who gallantly took on the job even though the design was to prove to be among the most difficult, not only in their short history, but in the field generally. The skill with which they have catered to the eccentricities of the designer is apparent on every page.

Peter T. Daniels
Chicago, 1981

Foreword

For some years it has been my practice from time to time to offer a course of lectures, "Introduction to the Semitic Languages and Literatures," in which, besides sketching the history of the more important Semitic languages and their literatures, I clearly display the languages themselves in brief specimens. After the last presentation of this course the publisher suggested to me that I offer its material in book form. I comply with this request gladly; I had been distributing to my auditors the most important grammatical facts and the texts in duplicated form, but had myself felt the need to be able to put a primer into their hands, and also hoped that it could be used by one or another of my colleagues for similar courses, or that it might help to a broader perspective those who know but a small part of the Semitic languages, by self-study; and, by using it, non-Semitic linguists could probably also achieve an insight into the Semitic linguistic stock.

In preparing this manual I have restricted myself to text specimens and grammatical sketches, since for the external history of the Semitic languages Nöldeke's article "Semitic Languages" (☐ 1:5) and the introduction to Brockelmann's presentation of the comparative grammar (☐ 1:3) can be consulted, and for histories of the literatures the references are well known. This restriction on the contents results in a Semitic counterpart — though a much more modest one — to Schleicher's *Indogermanische Chrestomathie*, including parts of his *Compendium*. Such a counterpart to the Indo-European chrestomathy, which came into my hands early, I sorely missed at the beginning of my concern with the Semitic languages; over the course of my teaching experience I have become more and more convinced that the learning of one or a few of the Semitic languages and the study of the comparative grammar of the whole requires an overview of the linguistic facts of all the important branches of the Semitic family, if the risk of a one-sided and distorted conception of the nature of the Semitic languages and their mutual relationship is to be avoided. To help fill this gap has been the goal of my introductory course, and is now also the goal of this book.

If I have reached this goal in any measure, if in particular I have succeeded in giving an accurate, up-to-date portrait of the languages that lie farther from my experience, I must thank the ready assistance of a large number of colleagues. My honored teacher A. Fischer (Leipzig) and J. J. Hess (Zürich) have increased the value of the book by contributing as yet unpublished texts from the Arabic dialects they know best;[1] Distinguished

1. The transcription of the texts has had to be considerably simplified in accordance with the character of the book.

Professor Fischer has also reviewed the entire Colloquial Arabic chapter. E. Littmann (Tübingen) has read the proofs of the section on Tigrē, H. Stumme (Leipzig) of the Maltese text specimen, and F. Hommel (Munich) of the word list. The most extensive cooperation was provided by E. Mittwoch (Berlin), who repeatedly checked the sections on Ge^{c}ez and Amharic, and by B. Landsberger (Leipzig), who raised the presentation of Akkadian to the level of his unrivaled knowledge of the language and who also advised me on many points in the chapter on proto-Semitic. I tender my warmest thanks to all these gentlemen; likewise to my student Dr. M. Plessner (Berlin), who read the proofs of the entire book.

On Chapter 1 all the rest are built; otherwise they are independent of each other, though here and there in one reference is made to another.[2] Within a chapter the treatment of the later forms presupposes in the reader a certain familiarity with the older, and so is on a somewhat less elementary level than the latter. The grammatical sketches chiefly utilize and explain the linguistic material in the text specimens, though they attempt to balance this principle against the determination that nothing of crucial importance remain entirely unmentioned. Qualifications — "mostly," "usually," etc., etc. — are not used sparingly; nevertheless, statements with no qualifications should not be taken as absolute: to simplify, one must coarsen. The notes to the texts are limited to the most sketchy key, principally to phonology and morphology; many merely repeat what is already said in the grammatical sketches.

A reader who is less familiar with the material might after studying Chapter 1 go next to Akkadian, Old Hebrew, and Classical Arabic.

Gotthelf Bergsträsser
Munich, February, 1928

2. The Aramaic chapter is a bit more closely connected to the Hebrew chapter.

Transcription

Consonants

A dot under a letter indicates emphatic pronunciation (§ 1.1.1). A line under or over a letter indicates pronunciation as a spirant, ˇ over a letter indicates *sh*-type sibilants, ′ after a consonant marks palatalization, and ° labialization.[a]

a. For typographical convenience and also on theoretical grounds, Bergsträsser's choice of symbols has been somewhat altered. Changes are generally in the direction of conformity with the International Phonetic Alphabet (IPA). The letters, *c*, *δ*, *γ*, *ŧ*, *ǰ*, *ɟ*, *θ*, and *y* and the signs ′ and ° (after consonants) replace Bergsträsser's *ţ*, *ḏ*, *ḡ*, *y*, *ǧ*, *ḑ*, *ṯ*, *j*, ʲ, and ʷ respectively. Cf. note d.

ᵓ glottal stop (§ 1.1.1)[3]

ᶜ glottal fricative (§ 1.1.1)

b

ḇ = *v*

c = *ts*

č = English *ch*

č̣ = emphatic *č*

d

ḍ emphatic *d* (see also § 6.1.1)

ḏ = *th* in *this*

ḏ̣ emphatic *ḏ* (see also § 6.1.1)

δ = *ḏ*

δ̣ = *ḏ̣*

f

g

ġ emphatic *g*

ḡ voiced velar fricative, Dutch *g*, French uvular *r*

γ = *ḡ*

h

ḥ hoarse, compressed *h* (§ 1.1.1)

ḫ = German *ch* in *auch*

ǰ = English *j*

ɟ = *dz*

k

ḵ = *ḫ*

l

ḷ = English dark *l*

m

n

p

ṗ = emphatic *p*

p̄ = *f*

q emphatic *k*

r = trilled *r*

ṛ emphatic *r*

s

ṣ emphatic *s*

š = *sh*

ś palatal *s*, lying between *s* and *š*, somewhat similar to German *ch* in *ich* (see also § 5/3.1.1)

t

ṭ emphatic *t*

ṯ = *th* in *thin*

ṯ̣ emphatic *ṯ*

θ = *ṯ*

θ̣ = *ṯ̣*

v

w

y

z

ẓ emphatic *z*

ž = *s* in *treasure*

3. For the sake of simplicity the letter is used only within words, but is to be supplied before an initial vowel, since with few exceptions in most of the Semitic languages initial vowels are introduced with a glottal stop ("strongly").

Vowels

In general, only the vowels *a e i o u* are distinguished; they also occur in diphthongs, in which each component retains its own pronunciation. In the specimens of living dialects *ä* and *å* (= IPA [æ] and [ɔ]) and *ɨ* are occasionally used. Only two quantities are distinguished, long (¯ on the letter) and short; on the use of the breve ˘ in Hebrew and Aramaic see § 3 n. 9. A dot · is occasionally used as the sign of a vocalic nucleus of uncertain quality.

Accent

ʹ indicates syllables with primary accent;[b] ˋ indicates secondary accent, and also the accented syllables of words that accentually depend on the following one (and occasionally of those that depend on the preceding one, in which case the two are joined by -). Further details of accent and the use of accent-marks are to be found under the individual languages. The hyphen - serves in Akkadian, South Arabic-Ethiopic, and Arabic for the analysis of single words into their components (most significantly to separate enclitic particles, in Amharic for deeper levels of analysis); but in Hebrew and Aramaic it joins words that form an accent unit.

Miscellaneous Signs

* not attested, but only hypothetical (reconstructed) form.

< developed from, > becomes.

In the translations of the text specimens parentheses enclose explanatory additions; in the transcribed examples within the grammatical sketches, sounds that may be absent; e.g., *ōz(i)* = *ōzi* or *ōz*.[c]

/ stands between interchangeable sounds; e.g., *ho/u* = *ho* or *hu*.

Alternative Transcriptions

For some sounds (besides the ones indicated in the table of consonants, *iyy* = approximately *īy*, *uww* = approximately *ūw*; *ayy* = approximately *aiy*, *aww* = approximately *auw*) two letters may be used; this has its explanation in the structure of the sound system and in the manner of transmission of the various languages.[d]

b. "Accent" here is a cover term for both stress (intensity, loudness) and pitch (tone) accent.

c. In the transcriptions, angle brackets enclose words supplied by Bergsträsser (i.e., not found in the texts designated in his bibliographic footnotes) and indications of ellipses he failed to mark.

d. This principle is here carried to a logical conclusion. In several passages it is clear that Bergsträsser understood (perhaps having independently devised) the phonemic principle (cf. § 3 note f and § 6/2 note b). To better exhibit the phonemic structures of the various languages, the diacritics _ (and ¯ over a consonant), ¨, °, and ʹ are meant to indicate positional variants, while different letters stand for contrasting segments within a language (thus *θ* is used in proto-Semitic, Arabic, etc., while the same phone occurring as a variant of *t* in Hebrew, Aramaic, etc. is written *ṯ*). Similarly, consonants that have undergone shifts are accorded new symbols: this is traditional in the use of *f* for Arabic (and not *p̄*); by extension *ǰ* is used for the affricate [dᶻ] rather than *ǧ*, which recalls the etymological *g*; etc.

Abbreviations of Language Names

Owing to the large number of authors and the variety of languages in which they have written on the Semitic languages, an annoying diversity of abbreviations is found, sometimes with no explanation ("Ar." is especially prone to abuse). While only a selection from this list occurs in this book, it is hoped that the following might become a standard set.

Ab	Arabic
Ag	Argobba
Ah	Amharic
Ak	Akkadian
Am	Aramaic
An	Ammonite
As	Assyrian
At	Amorite
Bd	Bedouin Arabic
Ba	Babylonian (recension)
BA	Biblical Aramaic
BH	Biblical Hebrew
Cl	Classical (Arabic)
Cn	Canaanite
Co	Colloquial (Arabic)
CPA	Christian Palestinian Aramaic
CS	Common Semitic
E	Ethiopic
EA	El-Amarna
Eb	Eblite
Ed	Edomite
Eg	Egyptian (Arabic)
ESA	Epigraphic South Arabic
GA	Galilean (Jewish Palestinian) Aramaic
Gu	Gurage
Gz	Ge^{c}ez
H	Hebrew
Hd	Ḥaḍramautian
Hr	Harari
Hs	Harsusi
IA	Imperial Aramaic
IH	Israeli Hebrew
Li	Liḥyanite
M^{c}	Ma^{c}lūla Aramaic
Ma	Maltese
Mb	Moabite
Md	Mandaic
MEA	Modern East Aramaic
Mh	Mehri
MH	Middle/Mishnaic Hebrew
Mn	Minean
Mo	Moroccan Arabic
MSA	Modern South Arabic
MStA	Modern Standard Arabic
MWA	Modern West Aramaic
N	New (Neo) . . .
Na	Nabatean
NWS	Northwest Semitic
O	Old . . .
Pa	Palmyran
PA	Palestinian Aramaic
Ph	Phoenician
PS	proto-Semitic
Pu	Punic
Qt	Qatabanian
S	Semitic
SA	South Arabic
Sb	Sabean
Sf	Safaitic
Sh	Ṣ́hauri
Si	proto-Sinaitic
Sm	Samaritan
Sq	Soqotri
SS	South Semitic
St	Standard . . .
Sy	Syriac
Ta	Tigrinya
TA	Talmudic Aramaic
Te	Tigrē
Th	Thamudic
Ti	Tiberian recension
Tu	Ṭūrōyō
Ug	Ugaritic
Ur	Urmia Aramaic

AA	Afro-Asiatic
B	Berber
Ch	Chadic
Cu	Cushitic
Om	Omotic

Introductory Note

This book deals with only a selection of Semitic languages. It omits all those that are known to us only or primarily from vowelless inscriptions, etc.; and of groups of closely related dialects it is limited to one or another characteristic member. There remain: Akkadian (Babylonian-Assyrian); Hebrew; Old Aramaic (represented by Biblical Aramaic, Syriac, and Mandaic) and Modern Aramaic (the dialects of Maᶜlūla and Urmia); South Arabic-Ethiopic, with Geᶜez as the representative of the old language and, for the living dialects, Tigrē and Amharic on the one side, and Mehri on the other; finally, North Arabic with Colloquial Arabic (the dialect of the Central Arabian Bedouins, Egyptian, Moroccan, and Maltese). — These languages may be grouped in various ways:[a] against Akkadian as East Semitic, all the others together form West Semitic;[b] on the other hand, against South Semitic (North[c] and South Arabic[d] and Ethiopic[e]) the other languages are grouped as North Semitic, and within this Hebrew and Aramaic belong closer together as Northwest Semitic.[f]

a. The *Stammbaum* ("family tree") model of the classification of Semitic may not be the most appropriate one. Rabin □0:2 suggests a *Wellentheorie* ("wave theory") that may better account for the various overlapping isoglosses observed particularly when the less well attested dialects are taken into consideration.

b. Eblite and Amorite are West Semitic, but they, with Old Akkadian, are treated in the notes to § 1 as being most relevant there.

c. There is some evidence that (North) Arabic might best not be classed with South Semitic, but rather belongs in a "Central Semitic" group having affinities with both Northwest and South Semitic. See Hetzron □0.6:1.

d. Epigraphic South Arabic is treated in the notes to § 5/3.

e. Geᶜez, Tigrē, and Tigrinya constitute North Ethiopic; the other Ethiopic languages are South Ethiopic.

f. Phoenician and a few minor languages join Hebrew in the Canaanite group; Ugaritic too is treated in the notes to § 3, as seeming most closely related to Canaanite.

Chapter 1

Proto-Semitic

§ 1/1.0

"Proto-Semitic" is not the name of a unified language that is clearly delimited temporally and spatially; it is a cover term for everything that we can infer to have temporally preceded the emergence of the individual Semitic languages (or at least the greater part thereof) as they are known to us. Since the various linguistic phenomena offer considerably different points of departure for deductions concerning their prehistory, and since furthermore we seek to understand the immediately recoverable proto-Semitic material as itself the outcome of earlier stages,[a] linguistic facts of very disparate age and diverse distribution all fall under the notion "proto-Semitic."

There is another way in which a description of proto-Semitic cannot have the same import and character as the description of a language transmitted in recorded form. In the first place the purported features of proto-Semitic are merely abstracted out of the individual Semitic languages, and hence are hypothetical;[b] and besides — and this is even more important — anything that chances not to be preserved in at least one Semitic language (and that will be no small amount) is simply not recoverable by us. Any description of proto-Semitic is thus necessarily uncertain and incomplete.[c] —

§ 1/1.1.1

Table 1 sets out the consonant inventory of proto-Semitic.[1] This table shows two noteworthy groups of sounds, the laryngeals and the emphatics. Of the laryngeals, only ʾ, the

1. The sound changes of the various languages are dealt with under the respective languages; for the purpose of an overview, the most divergent and most complicated of them, the vagaries of the dentals and sibilants, are collected in tabular form in Table 2.

a. The family of Afroasiatic languages includes Semitic, Egyptian, Cushitic, Omotic, Berber, and Chadic, and a proto-language is reconstructible to some extent as an "earlier stage" of Semitic. The former designation for this family, Hamito-Semitic, is going out of fashion because it erroneously suggests that the other five groups stand in closer relation among themselves than to Semitic.

b. Bergsträsser thus avoids the trap of claiming that proto-Semitic is a real language spoken by the ancestral Semites who must then have had a specific homeland that might be located, and makes possible the short step to saying that proto-Semitic represents underlying forms in the generative grammar sense.

c. It must be kept in mind that when Bergsträsser wrote, two of the four earliest Semitic languages were completely unknown (Eblite and Ugaritic), and two (Amorite and Old Akkadian*) were much less well understood than they are now. The reconstruction thus could not take into account all the data available today.

*A language different from Old Assyrian and Old Babylonian from which they cannot have developed directly.

Table 1

1. Laryngeals: ʾ ʿ h ḥ

2. Oral consonants:

a)

place of articulation		Stops Voiced	Stops Voiceless	Stops Voiceless Emphatic	Spirants Voiced	Spirants Voiced Emphatic	Spirants Voiceless	Spirants Voiceless Emphatic
place of articulation	labial	b	p					
place of articulation	dental	d	t	ṭ	δ	ẟ̣	θ	θ̣
place of articulation	velar	g	k	q	γ		ḫ	

b) sibilants: s-type   z   s   ṣ

       ś-type (palatal)   ś

       š-type   š

c) sonorants: r l

3. Nasal consonants: m n

4. Semivowels: w y

Table 2

d. The four earliest languages have phonemic θ and δ, but in all of them š includes ś, which is therefore a later West Semitic development, as are also θ and δ, and possibly γ (cf. § 3 note b). Gelb recommends a different set of symbols — ś for traditional š, š for θ, and ż for δ — to better reflect the subsequent realizations.

	non-emphatic voiced			non-emphatic voiceless					emphatic			
Proto-Semitic	d	δ	z	t	θ[d]	š	s	ś[d]	ṭ	θ̣[d]	ṣ	δ̣[d]
Akkadian	d	z		t	š		s	š	ṭ	ṣ		
Hebrew	d	z		t	š		s	ś	ṭ	ṣ		
Aramaic	d		z	t	š		s		ṭ	ṣ	ʿ	
South Arabic	d	δ	z	t	θ	ś	s	š	ṭ	θ̣	ṣ	δ̣
Ethiopic	d	z		t	s			š	ṭ	ṣ		ḍ
Arabic	d	δ	z	t	θ	s		š	ṭ	ẓ	ṣ	ḍ

simple glottal stop (or the corresponding glottal onset), as in the English exclamation *uh-oh*, and *h* are generally widespread in other languages; while ᶜ, a voiced growling sound, which encompasses numerous varieties from a stop to a continuant to a vowel pronounced with a growl, and *ḥ*, a strongly constricted, hoarse *h*, are elsewhere comparatively rare. The oldest pronunciation of the emphatics was probably with following release of the glottal stop, as is still the case in modern Ethiopic; this is widely replaced by a weakened pronunciation with velarization — broader contact between tongue and palate, particularly the soft palate. Laryngeal and emphatic phones lend Semitic a hard, rough sound, which is enhanced by a tendency toward energetic articulation of consonants.

In the table the asymmetry of the proto-Semitic consonantal system becomes apparent.[e] Only the laryngeals (and the nasals and semivowels) are fully represented. The dentals appear to lack only a voiced emphatic stop; but actually the two emphatic spirants as well are hardly fixed in their place in the system, and in the individual Semitic languages display a variability that must be ascribed to peculiarities of the original articulation. The velars exhibit only one emphatic, which tends in the individual languages to drift into places that had remained empty in the system — voiced stop, or even spirant; of the two spirants, at least *γ* is not entirely certified as proto-Semitic.[f] The series with the most gaps is the labials, though traces of emphatic stops may perhaps be found there. Among the sibilants, the position of emphatic voiced *s*-sound remains unfilled; one would also expect to find the voiced counterparts of the existing voiceless sounds *ś*[g] and *š*. On the whole, the system gives the impression that it is already the product of a long development with considerable disturbance.[h]

e. "Symmetry" of the proto-language must not be insisted upon too strongly. Aside from the fact that phonological systems tend to obey the principle of privative oppositions — whereby a less "marked" sound (a more ordinary one, requiring fewer features in its description) is likely to be paired with the absence of a more marked one — a totally symmetrical proto-system would leave it difficult to account for any subsequent changes: an ideal system would not have had to be altered.

f. *γ* is found in Ugaritic, and so is perhaps to be ascribed to proto-Semitic.

g. Steiner □ 1.1.1.3:3 has collected evidence that **ś* and its voiced counterpart **δ* were lateral fricatives.

h. But the Afroasiatic consonantal system has been reconstructed by Diakonoff □ 1:12 as essentially the same as the proto-Semitic one.

§ 1/1.1.2

There are three long vowels and three short ones *ā ī ū a i u*; but an older stage is still clearly recognizable, in which *i* and *u* were functionally equivalent as varying realizations of a reduced grade, and together were opposed to the vowel *a*, the single full short vowel.[i] Diphthongs as combinations of several vowels in one syllable are not found; *au* and *ai* do occur, but have the value vowel + consonantal *w* or *y*.

i. Such a two-short-vowel system is what Diakonoff reconstructs for Afroasiatic.

Already within proto-Semitic, some sound changes have taken place. ᵓ at the end of a syllable that begins with ᵓ disappears, with lengthening of the vowel; e.g., Ab *ākulu* 'I eat' < **ᵓaᵓkulu* (prefix *ᵓa* + root *ᵓkl*). After *ā*, *w* and *y* frequently become ᵓ; e.g., Ab *qāᵓilun* 'speaking' < *qāwilun* (from *qwl*). Adjacent to laryngeals, *i* and *u* are sometimes replaced by *a*; e.g., Ab *qaᶜ* 'fall' from *waqaᶜa* 'he fell,' where the loss of the first syllable indicates that the vowel of the imperative was originally *i* (see § 1/1.2.2.5). Assimilation of *n* to a following consonant under varying conditions is a feature common to North Semitic. —

§ 1/1.2.0

The complementary relationship between consonant and vowel is the signal characteristic of Semitic. The meaning of a root inheres exclusively in the consonants of the root; the vowels, along with consonant repetitions or lengthenings[j] and certain consonantal affixes, serve only to modify this root meaning through the formation of various nominal and verbal stems and their inflection. Each word is thus an individual representative of a formative pattern, either nominal or verbal. The pattern may be isolated by replacing the individual root consonants with general symbols, and that is how they are notated; Ab *qātilun* 'murderer' thus instantiates the nominal pattern C*ā*C*i*C*un* (C = consonant).[2] This system holds almost

j. This term is preferred to "doubling" and "gemination" because a long consonant does not last twice the duration of a short one, nor is the stop articulation of a long affricate repeated.

2. For practical use, the consonants of some paradigmatic root are usually used. The most common one, employed here, is *qtl*, except in Akkadian, where *prs* is preferred.

without limit in the realm of the verb and those nouns that stand in some relation to the verb; it does not pertain to the substantives proper, the primary nouns. Here an older state of affairs is clearly recognizable, in which the relation of consonant and vowel does not differ markedly from that in other languages, and in which the "root" is composed of both consonant and vowel in indivisible unity.

The unequal value of consonant and vowel is closely related to another prevailing trait of Semitic, triliterality — the fact that most consonantal roots (aside from pronouns and genuine particles) are composed of THREE consonants (radicals).[3] Many such roots can be identified as extensions of original biliterals. Traces of unaltered biconsonantal roots are found on the one hand in irregular, so-called weak verbs, and on the other in the primary nouns.

§ 1/1.2.0.2

Weak verbs are those that display shortening in their inflection as compared with triliteral (strong) verbs. In part these shortenings are secondary, chiefly the result of contractions, such as they undergo when one of the root consonants is a semivowel (or in some circumstances a laryngeal); but in part the shorter forms are the older, based directly on a root with no more than two consonants.[k] Their vowel (as well as the occasional doubling of the second consonant) determines the type of secondary extension to triliteral roots, chiefly to II *w* or *y* (i.e., with *w* or *y* as middle radical) and II geminate (with repetition of the second radical in the position of the third radical). Among the primary nouns some biliteral sub-

k. These statements constitute a compromise between the theory that all Semitic roots were originally biliteral with identifiable extensions with some semantic function, and the theory that all roots were triliteral with the ones involving the semivowels ᵓ *w y* becoming weak in inflection.

3. Groups of roots that are distinguished by sharing a particular type of radical (particularly the "weak" roots) are designated by the number of the radical and its distinguishing feature. So "I laryngeal" means roots whose first radical is a laryngeal; "II weak" roots are ones whose second radical is "weak," i.e., *w* or *y*; "II geminate" roots are those whose second radical is geminated or repeated, so that the last two radicals are the same; etc.

stantives have been retained, which judging by their meaning must belong to the oldest stratum of the language.[4]

The special relation between consonant and vowel has the result that consonant articulation is sharp and exact, with only a limited tendency toward assimilation to neighboring consonants;[l] the vowel articulation on the other hand is indefinite, the available range for it being very great and noticeable even in the long vowels. —

In pronoun, verb, and noun three numbers, singular, dual, and plural, are differentiated, and two genders, masculine and feminine, and these, in pronoun and verb, not merely in the third person but in the second as well. The dual is not so richly developed as the plural; in the noun it was from the first probably just a form for making pairwise-corresponding counterparts, pronoun and verb retain no trace of it in the first person at all, and no gender distinction is made in it in the second person.[m]

The personal pronouns of the first and second persons are: 'I' **anʾā*, 'thou' masculine **antā*, feminine **antī*; 'we' **niḥnū*, 'you' masculine **antumū*, feminine **antinnā*. — The third person personal pronoun is a determinative, which originally meant something like 'the same'; it is 'he' **hūʾa*, 'she' **šīʾa*,[n] masculine plural **humū*, feminine **šinnā* (reshaped after the second person). — The special treatment of the first and second persons versus the third recurs in the verb.

Besides the fully stressed forms just given, the personal pronouns also have enclitic forms, which on nouns (and prepositions) indicate the genitive, and on verbs and some particles the accusative; only the first person singular has different forms for the genitive and accusative. These pronominal suffixes are: 'my' *-*ya* and *-*ī*, 'me' *-*nī*; 'thy, thee'

4. There is even one monoliteral substantive: **pū* 'mouth.'

l. A further property of the consonantal root, identified by Landsberger □1.2.0:1 but statistically investigated only by Greenberg □1.2.0:2, is the incompatibility of root consonants. No triliteral root can contain more than one consonant from the same point of articulation (except II geminates). Greenberg's study is founded upon Arabic; Koskinen

§ 1/1.2.0.3

□3b.2.0:1 finds a similar principle operating in Hebrew. A preliminary investigation of the roots in Akkadian (Old Babylonian) suggests that a stronger principle operates in that language: no root may contain more than one consonant sharing any distinctive feature (place or manner of articulation, voicing).

m. It is now known that the dual was fully productive in Old Akkadian (and Old Assyrian).

§ 1/1.2.1.1

n. Not all authors accept the *h*/*š* distinction as germane to the gender distinction, preferring to ascribe it to dialectal variation within proto-Semitic or to dissimilation, perhaps of a consonant **s̱* (so Diakonoff). Cf. note v and § 5/3 note c.

masculine *-*kā*, feminine *-*kī*; 'his, him' *-*hū*, 'her' *-*šā*; 'our, us' *-*nā*; 'your, you' masculine *-*kumū*, feminine *-*kinnā*; 'their, them' masculine *-*humū*, feminine *-*šinnā*.

§ 1/1.2.1.2 No proto-Semitic forms for the demonstrative are known for sure, just elements that emerge quite diversely in the daughter languages: a deictic particle **hā*-, a stem *δ* + long vowel, also *l*, *θ* especially in adverbs, as well as (found in only some of the languages) *k* (for far deixis) and *n*.

There is no possessive pronoun of an adjectival character (the function of one is performed by the pronominal suffixes),[o] and likewise the demonstratives are not simply adjectives, but genuine substantives: when in construction with a substantive they can precede it, while adjectives must follow. Interrogatives and numbers are substantives as well; so is the expression of "allness": 'all men' is in Arabic *kullu n-nāsi* 'the totality of men' or *an-nāsu kulluhum* 'the men, their totality.' For many substantives, e.g., the names of materials, there are no corresponding adjectives; instead the substantive itself can occur with another substantive as appositive, genitive, or predicate, as in Ab *aθ-θaubu l-ḥarīru* 'the silken garment,' *θaubu ḥarīrin* (genitive) 'a silken garment,' *aθ-θaubu ḥarīrun* 'the garment is silk.' The Semitic languages do indeed have an ending, -*īy*- or -*āy*-, which derives adjectives from substantives; but it was used originally almost exclusively for forming place-of-origin indicators from place (or personal) names (Ab *nisbatun*, hence called nisbe endings): Ak *Yaudayyu* (As *Yaudayya*), Ab *Yahūdīyun* 'Jewish, Jew.' Also, where an adjective and a substantive are both available, it is often preferred to use the substantive (especially when it is an abstract) in the genitive rather than the related adjective: Ab *rağulu sauʾin* 'a bad man,' literally 'a man of badness'; cf. BA *kursē-malḵūṯēh* 'his royal throne,' literally 'the throne of his kingship.'

o. Though Old Akkadian and Old Assyrian had one; cf. § 2 note e.

In the interrogative pronoun a division between persons and things replaces the distinction between masculine and feminine. The stem is *m* + long vowel; the apportionment of forms between persons and things is different in the different languages. The interrogative pronoun can be strengthened with *-n*; the most widespread of these forms is **mān*, which usually means 'who?.' Beside the purely substantival interrogative pronouns 'who?,' 'what?,' many of the languages have an adjectival 'which?' with the stem *aiy-* (derived from an interrogative particle **ai* 'where?,' etc.), which, however, was probably also originally a substantive and in that guise especially is conjoined with an explicative or partitive genitive, as in Ab *aiyu šaiʾin* 'which thing?,' literally 'what of the thing?,' or *aiyuhum* 'which of them?.' — The interrogatives serve more generally as indefinites, especially *mā*, which is a particle of multitudinous uses (principally generalizing and topicalizing).

No proto-Semitic relative pronoun can be reconstructed,[p] but the relative CLAUSE is proto-Semitic, as the similarity of its formation in the various languages proves. It need not necessarily be introduced by a pronoun; but already in proto-Semitic the possibility must have existed either of topicalizing with a demonstrative the substantive to which it belonged, or of referring with an interrogative pronoun to an underlying concept of a general and indefinite nature. To this last possibility the interrogatives owe their use as generalized relatives, a function which any of them can also serve (e.g., 'who?' also 'who,' 'whoever,' 'each one that,' also plural 'all those who'). As opposed to what we are familiar with, no relative pronoun referring to its head can be a constituent of the relative clause, which must instead be an independent clause. The head is as a rule a constituent of this clause only in the form of a

p. Cf. OAk *šu ši ša*, a declined relative pronoun.

pronominal suffix; e.g., Ab *kitābun anzalnāhu* 'a book — we have sent IT away' = 'a book THAT we have sent away.' After a first or second person, therefore, the relative clause must be in the same person; e.g., Sy *allāhā att danḥett men šmayyā* 'you are God, this — you have come down from heaven' = 'who has come down from heaven.' With or without relative pronoun, the relative clause can be substantival (without head substantive): 'that which,' 'one who,' 'who,' etc.; e.g., BA *lŠšbṣr šmeh* 'to one whose name is Sheshbazzar.' —

§ 1/1.2 The opposition between noun and verb differs notably from that in most other languages. On one side stands a relatively small number of what are strictly substantives proper, not further analyzable, originally not obeying the rule of a consonantal root, which name things (kinship terms, animals, body parts, tools, etc.); on the other side is the large group of nominal-verbal roots, which designate attributes, states, or actions. The gulf between the two kinds of root is bridged only at a later stage through the formation of denominal verb stems on the one hand and deverbal names of things (e.g., nouns of instrument, **miptāḥ* 'key' from *ptḥ* 'open'). The distinguishable stems (themes) in which the nominal-verbal roots are embodied were early organized into a finely graded system of semantic categories; on the nominal side for example adjective, verbal adjective, noun of agent, noun of action, etc., etc., all in various subclasses; on the verbal side objective modes of action (*Aktionsarten*):[q] punctual (momentaneous), ingressive, terminative, durative-fientive,[r] stative, etc., etc. It is for the formal differentiation of these semantic categories that — however it may have come about — the singular behavior of the vowels in Semitic appears to have evolved: those stems belonging to the same group preserve the same structure, i.e., the same vocalism.

q. This use of the term *Aktionsart* (translated "mode of action" or simply "mode") is idiosyncratic; it usually refers to what Bergsträsser calls "aspect," but there seem to be as many usages of the term as there are authors using it. Cf. note ad.

r. "Fientive" is a term coined by Landsberger (who is responsible for much of this discussion of the verbal system), from the Latin *fiens* "becoming," that he never defined rigorously; it came to be used, if at all, to designate both verbs that are non-stative in inherent meaning, and inflections of a verb that are not permansive (stative) in form.

As in the nominal sphere, the possible verb stem formations are limited by the root meaning (e.g., naturally no noun of agent is formed from a root that designates an attribute, like 'white'); this also holds (originally) for the verbal category of mode of action: most verbs belong by virtue of their meaning to a particular mode, and can only form stems in another in an extended or transferred sense. Thus, 'go away' is punctual-ingressive, 'come' is punctual-terminative, 'run' durative-fientive, 'sleep' stative. Originally, therefore, most verbs probably belonged to a single, particular vocalization type.[s] The clearest traces left by this stage of development are in the

§ 1/1.2.2

s. This extremely concise presentation of Bergsträsser's view of the development of the Semitic verbal system (one of the most hotly disputed questions in Semitic linguistics) may be supplemented by the fuller one from □3b:6v2§3 (transcription altered to conform with that adopted here):

The oldest Semitic verb forms are the imperative and the imperfect, which has the same stem; to be exact, in the suffixless forms it ends with a consonant (short imperfect, H jussive and imperfect consecutive = Ab apocopate = Ak preterite). Being based on the imperative, this short imperfect had chiefly a jussive meaning; next, as the only declarative verb form at the outset, there fell to it the expression of the past (past action), since the nominal clause was available to express the present.

The polysemy of the short imperfect has been retained not only in Hebrew (jussive and imperfect consecutive), but also in Akkadian (precative and preterite) and to some extent in Arabic (jussive and negation of the past after *lam*). The antiquity of the form itself is apparent, among other reasons, from its wide distribution in the Hamitic languages.

The vocalization of these stems, in so far as those that were not biliteral (monovocalic) are concerned, could vary considerably; but they were unified early owing to various factors.

In addition, the possibility likewise existed from an early date of attaching pronominal suffixes to nouns, e.g., Ak *šarr-ākū* 'I am king.' By this means there was formed from the adjectival forms *qatil-* and *qatul-*[5] (biliteral **mit-*, **buš-*) a suffix conjugation, the Akkadian permansive and West Semitic neutral *i-* and *u*-perfect.[6] In the third person only gender and number indicators served as suffixes; in the first and second persons, on the other hand, the personal pronouns without the initial *an-* were used, i.e., **-akū* > *-ākū, -tā -tī, -nā, -tumū -tinnā*. Subsequently in Akkadian the *-ā-* of the first person singular was introduced into the other forms, while in West Semitic by analogy with these forms it fell away from the first person singular also.

Beside *qati/ul-* (and corresponding biliterals with *i/u*), neutral perfects *qatal-* (or biliterals with *a*) will also have been present; but, probably because of their limited number, they exerted no influence on subsequent developments.

The meaning of this suffix conjugation was by its nature chiefly that of a general present. Its great age is evidenced not only by the correspondences in the Semitic languages, but also by its occurrence in Egyptian and Berber in the same meaning.

A present-future split off from the preterite (jussive), and in different ways in East and West Semitic: while in Akkadian an accented *á* was inserted after the first radical — *ipqid* : *ipáqid* — in West Semitic a final vowel was attached — *yaqtul* : *yaqtulu* or *yaqtula*.

Since a suffixed *-u* also occurs in Akkadian (as subordination marker), perhaps the split itself is already proto-Semitic, and only the differention of the *u-* and *a*-forms and the Akkadian *á*-infixing are later. The fact that suffixed or infixed vowels are common as tense markers in Hamitic would also support this, as would the fact that there are similarities in usage between the Akkadian present and the West Semitic imperfect.

The relation between the Ethiopian indicative *yeqátel* (opposed to the subjunctive *yeqtel*) and the Akkadian present is unclear.

(Continued in note ac).

5. It is thus presupposed that the development of the permansive-perfect as verb form with specific vowel relations, despite the great age of the suffix conjugation per se, first occurs at a time when the formative value of the vocalism already prevailed.

6. Therefore I cannot accept the widely advocated idea that the permansive is identical with the full range of the West Semitic perfect; still less, of course, the opposite, first formulated by Barth and now newly advocated by Brockelmann and Bauer, that it is rather the Akkadian present that corresponds to the West Semitic perfect.

system of biliteral verbs, especially as it is found in Akkadian. Here, e.g., biliteral verbs with middle *ū*, if they are intransitive, form an ingressive-mode group, which particularly denotes the sudden reversal of a normal state into the opposite (*mūt* 'die,' *nūḫ* 'fall asleep,' *nūš* 'set in motion'); if they are transitive, they form a durative-terminative group (*ṣūd* 'hunt down a wild animal,' *dūk* 'strike dead').[t]

t. This analysis is presented in Landsberger □2/1.0:1,362. His suggestion □1.2.0:1 that roots must differ by at least two quanta — both a consonant and an ablaut pattern — though, does not seem supported by the collected data now available.

From these stems are derived ones that indicate verbwise an event (especially an action), and probably also some that indicate a state; this is done by means of prefixes. The forms of these derivations are already unified verbal forms at the earliest reconstructible stage, and their pronominal elements can no longer lead a separate existence; the meaning of this inflection is completely dependent on the mode of the stem; there is no tense difference. The stems that according to their kind of meaning are purely nominal, especially those that express an attribute, and to a great extent those that express a state, can serve as predicates of nominal clauses; in contrast to the verbal expression of an event, they express static existence. Out of such nominal clauses a second, non-genuine verbal inflection has developed, in which the postposed pronouns of the first and second persons, in hardly altered form, are fused with the stem into a word.

The various Semitic languages, particularly Akkadian as against West Semitic, have gone their own ways in gathering together the various prefixing- and suffixing-inflected themes into unified paradigms, in which "tense"-stems stand in specific ablaut relations to each other and in whose forms any verb can be inflected more or less without exception. They have also diverged regarding the disposition of the objective mode-differences for expressing the subjective time-stages past, present, and future. It is Common Semitic for the imperative to have the punctual stem-form: a command "set yourself in motion" is more obvious and more natural than a command "go for an hour-long walk." For non-punctual commands Semitic uses declarative forms of durative character. Declarative forms are also used for the expression of prohibitions; the imperative itself cannot be negated.

The imperative has no inflection apart from gender and number indication. The indication of gender and number is accomplished by endings that derive from pronouns: feminine singular *-*ī*, masculine plural *-*ū*, and feminine plural *-*nā*.[7] The prefix conjugation uses the same endings in the second person, and in the third person plural, while the first person remains without ending; the prefixes are *ᵓ- for the first person singular, **n*- for the first person plural, **t*- for the second person and for the third person feminine singular, and **y*- for the third person except feminine singular. The vowel of the prefixes varies; for the intensive and causative stems it is *u*.

§ 1/1.2.2.1

u. Gelb □ 1/2.2.2.1.2:1 suggests, on Old Akkadian and Amorite evidence, that the *-a* of the third person masculine singular goes back to a pronominal *-u*, originally copulative, that became a predicative marker on substantives and adjectives. It passed thence to stative verbs and then fientive verbs, and it became *-a* under the influence of the adverbal accusative marker. The ultimately pronominal origin is parallel to that which Bergsträsser suggests for the first and second persons.

The endings of the suffix conjugation are in the third person merely nominal gender and number markers,[u] namely feminine singular *-*at*, masculine plural *-*ū*, feminine plural *-*ā*. The suffixes of the first and second persons are the second parts of the personal pronouns: 'we' *-*nū*; 'thou' masculine *-*tā*, feminine *-*tī*; 'you' masculine *-*tumū*, feminine *-*tinnā*. Only for 'I' is there a divergent element *-*ākū*.[8]

The verb forms as a whole, both prefix and suffix conjugations, are of a purely predicative and not a possessive character: the pronominal elements contained in them, insofar as they are not recognizable immediately as subject pronouns, have no relation whatsoever with the possessive suffixes.

7. This is probably older than the *-ā* which appears in various of the languages in the feminine plural — in Akkadian in the masculine as well — of the imperative (but not of the prefix conjugation).

8. This *ā* seems to have spread to the other suffixes in Akkadian, while in the other languages it was instead abandoned under their influence.

§ 1/1.2.2.2 The means of formation of derived verb stems are chiefly the lengthening of the second radical for strengthening (intensive stem), and repetition, especially of the third radical; also the prefixes *ś* and *h* (ʾ) in causative, *n* in reflexive-passive, and *t* in reflexive-reciprocal meaning. These and other formative materials are used from earliest times with great versatility and combine freely with each other. As established types already found in proto-Semitic we may list, besides the unaltered basic stem, an *n*- and a *t*-stem for it, and also an *ś*-causative and an *h*- (ʾ-)causative (the contrast between which in proto-Semitic is not yet completely understood),[v] as well as a *t*-reflexive of the *ś*-causative, and finally an intensive with a *t*-reflexive.[w] The extraordinary multiplicity of modifications that the root meanings undergo in verb stem formation are only very inadequately suggested by categories like reflexive, etc.[x] The TENSE stem formation results from vowel alternation (ablaut), with regard to which the various languages diverge from each other. Already in proto-Semitic the vowel of an open first stem syllable disappears after a prefix; thus[y] the Akkadian basic stem *taprus*, Arabic *n*-reflexive *tanqatilu*, Akkadian *t*-reflexive *taptaras* (with metathesis), causative *tušapris*, and its reflexive *tuštapris* (with the same vowel loss again between the two stem-prefixes); contrast intensive *tuparris*, or its *t*-reflexive in Arabic *tataqattalu*. This phenomenon indicates that the prefixes (or the last of them) were accented. — In proto-Semitic the metathesis of the first radical and the *t*-prefix, by which it becomes an infix, occurs only with an initial sibilant, and is extended to other initial radicals only in the individual languages.

The stem patterns of the verbal nouns appear to have not yet been fixed in proto-Semitic, since they differ markedly in the different languages. Only the nominal form *qātilu* for the

v. The two forms do not contrast in any Semitic language; a postulated development *š* > *h* > ʾ seems preferable. See Bravmann □ 1.2.2.4.2:2 and note n.

w. The grammatical tradition for each language has assigned names to the different stems. These names and the cross-language correspondences are given in Table 3.

x. Henceforth these names are used for the formal categories they are attached to, and not for their syntactic or semantic functions.

y. Each of these examples has the second person prefix *ta*-.

participle of the basic stem (of verbs clearly expressing an action) and the use of *mu-* as participle prefix of the derived stems were already established in proto-Semitic. — The verbal nouns retain verbal government; infinitive and participle — in Akkadian only the infinitive — can under certain circumstances have an object accusative, and the infinitive a subject nominative as well.

§ 1/1.2.2.5 Among the classes of weak verbs, the II weak and II geminate verbs can be recognized as originally biliteral; they

---

Table 3

	Akkadian		Hebrew	Aramaic	Ethiopic		Arabic
basic	G (B)	I	qal, pa^{c}al	peal	I,1	A	Ist Form
t-reflexive	Gt	I/2		ethpeel	III,1	A/3	VIIIth Form
	Gtn	I/3					
passive			qal passive				
intensive	D	II	piel	pael	I,2	B	IInd Form
intensive-reflexive	Dt	II/2	hitpael	ethpaal	III,2	B/3	Vth Form
	Dtn	II/3					
intensive-passive			pual				
causative	Š	III	hifil	aphel	II,1	/2	IVth Form
causative-reflexive	Št	III/2		ettaphal	IV,1	/4	Xth Form
	Štn	III/3					
causative-passive				hofal			
n-reflexive	N	IV	nifal				VIIth Form
	Ntn	IV/3					
goal					I,3	C	IIIrd Form
goal-reflexive					III,3	C/3	VIth Form

The letter-system in the first Akkadian column (G = Ground-stem, [originally German *Grundstamm*], B = Basic Stem, D = Doubling Stem) can conveniently be used to describe the forms in the other languages, adding L (= Lengthening), R (= Reduplicating), and p (= internal passive) (see Appendix A).

have been adapted only partially to the forms of the triliteral patterns, to the extent that according to their vowel and the nature of their second consonant they either inserted a *w* or *y* as their middle radical or else repeated the second consonant as a third radical. Thus the II *w* group took on words with middle *a* along with those with *u*. Already in proto-Semitic the inflection of the I *w* verbs exhibits the alternation between biliteral forms — imperative **θib* (Ak *šib*, H *šeḇ*, Am *teḇ*) 'sit,' prefix conjugation **yaθib* (*ūšib*, *yēšeḇ*, *yetteḇ*), verbal noun **θibtu*[z] (*šubtu*, *šéḇeṯ*, *teḇtā*) — and triliteral ones (from **wθb*). —

z. With feminine ending — but note Eb *ṣiʾum* (**wṣʾ*) and *diʿum* (**ydʿ*), masculine; cf. also At *daʿum*, *daʿatum*.

§ 1/1.2.3 Nominal stem formation, except for the verbal nouns proper, is less normalized than verb stem formation; in proto-Semitic it must have still been in flux. Among nominal forms without affixes, the adjectives *qatīl* and *qatūl* (often derived from verbs and then commonly passive) and the intensive adjectives (customary activity, professional occupation) *qattal qattāl* stand out. The prefixes are by and large the same as on the verb; the most widespread is **ma-* **mi-*, which serves chiefly to form nouns of place and time and of instrument. The most important old suffix is the above-mentioned nisbe-ending **-īy-* and **-āy-*. Noun compounding is as rare as verb compounding, at least insofar as concerns distinct stems or words; roots (particularly ones with more than three consonants) may have occasionally developed from the compounding of two roots.

The oldest evidence of the predicative inflection of nouns is found in the suffix-forms of verbs, and in fact two stages of development are represented: an older one in the first and second persons, in which the nominal predicate is really without ending; and a younger one in the third person, which uses gender and number endings, but no case indication. Likewise, the noun before genitive, the so-called construct state, is inflected just like this predicative noun. Outside of the genitive construction (i.e., in the so-called absolute state), the non-predicative noun distinguishes three cases, a nominative with *-*u* as subject case, a genitive with *-*i* as adnominal case (all the prepositions govern the genitive as well), and an accusative with *-*a* as adverbal case in the broadest sense.[9] These endings are also attached to the feminine ending *-*at* (or just *-*t*). The dual and plural distinguish only two cases, a nominative and an oblique case; to the masculine nominative ending *-*ū* corresponds the oblique ending *-*ī*; the feminine plural has in the absolute state the endings nominative *-*ātu*, genitive-accusative *-*āti*. Besides these plural endings that are certainly proto-Semitic, a few others found in the individual languages probably go back to proto-Semitic time; the various endings had various uses. In addition, collectives of various kinds already played a great role in proto-Semitic. The use of the plural shows peculiarities, e.g., names of materials tend to be in the plural, as in Ak *šīpātu* 'wool.' — Also the feminine ending *-*at* *-*t* is one of several, which have clear differences in use. Furthermore there are groups of substantives that are feminine without having any feminine ending (the most important is that of the paired body parts, e.g., **yad* 'hand'). On the other hand, many masculines have the feminine ending. These phenomena as well as the opposition person : thing in the interrogatives show that Semitic once possessed a richer system of nominal classes.

The numbers except for 'one' and 'two' are substantives, which through 'ten' have two genders; 'twenty' is the dual

9. In a small group of biliteral (and monoliteral) substantives, namely the kinship terms **abū* 'father,' **aḫū* 'brother,' etc. as well as **pū* 'mouth,' the case vowels are long.

(plural) of 'ten,' 'thirty' through 'ninety' the plurals of 'three' through 'nine.' The numbers 'three' through 'ten' DIsagree in gender with their substantives so that a masculine substantive has a number in feminine form, and vice versa; traces of the same polarity in the use of the genders are, e.g., the Hebrew plurals *āḇōṯ* (feminine) of *āḇ* 'father,' against *nāšīm* (masculine) of *iššā* 'woman.' The counted substantive is often in the singular, and sometimes in the genitive but sometimes in the accusative; an explanatory accusative instead of an appositive in the same case is also to be found elsewhere than in the numeral syntax. Such a wealth of concord within the phrase has its parallel in the wealth of concord in the clause: an adverbal predicate nominal (introduced by a copula or otherwise occurring in a verbal clause, the so-called circumstantial clause) does not agree in case with the subject or the substantive of which it is predicated, but is in the accusative; a preceding (but not following) predicate, especially a verb, need correspond with the following subject neither in gender nor in number (it can be in the masculine singular); plurals are, for the purpose of concord, sometimes considered feminine singular. —

§ 1/1.3 The clause is to a large extent nominal; the predicative construction of nouns accords with the attributive-appositional. A verbal copula 'be' did not exist at all in early times. The third person personal pronoun serves in some circumstances as a copula: thus, e.g., Gz *weᵓetū-nī́ gèbra edawī́ka weᵓétū* 'he also the work of your hands he' = 'he too is the work of your hands'; and even after first or second person, e.g., BA *ănáḥnā himmō ᶜaḇḏṓhī* 'we they his servants' = 'we are his servants.' A special form of nominal clause is the compound clause, whose predicate is a complete clause that by some means resumes the subject; e.g., BA *baiṯā dnā saṯrēh* 'this house — he has torn it down' = 'he has torn down this house.' As the verb shows that the subject pronoun was prefixed in the purely verbal forms but suffixed in the originally nominal forms, the oldest word order of the verbal clause must have been subject-predicate, and of the nominal clause predicate-subject; later this was reversed, at least in the West Semitic languages. But the freedom always remains to alter the word order with a shift in topic. On other points firm rules have existed from of old: the adjectival and likewise the genitival attribute follow the substantive.

Beside the syndetic parataxis using **wa-* 'and,' **au* 'or,' etc., the possibility exists of asyndetic parataxis; in particular, a verb can stand in apposition to another, e.g., Sy *keṯbeṯ bᶜēṯ* 'I wrote, I asked' = 'I wrote, asking.' This construction is especially favored in imperatives, where a more general verb which principally incorporates the request-feature is specified by another more closely indicating the actual content of the request; e.g., BA *ĕzel aḥeṯ* 'go, put.'

Hypotaxis is just developing in proto-Semitic; headless subordinate clauses that represent a transitional phase from parataxis to hypotaxis prevail: in particular, besides the above-mentioned relative clauses without relative pronoun, object clauses and adverbial clauses (so-called circumstantial clauses, English 'while,' etc.). Subject to strict syntactic regulation, this type of headless subordinate clause has been preserved in the Semitic language with the most complicated sentence structure at its disposal, Arabic. The relative clause WITH relative pronoun also has, as shown above, clearly paratactic character.

§ 1/1.2.4 The following particles, among others, are proto-Semitic: a set composed of consonant and short vowel (so-called prefixes), including the conjunction **wa-* 'and' and the prepositions **la-* 'for, belonging to' (also dative particle), **bi-* 'in, with, by,' as well as the still substantive-like **ka* 'like';[aa] also the negation *l* that occurs in various ablaut forms (*lā al ul*), the preposition *min* 'from, out of,' and several prepositions that share the ending *-ai*, especially **ᶜalai* 'on,' **ilai* 'to.' *min* after an adjective compares; e.g., H *gāḇṓah mikkol-hāᶜām* 'high from the totality of the people' = 'greater than all people.' All the prepositions are syntactically substantives; they can therefore also be combined with each other, whereby the first effectively is in the accusative, the second in the genitive, e.g., Ab *min ᶜindihī* (here genitive formally as well) literally 'from at him' (not in Akkadian).[ab]

aa. Also the prepositions OAk Eb *ište* etc., E *westa*; OAk Eb *in*(*a*), SA *in* (reflecting the survival of archaisms in peripheral areas).

ab. But compare the Akkadian compound prepositions formed of preposition + substantive: *ina muḫḫi* 'on top of,' literally 'on the skull'; *ina libbi* 'therefrom, therein,' literally 'in the heart.' Cf. § 2 note o.

§ 1/1.4 The need to express certain grammatical relations is satisfied by a stylistic device also otherwise much favored in Semitic, paronomasia (using the same word or the same root in different syntactic functions in one sentence). Among its functions are strengthening, e.g., H *mōṯ yūmaṯ* 'he shall (indeed) be killed'; expression of adverbial modification, e.g., Ab *ḍarabūhu ḍarbata rajulin wāḥidin* 'they struck him the blow of one man,' i.e., 'as one man'; and expression of an indefinite pronoun, e.g., Ab *qāla qāᵓilun* 'a sayer said,' i.e., 'someone said.'

---

§ 1/2.0 After the departure toward Babylonia of the stock of Semites out of whose language Akkadian developed, the rest of Semitic underwent a further period of common development, which resulted in some features of West Semitic that distinguish it from Akkadian.[10] The most important of them are the

10. Some of the characteristics of proto-Semitic treated above are as it happens less prominent in Akkadian than in West Semitic, especially syntactic ones; they could thus be among the just post-Akkadian developments.

ac. (Continuing note s): While Akkadian in general remained

§ **1/2.2.2**

at this stage of development, in West Semitic the perfect developed from the general present meaning to a perfect in the Indo-European sense (a present state resulting from a past event) and further to the expression of the assertion of past events without consideration of the states resulting from them: **mit-* 'he is dead' > 'he has died'; **zaqin* 'he is old' > 'he has become old.' Then, on the model of the old present-imperfect, an imperfect and also a preterite-jussive were formed to go along with the past tense that thus developed: **yamut-* 'he dies,' **yamut* 'he died,' 'may he die.' Except where analogy prevailed (as in **yamut-* influenced by *maut-* 'death'), the principle of polarity† was decisive here in the choice of imperfect vowel: in place of the reduced vowel *i/u* in the perfect, the full vowel *a* occurred in the imperfect.[11]

A switch of the vowels may have taken place: **yiqtal-* as imperfect of *qatil*, **yuqtal-* of *qatul*.

On the basis of the neutral system that thus developed, perfect *qati/ul-* : imperfect *yiqtal-* or the like, a new active perfect *qatal-* was added to the old imperfect *yaqti/ul-* (preterite-jussive + present), where for the choice of perfect vowel the principle of polarity again operated, but the opposition to the old *qati/ul* was crucial. The old active *a*-imperfect followed to a small extent the neutral scheme (new formation of an *i*-imperfect); to a greater extent, as a result of the predominance by this time of the neutral meaning of the *a*-imperfect, they went over to *i/u*-imperfects.

†Speiser □ 1.2.2:2 fiercely attacks the notion of "polarity."

11. This assumes that the Arabic scheme *qatula* : *yaqtulu* is secondary.

further development of the verbal system[ac] and the sharp distinction between definite and indefinite.

The system of objective modes is relegated to the background by two interrelated subjective distinctions: subjective tenses (past, present, future) on one side and subjective aspects on the other.[ad] In this context, aspects are understood as the speaker's manners of insight, observation, and description, which in Akkadian generally do not find expression: whether the subject wishes to assert facts or relate events and describe situations, whether he himself is certain or doubtful, whether he participates intentionally or demandingly in the matter presented. The relations to the modes and the tenses are clear: narration, e.g., is preeminently past punctual, description present stative. Besides that, threads are also discernible that lead to modal distinctions: subjunctive as willed by the superordinate subject, etc. Thus it makes sense that certain moods

The perfect was not confined to the assertion of past events, but developed further, as often in Indo-European as well, to the narrative tense, thus beginning to encroach on the sphere of the old preterite. The confrontation between the two forms had different consequences in the various West Semitic languages. In Ethiopic and in Aramaic the preterite disappeared entirely. In Arabic it was retained principally after the negation *lam*, where again polarity operated, which also in the Hamitic languages has led to the use of opposite tense forms for negation and for affirmation. In Hebrew except in poetry, the old preterite is found almost exclusively in the imperfect consecutive. Therein is reflected the original difference in meaning between perfect and preterite; the first establishes a fundamental event, and the latter narrates the further progress thereof. Elsewhere, polarity operates not just in the opposition perfect + imperfect consecutive, but originally probably also in another one, negative perfect (as still in attested Hebrew always) : affirmative imperfect consecutive (in attested Hebrew at least predominantly).

Finally, to go with the opposition perfect : imperfect consecutive was created the other one, imperfect : perfect consecutive, whereby the polar schema reached its fulfillment. This development was facilitated by the general-present meaning, never lost, of the old neutral perfect.

ad. "Aspect" normally refers to the "objective" time-distinctions of completed versus incomplete action, punctual versus durative, etc. The usage found here does not recur in the book.

are present in West Semitic that are lacking in Akkadian.[ae] — The old modes are also in part built into the new tense system, especially the contrasts punctual, durative-fientive, stative; the others retain some significance in verb-stem formation, though on the whole they are reduced to the opposition active (action) : neutral (event, state, property). Active and neutral modes have differing vocalizations in the same tense.[af]

In this new system the suffix conjugation, which at the older stage was equivalent to the nominal clause and had a neutral character, has been transformed to the principal past tense of active-transitive verbs as well, the so-called perfect. It serves for both narration and assertion of past events and also expresses other kinds of completion, termination of the action, e.g., in cases like H *bēráḵtī* 'I hereby bless,' where the action is accomplished with or in the utterance.[ag] The old uses of the suffix conjugation remain as well. The forms of the prefix conjugation, the so-called imperfect, take over principally present and future, along with simultaneity as opposed to precedence; repetition (habit) and state (description) in the past; and modal modifications, such as we express with "can," "should," etc. To the single West Semitic imperfect of the form **yaqtul-* (also with *i a* in the second syllable) correspond in Akkadian[ah] two prefixing "tenses," in form the preterite (properly speaking punctual) *iprus* (others with *i a*) but in meaning, rather, the present (properly speaking durative) *ipáras*, whose form has a West Semitic counterpart only in the Ethiopic (-South Arabic) *yeqátel.*[ai] — The tense system is filled out with the inclusion of the participle, which as well as the present expresses a special nuance of the future, corresponding somewhat to the English "I am going to . . .," e.g., Sy *sāleq-nā* 'I am going to rise, I am about to rise, will (shortly) rise.'

The active perfect of West Semitic as a rule has *a* in the

ae. Gelb □ 1/2.2.2.1.2:1 on the basis of Old Akkadian evidence suggests that *-u* is the proto-Semitic indicative marker, and *-a* the subjunctive marker (reflecting also the situation in Arabic, see § 6.2.2).

af. This, rather than the normal opposition to "passive," is the usage of "active" henceforth in this book (with a few clear exceptions).

ag. I.e., the speech act now called "performative."

ah. And in Eblite and Amorite as well.

ai. Leslau □ 5.2.2.1:1 disputes the identification of Ak *iparras* (see § 2.2.2 with note i) with Gz *yeqáttel* on the grounds that the Common Ethiopic form could not have had a geminate middle radical. Christian's □ 1.2.2.1.1:5 and Rundgren's □ 1.2.2:4 theories, based on this supposed correspondence, may thus founder.

basic stem as the vowel of the second syllable of the stem, while the corresponding imperfect has *u* or *i*; to the neutral *i*-perfect corresponds an imperfect with *a*.[12] Transitive verbs also inflect neutrally, if they do not express an active happening; e.g., Ab *sami*^{c}*a* 'he heard' (mental conception conceived as a more passive function).

Before the development of this new perfect the suffix conjugation, since it had a stative meaning, could be used with transitive verb-roots only in a passive sense. This older stage, which Akkadian preserves, is probably the origin of the development of a special passive distinguished from the active by its vocalization in West Semitic.

§ 1/2.2.3 As for definiteness, the West Semitic languages diverge from each other in the means they use to express it,[13] but agree so closely in the rules applying to it that a pre-divergence common origin is probable.[aj] Serving as the article is a demonstrative element whose original character is still occasionally revealed. The article expresses not just already-established individual definiteness, but also that first effected by the context (e.g., H *kāṯaḇ bassép̄er* 'he wrote in the book,' namely the one in question, English 'in a book')[ak] as well as the generic (especially in comparisons, e.g., Ab *miθlu l-ḥimāri* 'like the ass,' English usually 'like an ass'). A definite genitive (including pronominal suffix) definitizes the governing substantive, so that it cannot take the article; e.g., Ab *bintu l-maliki* 'THE daughter of the king.' If it is to remain indefinite, then the genitive must be periphrased, for which periphrasis the preposition *la- is usually used, e.g., BA *méleḵ lYiśrā*$^{\supset}$*ēl raḇ* 'a great king of Israel.' An adjective as attribute of a definite

aj. Nowadays considered extremely unlikely.

ak. A translation conveying both the form and the meaning of this usage might be 'he wrote in a certain book.'

12. As regards the imperfect vowel of the neutral-mode *u*-perfect, the West Semitic languages differ.

13. Ethiopic has no definite article, but probably gave it up only secondarily.

substantive takes the article, e.g., H *hāʿīr haggḏōlā* 'the big city.' Correspondingly, the relative clause following a definite object has a relative pronoun (which as a former demonstrative is definite); following an indefinite it does not.

Chapter 2
Akkadian

§ 2.0 Akkadian, to use its native name, is what we call the Semitic language of the cuneiform inscriptions. A great quantity of written material in Akkadian has come down to us, which represents, however, but a fraction of the abundant texts written by the Babylonians and Assyrians (we can speak of literature proper only to a limited extent). In conformity with the division of the peoples, Akkadian can be separated into two markedly different dialects, a Babylonian and an Assyrian. Both can be followed through two or three millennia. The classical era of Babylonian is the Old Babylonian period of the Dynasty of Hammurabi; the largest number of Assyrian texts belongs to the period of the Neo-Assyrian Empire. —

Cuneiform writing, which was by nature unsuited to record Akkadian, does not use all the capabilities inherent in the system to render all the sounds exactly; thus to a greater extent than for the other Semitic languages the transcription of an Akkadian text is a reconstruction, and this results in some uncertainty and doubt concerning particular matters.[a]

We have already written of the peculiarities of Akkadian as compared with West Semitic. The two groups of languages contrast utterly in many ways, even in overall character: in Akkadian dead objective rigidity; in West Semitic, most clearly in Hebrew, living subjective flexibility. Thus from the West Semitic point of view, Akkadian represents generally a more archaic stage of development of the Semitic language-type, although in details it has gone its own way. This is most

a. Bergsträsser's adviser Landsberger never himself organized his understanding of Akkadian grammar. Not only is this chapter the only first-hand systematic presentation of his views; it is also the first time that the distinguishing feature of the present was identified, the perfect tense was described — and that the name "Akkadian" itself was given wide currency.

obvious in the phonology; here Akkadian has the character of a language taken over by a linguistically alien population and influenced by its phonological habits. The language of this older population was Sumerian.[b] —

b. A schematic presentation of grammatical features that may be ascribed to — or that at least correlate with — Sumerian is given in Edzard □2/1.0:2.

§ 2.1.1 The rich consonantal system of Semitic is simplified in Akkadian, by the loss of the laryngeals, dental spirants, and in large measure the semivowels. The laryngeals *ḥ* ʿ ʾ have largely disappeared, sometimes remaining as ʾ; forms with and without ʾ often occur side by side. *w* is present only in the older period; later it becomes ʾ initially, and medially it sometimes disappears but sometimes is written *m* instead: *awīlum* 'man,' later *amēlu*, *awatum* 'word,' later *amatu* (probably still pronounced *awēlu awatu*).[c] Initial *y* has already disappeared at the earliest stage (exceptions are rare, e.g., *yāti* 'me'); intervocalically it remains in certain cases until a late stage. Also, where ʾ or a semivowel are no longer written with their own signs, the presence of at least traces of them is recognizable in the non-occurrence of vowel contraction (*dārium* 'eternal,' later *dārū*) or in the written syllable division (*šum-ud* 'make many' for *_šumʾud_). A disappearing ʾ before or after a consonant induces lengthening of the preceding vowel; thus *zību* 'wolf' for *_ziʾbu_, or the other way *ḫīṭu* 'sin' for *_ḫiṭʾu_ (dialectally *ḫiṭṭu* instead). — The dental spirants are replaced by sibilants — strikingly, not always by the closest corresponding one: *δ* does indeed become *z*, but *θ* is replaced not by *s* but rather by *š*, and *δ̣* merges with *θ̣* as *ṣ*, which, however, in spite of the conventional transcription seems actually to have been voiced.

c. The various etymological correspondences of ʾ can be indicated as follows: ʾ$_1$ = *ʾ; ʾ$_2$ = *_h_; ʾ$_3$ = *_ḥ_; ʾ$_4$ = *ʿ; ʾ$_5$ = *_γ_; ʾ$_6$ = *_w_; ʾ$_7$ = *_y_.

Among the sibilants themselves a sound change took place whereby *ś* merged into *š*. In later Assyrian *š* is pronounced *s*.

Akkadian displays consonant assimilation to a rather surprising extent for a Semitic language. Peculiar to it is the assimilation of *š* to a preceding dental as *s*: **ēmidšu* 'I imposed on him' > *ēmidsu*, and further **bītšu* 'his house' > *bīssu* (at an earlier stage the dental + *š* instead occasionally became *šš*:[d] **edšu* 'new' > *eššu*). In the opposite order, BEFORE a dental (or sibilant), *š* goes rather to a sound written *l*: *aštapar* 'I sent' > *altapar*; Neo-Assyrian carried the development of this combination further to *ss*: *aštakan* 'I made' > *assakan*.

The result of assimilation is in many cases a long consonant: *ibbī* 'he named' < **inbī*. In addition to this developmental tendency, though, Akkadian also exhibits the contrary, the resolution of "double" consonants by geminate dissimilation, i.e., replacement of the first half of a long consonant with *n* (*m*); e.g., *inaddin* 'he gives' > *inandin inamdin*, *ṣubbu* 'wagon' > *ṣumbu*.

An example of consonant dissimilation is that the nominal prefix *m-* becomes *n* before a stem containing a labial; e.g., *narkabtu* 'war chariot.'

The numerous suffixes that end in *-m* (noun mimation, dative pronouns, energic[e]) later lost this consonant. A considerable number of forms with varying meanings have thereby become homophonous, and so the expressive efficiency of the inflectional system is notably circumscribed.

§ 2.1.2

The diphthongs are almost all monophthongized, with *ai* usually > *ī*, in some circumstances > *ē*, *au* > *ū*: **baitu* 'house' > *bītu*, but **ušaidi*^{c} 'he caused to know' (from *yd*^{c}) > *ušēdī*; **yaumu* 'day' > *ūmu*. *ē* also develops from *a* - *i* *ā* - *i*, when a consonant is lost between the vowels.[f]

a (*ā*) very commonly becomes *e* (*ē*). This change is the rule in the vicinity of a *ḥ* ^{c} that was at one time present: *rēmu* 'to pity' < **raḥāmu*; *emēdu* 'to meet, impose' < *^{c}*amādu*, *bēlu* 'lord' < **ba*^{c}*lu*; it also happens occasionally elsewhere, e.g., *erṣetu* 'land' < **arḍ̣atu* (Ab *arḍun*), here under the influence of the *ḍ̣*. Moreover, *e* can develop out of *i*, especially before *ḫ r*.

d. This assimilation occurs within the root only; spellings of dental + *-šu* as *-ds-* are probably morphophonemic spellings of *-ss-*, i.e., *ēmissu* like *bīssu*.

e. This is the etymological term for what in Assyriology is called, from one of its functions, the ventive (see § 2.2.2).

f. Long vowels resulting from such contractions are normally marked with a circumflex accent; Bergsträsser omits this distinction, marking all long vowels with a macron. Vowel and consonant length in Akkadian words have in some cases been revised here to reflect current information.

§ **2.1.3**

The accent is not indicated; in some cases it is detectable through secondary consonant lengthing after a stressed short vowel, as in *imáḫḫaṣ* 'he strikes' beside *imáḫaṣ*.[g] —

g. It is now recognized that accent is not significant (phonemic) in Akkadian, or at least that any significance it may have had is not recoverable from the extant documents. It is preferable to take the consonant lengthening as primary and to suppose an accentual system something like that of Arabic (where the closed syllable or one with a long vowel nearest the end of the word is automatically accented).

§ **2.2.1.1**

Akkadian has initial *š* in the third person pronouns — and in the causative prefix; *n* has spread throughout the second and third person plural, and length is not retained. Thus *šū* 'he,' -*š*(*u*) 'his, him,' *šunu* masculine and *šina* feminine 'they.' 'I,' extended by *k*, is *anāku*. There are independent pronouns not just for the nominative, but for the dative and accusative as well; e.g., *yāšim* 'to me,' *yāti* 'me'; *šuāšim* 'to him,' *šuāti* 'him' (later, confusions and innovations, e.g., *šāšu* 'him'). Some of the suffixes also have three forms, like -*ša* 'her' (possessive), -*šim* 'to her,' -*ši* 'her' (accusative); and plural -*šun*(*u*) 'their' (masculine), -*šunūšim* 'to them,' -*šunūti* 'them' (masculine) — and others only two, e.g., beside -*š*(*u*) 'his, him' a specific -*šum* 'to him.' The *m* of the dative is doubtless identical with the ventive ending (see § 2.2.2). 'My' postvocalically is in certain cases -*ya*, e.g., (with elision of *y*) *rēʾūa* 'my shepherd,' and especially in the genitive: 'my lord's' *bēliya*, since the genitive ending -*i* is present before genitive and pronominal suffixes, whereas the nominative and accusative endings are not: *bēlī* 'my lord' (nominative or accusative). — Akkadian also has an independent possessive *yāʾum* 'my,' feminine *yattum*, etc.; but it disappeared early.[h]

h. It is hard to tell what Bergsträsser meant by this statement about the disappearance of *yāʾum*; it is found in Late Babylonian.

Owing to the presence of the independent accusative pronouns, there is no need for an accusative particle to which suffixes are attached (as in other Semitic languages).

§ **2.2.1.2**

Akkadian uses the third person personal pronouns as demonstratives, along with the stem *n*-, *annium* (later *annū*) 'this.' The demonstratives are postposed: *awīlum šū* 'that man.' The relative is *ša* 'which,' which is also used for genitive periphrasis; interrogatives *mannum* 'who?,' *mīnum* 'what?'; indefinite *manma mamma* 'someone, whoever,' *minma mimma* 'something, whatever.' —

§ 2.2.2.1

As already mentioned, besides the so-called permansive, a suffixing form, the Akkadian verb has two prefixing forms, the so-called present and the so-called preterite, which are distinguished in the basic stem by the present having an accented *a* after the first radical: preterite *iprus*, present *ipáras* (often with secondary lengthening *ipárras*).[i] The primary semantic difference between these forms is purely objective, a difference of mode of action: the permansive is stative, the present fientive-durative, the preterite punctual. Furthermore, present and preterite are used also for the expression of time, but predominantly again in objective sense: it is the sequence of tenses that renders the reciprocal time-relations of anteriority and posteriority of the events described. Then the binary opposition *íprus* : *ipárras* is augmented to a ternary one by the inclusion of the *t*-stem *íptaras*. Punctual narration uses only *íprus* as earlier, *íptaras* as later stage.[j] The conditional sentence requires *ipárras* in the apodosis; the protasis can be simple with either *íprus* or *íptaras*, or else compound, *íprus* followed by *íptaras*. Each of these stages can itself be composed of several verbs in the same form. Only secondarily and to a limited extent does subjective time find expression; *íprus* past, *íptaras* present (punctual), *ipárras* future (and durative present). This use of the *t*-forms is peculiar to Akkadian.

i. The lengthening of the middle radical is the actual mark of the present; the freedom of cuneiform writing permits it to go unexpressed sometimes.

j. The common name of the *iptaras* tense is now "perfect," though it is not clear why.

The preterite is often strengthened with *lu* (which is also the precative particle); the present with the negation *la* is also the prohibitive. — The permansive of transitive verbs and verbal stems is mostly passive: *katim* 'he is covered.'

Permansive, present, and preterite also form, besides the indicative, a subjunctive or relative and an energic or ventive (the latter also occurs with the imperative). The subjunctive, though only in the unsuffixed forms, ends with *-u*; it occurs in subordinate clauses, especially relative clauses (but not in a conditional clause). The energic is at first limited to verbs of motion and gives them a terminative sense (reaching a goal); it has also been transferred to verbs of speaking and also to verb forms occurring in close relation with genuine energics. The ending is *-am*, after a vowel *-m*, plural *-nim*; the *m* assimilates to the initial consonant of a suffix: *-annī* < **-am-nī*, *-aššu* < **-am-šu* (*-annī* is later used in forms other than ventives).

The prefixes are (whenever the prefix-vowel is not *u*) third person *i-*, first person singular *a-* (*lu* + *i-* > *li-*, *lu* + *a* > *lu-*); the other forms are *ta- ni-*.

§ 2.2.2.3 In the basic stem the vowel of the last syllable in the present and preterite is *a*, *i*, or *u*; in the present *a* predominates, but when the preterite has *i*, this is also usual in the present. E.g., *imḫaṣ imaḫ(ḫ)aṣ* 'strike,' *iplaḫ ipal(l)aḫ* 'fear,' *ikrub ikar(r)ab* 'pray,' *ikšud ikaš(š)ad* 'arrive at, conquer,' *iškun išak(k)an* 'set, make,' *išpur išap(p)ar* 'send,' *išqul išaq(q)al* 'weigh'; but intransitive *iknuš ikan(n)uš* 'bend,' *iqrib iqar(r)ib* 'near,' *išbir išeb(b)ir* 'break.' The imperative is two-vowelled with the vowel of the preterite: *šupur* 'send.' The permansive has the form *kašid*; before a vowel the *i* disappears: *marṣat* 'she is sick.' The participle is, e.g., *pāliḫu* 'fearing,' the infinitive *amāru* 'to see.'

§ 2.2.2.4 The derived stem morphology is unusually rich and complex, using various combinations of relatively few formatives: lengthening of the second radical, *t* (always infixed after the first radical), *n* (and both together infixed as *-tan-*), *š*. The last vowel is in general *i* in the preterite and the participle, *a* in the present (and in the other syllables); e.g., intensive *uḫappid uḫappad* 'gouge out (eyes),' *ugammir ugammar mugammiru* 'complete'; its *t*-stem *uḫtappid uḫtappad*; causative *ušaklil ušaklal mušaklilu*, imperative *šuklil* (*šaklil*) 'complete.' The permansive and infinitive have *u* in the last syllable (and usually in preceding ones also): intensive *ḫulluq*(*u*) 'to annihilate,' causative *šuršud*(*u*) 'to found,' *t*-stem of the causative *šutaprus*(*u*).

The *t*-stem of the basic stem is formed differently. It has but one prefix form, in which the vowel of the last syllable generally is that of the present of the basic stem: *imtaḫaṣ*, *iktašad ištakan*, *ištebir*; as punctual it is accented on the first syllable, as durative on the second: *íktašad iktáš*(*š*)*ad*.[k]

k. The distinction must be kept in mind between the perfect tense with *t*-infix and the *t*-stem; the latter has the normal two prefixing tense forms, the preterite homophonous with the basic stem perfect, and the present exhibiting the characteristic consonant lengthening (the accent difference is incidental); note the *t*-infixed perfect tense of the *t*-stem, *iptatras*.

The meaning of the *t*-stem, leaving aside the above-mentioned time-modifying forms, is reciprocal, and in the causative also passive; the *n*-stems are mostly passive.

The number of weak verbs is quite large as a result of the loss of the laryngeals, although strong laryngeal verbs (especially II laryngeal) are also found.

§ 2.2.2.5.1

The I *n* verbs lose the first radical in the imperative: *idin* 'give.' In this verb, besides the regular present form *inaddin* 'he gives,' there is an innovation based on the preterite *iddin*: *iddan*.

The following groups of I weak verbs are still distinguished in the basic stem: I *w* *ūšib* 'he sat,' present *uššab*; *ūbil* 'he brought,' *ubbal* (these have a weak imperative *šib bil*); I *y* *īšir* 'I straightened up' (but *ēṣip* 'I added'); I laryngeal either with *a*, as in *ākul* 'I ate,' *akkal*; *ālul* 'I suspended,' *allal*; *āmur* 'I saw,' *ammar*; *āpul* 'I answered, compensated,' *appal*; or with *e*, as in *ēpuš* 'I made,' *eppuš* (with the vowel of the preterite for older *eppaš*), having infinitive *epēšu*, participle *ēpišu*; *ēsir* 'I enclosed.' *alāku* 'to go' is irregular (with consonant lengthening instead of vowel lengthening): *illik* 'he went,' present *illak*. In the derived stems *ū* occurs as the result of contraction only when one of the contracting vowels is *u*, e.g., causative *šūbil* 'bring,' *šūḫuzu* 'to make seize'; otherwise there are only an *a*-series and an *e*-series, with I *w* verbs falling in both classes: causative *ušābil* 'he sent,' but *ušēšib* 'he caused to sit,' and I and III weak *ušēdī* 'he informed,' *ušēṣī* 'he let go out.'

§ 2.2.2.5.2 The different groups of II weak verbs are distinguished principally in the preterite (and imperative) of the basic stem: II *w idūk* 'he killed,' *imūt* 'he died,' *išūṭ* 'he pulled'; II *y iṭīb* 'he became good'; II laryngeal *a*-series *irām* 'he loved,' *e*-series *ibēl* 'he subjugated.' In addition there are also *a*-preterites of II *w y*, e.g., *ibāš* 'he came to shame.' The present of all groups has as a rule *ā* (*ē*): *idāk imāt išāṭ*, *iṭāb*; besides these, forms are found that are influenced by the preterite. Furthermore, the characteristic vowel, at least of the *u*-series, appears in the *t*- form of the basic stem: *imtūt* 'he dies.' The other stems have the vowel that would result from the contraction of the vowels of the corresponding strong form. The intensive is *ukīn* 'he strengthened,' *utīr* 'he led back,' or else with short vowel like *uṭib* 'he made good'; many forms secondarily lengthen the last radical, e.g., present *ukannu*, infinitive *ṭubbu*.[1] The causative deviates from the strong pattern *ušakšid*: *ušmīt* 'he killed,' its *t*-stem *uštamīt*.

1. Actually, ALL unsuffixed intensive forms have a long vowel (*uṭīb*) and ALL forms but the preterite lengthen the last radical before a vowel.

§ 2.2.2.5.3 In the III weak verbs the ending *ī* predominates; some of the laryngeal verbs have *ē*, e.g., *išmē* 'he heard.' In the basic stem some III *w* verbs retain their inherent inflection, e.g., *imnū* 'he paid,' and there are occasional *a*-forms, e.g., *itmā* 'he swore,' present *itammā*. The final *-ū* combines with the ending *-ū*/*u* (plural or relative), as also happens in the related nominal forms with the nominal ending *-u* (nominative *-ū*, genitive *-ē*, accusative *-ā*; feminine *-ītu*). — The auxiliary verb *īšū* 'he has' (first person the same) belongs to the III weak class (as well as I *y*). —

§ 2.2.3 The three cases are clearly distinguished in the older language, while later, both in the noun and in those pronouns that distinguish cases, they are confused. The old endings are nominative *-um*, genitive *-im*, accusative *-am*; later they lose the final *-m* (mimation).[1] Divine names often have no case ending (probably a vocative in origin): *Šamaš* as the name of the Sun god, versus *šamšum* 'sun.' In the construct state (before a following genitive) the mimation falls away, and in the nominative and accusative the case-vowel does as well; the *-i* of the genitive remains. After long consonants or consonant clusters the nominative and accusative often retain a final vowel, usually *i* (but also, e.g., *šamšu Bābili* 'the sun of Babylon'), and before a pronominal suffix usually *a* (*bābtašu* 'his kin' nominative). Forms without endings shorten final long consonants, e.g., *šar* from *šarrum* 'king' (more commonly *šarri*),[m] and break up final consonant clusters with an intrusive vowel, which can be either an original stem vowel that has disappeared before a vocalic ending, or else an epenthetic vowel: *alap* from *alpu* 'ox,' *arad* from *ardu* 'slave,' *kalab* from *kalbu* 'dog,' *qabal* from *qablu* 'battle'; *mišil* from *mišlu* 'half,' *miger* from *migru* 'favorite.' The plural ending is *-ū*, genitive and accusative *-ī* (*ilū ilī* 'gods,' *nišū nišī* 'men'), dialectally also *-ānu -āni*; later *-āni* (*ilāni*) or *-ē* (*nišē*). The noun (but no longer the verb) has a dual with *-ān*, genitive and accusative *-ēn* (before a genitive just *-ā -ē*), which later survives only as the relic *-ā*: *qātā* 'hands,' *šēpā* 'feet.' The feminine ending is *-tu*, plural *-ātu*, genitive and accusative *-āti* (later only *-āti*). After a long consonant or a cluster the ending is *-atu* (*-etu*): *šarratu* 'queen,' *erṣetu* 'earth'; or, as in the masculine forms without ending, it incorporates an epenthetic vowel: *tukultu* 'help,' construct state *tukulti* or rarely *tuklat* (likewise also

m. This is an unfortunate example, as a construct **šarri* is not attested; cf. *kak* beside *kakki* 'weapon.'

1. From the name of the Hebrew letter *mīm*.

bēlet 'lady' construct state beside *bēlti*), plural *tuklātu.* The adjectives form their plurals the same way in the feminine only; in the masculine they have the ending *-ūtu*, genitive and accusative *-ūti* (later only *-ūti*).

§ 2.2.4 Akkadian differs from the other Semitic languages in the richness of its adverbial endings. The most important are *-iš*, e.g., *arḫiš* 'promptly,' *nakriš* 'hostilely,' *danniš* 'mightily' (also *an*(*a*) *danniš* > *adanniš*); and *-um*, which, usually with suffixes attached, is equivalent to a combination with preposition (especially 'in'): *ṣēruššu* 'on, to him' = *ina ṣērišu* 'on, to his back' (with the first person: *ellamūa* 'before me'). The abstract ending *-ūt* is also used adverbially: *balṭūssun* 'alive' (plural), literally 'their aliveness.'—

Akkadian does not have any monoconsonantal prefixed particles: 'like' is *kī*, as an independent word, strengthened *kīma*; 'in' is *in*(*a*); the dative particle is *an*(*a*), also 'to'; 'and' is generally omitted between single words, otherwise the independent word *u* is 'and, or.'[n] *kī, ina,* and *ana* cannot take pronominal suffixes, nor can several other genuine prepositions: *ištu ultu* 'from,' *adi* 'up to, including,' *lām* 'before.'[o] For sentence conjunction, the enclitic emphatic particle *-ma* is attached to the last word of the first sentence; before it, otherwise shortened final vowels remain long and otherwise lost final *m* is retained; the preceding syllable is accented. Negation is *ul* for statement, *la* for prohibition and for single words, dialectally also for statement.

n. Sometimes distinguished as *u* 'and,' *ū* 'or.'

o. Pronominal suffixes can be used with prepositions by attaching them to a dummy substantive, cf. § 1 note ab.

§ 2.3 The Akkadian sentence makes an utterly non-Semitic impression, since contrary to the general rule the verb normally goes at the end and its occasional advancement conforms not to a shift in psychological allotment of emphasis (as is the case with change in order elsewhere in Semitic), but rather to clearly defined principles of word order. Also, the infinitive, along with a preposition governing it, follows its object: *raggam ana ḫulluqim* 'in order to destroy the evil' (also, with preposition preposing and case attraction: *ana usim šūḫuzim* 'to teach good behavior'). — There are numerous subordinate clauses with no conjunction, especially relative clauses, before which the governing substantive occurs in the construct state (*awat iqbū* 'the word that he spoke'), and declarative clauses (*ina idū la amḫaṣu itammā* 'he shall swear: "I did not knowingly strike [him]"'). Assyrian has, besides the *-u* (which occurs in the last two examples) of the relative, a special suffix *-ni* marking subordination. —

§ 2.4 The Akkadian vocabulary was heavily influenced by Sumerian: with the adoption of Sumerian religion and both intellectual and material culture the Akkadians also adopted a wealth of terms for the new concepts, occupations, and realia of culture.

In the realms of public administration and legal and commercial life, Akkadian has an expressive capability adequate to the rendering even of complicated circumstances, and in religious and narrative poetry is not deficient in verve and forcefulness. In liveliness, flexibility, versatility, and vividness it remains, in part as a result of an excessive tendency toward familiar phrase and formula, far behind Hebrew, which is closest to it among the Semitic languages in archaism of spirit.

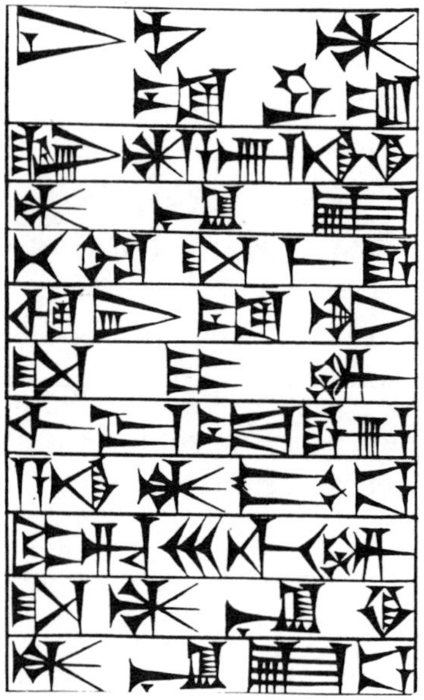

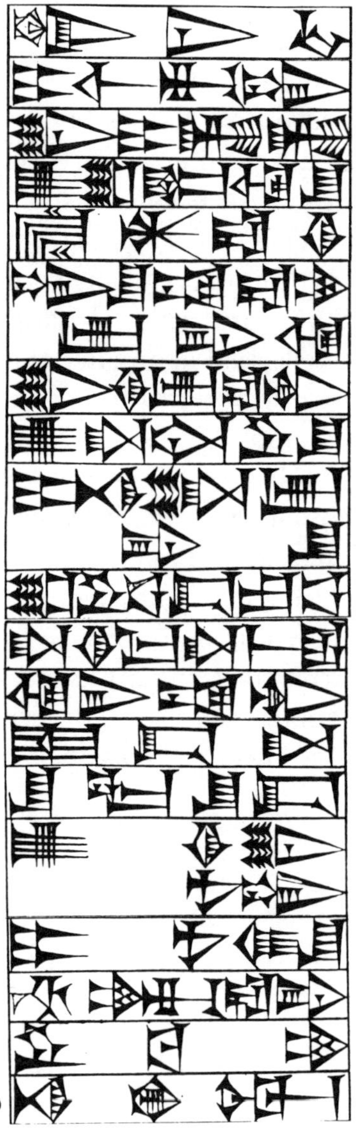

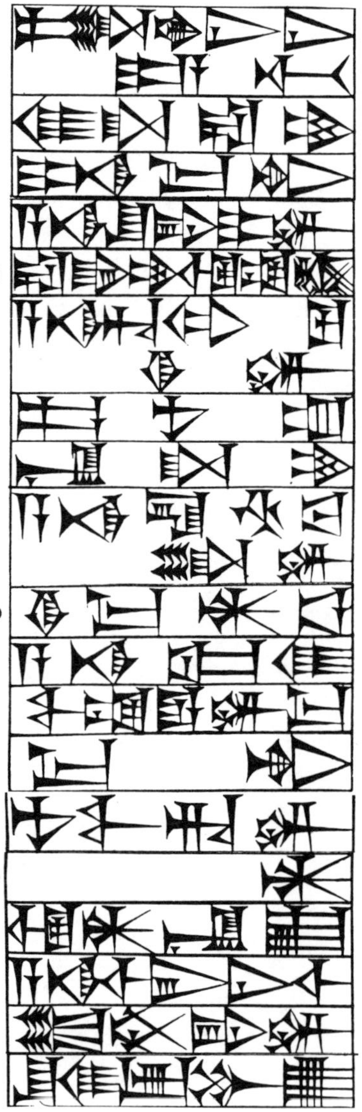

p. Cuneiform text reproduced from Robert F. Harper, *The Code of Hammurabi King of Babylon about 2250 B.C.* (Chicago: Univ. of Chicago Press, 1904[2]), pls. 1, 2, 7, 57, 58, 59, 66, drawn by A. H. Godbey; transliteration after R. Borger, *Babylonisch-Assyrische Lesestücke* (Rome: Pontifical Biblical Institute, 1979[2]), vol. 1, pp. 5ff., 38, 42 (AnOr 54). Consulted in translating: G. R. Driver and John C. Miles, *The Babylonian Laws* (Oxford: Clarendon, 1955), vol. 2, pp. 7, 13, 77, 79, 87, 89; Theophile J. Meek in J. B. Pritchard, *Ancient Near Eastern Texts Relating to the Old Testament* (Princeton: Princeton University Press, 1969[3]), pp. 164f., 175f.

q. The Amorite name *ᶜAmmu-rāpi* 'Ammu is healer.'

Text Specimens

[S] after a word indicates Sumerian origin.

1. From the Code of Hammurabi[P]

a) Beginning and End of the Prologue

i [1]*ì-nu* AN *ṣi-ru-um* [2] LUGAL ^{d}*A-nun-na-ki* [3] ^{d}EN.LÍL [4] *be-el ša-me-e* [5] *ù er-ṣe-tim* [6] *ša-i-im* [7] *ši-ma-at* KALAM [8] *a-na* ^{d}AMAR.UD [9] DUMU *re-eš-ti-im* [10] *ša* ^{d}EN.KI [11] ^{d}EN.LÍL-*ut* [12] KIŠ *ni-ši* [13] *i-ši-mu-šum* [14] *in I-gi$_4$-gi$_4$* [15]*ú-šar-bí-ù-šu* [16] KÀ.DINGIR.RA^{ki} [17] *šum-šu ṣi-ra-am ib-bi-ù*	*īnum Anum ṣīrum šar Anunnakī, Enlil bēl šamē u erṣetim šāʾim*[2] *šīmāt*[2] *mātim ana Marduk mārim rēštîm*[3] *ša Ea illilūt*[S] *kiššat nišī išīmūšum, in Igigi ušarbiūšu,*[4] *Bābili šumšu ṣīram ibbiū,*[5]	When august Anu, king of the Anunnaki, (and) Enlil, lord of heaven and earth, allotter of the destinies of the land, | allotted to Marduk, the firstborn son of Ea, divine lordship over the totality of mankind, magnified him among the Igigi, called Babylon by its exalted name, |
[18] *in ki-ib-ra-tim* [19] *ú-ša-te-ru-šu* [20] *i-na li-ib-bi-šu* [21] *šar-ru-tam da-rí-tam* [22] *ša ki-ma ša-me-e* [23] *ù er-ṣe-tim* [24] *iš-da-ša* [25] *šu-úr-šu-da* [26] *ú-ki-in-nu-šum*	*in kibrātim ušāterūšu,*[6] *ina libbišu šarrūtam darītam, ša kīma šamē u erṣetim išdāša šuršudā, ukinnūšum:*[7]	made it supreme in the world (lit. [four] regions), (and) therein established for him eternal kingship, whose foundations are as solidly grounded as heaven and earth: |
[27] *i-nu-mi-šu* [28] *Ḫa-am-mu-ra-pí* [29] *ru-ba-am* [30] *na-aʾ-dam* [31] *pa-li-iḫ ì-lí ya-ti* [32] *mi-ša-ra-am* [33] *i-na ma-tim* [34] *a-na šu-pí-i-im* [35] *ra-ga-am ù ṣe-nam* [36] *a-na ḫu-ul-lu-qí-im* [37] *da-nu-um* [38] *en-ša-am* [39] *a-na la ḫa-ba-li-im*	*inūmišu Ḫammurapi*[q] *rubām naʾdam pāliḫ ilī yāti mīšaram*[8] *ina mātim ana šūpîm,*[9] *raggam u ṣēnam ana ḫulluqim, dannum enšam ana la ḫabālim,*	at that time Anu and Enlil named me (lit. called my name), Hammurabi, the reverent prince, god-fearer, to make justice prevail in the land, to destroy the wicked and the evil, that the strong might not oppress the weak, |
[40] *ki-ma* ^{d}UTU [41] *a-na* SAG.GI$_6$ [42] *wa-ṣe-e-em-ma* [43] *ma-tim* [44] *nu-wu-ri-im* [45] AN [46] *ù* ^{d}EN.LÍL [47] *a-na ši-ir ni-ši* [48] *ṭu-ub-bi-im* [49] *šu-mi ib-bu-ú*	*kīma Šamaš ana ṣalmāt*[10] *qaqqadim waṣēm*[11]*-ma mātim nuwwurim Anum u Enlil ana šīr nišī ṭubbim*[12] *šumī ibbū.*	to rise like Shamash over the black-headed (i.e., mankind) and give light to the land, to promote the welfare (lit. to make good the flesh) of the people. |

2. *šym.* 3. Nisbe from *rēštu* 'tip, beginning' (*rēšu* 'head,' from *rʾš*). 4. *rby.* 5. *nbʾ.* 6. *wtr.* 7. *kwn* intensive. 8. *yšr.* 9. *wpy.* 10. Feminine, because the understood *nišī* 'people' is feminine plural. 11. *wṣʾ.* 12. *ṭyb* intensive.

col. ii.

col. iv.

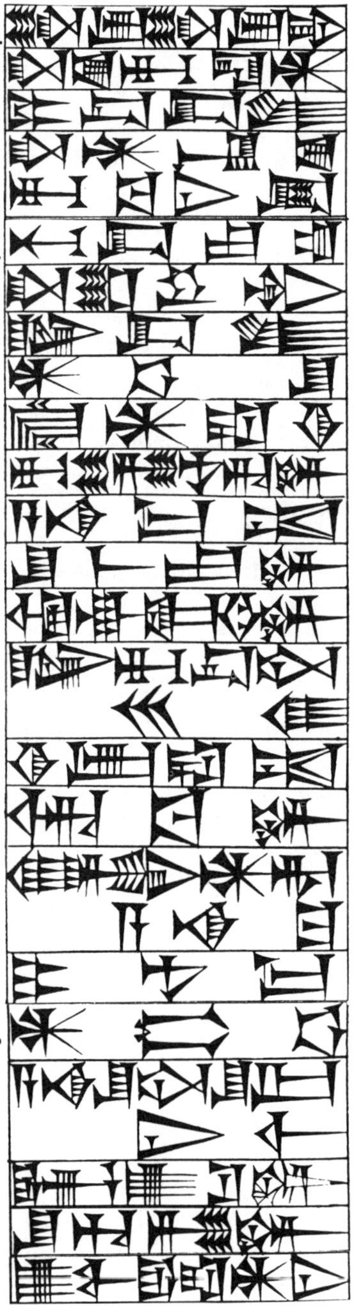

col. v.

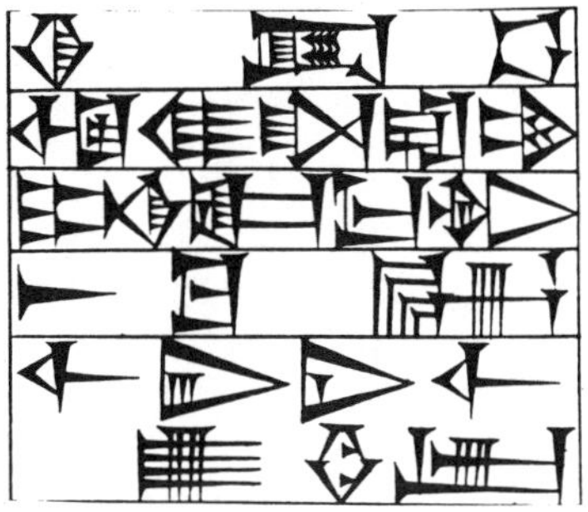

col. xl.

r. Probably to be read as Sumerian Duranki.

s. The Amorite name *Śumu-la-Il* 'progeny for Il.'

t. 'Sin is the preserver of life.'

50 *Ḫa-am-mu-ra-pí* 51 *re-yu*(I+A)*-um* 52 *ni-bi-it* 53 ^{d}EN.LÍL *a-na-ku* 54 *mu-kam-me-er* 55 *nu-úḫ-ši-im* 56 *ù ṭú-uḫ-di-im* 57 *mu-ša-ak-li-il* 58 *mi-im-ma šum-šu* 59 *a-na* EN.LÍL^{ki} DUR.AN.KI

Ḫammurapi rēʾūm[13] *nibīt*[14] *Enlil anāku: mukammir nuḫšim u ṭuḫdim, mušaklil mimma šumšu ana Nippurim rikis šamē erṣetim,*[r]

I am Hammurabi, the shepherd, called by Enlil: who heap up abundance and plenty, provider of everything (lit. whatever its name) for Nippur, 'bond of heaven and earth,' |

60 *za-ni-nu-um* 61 *na-aʾ-du-um* 62 *ša* É.KUR 63 LUGAL *le-yu-um* 64 *mu-te-er* ^{uru}NUN^{ki} 65 *a-na aš-ri-šu* 66 *mu-ub-bi-ib* ii 1 *šu-luḫ* É-ZU.AB

zāninum naʾdum ša Ekur, šarrum lēʾūm,[15] *mutēr*[16] *Eridu ana ašrišu, mubbib*[17] *šuluḫ Eabzu,*

the devout patron of Ekur, the able king, restorer of Eridu (lit. to its place), purifier of the cult of Eabzu, |

iv 67 *li-ip-li-ip-pí* 68 *ša Su-mu-la-ìl* 69 IBILA *da-núm* 70 *ša* ^{d}EN.ZU*-mu-ba-lí-iṭ* v 1 NUMUN *da-rí-um* 2 *ša šar-ru-tim* 3 LUGAL *da-núm*

. . . *liblibbi ša Sumulaʾil,*[s] *aplum dannum ša Sīn-muballiṭ,*[t] *zērum*[18] *dārium ša šarrūtim, šarrum dannum,*

. . . grandson of Sumulael, powerful heir of Sinmuballit, everlasting seed of kingship, the powerful king, |

4 ^{d}UTU*-šu* 5 KÁ.DINGIR.RA^{ki} 6 *mu-še-ṣí nu-ri-im* 7 *a-na ma-at* 8 *Šu-me-rí-im* 9 *ù Ak-ka-di-im* 10 LUGAL *mu-uš-te-eš-mi* 11 *ki-ib-ra-at* 12 *ar-ba-im* 13 *mi-gi₄-ir* ^{d}INANNA *a-na-ku*

šamšu Bābili, mušēṣī[19] *nūrim ana māt Šumerim u Akkadim, šarrum muštešmī*[20] *kibrāt arbaʾim, miger Inanna anāku.*

the sun of Babylon, dispenser of light over the land of Sumer and Akkad, bringer of the four regions to obedience, favorite of Inanna am I. |

14 *i-nu-ma* 15 ^{d}AMAR.UD 16 *a-na šu-te-šu-ur ni-ši* 17 KALAM *ú-si-⌜im⌝* 18 *šu-ḫu-zi-im* 19 *ú-wa-e-ra-an-ni* 20 *ki-it-tam* 21 *ù mi-ša-ra-am* 22 *i-na* KA *ma-tim* 23 *aš-ku-un* 24 *ši-ir ni-ši ú-ṭi-ib*

inūma Marduk ana šutēšur[21] *nišī, mātim usim šūḫuzim*[22] *uwaʾʾeranni,*[23] *kittam*[24] *u mīšaram ina pī mātim aškun, šīr nišī uṭīb.*[25]

When Marduk commissioned me to guide the people and to teach good behavior to the land, I established truth and justice in the mouth of the land, and promoted the welfare of the people.

b) Law of Retribution (§§ 196-199, 206-208, 250-252)[26]

xl 45 *šum-ma a-wi-lum* 46 *i-in* DUMU *a-wi-lim* 47 *úḫ-tap-pí-id* 48 *i-in-šu* 49 *ú-ḫa-ap-pa-du*

§ 196. *šumma awīlum īn mār awīlim uḫtappid, īnšu uḫappadū.*

§ 196. If a man puts out the eye of a free man (lit. son of a man), they shall put out his eye.

50 *šum-ma* GÌR.PAD.DU *a-wi-lim* 51 *iš-te-bi-ir* 52 GÌR.PAD.DU*-šu* 53 *i-še-eb-bi-ru*

§ 197. *šumma eṣemti awīlim ištebir, eṣemtašu išebbirū.*

§ 197. If he breaks the bone of a free man (lit. a man), they shall break his bone.

54 *šum-ma i-in* MAŠ.EN.KAK 55 *úḫ-tap-pí-id* 56 *ù lu* GÌR.NÍG (read .PAD).DU MAŠ.EN.KAK 57 *iš-te-bi-ir* 58 1 MA.NA KÙ.BABBAR 59 *i-ša-qal*

§ 198. *šumma īn muškēnim uḫtappid ū lu eṣemti muškēnim ištebir,* 1 *mana kaspam išaqqal.*

§ 198. If he puts out the eye of a commoner or breaks the bone of a commoner, he shall pay one mina of silver.

13. *rʿy*. 14. *nbʾ*. 15. *lʾy*. 16. *twr* intensive 17. *ʾbb*. 18. *zrʿ*. 19. *wṣʾ*. 20. *šmʿ*. 21. *yšr*. 22. *ʾḫz*. 23. *wʾr*. 24. < **kēntu* from *kwn*. 25. *ṭyb* intensive. 26. For the content cf. below pp. 70f.

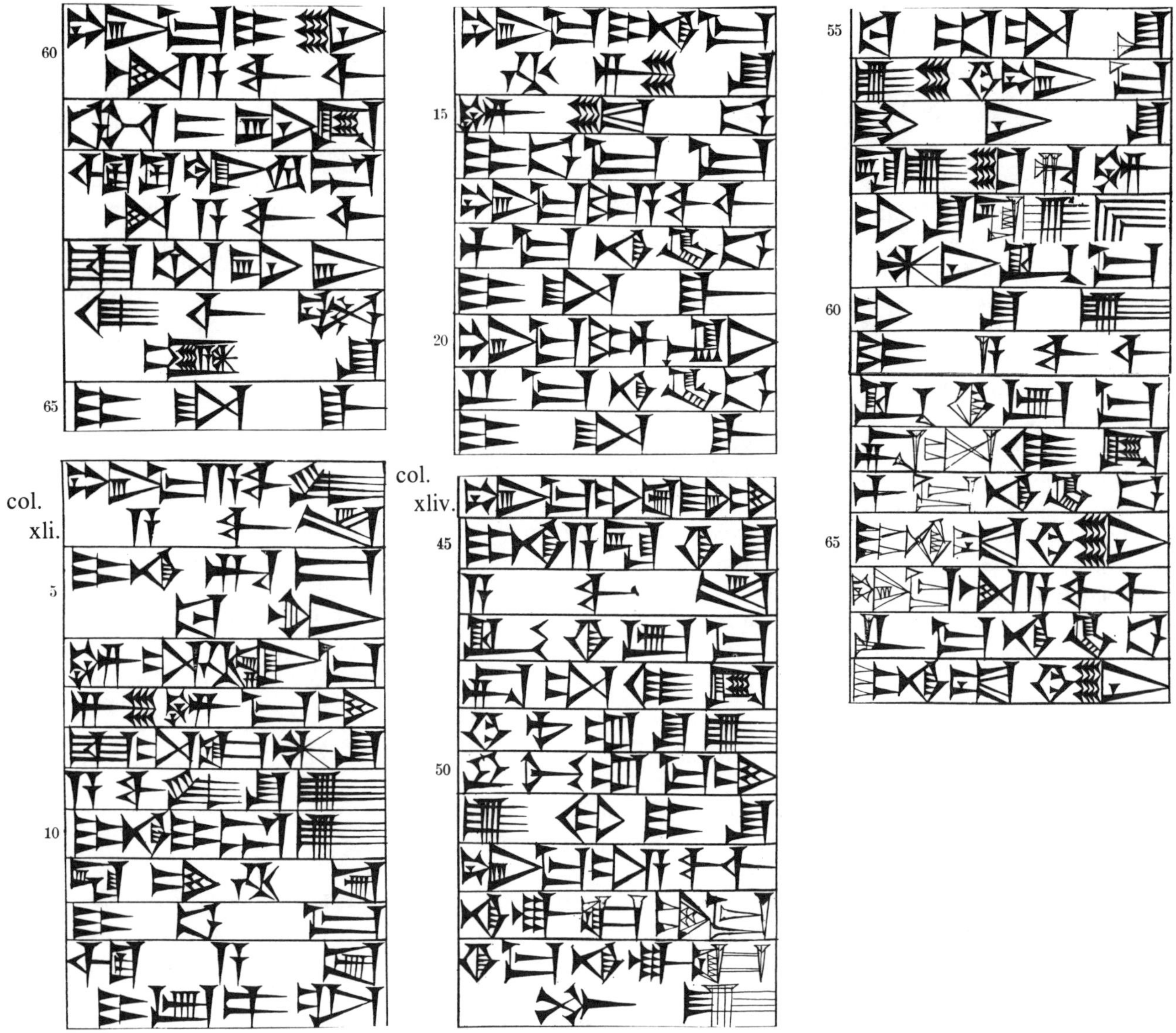
col. xli.
col. xliv.

60 *šum-ma i-in* ARAD *a-wi-lim* 61 *úḫ-tap-pí-id* 62 *ù lu* GÌR.PAD.DU ARAD *a-wi-lim* 63 *iš-te-bi-ir* 64 *mi-ši-il* ŠÁM-*šu* 65 *i-ša-qal*

§ **199.** *šumma īn warad awīlim uḫtappid ū lu eṣemti warad awīlim ištebir, mišil šīmišu išaqqal.*

§ **199.** If he puts out the eye of a man's slave or breaks the bone of a man's slave, he shall pay half his value.

---

xli 4 *šum-ma a-wi-lum a-wi-lam* 5 *i-na ri-is-ba-tim* 6 *im-ta-ḫa-aṣ-ma* 7 *sí-im-ma-am* 8 *iš-ta-ka-an-šu* 9 *a-wi-lum šu-ú* 10 *i-na i-du-ú* 11 *la am-ḫa-ṣú* 12 *i-tam-ma* 13 *ù* A.ZU *i-ip-pa-al*
14 *šum-ma i-na ma-ḫa-ṣí-šu* 15 *im-tu-ut* 16 *i-tam-ma-ma* 17 *šum-ma* DUMU *a-wi-lim* 18 ½ MA.NA KÙ.BABBAR 19 *i-ša-qal*
20 *šum-ma* DUMU MAŠ.EN.KAK 21 ⅓ MA.NA KÙ.BABBAR 22 *i-ša-qal*

§ **206.** *šumma awīlum awīlam ina risbātim imtaḫaṣ-ma simmam ištakanšu, awīlum šū "ina*[27] *idū*[28] *la amḫaṣu" itammā u asām*[S] *ippal.*[29]

§ **207.** *šumma ina maḫāṣišu imtūt,*[30] *itammā-ma, šumma mār awīlim, ½ mana kaspam išaqqal;*

§ **208.** *šumma mār muškēnim, ⅓ mana kaspam išaqqal.*

§ **206.** If a man strikes a man in a brawl and inflicts a wound on him, that man shall swear "I did not strike him deliberately" and he shall pay the physician.
§ **207.** If he dies from his blow, he shall swear and, if he is a free man, he shall pay one-half mina of silver;

§ **208.** If he is a commoner (lit. son of a commoner), he shall pay one-third mina of silver.

---

xliv 44 *šum-ma* GU4 *sú-qá-am* 45 *i-na a-la-ki-šu* 46 *a-wi-lam* 47 *ik-ki-ip-ma* 48 *uš-ta-mi-it* 49 *di-nu-um šu-ú* 50 *ru-gu-um-ma-am* 51 *ú-ul i-šu*
52 *šum-ma* GU4 *a-wi-lim* 53 *na-ak-*⸢*ka-pí*⸣*-*[*ma*] 54 *ki-ma na-ak-*⸢*ka*⸣*-pu-ú* 55 *ba-ab-ta-šu* 56 *ú-še-di-šum-ma* 57 *qar-ni-šu* 58 *la ú-šar-ri-im* 59 GU4-*šu la ú-sa-an-ni-iq-ma* 60 GU4 *šu-ú* 61 DUMU *a-wi-lim* 62 *ik-ki-ip-ma* 63 *uš-*⸢*ta*⸣*-mi-it* 64 ½ [MA].NA KÙ.BABBAR 65 *i-*[*na*]*-ad-di-in*
66 [*šum*]*-ma* ARAD *a-wi-lim* 67 ⸢⅓⸣ MA.NA KÙ.BABBAR 68 ⸢*i*⸣*-na-ad-di-in*

§ **250.** *šumma alpum sūqam ina alākišu awīlam ikkip*[31]*-ma uštamīt,*[32] *dīnum šū rugummām ul išū.*

§ **251.** *šumma alap awīlim nakkāpī*[33]*-ma kīma nakkāpū*[34] *bābtašu ušēdīšum*[35]*-ma qarnīšu la ušarrim alapšu la usanniq-ma alpum šū mār awīlim ikkip-ma uštamīt, ½ mana kaspam inaddin;*

§ **252.** *šumma warad awīlim, ⅓ mana kaspam inaddin.*

§ **250.** If an ox while walking along the street gores and kills a man, that case has no claim.

§ **251.** If a man's ox is a gorer and his district has informed him that it is a gorer, and he has not polled its horns or tied up his ox, and that ox gores and kills a free man, he shall give one-half mina of silver;

§ **252.** If a man's slave, he shall give one-third mina of silver.

27. *ina* as conjunction: "while he knows." 28. *ydʿ*. 29. *ʾpl*. 30. *mwt*. 31. *nkp*. 32. *mwt*.
33. Comparative adjective with nisbe ending. 34. *nakkāpī* + *-u* of the relative. 35. *ydʿ*.

u. Cuneiform text reproduced from *OLZ* 1914 112, drawn by Viktor Shileiko.

v. 'Sin gave (him) to me.'

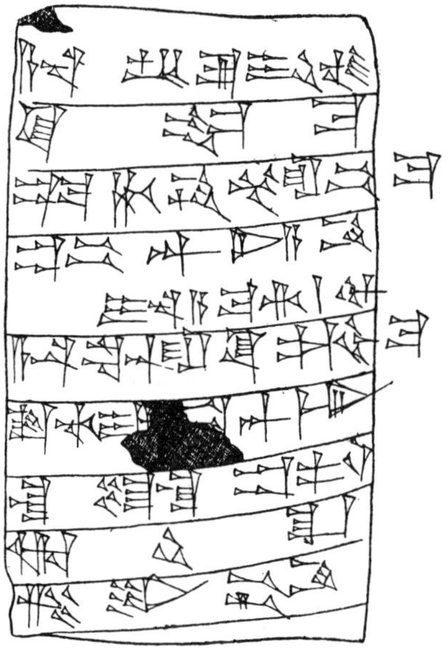

w. Cuneiform text reproduced from L. W. King, *The Letters and Inscriptions of Ḫammurabi, King of Babylon, about B.C. 2200* . . . (London: Luzac and Co., 1898), No. 55; consulted in transliterating and translating: R. Frankena, *Briefe aus dem British Museum* (Leiden: E. J. Brill, 1966), No. 53 (Altbabylonische Briefe 2).

x. Root *mkr*, loanword INTO Sumerian.

y. The Amorite name ᶜ*Ammī-ditana* 'my uncle is bison.'

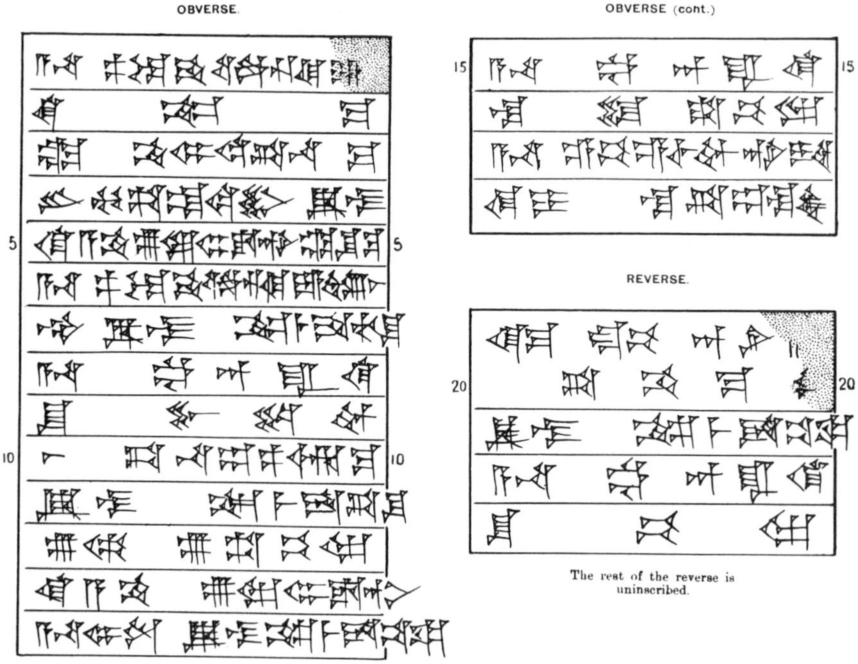

2. Two Hammurabi Letters

1 *a-na* ^{d}EN.ZU-*i-di-nam* 2 *qí-bí-ma* 3 *um-ma Ḫa-am-mu-ra-pí-ma* 4 *ṭup-pí an-ni-a-am i-na a-ma-ri-im* 5 *a-na* KÁ.DINGIR.RA^{ki} *al-kam-ma* 6 *it-ti-*⸢*ya na*⸣*-an-me-er* 7 *la tu-la-ap-pa-tam* 8 *ar-ḫi-iš* 9 *sí-in-qá-am*

a)[36,u] *ana Sīn-iddinam*[v] *qibī-ma umma*[37] *Ḫammurapi-ma: "ṭuppi*[S] *anniam ina amārim ana Bābili alkam*[38]*-ma, ittiya nanmer,*[39] *la tulappatam, arḫiš sinqam!"*

a) Say to Siniddinam: thus (says) Hammurabi: "Upon seeing this tablet, come to Babylon and meet with me, do not delay, come here at once!"

1 *a-na* UGULA DAM.GÀR ZIMBIR^{ki}*-ya-[aḫ-ru-rum]* 2 *qí-bí-ma* 3 *um-ma Am-mi-di-ta-na-ma* 4 LÚ *mu-ša-ad-di-in* SÍG.ÙZ 5 *ki-a-am ú-lam-mi-da-an-ni um-ma šu-ma*

b)[40,w] *ana wakil tamkārī*[S,x] *Sippar-yaḫrurum qibī-ma umma Ammiditana*[y]*-ma mušaddin šīpāt enzim kīam ulammidanni umma šū-ma:*

b) To the overseer of merchants of Sipparyahrurum say: thus (says) Ammiditana: the collector for goat-hair has reported the following to me: |

6 *a-na* UGULA DAM.GÀR ZIMBIR^{ki}*-ya-aḫ-ru-rum* 7 *aš-šum* SÍG.ÙZ *ne-me-et-ti-šu* 8 *a-na* KÁ.DINGIR.RA^{ki} 9 *šu-bu-li-im* 10 *aš-ta-na-ap-pa-ar-ma*

"ana wakil tamkārī Sippar-yaḫrurum aššum[41] *šīpāt enzim nēmettišu*[42] *ana Bābili šūbulim*[43] *aštanappar-ma*

"I have repeatedly written to the overseer of merchants of Sippar-yahrurum to send the goat-hair, his tax, to Babylon |

11 SÍG.ÙZ *ne-me-et-ta-šu* 12 *ú-ul ú-ša-bi-lam* 13 *ki-a-am ú-lam-mi-da-an-ni*

šīpāt enzim nēmettašu ul ušābilam"; kīam ulammidanni.

but he has not sent the goat-hair, his tax"; thus has he reported to me. |

14 *a-na mi-nim* SÍG.ÙZ *ne-me-et-ta-ka* 15 *a-na* KÁ.DINGIR.RA^{ki} 16 *la tu-ša-bi-lam*

ana mīnim šīpāt enzim nēmettaka ana Bābili la tušābilam?

Why have you not sent the goat-hair, your tax, to Babylon? |

17 *a-na e-pé-ši-im an-ni-im* 18 *ki-i la ta-ap-la-aḫ* r. 19 *ki-ma ṭup-pí an-ni-*⸢*a*⸣*-[am]* 20 *ta-am-ma-*⸢*ru*⸣ 21 SÍG.ÙZ *ne-me-et-ta-ka* 22 *a-na* KÁ.DINGIR.RA^{ki} 23 *šu-bi-lam*

ana epēšim annīm kī la taplaḫ? kīma ṭuppi anniam tammaru,[44] *šīpāt enzim nēmettaka ana Bābili šūbilam!*

How could you dare (lit. not fear) to do such a thing? As soon as you see this tablet, send the goat-hair, your tax, to Babylon!

36. A. Ungnad, *Bab. Briefe aus d. Zeit d. Hamm.-Dyn.* 1914, p. V note. 37. Introduction of direct speech. 38. *ʾlk.* 39. Instead of *nāmer* (*n*-stem of *ʾmr*) after the preterite *innamer* < **inʾamer.* 40. A. Ungnad, *Bab. Briefe aus d. Zeit d. Hamm.-Dyn.* 1914, No. 82. 41. < *ana šum* 'for the name.' 42. *ʿmd.* 43. *wbl*, infinitive of the causative. 44. *ʾmr.*

col. ii

z. Cuneiform text reproduced from H. C. Rawlinson, *A Selection from the Historical Inscriptions of Chaldæa, Assyria, and Babylonia* (London: British Museum, 1861), pls. 38, 39 (The Cuneiform Inscriptions of Western Asia 1); transliteration after R. Borger, op. cit. note p, pp. 73ff. Consulted in translating: D. D. Luckenbill, *The Annals of Sennacherib* (Chicago: Univ. of Chicago Press, 1924), pp. 30-32, and A. Leo Oppenheim in J. B. Pritchard, *Ancient Near Eastern Texts Relating to the Old Testament* (Princeton: Princeton University Press, 1969³), pp. 287f.

aa. 'May the king (live) forever.'

3. From the Prism of Sennacherib (ii 58 - iii 11)[z]

ii 58 *ù* ^{I}*Ṣi-id-qa-a* LUGAL ^{uru}*Is-qa-al-lu-na* 59 *ša la ik-nu-šú a-na ni-ri-ya* DINGIR.MEŠ É AD-*šú šá-a-šú* 60 DAM-*su* DUMU.MEŠ-*šú* DUMU.SAL.MEŠ-*šú* ŠEŠ.MEŠ-*šú* NUMUN É AD-*šú* 61 *as-su-ḫa-am-ma a-na* ^{kur}*Aš-šur*^{ki} *ú-ra-áš-šú*	*u Ṣidqa šar Isqalūna, ša la iknušu ana nīriya, ilāni bīt abīšu šāšu aššassu mārīšu mārātišu aḫḫīšu*[45] *zēr bīt abīšu assuḫam*[46]*-ma ana Aššur ūraššu.*[47]	But Sidka, king of Ashkelon, who had not submitted to my yoke, — the gods of his family (lit. father-house), himself, his wife, his sons, his daughters, his brothers, the seed of his family I deported and brought to Assyria. |
62 ^{I}LUGAL-*lu-dà-ri* DUMU ^{I}*Ru-kib-ti* LUGAL-*šú-nu maḫ-ru-ú* 63 UGU UN.MEŠ ^{uru}*Is-qa-al-lu-na áš-kun-ma na-dan* GUN 64 *kàt-re-e be-lu-ti-ya e-mid-su-ma i-šá-aṭ ab-šá-a-ni*	*Šarru-lu-dāri*[aa] *mār Rukibti šarrišunu maḫrū*[48] *eli nišī Isqalūna aškun-ma nadān bilti katrē bēlūtiya*[49] *ēmissū*[50]*-ma išāṭ*[51] *abšānī.*	Sharruludari, son of Rukibti, their former king, I set over the people of Ashkelon and imposed on him the payment of tribute (and) presents to my lordship, and he was pulling my yoke. |
65 *i-na me-ti-iq gir-ri-ya* ^{uru}É-DA.GAN.NA 66 ^{uru}*Ya-ap-pu-ú* ^{uru}*Ba-na-a-a-bar-qa* ^{uru}*A-zu-ru* 67 URU.MEŠ-*ni ša* ^{I}*Ṣi-id-qa-a ša a-na* GÌR^{II}-*ya* 68 *ár-ḫiš la ik-nu-šú al-me* KUR-*ud áš-lu-la šal-la-sún*	*ina mētiq*[52] *girriya Bīt-Dagan Yappū Banai-barqa Azuru maḫāzāni ša Ṣidqā, ša ana šēpīya arḫiš la iknušū, almē*[53] *akšud ašlula šallassun.*	In the course of my campaign, Beth-Dagon, Joppa, Bnebrak, (and) Asuru, cities of Sidka, which had not promptly bowed at my feet, I besieged, I conquered, I carried off their spoil. |
69 LÚ.GÌR.NITÁ.MEŠ LÚ.NUN.MEŠ *ù* UN.MEŠ ^{uru}*Am-qar-ru-na* 70 *ša* ^{I}*Pa-di-i* LUGAL-*šú-nu* EN *a-de-e ù ma-mit* 71 *ša* ^{kur}*Aš-šur*^{ki} *bi-ri-tu* AN.BAR *id-du-ma*	*šakkanakkī*[S] *rubē*[54] *u nišī Amqarrūna, ša Padī šarrašunu, bēl adē*[55] *u māmīt*[56] *ša Aššur, birītu parzilli*[57] *iddū*[58]*-ma*	The governors, nobles, and people of Ekron, who had thrown Padi, their king, bound by (lit. lord of) oath and curse of Asshur, into fetters of iron |
ana ^{I}*Ḫa-za-qi-ya-ú* 72 ^{kur}*Ya-ú-da-a-a id-di-nu-šú nak-riš a-na an-zil-li e-pu-šú*	*ana Ḫazaqiau Yaudayya iddinūšu*[59] *nakriš — ana anzilli ēpušū*	and had delivered him to Hezekiah the Jew as an enemy — on account of the evil deed they had committed |
73 *ip-laḫ lib-ba-šú-un* LUGAL.MEŠ-*ni* ^{kur}*Mu-ṣu-ri* 74 LÚ.ERÉN.MEŠ GIŠ.PAN GIŠ.GIGIR.MEŠ ANŠE.KUR.RA.MEŠ *ša* LUGAL ^{kur}*Me-luḫ-ḫi* 75 *e-mu-qi la ni-bi ik-te-ru-nim-ma il-li-ku* 76 *re-ṣu-su-un*	*iplaḫ libbašun, šarrāni Muṣuri ṣābī*[60] *qašti narkabāti sīsē*[61] *ša šar Meluḫḫi, emūqī la nībi,*[62] *ikterūnim-ma illikū rēṣūssun.*[63]	their heart(s) feared, and they called upon the kings of Egypt, the bowmen, chariots, and horses of the king of Meluhha, an army beyond counting, and these came to their aid. |

45. Irregular plural of *aḫu*. 46. *nsḫ*. 47. *wrʾ*, ventive. 48. Nisbe of *maḫru* 'front, earlier time.' 49. *bʿl*. 50. *ʿmd*. 51. *šwṭ* present. 52. *ʿtq*. 53. *lwy*. 54. *rby*. 55. *wdʿ*. 56. *ḥwy*. 57. Loanword from Anatolia. 58. *ndy*. 59. *ndn*. 60. *ṣbʾ*. 61. Loanword of uncertain origin. 62. *nbʾ*. 63. *rwṣ*.

col. iii

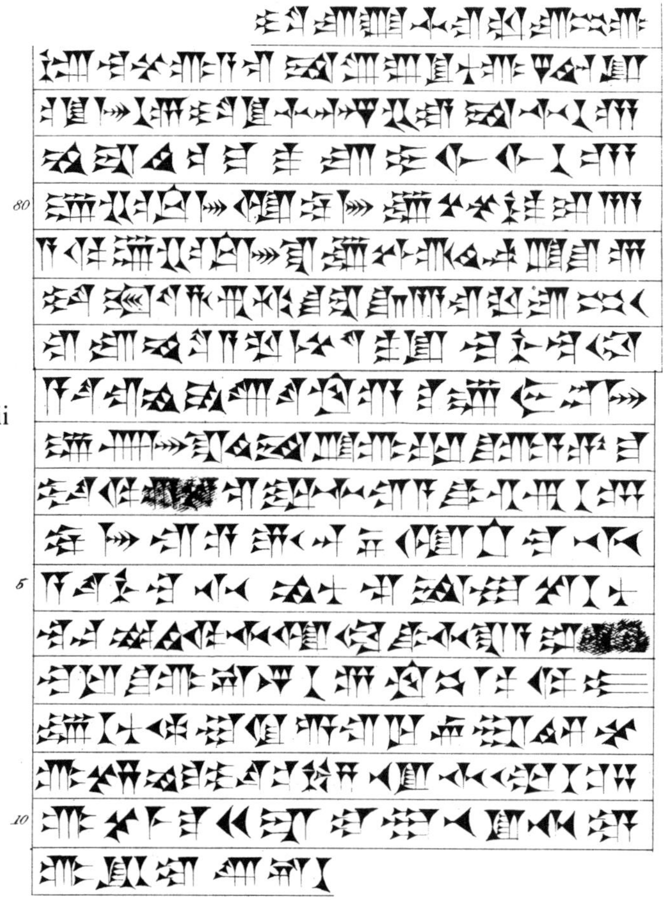

i-na ta-mir-ti ^{uru}*Al-ta-qu-ú* 77 *el-la-mu-ú-a si-id-ru šit-ku-nu ú-šá-ʾi-lu* 78 GIŠ.TUKUL.MEŠ-*šú-un*	*ina tamirti Altaqū ellamūa sidrū šitkunū ušaʾilū kakkīšun.*$^{S?}$	In the environs of Eltekeh their ranks were drawn up against me (and) they sharpened their weapons.
i-na tukul-ti ^{d}*Aš-šur* EN-*ya it-ti-šú-un* 79 *am-da-ḫi-iṣ-ma áš-ta-kan* BAD5.BAD5-*šú-un*	*ina tukulti Aššur bēliya ittišun amdaḫiṣ*[64]*-ma aštakan taḫtāšun.*[65]	With the aid of Asshur, my lord, I fought with them and brought about their defeat.
80 LÚ.EN GIŠ.GIGIR.MEŠ *ù* DUMU.MEŠ LUGAL ^{kur}*Mu-ṣu-ra-a-a* 81 *a-di* LÚ.EN GIŠ.GIGIR.MEŠ *ša* LUGAL ^{kur}*Me-luḫ-ḫi bal-ṭu-su-un* 82 *i-na* MURUB4 *tam-ḫa-ri ik-šu-da* ŠU^{II}*-a-a* ^{uru}*Al-ta-qu-u* 83 ^{uru}*Ta-am-na-a al-me* KUR-*ud áš-lu-la šal-la-sún*	*bēl narkabāti u mār šar Muṣurayya adi bēl narkabāti ša šar Meluḫḫi balṭūssun ina qabal tamḫāri ikšudā qātāya. Altaqū Tamnā almē akšud ašlula šallassun.*	The Egyptian charioteers and princes, together with the charioteers of the king of Meluhha, I personally (lit. my hands) captured alive in the midst of battle. Eltekah (and) Timna I besieged, I conquered, I carried off their spoil.
iii 1 *a-na* ^{uru}*Am-qar-ru-na aq-rib-ma* LÚ.GÌR.NITÁ.MEŠ 2 LÚ.NUN.MEŠ *ša ḫi-iṭ-ṭu ú-šab-šu-ú a-duk-ma* 3 *i-na di-⌜ma-a-te⌝ si-ḫir-ti* URU *a-lul pag-ri-šú-un*	*ana Amqarrūna aqrib-ma šakkanakkī*^{S} *rubē, ša ḫiṭṭu*[66] *ušabšū,*[67] *adūk-ma ina dimāti siḫirti maḫāzi ālul*[68] *pagrīšun.*	I came to Ekron, slew the officials and nobles who had committed sin, and hung their bodies on poles around the city.
4 DUMU.MEŠ URU *e-piš an-ni ù gíl-la-ti* 5 *a-na šal-la-ti am-nu si-it-tu-te-šú-nu* 6 *la ba-bil ḫi-ṭi ù gul-lul-ti ša a-ra-⌜an-šú-nu⌝* 7 *la ib-šu-ú uš-šur-šú-un aq-bi*	*mār āli ēpiš*[69] *anni*[70] *u gillati ana šallati amnū, sittūtišunu la bābil*[71] *ḫiṭṭi ū gullulti, ša aranšunu la ibšū, uššuršun*[72] *aqbī.*	The city-dwellers who were criminals and evil-doers I counted as spoil, and the rest, who were not guilty of sin or misdeed, not charged with any crime (lit. their guilt did not exist), I ordered their release.
^{I}*Pa-di-i* 8 LUGAL-*šú-nu ul-tu qé-reb* ^{uru}*Ur-sa-li-im-mu* 9 *ú-še-ṣa-am-ma i-na* GIŠ.GU.ZA *be-lu-ti* UGU-*šú-un* 10 *ú-še-šib-ma man-da-at-tu be-lu-ti-ya* 11 *ú-kin ṣe-ru-uš-šú*	*Padī šarrašunu ultu qereb Ursalimmu ušēṣām*[73]*-ma ina kussī*^{S} *bēlūti elišun ušēšib*[74]*-ma mandattu*[75] *bēlūtiya ukīn*[76] *ṣēruššu.*	Padi, their king, I brought out of Jerusalem and set on the throne of lordship over them, and imposed on him tribute for my lordship.

64. *mḫṣ*, *t*-stem. 65. *ḫty*. 66. *ḫṭʾ*. 67. *bšy*. 68. *ʾll*. 69. Participle. 70. *annu* = *arnu*. 71. Participle. 72. *yšr*, infinitive of the intensive. 73. *wṣʾ*. 74. *wšb*. 75. *ndn*. 76. *kwn* intensive.

a)

OBVERSE.

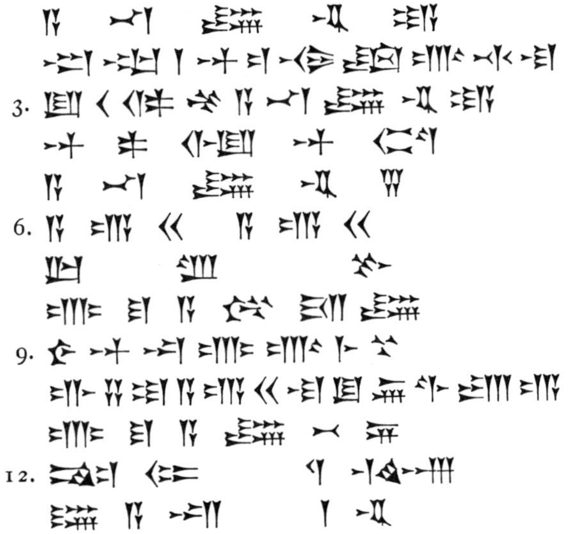

REVERSE.

ab. Cuneiform text reproduced from R. F. Harper, *Assyrian and Babylonian Letters belonging to the Kouyunjik Collections of the British Museum* (Chicago: Univ. of Chicago Press, 1896), vol. 4, No. 341; transliteration after L. Waterman, *The Royal Correspondence of the Assyrian Empire* (Ann Arbor: Univ. of Michigan Press, 1931), vol. 1, p. 236.

ac. 'Shamash has revived the dead.'

ad. 'Bau is merciful.'

ae. Cuneiform text reproduced from R. F. Harper, op. cit. note ab, No. 435; transliteration after L. Waterman, op. cit. note ab, pp. 300ff. Consulted in translating: A. Leo Oppenheim, *Letters from Mesopotamia* (Chicago: Univ. of Chicago Press, 1967), No. 89.

af. E. Reiner suggests emending the verb to the idiomatic *liṭīb* 'be pleasing to.'

ag. Translation uncertain.

b)

OBVERSE.

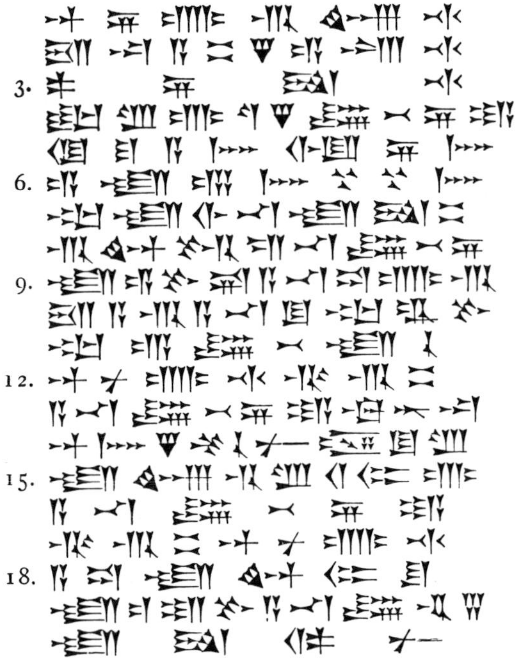

REVERSE.

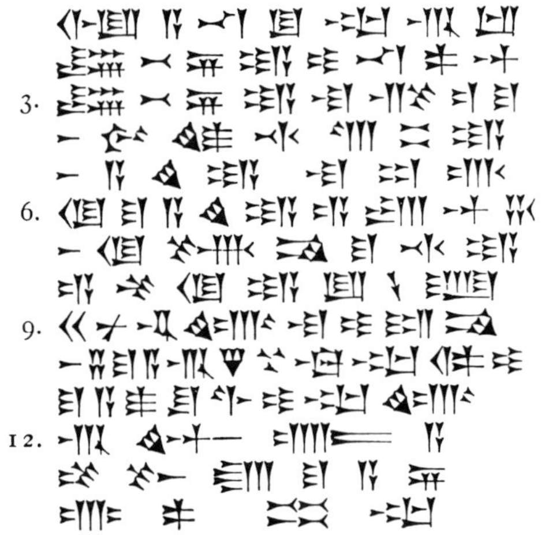

4. Two Neo-Assyrian Letters[77]

1 *a-na* LUGAL EN-*ya* 2 ARAD-*ka* {lú}GIŠ.ŠIR-UG5.GA-TI.LA 3 *lu-u šul-mu a-na* LUGAL EN-*ya* 4 {d}PA *ù* {d}AMAR.UD 5 *a-na* LUGAL EN-*yá* 6 *a-dan-niš a-dan-niš* 7 *lik-ru-bu*	**a)**[ab] *ana šarri bēliya aradka Šamaš-mīt-uballiṭ.*[ac] *lu šulmu ana šarri bēliya! Nabū u Marduk ana šarri bēliya adanniš adanniš likrubū!*	**a)** To the king, my lord, your slave Shamashmituballit. Greetings to the king, my lord! May Nabu and Marduk bless the king, my lord, mightily, mightily! |
8 *ú-ma-a* GEMÉ *ša* LUGAL 9 {fd}*Ba-ú-ga-me-lat* 10 *mar-ṣa-at a-dan-niš la ku-sa-pi ta-kal* 11 *ú-ma-a* LUGAL *be-lí* 12 *ṭè-mi liš-kun* 13 LÚ.A.ZU 1-*en* r. 1 *lil-li-ka* 2 *li-mur-ši*	*umā amtu ša šarri Bau-gāmilat*[ad] *marṣat adanniš, la kusāpi takkal;*[78] *umā šarru bēlī ṭēmi*[79] *liškun, asū ištēn lillika*[80] *līmurši.*[81]	Now: a slave-girl of the king, Bau-gamilat, is seriously ill, she does not eat a bite; now let the king, my lord, give an order, that a physician come (and) examine her.
1 *an-ni-ú ri-iḫ-ti* 2 *da-ba-a-bi ša e-gír-ti* 3 *pa-ni-it-ti* 4 *šar-ru-ú-tú ša* LUGAL *be-lí-ya* 5 *ki-ma* A.MEŠ *ù* Ì.MEŠ 6 *e-li* UN.MEŠ KUR.KUR.MEŠ 7 *ka-li-ši-na li-it-bi*	**b)**[ae] *anniu rīḫti dabābi ša egerti panitti.*[82] *šarrūtu ša šarri bēliya kīma mē u šamnē eli nīšē mātāti kalīšina litbī!*[af]	**b)** This is the rest of the content of the earlier letter. May the kingship of the king, my lord, like water and oil rise over all the people of the world (lit. lands)! |
8 *re-eʾ-us-si-na* LUGAL *be-lí* 9 *le-e-pu-uš a-na du-ú-ri* 10 *da-a-ri a-na-ku ka-al-bu* 11 *ka-rib* LUGAL *be-li-šú*	*rēʾūssina*[83] *šarru bēlī lēpuš*[84] *ana dūri dāri! anāku kalbu, kārib šarri bēlišu!*	May the king, my lord, exert shepherdship over them for everlasting eternity! I am a dog who greets the king, his lord. |
12 *an-nu-ú-ti ik-ri-bi* 13 *a-na* LUGAL *be-lí-ya ak-tar-ba* 14 DINGIR.MEŠ *šá* MU-*šú-nu az-ku-ru* 15 *li-iḫ-ḫu-ru liš-mi-ú* 16 *a-na* LUGAL *be-lí-ya* 17 *ik-ri-bi an-nu-ú-ti* 18 *a-du li-iʾ-mi-šu* 19 *li-iṣ-ṣi-pu a-na* LUGAL EN-*yá* 20 *li-id-di-nu*	*annūti ikribī ana šarri bēliya aktarba, ilāni ša šumšunu azkuru liḫḫurū*[85] *lišmiū,*[86] *ana šarri bēliya ikribī annūti adu*[87] *liʾmišu liṣṣipū,*[88] *ana šarri bēliya liddinū!*[89]	As for these blessings which I have invoked on the king, my lord, may the gods whose names I have spoken accept (and) hear (them) and may they multiply these blessings for the king, my lord, a thousandfold, and bestow them on the king, my lord. |
r. 1 *ù a-na-ku ka-ri-ib* 2 LUGAL *be-lí-ya i-na pa-an* 3 LUGAL *be-lí-ya la-zi-iz-ma* 4 *ina gu-mur-ti lìb-bi-ya* 5 *ina a-ḫi-ya la-ap-laḫ* 6 *ki-ma a-ḫi-ya e-ta-an-ḫa* 7 *ina ki-ṣir am-ma-ti-ya* 8 *e-mu-qí-ya lu-gam-mir*	*u anāku, kārib šarri bēliya, ina pan*[90] *šarri bēliya lazziz*[91]*-ma ina gumurti libbiya ina aḫēya laplaḫ; kīma aḫēya ētanḫā,*[92] *ina kiṣir ammātiya emūqīya lugammir!*	And I, who do homage to the king, my lord, would stand before the king, my lord, and from my whole heart honor (lit. fear) with my arms; if my arms tire, I will exert my strength to the utmost with my arms bent![ag] |
9 *man-nu* EN DÙG.GA *la i-ra-am* 10 *ina za-ma-a-ri šá* KUR *Ak-ka-di-i* 11 *ma-a áš-šu pi-i-ka* DÙG.GA 12 *re-eʾ-ú-a* 13 *gab-bu um-ma-a-ni* 14 *ú-pa-qu-ka*	*mannu bēla ṭāba la irām?*[93] *ina zamāri ša māt Akkadī mā: "aššu*[94] *pīka ṭābi, rēʾūa, gabbu ummāni upaqqūka!"*[95]	Who does not love a good lord? In the song of the land of Akkad (it says): "On account of your sweet voice, my shepherd, all people heed you."

77. Frdr. Delitzsch, *Assyrische Lesestücke*[5] 1912, p. 88b; p. 90-91h. 78. *ʾkl.* 79. *ṭʿm.* 80. *ʾlk.* 81. *ʾmr.* 82. = *panīti*, nisbe of *panū* 'face.' 83. *rʿy.* 84. I laryngeal. 85. *mḫr.* 86. *šmʿ.* 87. = *adi.* 88. *yṣp* intensive. 89. *ndn.* 90. From *panū* 'face.' 91. *nzz.* 92. *ʾḫn.* 93. *rʾm.* 94. = *ana šum.* 95. *pqḫ.*

Chapter 3

Hebrew

§ 3/1.0

Old Hebrew, the language of the Old Testament and a few inscriptions, preserves the spirit of old West Semitic best in sentence structure: it has not advanced to the strict systematization of Arabic, but clings to an archaic freedom, and has grown even more flexible and variable thanks to the richness of its complicated tense system; while on the other hand, it has not regressed to the syntactic amorphousness of Aramaic, although due to the loss of the short-vowel endings its sharpness of expression has been mitigated. This loss of final short vowels is one of the results of an alteration of accent that has led in the long run to far-reaching vowel lengthenings and reductions; some less striking changes in the quality of vowels go along with this. The original inventory of consonants is somewhat reduced. The characteristic feature of the consonantism, the spirantization of all stops, along with the vowel reductions, classes Hebrew with Aramaic; it may have taken on both these features relatively late under Aramaic influence, which after the exile grew stronger and stronger.[a]

a. Some information about Ugaritic (and Phoenician) is added in the notes. Because the data on the vowels in these languages are limited, only interesting points of difference with Hebrew are mentioned. Such vocalizations as are given are those of Gordon □3a:3.

The vocalization of Hebrew has come down to us in several traditions, of which the received (the Tiberian) and the Babylonian are considered here.[1]—

§ 3/1.1.1

Hebrew deals with the dental spirants in just about the same way as Akkadian; the only difference from Akkadian in the realm of dentals and sibilants is that Hebrew does not alter

1. The transcription proceeds under the assumption that the vowel signs in principle indicate only the quality, not the quantity of the vowels; the quantities are supplied in accordance with phonological rules.

the original palatal sibilant *ś* to *š*, but retains it and later merges it with *s*. The velar spirant *ḫ* merges with the neighboring laryngeal *ḥ* to *ḥ*[2] (ʿ likewise includes South Semitic *γ*).[b] The laryngeals show signs of weakening: ʿ ʾ and, rarely, *h* disappear in some circumstances (e.g., *rōš* 'head' < **rāš* < **raʾš*; *yōmar* 'he says' < **yaʾmar*, *yimṣā* 'he finds' < **yimṣaʾ*). The laryngeals as a group, and *r* as well, can no longer be lengthened; instead, compensatory lengthening of the preceding vowel generally takes place (sometimes, particularly with *h* and even more often with *ḥ*, it does not). Elsewhere, too, vowel length and lengthening of a following consonant are, within narrow limits, equivalent (secondary consonant lengthening can replace vowel lengthening and vice versa). Consonant length is always given up finally without compensatory lengthening (*ʿām* 'people' < **ʿam* [by stress lengthening] < **ʿamm-*), and also in some consonants when they are vowelless[3] (e.g., *wayhī* 'and he was' for **wayyhī*). — The semivowel *w* has become *y* initially[d] (though 'and' is still *w-*), and in part also medially. Both semivowels often mutate into the homorganic vowels, especially after prefixes (*bi* + vowelless[3] *y-* > *bī*, also *min* + vowelless[3] *y-* > *miyy* > *mī*) and in the conjugation of III weak verbs; in the Babylonian vocalization, initial vowelless[3] *y-* generally becomes *i*, e.g., *iḥī* 'may he live' = Ti *yḥī*. — The non-emphatic stops *b d g p t k* become the corresponding spirants postvocalically,[4] even across a boundary between two words when they are closely connected, and also after an originally present vowel that later disappeared (e.g., *alp̄ē* 'thousands of . . .' < **alapai*). *n* usually assimilates to a following consonant.

b. Ugaritic keeps *ḫ*, *γ* (which regularly corresponds to both Ab *γ* and Ab *ḍ*: does this represent a further proto-Semitic phoneme?), *θ*, *θ̣*, and *δ*. The proto-Semitic laterals *δ̣* and *ś* are not found. Phoenician has the same consonants as Hebrew except for *ś*.

c. They were lost late in the history of Phoenician.

d. To this extent, so also in Ugaritic.

2. In modern Israeli Hebrew much more often pronounced *ḫ*.

3. Cf. n. 6.

4. In Modern Hebrew spirantization does not affect *d g t*.

§ 3/1.1.3

Northwest Semitic had penultimate accent, which predominantly turned into final accent as a result of the subsequent loss of final short vowels.[5] The strong stress-accent completely altered the vocalism.[e] Hebrew lost almost all its final short vowels (above all its case endings) and many long ones, e.g., *-ēḵ* 'thy, thee' (feminine) < **-ikī*, ^{c}*al* 'on' < *^{c}*alai*. Medially, short vowels were lengthened in accented syllables and in open pretonic syllables, while they disappeared from other open syllables[6] (in a sequence of several such syllables, only from the last and third from last of them). Thus **la-δahabi* 'gold' (dative) > *lzāhāḇ*, **wa-la-ba*^{c}*alaihu* 'and to his masters' > *wliḇ*^{c}*ālāu*. The rule of pretonic lengthening admits of numerous exceptions, particularly in cases of *i* and *u*. The verb forms (without pronominal suffix) were originally accented on the antepenult, and thus after the loss of final short vowels the penult; only later did they switch to final accent, without alteration of the vowels. In this way we can explain *ā́mar* 'he spoke' with short tonic syllable, and *āmrā́* 'she spoke' < **amarat* with vowel loss in the pretonic syllable. The principal items (in addition to particles, etc.) that were entirely unaccented were nouns in the construct state and some imperatives; thus construct *alp̄ē* < **alapai*, *dḇar* 'word' from *dāḇār*, imperative *šlop̄* 'draw (the sword)' < **šulup* with vowel loss. The end of an utterance (the pause) has a special status with regard to accent; there even verbs follow the regular stress rules.[7]

When final consonant clusters result from the loss of final short vowels, they are usually resolved by an epenthetic vowel

e. Any number of schemes to explain the elaborate system of accent and vowel lengthening and reduction have been proposed. Noteworthy about Bergsträsser's solution as summarized here is the insistence that it is particularly stress (as opposed to pitch) accent that causes vowels to disappear. This position requires some hedging concerning Arabic, where long strings of short vowels in open syllables are preserved with the first one stressed.

f. Bergsträsser was criticized for omitting the reduced vowels from his transcription; but in fact since spirantization is indicated, the result is in effect a phonemic transcription. Cf. § 6/2 note b.

5. All words not finally accented are here marked with their accent.

6. To be more precise: were reduced to the "murmured" vowel (shwa) *ĕ*, which is not sharply distinguished from complete disappearance; the shwa is here omitted for simplicity's sake.[f]

7. Sentence-end (pause) forms that differ from the forms found within the sentences are marked ^{P} in the texts.

(Tiberian usually *e*, Babylonian more commonly *a*): **šibṭu* 'tribe' > **šibṭ* > Ti *šébeṭ*, Ba *šébaṭ*.

§ 3/1.1.2

The diphthongs *au* and *ai* are monophthongized to *ō* and *ē*, except that in closed accented syllables they are disyllabically resolved (like final clusters): *ḥáyil* 'power,' *máweṯ* 'death' (but construct state *ḥēl mōṯ*).[g] In the Babylonian recension, *ai* is occasionally retained: *-áihā* = *-ai* (masculine plural construct ending) + *-hā* (third person feminine singular pronominal suffix), Ti *-ḗhā*. Long accented *ā* becomes *ō* — the sound change that most clearly demarcates Hebrew from Aramaic.[h] *i* often replaces *a* in closed unaccented syllables;[i] in the Babylonian recension, more often, *a* is preserved. Contrariwise original *i* in a closed accented syllable becomes *a*: *baṯ* 'daughter' < **bint* (likewise Am *barṯā* 'daughter'); secondarily *i* (*e*) is often reintroduced. In closed accented syllables *i* and *u* become *e* and *o* (and lengthened *ē ō*); in the Tiberian recension *u* is sometimes altered in closed unaccented syllables to a particular open *o*,[8] unknown to the Babylonian recension. Correspondingly, the latter also lacks the open *e* (*ē*)[8] which is found in the Tiberian recension as an umlaut of *a* (*ā*), less commonly of *i* (*ē*), and also as epenthetic vowel. The laryngeals have considerable influence on the vocalization; they often alter adjacent *i u* to *a* (in the Tiberian recension, sometimes at least, *i* to open *e*)[j] and give occasion for the retention of old vowels or the development of epenthetic vowels (in the Babylonian recension especially after initial ʾ[9] and amidst sequences of consonants within words; in the Tiberian recension before a word-final laryngeal after long vowel other than *ā*: *Gilbṓaᶜ* for **Gilbōᶜ*). —

g. In Ugaritic and Phoenician all *au ai* > *ō ē*.

h. This change does not take place in Ugaritic (this is the main basis for the argument that Ugaritic is not a Canaanite language); on the other hand, in Phoenician all *ā* > *ō*.

i. This "Barth's" law was demonstrated to hold for Ugaritic by Ginsberg.

j. All Ugaritic *a*ʾC > *e*ʾC.

8. For simplicity's sake, the two *o*'s and the two *e*'s are not distinguished; also isolated variations in quality of *a ā* are not indicated.

9. Accordingly, a vowel is indicated here in the Tiberian recension (with breve). In this case and very often, if the laryngeal was otherwise vowelless then the Tiberian recension writes reduced vowels *ă*, *ĕ* (open), *ŏ*; these, like the ordinary reduced vowel *ĕ* (see n. 6), are omitted from the transcription.

§ 3/1.2.1.1 For 'I,' beside *ănī* there is the form, found also in Akkadian, extended by a *-k-*, *ānōḵī*; both forms have incorporated the ending of the suffix *-ī*. Conversely, in 'we' the ending of the independent pronoun *ănáḥnū* has been taken over as the suffix *-nū*. The original final long vowels of the pronouns and pronominal suffixes have in part disappeared. The masculines 'you; your, you' and 'they; their, them' have kept the *e*-vowel: *attem -ḵem hem -hem* (the Babylonian recension on the contrary has *a*). After a word ending originally with a short vowel and now with a consonant, a linking vowel, which developed from the former final vowel, is inserted before the suffix; only before the second person plural suffixes *-ḵem -ḵen* (always with *ḵ*, not *k*) is it lacking. In the second person singular the linking vowel is unchangeable: masculine pausal form *-ḗḵa* or *-āḵ* (elsewhere, in both the Tiberian and Babylonian recensions the form *-ḵā* occurs, which violates the sound laws; it replaces the expected *-āḵ* as found in other recensions), feminine *-ēḵ*; otherwise it depends on the kind of word the suffix is attached to, and in fact is usually *a*, but in the imperfect and imperative *e*. Furthermore, the affix *-en-* can occur before the suffix on these two forms as well as on several particles that originally took the accusative, and then the linking vowel is absent: *-énnī -ékkā* (< **-enkā*) *-énnū* (< **-enhū*) *-énnā* (< **-enhā*), etc. — The third person suffixes commonly lose their *h*; **-ahū* is then contracted to *-ō*, **-aihu* to *-āu*, **-ahem* to *-ām*, **-ehem* to *-ēm*, etc. (but **-ahā* is replaced by *-āh*).

§ 3/1.2.1.2 Hebrew has a definite article *ha-* (plus lengthening of the following consonant), which in, e.g., *hayyōm* 'today' (literally 'this day') retains its demonstrative character. For the demonstrative the stem *δ-* is used in the singular, and the stem *l-* in the plural: *zē* 'this,' feminine *zōṯ* (rarely *zō*, which predominates in post-Biblical Hebrew), plural *éllē*.[k] 'That' is expressed by the personal pronoun *hū* 'he.' When used adjectivally beside a definite noun, the demonstrative, like other adjectives, takes the article, and also like them follows the noun: *hāʾīš hazzē* 'this man.' 'Who?' is *mī*, 'what?' is *mā* (*mē*).[l] The relative particle and conjunction 'that' (often following prepositions) is *ăšer* (Ba *ašar*).[m] —

k. The Ugaritic demonstrative is *dū*, feminine *dāt* or *d*, plural *dūt* or *dū*.

l. Ugaritic has an indefinite, both animate and inanimate, *mn*.

m. The relative in Ugaritic is *d*, reminiscent of the situation in Aramaic.

§ 3/1.2.2

The first and second person perfect suffixes are the same as the endings of the personal pronouns; the first person singular -*tī* exhibits only the vowel. The suffix of the third person feminine singular is -*ā* like the nominal feminine ending. In the imperfect the third person feminine plural prefix is *t*-. The plural ending -*ū* is later supplemented by -*ūn*.

§ 3/1.2.2.1

Besides the indicative, the imperfect has a "cohortative" in -*ā* (first person only, = 'I, we will, intend to') and a jussive (wish form), which often merges with the indicative, but is elsewhere distinguished from it by its shorter form or regressed accent (or both).[n] The jussive serves, sometimes with minor changes of form, as the most common means of expression of the past, but only after the particle 'and,' which in this case is *wa*- (plus lengthening of the following consonant) (*waw*-consecutive, imperfect consecutive). Correspondingly, the perfect after 'and' (here in its regular form *w*-)[10] occurs in the sense of the imperfect (jussive, imperative). All this results in a complicated tense syntax for Hebrew which has no parallel in any other Semitic literary language.[o] — Imperfect and perfect consecutives are used to continue not just finite verbs, but also infinitives and participles; e.g., *makkē īš wāmēṯ*[11] 'the striker of

n. Ugaritic has an indicative *yaqtulu*, subjunctive *yaqtula*, jussive *yaqtul*, and energic *yaqtulan*(*na*).

o. One Old Aramaic inscription, discovered since Bergsträsser wrote, has a few *waw*-consecutive forms. Ugaritic prose uses *qtl* for the past and *yqtl* for the future, as well as *waw*-consecutives; in poetry, *yqtl* is the narrative form. The Phoenician system is very like the Hebrew, though *waw*-consecutives are rare; nowhere near enough poetry is preserved to determine anything about poetic verb usage.

10. But a shift of the accent to the end of the word often takes place: *śámtī* 'I put,' but *wśamtī́*.

11. *wā*- here is the pretonic form of *w*-.

a man and he dies,' i.e., 'if someone strikes a man and he dies.' This capability of passing from verbal nouns to finite verbs is one of the characteristic syntactic freedoms of Hebrew. The consecutive tenses often constitute the apodosis of a conditional etc. protasis; e.g., *im āsōn yihyē, wnāṯattā* . . . 'if there is lasting harm, you shall give . . . .' Moreover, this is an archaic form, in which hypotaxis is used in the protasis, but the apodosis is paratactically connected with it. In longer sequences of imperfect consecutives only the content can decide which of the elements belong more closely together, in a relation which we express by subordination with "when"; Hebrew in such cases relinquishes the characteristics of hypotaxis entirely.

Of the two infinitives in Hebrew, the ordinary one, the so-called infinitive construct, has by and large the normal functions of an infinitive (by preference combined with *l-* to correspond to some extent with our infinitive with "to," but also occurring gerundively — = 'while' — in construction with another form of the same verb); the infinitive absolute, a peculiarly Hebrew hybrid of verbal noun and verbal interjection of imperative character, is limited to use as paranomastic object and rarely as nominal substitute for a finite verbal form (usually an imperative). In the basic stem and some of the derived stems it has *ō* in the second syllable, e.g., *sāqōl* 'to stone,' intensive *rappō* (from *rpʾ*) 'to heal.'

p. The passive of the basic stem may be much more frequent in the Hebrew Bible than the traditional vocalization indicates: the text was so pointed only when context and consonants admitted no other alternative, but this results in not uncommon cases of, e.g., intensive passives of verbs that are not attested in the intensive active.

§ 3/1.2.2.2

From the full complement of verbal stems, besides the basic stem Hebrew uses only the *n*-reflexive, the intensive and its *t*-reflexive, and the causative (with prefix *h-*); there are passives of the intensive and causative, and, in traces, of the basic stem.[p, q]

q. To this assortment Ugaritic adds a *t*-reflexive of the basic stem. Its causative is formed with *š*, while the Phoenician causative has the formative *y*.

§ 3/1.2.2.3

In the basic stem the neutral mode, particularly the *u*-perfect, is in decline. Except in a few deviant groups of verbs only traces of the *i*-imperfect remain. Imperative and infinitive look the same, e.g., *šlop̄* 'draw (the sword)' and 'to draw' (as infinitive, *šlōp̄*); when endings are added, forms with a vowel in the first syllable predominate: *doqrénī* 'thrust me through,' *horḡō* 'his death' or 'to kill him.' When an infinitive like *pṯṓaḥ* 'to open' takes the prefix *l-* it is *lip̄tṓaḥ*, without spirantization of the second consonant; with this discrimination the independent semantic development of the infinitive with *l-* becomes operative. The stem underlying the perfect serves as the neutral-mode participle, e.g., *śāmḗaḥ* 'rejoicing' and 'he rejoices, rejoiced' (pause form); *yāḵōl* 'being able' and (*yāḵol*) 'he can, could.' The *ā* of the active participle becomes *ō*: *lōḥēṣ* 'oppressing' (plural *lōḥṣīm*); the passive participle is *pāᶜūl*.

§ 3/1.2.2.4 The *n*-reflexive has the form *nip̄ᶜal*; various groups of verbs have kept the older *a* of the prefix. In the imperfect the *n* assimilates to the first radical: *yissāqel* 'he will be stoned' (the Babylonian recension instead has secondary *a* in the last syllable: *yillāḵaḏ* 'he will be conquered'); the forms formed from the imperfect stem without prefix have a prothetic *h-*, e.g., *hikkānēs* 'to enter.' The participle, as in the neutral-mode basic stem, is the same as the perfect (*nip̄ᶜāl*). The *n*-reflexive is the most usual expression of the passive of the basic stem. The passives retain an active semantic element, so that the logical patient can be introduced using the object particle *eṯ*: *yēᵓāḵel eṯ-bśārō* 'his flesh will be eaten.'

The intensive and causative have *i* (*e*) in their last syllable, and in the first *i* in the perfect and *a* in the imperfect etc. Not uncommon is the older *a* in the last syllable of the intensive perfect (predominant in the Babylonian recension), and the older *a* of the first syllable of the causative perfect remains in various groups of verbs. In the causative, the *i* of the last syllable has secondarily lengthened to *ī* in many forms. The *h* of the preformative elides after prefixes. Thus perfect *hiḏbī́qū* 'they pursued,' imperfect *yaḏbī́qū*; but imperative *haḏbeq*, imperfect consecutive *wayyaṣ̌ᶜeq* 'and he summoned.' The participle has *a* in the prefix, or in a few anomalous groups of verbs *i*. The infinitives of both stems are like imperfects without personal prefix: *baśśer* 'to announce,' *haqrīḇ* 'to offer.'

The intensive reflexive has the form *hiṯhallek* 'he wandered' (with prothetic *h*), imperfect *yiṯhallek̲*; *a* is common in the last syllable of the perfect, while in the imperfect it is found only in the Babylonian recension. The *t* of the prefix metathesizes with a first-radical sibilant; and in some circumstances it can assimilate. E.g., *mištammśīn* 'using,' *yiṣṭārk̲ū* 'they will need.'

The passives uniformly have the sequence of vowels *u* (*o*) - *a*.

§ **3/1.2.2.5.1**   Verbs I *n* with *a*- or *i*-imperfects lose the first radical in the imperative and infinitive of the basic stem; e.g., from *nāḡaš* 'he drew near' *gaš* and *géšet̲* (< *gašt*, with feminine ending), and *ten* 'give' from *nāt̲an*, imperfect *yitten*. The antonym of 'give,' *lāqaḥ* 'take,' has been attracted into this group; therefore imperfect *yiqqaḥ*, imperative *qaḥ*.

The verbs I *w* (in Hebrew beginning with *y*) with *i*-imperfect have weak imperfects etc.: e.g., *yāšaḇ* 'he sat': imperfect *yēšeḇ*, imperative *šeḇ*, infinitive *šiḇtō* 'his sitting' (with feminine ending); *yāṣā* 'he went out': *yēṣē*; in this group also (with secondary *a* because of the laryngeal) *yāḏaᶜ* 'he knew': *yēḏaᶜ*, infinitive *dáᶜat̲* < *daᶜt*.[12] The group has annexed *hālak̲* 'he went': *yēlek̲*. Entirely in a class by itself is *yāk̲ol* 'he could, can,' imperfect *yūk̲al*. The perfects of the *n*-reflexive and the causative have the original prefix vowel *a*: *nōsap̄* 'he was added,' *hōqī́ᶜū* 'they suspended(?).' The passive

12. Actually I *y*, but almost everywhere in West Semitic changed to the I *w* group.

of the causative is *hūšaḇ* 'it (the place) was settled'; all biliteral stems follow this pattern, e.g., II weak *hūmaṯ* 'he was killed,' imperfect *yūmaṯ*. — Some I weak verbs are inflected like I *n* verbs: e.g., *niṣṣaṯ* 'he was burned' from *yāṣaṯ*.

§ 3/1.2.2.5.2

The very complicated inflection of the II geminate verbs incorporates many biradical forms; e.g., with the triliteral perfect of the simple stem *sāḇaḇ* 'he surrounded' (but neutral-mode verbs are biliteral, like *mar* 'it was, is bitter') goes the imperfect *yāsoḇ* (neutral *yēra*^{c} 'it is bad'), *n*-reflexive perfect *nāsaḇ*, imperfect *yissaḇ*, causative perfect *hēseḇ*, imperfect *yāseḇ*, participle *mēsēḇ*[r] (with a prefix vowel at variance with that of the strong verb). Before a vocalic suffix the second radical is geminated: *yasóbbū* 'they surround,' even before the linking vowel that such forms require before consonantal affixes: *sabbṓṯā* 'thou surroundest,' *tsubbḗnā* 'they (feminine) surround.' Like the II weak verbs, these verbs usually form the intensive on the pattern *sōḇeḇ*, *ysōḇeḇ*.

r. Nyberg □1:6R4,109 *mēseḇ*. Bergsträsser's flouting of transcriptional convention — hinted at in nn. 1 and 8, but not made explicit — seems to be based on assigning short vowels to verbal forms and long vowels to nominal forms of verb roots. The justification may be found in □3b:6v2§14s.

The II weak verbs occur in the basic stem perfect in active-mode and neutral-mode vocalizations: *qām* 'he stood up,' *śām* 'he put' (with first person *śámtī*, etc.), but *mēṯ* 'he has died, is dead.' In the imperfect only the *w*-series and *y*-series are distinguished: *yāqūm yāmūṯ*, but *yāśīm* (the imperfect consecutive has stress retraction and vowel shortening: *wayyā́qom wayyā́moṯ*, *wayyā́śem*); so also the imperative and infinitive *qūm mūṯ*, *śīm* (but infinitive absolute with its characteristic *ō*: *śōm*). 'Come,' among others, is inflected irregularly: perfect *bā*, imperfect *yāḇō*. The participle is the same as the perfect. The *n*-reflexive is *nāqōm* (with the older prefix vowel, as in the II geminate), *yiqqōm*; the causative is *hēmīṯ* 'he killed,' *yāqīm*, participle with the same variant prefix vowel as in the II geminate *mē*^{c}*īḏ* 'testifying.'

The III weak verbs have generalized single endings for all the unsuffixed forms: perfect *-ā*, imperfect etc. *-ē*, infinitive *-ōṯ* (with feminine ending). Before vocalic endings the final *-ā -ē* simply drop out; before consonantal suffixes the stem ends with *-ē* or *-ī* in varying distribution. Thus a rather simple conjugation results, disturbed only by the imperfect consecutive and related forms. These lose the second syllable of the stem entirely, resulting in forms in the basic stem and in the causative with final clusters that usually receive an epenthetic vowel, e.g., *wayyáᶜaś* 'and he did' < **yaᶜś*; also *wayhī* 'and it was, happened' from *yihyē*, *yḥī* 'may he live' from *yiḥyē*, *wayyar* 'and he saw' from *yirᵓē*. —

§ 3/1.2.3

As a result of the loss of short vowel endings, Hebrew retains only traces of case inflection,[s] principally a (mostly unstressed) locative ending *-ā*:[t] *Yāḇḗšā* 'to (in) Jabesh.' To introduce a definite direct object the particle *eṯ* (with suffixes *ōṯī* 'me,' etc.) is used. The dual ending is *-áyim*,[u] the plural ending *-īm*, construct state for both is *-ē*. The dual is in decline; pronoun and verb have already lost it. The feminine ending **-atu* has retained its *t* only in the construct state *-aṯ*; in the absolute state *-ā* it has disappeared (originally only in pause, **-aṯ* > **-ah*). Beside this feminine ending, **-tu*, beginning with a consonant, is not rare: *merkaḇtō* 'his wagon,' and without pronominal suffix with biconsonantal ending and therefore epenthesis: *šlṓšeṯ* 'three.' A rare feminine ending is *-ē*: *ᶜeśrē* 'ten.' The *ā* of the feminine plural ending **-ātu* has become *-ō*: *-ōṯ*; before a pronominal suffix the masculine construct state ending *-ē* is added to this ending (*-ōṯāu -ōṯḗhā*).

In forms without endings, the monovocalic nouns break up their final clusters by epenthesis. With stem vowel *a* the result is *népeš* (Ba *nápaš*) 'soul,' with *i*: *séper* (*sépar*) 'book,' with *u*: *ḥómeš* (*ḥómaš*) 'one fifth'; with pronominal suffix

s. Ugaritic has the historical three cases; furthermore, the third person personal pronouns have an oblique case ending in *-t*.

t. This can now be recognized not as a vocalic case ending, but as a locative suffix *-ah* reflected in Ugaritic *-h*.

u. The dual is fully productive in Ugaritic, in pronoun, verb, and noun.

monovocalic *nap̄šō* 'his soul,' etc. Rarely, these nouns have the vowel between the last two consonants: *šk̲em* 'shoulder' (but *šik̲mō* 'his shoulder'), *klī* (from *kly*) 'vessel, implement.' They form the plural on a bivocalic subsidiary stem:[v] *ṣᶜād̲īm* 'steps' < **ṣaᶜad-*, *ărāṣōt̲* 'lands' < **araṣ-*, construct state *alp̄ē* 'thousands of . . .' (with spirantized *p̄*) < **alap-*. —

v. Thus the broken plural is not an exclusively South Semitic phenomenon; this is an important argument in denying a special unity between Arabic and Ethiopic as against Northwest Semitic.

§ 3/1.2.4

Of the monoconsonantal prepositions *b-* 'in, with, by,' *l-* (dative particle), *k-* 'like,' the first two can have suffixes joined to them directly, the third only with the mediation of the indefinite *mā* > *mō*: *kāmṓhū* 'like him.' The *n* of *min* 'from, out of' is generally assimilated to following consonants: *mikkem* 'from you' (before laryngeal, without gemination *mē-*); it can be doubled before a suffix: *mimménnū* 'from him' (and always has *nn* before a vowel). The original final *-ai* of the prepositions *el* 'to,' *ᶜal* 'on, against' is retained before a suffix (*ᶜālāu* 'on him,' *ᶜālḗnū* 'on us'), and has spread to some other prepositions.[w]

w. Ugaritic derives adverbs with *-ny* and *-m*. Enclitic *-m* is widespread, but its significance is less than clear. It may even sometimes occur "for euphony."

The negation for description is *lō*, for command *al*; for a nominal sentence *ēn* is used, literally 'nonexistence' (also with pronominal suffix *ēnō* 'he, it is not'). Hebrew has an interrogative particle *h-* and a deictic particle *hinnē* used very frequently to introduce nominal clauses. 'And' is *w-* (in the Tiberian recension, before a labial or before a vowelless initial consonant *u-*).[x] Hebrew is poor in subordinating conjunctions; the most important, besides the above-mentioned *ăšer* and its combinations, are the versatile *kī* 'since, but, that, if' and *pen* 'lest,' both, fundamentally, introducing main clauses, as is still often clear, as well as *im* 'if.'

x. Ugaritic also has a less common 'and' *p-*.

§ 3/1.3

The principal syntactic means of expression in Hebrew are the richly developed verbal system; the alternation between basic syndesis and asyndesis, which occasionally serves particular expressive purposes; and the use of word order types —

from the simple distinction between the orders subject-verb and the opposite through complicated formations. These means are in themselves capable of expressing subordination as well, and a fair amount of freedom exists in their use. Thus Hebrew is a language rich in nuance and color, exceptionally suited to the expression of elevated experience as well as to lively description and vivid narration, though without reaching a high level of intellectual acuity: a language of poets and prophets, not of thinkers.

§ 3/1.4 The vocabulary too is concrete and is distinguished for its richness in terms for affective, religious, moral affairs. Later stages of the language are enriched with Aramaic words, including some that were themselves borrowed from Akkadian.

---

§ 3/2 Middle Hebrew, the language of the Tannaitic period and its literature (the Mishna and the oldest Midrashim), repeatedly renewed in literature in post-Talmudic times and finally reborn in Modern Israeli Hebrew, differs markedly in both grammar and lexicon from Old Hebrew, due in part to Aramaic influence. 'I' is always *ănī*, 'we' *ănū*,[y] 'they' *hen* (masculine as well as feminine). Besides the old demonstratives new forms have emerged; among them *ōṯō* 'that,' *ōṯāh* (feminine), etc., from the object particle with pronominal suffix. The relative *ăšer* is replaced by *še-* (plus lengthening of the following consonant), which is already found in Old Hebrew, and from this in combination with the dative preposition *l-* has emerged a genitive particle *šel* (literally 'what belongs to . . .'), used in an Aramaic fashion (*almnāṯo šel-méleḵ*[z] 'the widow of the king'), which itself forms a possessive by adding pronominal

y. Subsequent manuscript discoveries have shown this form to be *ānū*.

z. This form is now known to be *šellamméleḵ*, see note ad.

aa. The old pattern whereby the article occurs on both a definite noun and its adjective is supplemented by a pattern conformed to that of the definite construct chain, with the article only on the second element, viz., the adjective; e.g., *mélek̠ haṭṭōḇ* 'the good king.'

suffixes: *šellī* 'my,' etc.[aa] The consecutive tenses have been abandoned, the nominal forms of the verb overrun the finite verb; the participle constitutes a new present. The old infinitives recede before new formations on the Aramaic model: *ḥqīrā* and *meḥqār* 'to investigate' in the basic stem, *limmūd* 'to teach' in the intensive, *hanhālā* 'to lead' in the causative, etc. (also with the abstract ending *-ūṯ*: *hiṯpattḥūṯ* 'development'). The III ᵓ verbs cross over to the III weak class, as in Aramaic, e.g., *māṣ́īnū* 'we found' for *māṣ́ānū* < **-aᵓnū*; the verb 'to be' is shortened: *yhē* 'may he be' for *yihyē*, *yhū* 'may they be' for *yihyū*. The masculine plural ending is *-īn*, as in Aramaic. *hinnē* is replaced by the Aramaic *hrē*. The conjunctions proliferate by paraphrase and combination, in part with Aramaic elements, like *ellā* 'besides, but,' and *ăpillū* 'even if,' both containing *in* (*en*) 'if,' which corresponds to the Hebrew *im*. In addition to novel formations, particularly of abstracts (with the abstract ending *-ūṯ* already found in Old Hebrew, before which the nisbe ending often occurs, as in *ĕnōšiyyūṯ* 'mankind,' or with Aramaic nominal forms, like *taᶜnūḡ* 'pleasure'), borrowings from Aramaic and the Classical and, recently, European languages enrich the vocabulary.

Medieval Hebrew is one of the most neglected languages. The Spanish heyday of Jewish literature brought a decided improvement; the literature of the Enlightenment since the eighteenth century inaugurated a renewal of recourse to the Old Testament. The present rebirth of Hebrew[13] entails the necessity of saying everything in Hebrew and the very urgent task of so broadening the range of expression of Hebrew that it becomes apt for discussing the entire scope of modern culture. The completion of this task can only be brought into

13. On the pronunciation see notes 2 and 4.

view and ultimately succeed if a sure feel for the Hebrew language develops anew; even then would the risk be great, as the example of other Oriental languages which face the same task even with a living and strong linguistic consciousness indicates. The attempt to perform that task without this preparation can only lead to illusory success: to a Hebrew that is in reality a European language in transparent Hebrew clothing, with Common European characteristics and language-particular peculiarities, but only outwardly Hebrew in character. The break between present-day Hebrew and the older varieties is thus incomparably greater than that between Middle Hebrew and Old Hebrew.[ab]

ab. Some fifty years after this was written, we are in a position to evaluate Bergsträsser's prophetic ability. Modern Hebrew has, in fact, in large measure "succumbed" to European influence. The phonology is simplified, the tense system is completely changed to the European model (perfect > past, participle > present, imperfect > future) while some limited productivity remains to the stem system, the syntax looks more European than Semitic, and the vocabulary borrows heavily from the many languages Hebrew has been in contact with (despite massive and erudite achievements in bringing older Hebrew words back to consciousness with new meanings). But the rift is not absolute, and it cannot be said that had Hebrew been continually used as a living language while its speakers participated fully in Western culture it would not have changed just as much.

Text Specimens

P after a word indicates pause form, Ak Akkadian origin, and Am Aramaic origin.

1. Old Hebrew[14,ac]

a) Saul's Coronation (I Sam. 10:17-25, in the Babylonian vocalization)[15]

ויצעק שמואל את העם אל יהוה המצפה: ויאמר אל בני ישראל	*wayyaṣʿeq Šmūʾēl eṯ-hāʿām el-Yhwh*[16] *ham Maṣpā*[17] *wayyṓmar*[18] *el-bnē*[19]*-Yiśrāʾēl:*	Then Samuel called the people together to the Lord at Mizpah and said to the sons of Israel: |
כה אמר יהוה אלהי ישראל אנכי העליתי את ישראל ממצרים ואציל אתכם מיד מצרים ומיד כל הממלכות הלחצים אתכם:	*"kō āmar Yhwh elōhē Yiśrāʾēl: 'ānōḵī haʿalḗṯī eṯ-Yiśrāʾēl mim Miṣráyim wāʾaṣṣīl*[20] *eṯḵam miyyaḏ-Miṣráyim*[21] *wmiyyaḏ-kol-hammamlāḵōṯ hallōḥṣīm eṯḵam;*	"Thus says the Lord, the God of Israel: | 'I brought up Israel out of the land of Egypt and delivered you from the hand (power) of the Egyptians and from the hand of all the kingdoms that were oppressing you; |
ואתם היום מאסתם את אלהיכם אשר הוא מושיע לכם מכל רעותיכם וצרתיכם	*wʾattam hayyōm mʾastam eṯ-elōhēḵam, ašar-hū*[22] *mōšīʿ*[23] *lāḵam mikkol-rāʿōṯēḵam*[24] *wṣārōṯēḵam,*[24]	but you have this day rejected your God, who saves you from all your calamities and your distresses; |
ותאמרו לו כי מלך תשים עלינו	*wattōmrū lō: "kī málaḵ tāśīm*[25] *ālḗnū!"'*	and you have said to him: "Rather should you set a king over us!"' |
ועתה התיצבו לפני יהוה לשבטיכם ולאלפיכם:	*wʿattā*[26] *hiṯyaṣṣḇū lip̄nē*[27]*-Yhwh lšiḇṭēḵam wilʾalp̄ēḵam!"*	Now therefore present yourselves before the Lord by your tribes and by your thousands." |
ויקרב שמואל את כל שבטי ישראל וילכד שבט בנימן:	*wayyaqreḇ Šmūʾēl eṯ-kol-šiḇṭē-Yiśrāʾēl, wayyillāḵaḏ šéḇaṭ-Binyāmīn;*	Then Samuel brought all the tribes of Israel near (the Lord), and the tribe of Benjamin was taken by lot;

ac. Consulted in translating: Revised Standard Version. Text of b-d as in K. Elliger and W. Rudolph, eds., *Biblia Hebraica Stuttgartensia* (Stuttgart: Deutsche Bibelstiftung, 1977).

14. In the texts the necessary emendations are incorporated; only restorations of lacunae are expressly marked. 15. P. Kahle, *Masoreten des Ostens* 1913, pp. 24-25. 16. Vocalization not transmitted. 17. Accusative (without the locative suffix *-ā*) for the expression of direction. 18. *ʾmr.* 19. Construct state of *bānīm*, plural of *bēn* (biliteral). 20. *nṣl.* 21. Ending only superficially the same as the dual ending; likewise *Yrūšāláyim, šāmáyim* 'heaven,' *máyim* 'water.' 22. Resumptive pronoun of the relative clause ('he'). 23. *wšʿ.* 24. *rāʿā* < **raʿʿat-*, therefore the *ā* not reducible; likewise *ṣāra* < **ṣarrat-*. 25. *śym.* 26. Locative of *ʿēṯ* < **ʿint* 'time.' 27. Construct state of *pānīm* 'face,' plural (*pny*).

ויקרב את שבט בנימן למשפחתו ותלכד משפחת המטרי	*wayyaqreḇ eṯ-šéḇaṭ-Binyāmīn lmaš-p̱ḥōṯāu, wattillāḵaḏ mašpáḥaṯ*[28]*-ham Maṭrī;*[29]	he brought the tribe of Benjamin near (him) by its families, and the family of the Matrites was taken by lot; |
וילכד שאול בן קיש	[30]*wayyaqreḇ mašpáḥaṯ-ham Maṭrī lʾanšáihā,*[31,30] *wayyillāḵaḏ Šāʾūl ben-Qīš.*	then he brought the family of the Matrites near by its men, and Saul the son of Kish was taken by lot. |
ויבקשהו ולא נמצא:	*waybaqqšū́hū wlō-nimṣā.*[32]	But when they sought him, he could not be found. |
וישאלו עוד ביהוה הבא עוד הלם איש	*wayyišʾalū ʿōḏ bYhwh: "hḇā*[33] *<. . .> hlōm <hā>ʾīš?"*	So they inquired again of the Lord: "Did the man come hither?" |
ויאמר יהוה הנה הוא נחבא אל הכלים:	*wayyṓmar Yhwh: "hinnē-hū niḥbā*[34] *el-hakkēlīm."*[35]	And the Lord said: "Behold, he has hidden himself among (lit. in the direction of) the baggage." |
וירצו ויקחהו משם	*wayyārū́ṣū*[36] *wayyiqqāḥū́hū*[37] *miš-šām,*	Then they ran and fetched him from there, |
ויתיצב בתוך העם ויגבה מכל העם משכמו ומעלה:	*wayyiṯyaṣṣaḇ bṯōḵ-hāʿām wayyiḡbah mikkol-hāʿām miššiḵmō wā-mā́ʿalā.*[38]	and he stood among the people and was taller than any of the people from his shoulders up (lit. and up) (i.e. when he stood . . . he was . . .). |
ויאמר שמואל אל כל העם הראיתם אשר בחר בו יהוה כי אין כמהו בכל העם	*wayyṓmar Šmūʾēl el-kol-hāʿām: "harʾīṯam*[39] *ašar-bāḥar bō Yhwh? kī ēn ḵāmṓhū bḵol-hāʿām."*	And Samuel said to all the people: | "Do you see him whom the Lord has chosen? There is none like him among the people." |
וירעו כל העם ויאמרו יחי המלך:	*wayyārī́ʿū*[40] *ḵol-hāʿām wayyōmrū: "iḥī*[41] *hammálaḵ!"*	And all the people rejoiced and said: "Long live the king!" |
וידבר שמואל אל העם את משפט המלכה ויכתב בספר וינח לפני יהוה	*wayḏabbar Šmūʾēl el-hāʿām eṯ-mašpaṭ hammlūḵā wayyiḵtoḇ bas-sēp̄ar wayyannaḥ*[42] *lip̄nē-Yhwh.*	Then Samuel told the people the rights and duties of the kingship and wrote (them) in a (lit. the) book and laid it before the Lord. |
וישלח שמואל את כל העם איש לביתו:	*wayyišlaḥ Šmūʾēl eṯ-kol-hāʿām īš lḇēṯō.*	Then Samuel sent all the people away, each one (lit. a man) to his house.

28. Construct state with feminine ending *-t* of *mašpāḥā* (with *-at*). 29. Nisbe. 30. Restored. 31. Construct state of *ănāšīm*, singular divergently *īš*. 32. *mṣʾ*. 33. Interrogative particle; *bwʾ*. 34. *ḥbʾ*. 35. Plural of *klī*. 36. *rwṣ*. 37. *lqḥ*. 38. Locative. 39. Interrogative particle: *rʾy*. 40. *rwʿ* causative. 41. *ḥyy* (<*ḥwy*). 42. *nwḥ* causative with secondary lengthening.

b) The Death of Saul
(I Sam. 31:1-6, 8-13)

וּפְלִשְׁתִּים נִלְחָמִים בְּיִשְׂרָאֵל וַיָּנֻסוּ אַנְשֵׁי יִשְׂרָאֵל מִפְּנֵי פְלִשְׁתִּים וַיִּפְּלוּ חֲלָלִים בְּהַר הַגִּלְבֹּעַ׃	*uP̱lištīm nilḥāmīm bYiśrāʾēl, wayyānū́sū*[43] *anšē-Yiśrāʾēl mippnē-P̱lištīm wayyipplū*[44] *ḥlālīm bhar-hagGilbṓaᶜ.*	While the Philistines were fighting against Israel, the men of Israel fled before the Philistines and fell slain on Mount Gilboa. |
וַיַּדְבְּקוּ פְלִשְׁתִּים אֶת־שָׁאוּל וְאֶת־בָּנָיו וַיַּכּוּ פְלִשְׁתִּים אֶת־יְהוֹנָתָן וְאֶת־אֲבִינָדָב וְאֶת־מַלְכִּי־שׁוּעַ בְּנֵי שָׁאוּל׃	*wayyaḏbīqū P̱lištīm eṯ-Šāʾūl wʾeṯ-bānāu, wayyakkū*[45] *P̱lištīm eṯ-Yhōnāṯān wʾeṯ-Ăḇīnāḏāḇ wʾeṯ-Malkīšū́aᶜ, bnē-Šāʾūl.*	And the Philistines pursued Saul and his sons, and the Philistines slew Jonathan and Abinadab and Malchishua, the sons of Saul. |
וַתִּכְבַּד הַמִּלְחָמָה אֶל־שָׁאוּל וַיִּמְצָאֻהוּ הַמּוֹרִים בַּקָּשֶׁת וַיָּחֶל מְאֹד מֵהַמּוֹרִים׃	*wattiḵbaḏ hammilḥāmā ᶜal-Šāʾūl, wayyimṣāʾū́hū hammōrīm*[46] <...> *baqqā́šeṯ,*[P] *wayyēḥal*[47] *baḥómeš*[48] *mēhammōrīm.*	The battle pressed hard upon Saul, the archers found him, and he was badly wounded by the archers. |
וַיֹּאמֶר שָׁאוּל לְנֹשֵׂא כֵלָיו שְׁלֹף חַרְבְּךָ וְדָקְרֵנִי בָהּ פֶּן־יָבוֹאוּ הָעֲרֵלִים הָאֵלֶּה וְהִתְעַלְּלוּ־בִי	*wayyṓmer Šāʾūl lnōśē*[49]*-ḵēlāu: "šlop̄-ḥarbḵā wḏoqrénī ḇah, pen-yāḇṓʾū hāᶜrēlīm hāʾēllé* <...> *whiṯᶜall·lū ḇī!"*	Then Saul said to his armorbearer: "Draw your sword and thrust me through with it, lest these uncircumcised come and make sport of me!" |
וְלֹא אָבָה נֹשֵׂא כֵלָיו כִּי יָרֵא מְאֹד וַיִּקַּח שָׁאוּל אֶת־הַחֶרֶב וַיִּפֹּל עָלֶיהָ׃	*wlō-āḇā*[50] *nōśē-ḵēlāu; kī yārē*[51] *mʾōḏ. wayyiqqaḥ Šāʾūl eṯ-haḥéreḇ wayyippol ᶜālḗhā.*	But his armorbearer would not; for he feared greatly. Therefore Saul took his own sword, and fell upon it. |
וַיַּרְא נֹשֵׂא־כֵלָיו כִּי מֵת שָׁאוּל וַיִּפֹּל גַּם־הוּא עַל־חַרְבּוֹ וַיָּמָת עִמּוֹ׃	*wayyar*[52] *nōśē-ḵēlāu, kī-mēṯ*[53] *Šāʾūl, wayyippol gam-hū ᶜal-ḥarbō wayyā́mōṯ ᶜimmō.*	And when his armorbearer saw that Saul was dead, he also fell upon his sword, and died with him. |
וַיָּמָת שָׁאוּל וּשְׁלֹשֶׁת בָּנָיו וְנֹשֵׂא כֵלָיו בַּיּוֹם הַהוּא יַחְדָּו׃	*wayyā́mōṯ Šāʾūl ušlṓšeṯ-bānāu wnōśē-ḵēlāu* <...> *bayyōm hahū yaḥdāu.*	Thus Saul died, and his three sons, and his armorbearer, on the same day together. |
וַיְהִי מִמָּחֳרָת וַיָּבֹאוּ פְלִשְׁתִּים לְפַשֵּׁט אֶת־הַחֲלָלִים וַיִּמְצְאוּ אֶת־שָׁאוּל וְאֶת־שְׁלֹשֶׁת בָּנָיו נֹפְלִים בְּהַר הַגִּלְבֹּעַ׃	*wayhī*[54] *mimmoḥrāṯ, wayyāḇṓʾū P̱lištīm lpāššēṯ eṯ-haḥlālīm wayyimṣʾū eṯ-Šāʾūl wʾeṯ-šlṓšeṯ-bānāu nōp̄līm*[55] *bhar-hagGilbṓaᶜ.*	But when on the next day (lit. and when it was on the next and) the Philistines came to strip the slain, and found Saul and his three sons fallen on Mount Gilboa. |

43. *nws.* 44. *npl.* 45. *nky* causative. 46. *wry* causative, singular *mōrē.* 47. *ḥll* *n*-stem (< **yiḥḥal* < **yinḥal*). 48. Restored. 49. *nśʾ.* 50. *ʾby.* 51. *yrʾ.* 52. *rʾy.* 53. *mwt.* 54. *hyy* (< *hwy*). 55. Participle of 'fall' in perfective sense.

וַיִּכְרְתוּ אֶת־רֹאשׁוֹ וַיַּפְשִׁטוּ אֶת־כֵּלָיו וַיְשַׁלְּחוּ בְאֶרֶץ־פְּלִשְׁתִּים סָבִיב לְבַשֵּׂר בֵּית עֲצַבֵּיהֶם וְאֶת־הָעָם׃	*wayyikrṯū eṯ-rōšō waypāššṭū eṯ-kēlāu wayšallḥū bʾéreṣ-Plištīm sāḇīḇ lḇaśśēr eṯ-ᶜṣabbēhem wʾeṯ-hāᶜām;*	they cut off his head, and stripped off his armor, and sent (both) throughout the land of the Philistines, to announce the good news to their idols and to the people; |
וַיָּשִׂמוּ אֶת־כֵּלָיו בֵּית עַשְׁתָּרוֹת וְאֶת־גְּוִיָּתוֹ תָּקְעוּ בְּחוֹמַת בֵּית שָׁן׃	*wayyāśī́mū eṯ-kēlāu bēṯ[56]-ᶜAštéreṯ, wʾeṯ-gwiyyāṯō hōqī́ᶜū[57] bḥōmaṯ-Bēṯšān.*	they put his armor in the temple of Astarte, but they hung up(?) his corpse on the wall of Beth-shan. |
וַיִּשְׁמְעוּ אֵלָיו יֹשְׁבֵי יָבֵישׁ גִּלְעָד אֵת אֲשֶׁר־ עָשׂוּ פְלִשְׁתִּים לְשָׁאוּל׃	*wayyišmᶜū ᶜālāu yōšḇē-Yāḇeš-Gilᶜāḏ,[58] eṯ-ăšer-ᶜāśū[59] Plištīm lŠāʾūl,*	But when the inhabitants of Jabesh in Gilead heard about him what the Philistines had done to Saul, |
וַיָּקוּמוּ כָּל־אִישׁ חַיִל וַיֵּלְכוּ כָל־הַלַּיְלָה וַיִּקְחוּ אֶת־גְּוִיַּת שָׁאוּל וְאֵת גְּוִיֹּת בָּנָיו מֵחוֹמַת בֵּית שָׁן	*wayyāqū́mū[60] kol-īš-ḥáyil way-yēlḵū[61] ḵol-halláylā wayyiqḥū[62] eṯ-gwiyyaṯ-Šāʾūl wʾeṯ-gwiyyōṯ-bānāu mēḥōmaṯ-Bēṯšān;*	all the valiant men (lit. men of strength) arose, and went all night, and took the body of Saul and the bodies of his sons from the wall of Bethshan; |
וַיָּבֹאוּ יָבֵשָׁה וַיִּשְׂרְפוּ אֹתָם שָׁם׃ וַיִּקְחוּ אֶת־ עַצְמֹתֵיהֶם וַיִּקְבְּרוּ תַחַת־הָאֶשֶׁל בְּיָבֵשָׁה וַיָּצֻמוּ שִׁבְעַת יָמִים׃	*wayyāḇṓʾū Yāḇḗšā wayyiśrpū ōṯām šām wayyiqḥū eṯ-ᶜaṣmōṯēhem way-yiqbrū ṯáḥaṯ-hāʾéšel bYāḇḗšā way-yāṣū́mū[63] šiḇᶜaṯ-yāmīm.[64]*	and when they came (back) to Jabesh they burnt them there and took their bones and buried them under the tamarisk in Jabesh and fasted seven days.

c) Nehemiah's Appointment as Governor of Jerusalem (Neh. 1:1-4, 2:1-6)

וַיְהִי בְחֹדֶשׁ־כִּסְלֵו שְׁנַת עֶשְׂרִים וַאֲנִי הָיִיתִי בְּשׁוּשַׁן הַבִּירָה׃ וַיָּבֹא חֲנָנִי אֶחָד מֵאַחַי הוּא וַאֲנָשִׁים מִיהוּדָה	*wayhī ḇḥṓḏeš[65]-kisleu*[AkAm] *šnaṯ[66]-ᶜeśrīm,[67] waʾănī hāyī́ṯī[68] bŠūšan habbīrā, wayyāḇō[69] Ḥnānī, ēḥāḏ[70] mēʾaḥai,[71] hū waʾănāšīm mĪhūḏā.*	Now it happened in the month of Kislev, in the twentieth year, as I was in Susa the capital, that Hanani, one of my brothers (i.e. close friends), he and (other) men came out of Judah. |
וָאֶשְׁאָלֵם עַל־הַיְּהוּדִים הַפְּלֵיטָה אֲשֶׁר־נִשְׁאֲרוּ מִן־הַשֶּׁבִי וְעַל־יְרוּשָׁלָםִ׃	*wāʾešʾālēm ᶜal-hayYhūḏīm hap-plēṭā, ašer-nišʾrū min-haššéḇī,*[P] *wᶜal-Yrūšāláyim*	And I asked them concerning the Jews that survived, who had escaped exile, and concerning Jerusalem. |

56. For *bḇēṯ* (dissimilation). 57. *wqᶜ* (uncertain). 58. Genitive phrase. 59. *ᶜśy*. 60. *qwm*. 61. *hlk*. 62. *lqḥ*, for **yiqqḥū*. 63. *ṣwm*. 64. Plural of *yōm*. 65. Sic, each time different! 66. From *šānā* (biliteral). 67. Plural of *ᶜéśer* 'ten.' 68. *hyy*. 69. *bwʾ*. 70. < **aḥḥad* (with secondary lengthening). 71. **aḥḥīm* with lengthening, as in Akkadian; *-ai* < **-ai-ya*.

וַיֹּאמְרוּ לִי הַנִּשְׁאָרִים אֲשֶׁר־נִשְׁאֲרוּ מִן־הַשְּׁבִי שָׁם בַּמְּדִינָה בְּרָעָה גְדֹלָה וּבְחֶרְפָּה	*wayyōmrū lī: "hannišʾārīm, ăšer-nišʾrū min-haššḇī šām bammdīnā,*[Am] *brāʿā gḏōlā uḇḥerpā;*	And they said to me: "The survivors there in the province who escaped exile are in great trouble and shame;
וְחוֹמַת יְרוּשָׁלַםִ מְפֹרָצֶת וּשְׁעָרֶיהָ נִצְּתוּ בָאֵשׁ׃	*wḥōmaṯ-Yrūšāláyim mpōrā́ṣeṯ,*[P72] *ušʿārḗhā*[73] *nissṯū*[74] *ḇāʾēš."*	the wall of Jerusalem is broken down, and its gates are destroyed by fire."
וַיְהִי כְּשָׁמְעִי אֶת־הַדְּבָרִים הָאֵלֶּה יָשַׁבְתִּי וָאֶבְכֶּה וָאֶתְאַבְּלָה יָמִים וָאֱהִי צָם וּמִתְפַּלֵּל לִפְנֵי אֱלֹהֵי הַשָּׁמָיִם׃	*wayhī kšomʿī eṯ-haddḇārīm hāʾḗllē, yāšā́ḇtī wāʾeḇkē*[75] *wāʾeṯʾabblā*[76] *yāmīm wāʾĕhī ṣām umiṯpallēl lip̱nē-ĕlōhē-haššāmā́yim.*[P]	When (lit. as) I heard these words, I sat down and wept and mourned for days and continued (lit. was) fasting and praying before the God of heaven.
וַיְהִי בְּחֹדֶשׁ נִיסָן וָאֶשָּׂא אֶת־הַיַּיִן וָאֶתְּנָה לַמֶּלֶךְ׃	*wayhī bḥṓḏeš*[65]*-nīsān,*[AkAm] <...> *waʾeśśā*[77] *eṯ-hayyáyin wāʾettnā*[78] *lammélek̲.* <...>	And in the month of Nisan I took up the wine and gave it to the king.
וַיֹּאמֶר לִי הַמֶּלֶךְ מַדּוּעַ פָּנֶיךָ רָעִים וְאַתָּה אֵינְךָ חוֹלֶה אֵין זֶה כִּי־אִם רֹעַ לֵב	. . . *wayyṓmer lī hammélek̲: "maddū́aʿ pānḗk̲ā rāʿīm, wʾattā ēnk̲ā ḥōlē?*[79] *ēn zē kī-im rṓaʿ-lēḇ!"*	. . . And the king said to me: "Why is your face sad, seeing you are not sick? This is nothing else but sadness of heart."
וָאִירָא הַרְבֵּה מְאֹד׃ וָאֹמַר לַמֶּלֶךְ הַמֶּלֶךְ לְעוֹלָם יִחְיֶה	*wāʾīrā*[80] *harbē-mʾōḏ wāʾōmar lammélek̲: "hammélek̲ lʿōlām yiḥyē!*	Then I was very much afraid and said to the king: "Let the king live forever!
מַדּוּעַ לֹא־יֵרְעוּ פָנַי אֲשֶׁר הָעִיר בֵּית־קִבְרוֹת אֲבֹתַי חֲרֵבָה וּשְׁעָרֶיהָ אֻכְּלוּ בָאֵשׁ׃	*maddū́aʿ lōyērā́ʿū*[81,82] *pānai, ăšer-hāʿīr, bēṯ-qiḇrōṯ*[83]*-ăḇōṯai, ḥrēḇā ušʿārḗhā ukklū ḇāʾēš?"*	Why should my face not be sad, when the city, the house of the graves of my fathers, lies waste and its gates have been destroyed by fire?"
וַיֹּאמֶר לִי הַמֶּלֶךְ עַל־מַה־זֶּה אַתָּה מְבַקֵּשׁ וָאֶתְפַּלֵּל אֶל־אֱלֹהֵי הַשָּׁמָיִם׃ וָאֹמַר לַמֶּלֶךְ	*wayyṓmer lī hammélek̲: "ʿal-mazzē*[84] *attā mḇaqqēš?" wāʾeṯpallel el-ĕlōhē-haššāmā́yim*[P] *wā-ʾōmar lammélek̲:*	Then the king said to me: "For what do you ask?" So I prayed to the God of heaven and said to the king:
אִם־עַל־הַמֶּלֶךְ טוֹב וְאִם־יִיטַב עַבְדְּךָ לְפָנֶיךָ אֲשֶׁר תִּשְׁלָחֵנִי אֶל־יְהוּדָה אֶל־עִיר קִבְרוֹת אֲבֹתַי וְאֶבְנֶנָּה׃	*"im-ʿal-hammélek̲ ṭōḇ wʾim-yīṭaḇ*[85] *ʿaḇdk̲ā*[86] *lpānḗk̲ā, ăšer-tišlāḥḗnī el-Yhūḏā, el-ʿīr-qiḇrōṯ-ăḇōṯai, wʾeḇnénnā!"*[87]	"If it pleases (lit. is good to) the king, and if your servant has found favor before you, (I ask) that you send me to Judah, the city of my fathers' graves, that I may rebuild it."

72. Passive of the intensive, *-ōr-* < **-urr-*. 73. Plural of *šáʿar*. 74. *n*-stem of *yṣt*. 75. *bky*. 76. Cohortative, in the later language also after *wa-*. 77. *nśʾ*. 78. *ntn*, cohortative. 79. *ḥly*. 80. *yrʾ*. 81. The text has the irregular form *yērʿū*. 82. *rʿʿ*. 83. Plural of *qéḇer*. 84. *mā* 'what?' strengthened by the demonstrative; secondary lengthening. 85. Imperfect (root *yṭb*) of the perfect = adjective *ṭōḇ* (root *ṭyb*). 86. From *ʿéḇeḏ*. 87. *bny*.

וַיֹּאמֶר לִי הַמֶּלֶךְ וְהַשֵּׁגַל יוֹשֶׁבֶת אֶצְלוֹ עַד־מָתַי יִהְיֶה מַהֲלָכְךָ וּמָתַי תָּשׁוּב	*wayyṓmer lī hammélek̲, whaššēgāl*[Am] *yōšéb̲et̲ eṣlō: "ʿad̲-māt̲ai yihyē mahlāk̲k̲ā umāt̲ai tāšūb̲?"*[88]	And the king said to me, with the queen sitting beside him: "Until when will your journey last, and when will you return?" |
וַיִּיטַב לִפְנֵי־הַמֶּלֶךְ וַיִּשְׁלָחֵנִי׃	*wayyīṭab̲ lip̄nē-hammélek̲ wayyišlāḥénī.*	So it pleased the king (lit. it was good before the king) and he sent me.

d) Law of Retribution
(Ex. 21:12-14, 18-19, 23-30)[89]

מַכֵּה אִישׁ וָמֵת מוֹת יוּמָת׃	*makkē*[90]*-īš wāmēt̲, mōt̲*[91] *yūmāt̲;*[P]	If anyone strikes a man and he dies, then he shall be put to death; |
וַאֲשֶׁר לֹא צָדָה וְהָאֱלֹהִים אִנָּה לְיָדוֹ וְשַׂמְתִּי לְךָ מָקוֹם אֲשֶׁר יָנוּס שָׁמָּה׃	*waʾăšer-lō-ṣād̲ā*[92] *whāʾĕlōhīm innā*[93] *lyād̲ō, wśamtī*[94] *lk̲ā māqōm*[95] *ăšer-yānūs šā́mmā.*	but if he (lit. who) had had no evil intention but God let him fall into his hand, then I will appoint for you a place to which he may flee. |
וְכִי־יָזִד אִישׁ עַל־רֵעֵהוּ לְהָרְגוֹ בְעָרְמָה מֵעִם מִזְבְּחִי תִּקָּחֶנּוּ לָמוּת׃	*wk̲ī-yāzīd̲*[96] *īš ʿal-rēʿḗhū lhorgō b̲ʿormā, mēʿim-mizbḥī*[97] *tiqqāḥénnū lāmūt̲.*[P 98]	If a man willfully attacks his neighbor to kill him treacherously, you shall take him from my altar, that he may die. |
וְכִי־יְרִיבֻן אֲנָשִׁים וְהִכָּה־אִישׁ אֶת־רֵעֵהוּ וְלֹא יָמוּת וְנָפַל לְמִשְׁכָּב׃	*wk̲ī-yrīb̲ūn*[99] *ănāšīm whikkā īš et̲-rēʿḗhū* <...> *wlō-yāmūt̲ wnāpal lmiškāb̲,*	When men quarrel and a man strikes his neighbor and he does not die but keeps to his bed, |
אִם־יָקוּם וְהִתְהַלֵּךְ בַּחוּץ עַל־מִשְׁעַנְתּוֹ וְנִקָּה הַמַּכֶּה	*im-yāqūm whit̲hallek̲ baḥūṣ ʿal-mišʿantō,*[100] *wniqqā*[101] *hammakkē;*	then if he rises (again) and walks about with his staff, he that struck him shall be cleared; |
רַק שִׁבְתּוֹ יִתֵּן וְרַפֹּא יְרַפֵּא׃	*raq šib̲tō*[102] *yitten wrappō yrappē.*[103]	only he shall pay for the loss of his time (lit. his sitting), and shall have him thoroughly healed. |

88. *šwb*. 89. For the content compare pp. 38-41. 90. *nky* causative. 91. Infinitive absolute. 92. *ṣdy*. 93. *ʾny*. 94. *śym*. 95. Noun of place from *qām* (*qwm*) 'he stood up.' 96. *zyd*. 97. Noun of place from *zāb̲aḥ* 'he offered.' 98. Infinitive construct. 99. *ryb*. 100. Noun of instrument from *nišʿan* 'he supported himself.' 101. *n*-stem of *nqy*. 102. *wšb*. 103. *rpʾ*.

<table>
<tr><td>וְאִם־אָסוֹן יִהְיֶה וְנָתַתָּה נֶפֶשׁ תַּחַת נָפֶשׁ: עַיִן תַּחַת עַיִן שֵׁן תַּחַת שֵׁן יָד תַּחַת יָד רֶגֶל תַּחַת רָגֶל: כְּוִיָּה תַּחַת כְּוִיָּה פֶּצַע תַּחַת פָּצַע חַבּוּרָה תַּחַת חַבּוּרָה:</td><td>wᵓim-āsōn yihyē, wnāṯattā népeš táḥaṯ-nā̃peš,[P] ᶜáyin tāḥaṯ-ᶜáyin, šēn[104] táḥaṯ-šēn, yād táḥaṯ-yāḏ, régel táḥaṯ-rā̃ḡel,[P] kwiyyā táḥaṯ-kwiyyā, péṣaᶜ táḥaṯ-pā̃ṣaᶜ,[P] ḥabbūrā táḥaṯ-ḥabbūrā.</td><td>But if any lasting harm results, then you shall give life (lit. soul) for life, eye for eye, tooth for tooth, hand for hand, foot for foot, burn for burn, wound for wound, stripe for stripe. |</td></tr>
<tr><td>וְכִי־יַכֶּה אִישׁ אֶת־עֵין עַבְדּוֹ אוֹ־אֶת־עֵין אֲמָתוֹ וְשִׁחֲתָהּ לַחָפְשִׁי יְשַׁלְּחֶנּוּ תַּחַת עֵינוֹ:</td><td>wkī-yakkē īš eṯ-ᶜēn-ᶜaḇdō ō-eṯ-ᶜēn-ămāṯō[105] wšiḥṯāh,[106] laḥopšī yšallḥénnū táḥénnū táḥaṯ-ᶜēnō;</td><td>If a man strikes the eye of his male slave or the eye of his female slave and destroys it, he shall let him go free for the sake of his eye; |</td></tr>
<tr><td>וְאִם־שֵׁן עַבְדּוֹ אוֹ־שֵׁן אֲמָתוֹ יַפִּיל לַחָפְשִׁי יְשַׁלְּחֶנּוּ תַּחַת שִׁנּוֹ:</td><td>wᵓim šēn-ᶜaḇdō ō-šēn-ămāṯō yappīl,[107] laḥopšī yšallḥénnū táḥaṯ-šinnō.</td><td>and if he knocks out the tooth of his male slave or of his female slave, then he shall let him go free for the sake of his tooth. |</td></tr>
<tr><td>וְכִי־יִגַּח שׁוֹר אֶת־אִישׁ אוֹ אֶת־אִשָּׁה וָמֵת סָקוֹל יִסָּקֵל הַשּׁוֹר וְלֹא יֵאָכֵל אֶת־בְּשָׂרוֹ</td><td>wkī-yiggaḥ[108] šōr eṯ-īš ō-eṯ-iššā wāmēṯ, sāqōl yissāqel haššōr wlō-yēᵓāḵel eṯ[109]-bśārō;[110]</td><td>If an ox gores a man or a woman and he dies, then the ox shall be stoned and its flesh shall not be eaten; |</td></tr>
<tr><td>וּבַעַל הַשּׁוֹר נָקִי:</td><td>uḇáᶜal-haššōr nāqī.</td><td>but the owner of the ox is cleared. |</td></tr>
<tr><td>וְאִם שׁוֹר נַגָּח הוּא מִתְּמֹל שִׁלְשֹׁם וְהוּעַד בִּבְעָלָיו וְלֹא יִשְׁמְרֶנּוּ וְהֵמִית אִישׁ אוֹ אִשָּׁה</td><td>wᵓim-šōr naggāḥ hū mittmōl šil-šōm[111] whūᶜaḏ[112] biḇᶜālāu[113] wlō-yišmrénnū whēmīṯ[114] īš ō-iššā,</td><td>But if the ox has been accustomed to gore in the past and this has been told to the owner but he has not kept it in and it kills a man or a woman, |</td></tr>
<tr><td>הַשּׁוֹר יִסָּקֵל וְגַם־בְּעָלָיו יוּמָת:</td><td>haššōr yissāqel wgam-bᶜālāu yūmāṯ;[P]</td><td>then the ox shall be stoned and its owner shall be killed; |</td></tr>
<tr><td>אִם־כֹּפֶר יוּשַׁת עָלָיו וְנָתַן פִּדְיֹן נַפְשׁוֹ כְּכֹל אֲשֶׁר־יוּשַׁת עָלָיו:</td><td>wᵓim-kóper yūšaṯ[115] ᶜālāu, wnāṯan piḏyan-napšō kḵol-ăšer-yūšaṯ ᶜālāu.</td><td>but if a ransom is placed upon him, then he shall give for the redemption of his life all that is placed upon him.</td></tr>
</table>

104. < **šinn*. 105. From *āmā* (biliteral). 106. Intensive. 107. *npl.* 108. *ngḥ.* 109. The accusative particle *eṯ* also occurs with the logical patient of the passive. 110. From *bāśār.* 111. From *šālōš* 'three.' 112. *wᶜd.* 113. From *báᶜal*; plural in singulative sense. 114. *mwt.* 115. *šyt.*

2. Middle Hebrew

The Law of the King
(Mishna Sanhedrin 2:2-5)[ad]

הַמֶּלֶךְ לֹא דָּן וְלֹא דָּנִין אֹתוֹ לֹא מֵעִיד וְלֹא מְעִידִים אֹתוֹ

hammélek̲ lō d̲ān,[AkAm116] *wlō-d̲ānīn ōt̲ō; lō mēʿīd̲,*[117] *wlō-mʿīd̲īn ōt̲ō;*

לֹא חוֹלֵץ וְלֹא חוֹלְצִין לְאִשְׁתּוֹ וְלֹא מְיַבֵּם וְלֹא מְיַיבְּמִים אֶת אִשְׁתּוֹ וְאֵין נוֹשְׂאִין אֶת אַלְמַנְתּוֹ

lō-ḥōlēṣ, wlō-ḥōlṣīn lʾištō;[118] *lō myabbēm, wlō myabbmīn et̲-ištō; . . . wʾēn nōśʾīn et̲-almnāt̲ō.*[119]

The king does not judge, nor does anyone judge him; he is not a witness, nor is anyone a witness against him; | he may not perform halitzah (removal of the shoe denoting refusal to perform levirate marriage), nor does anyone perform halitzah on behalf of his wife; he does not contract levirate marriage, nor does any contract levirate marriage with his wife; . . . nor does anyone wed his widow. |

ר׳ יְהוּדָה א׳ נוֹשֵׂא הוּא הַמֶּלֶךְ אַלְמַנְתּוֹ שֶׁלָּמֶלֶךְ שֶׁכֵּן מָצִינוּ בְּדָוִיד שֶׁנָּשָׂא אַלְמַנְתּוֹ שֶׁל שָׁאוּל:

rabbī[120] *Yhūd̲ā ōmēr: "nōśē hū hammélek̲ almnāt̲ō šel-mélek̲, šekkēn māṣīnū*[121] *b̲ D̲āwīd̲, šennāśā almnāt̲ō šel-Šāʾūl."*

Rabbi Judah says: "The king himself marries (i.e. may marry [and so in the following]) the widow of a king, since so we find with David, who wed the widow of Saul." |

מֵת לוֹ מֵת אֵינוֹ יוֹצֵא מִפֶּתַח פַּלָטוֹרִין שֶׁלּוֹ

. . . mēt̲ lō mēt̲, ēnō yōṣē[122] *mippét̲aḥ-plāṭōrīn*[123] *šellō;*

. . . If one of his (kin) (lit. a dyer) dies, he does not go out the door of his palace; |

וּכְשֶׁמַּבְרִים אֹתוֹ כָּל הָעָם מְסוּבִּין עַל הָאָרֶץ וְהוּא מֵסֵב עַל הַדַּרְגֵּשׁ:

. . . uk̲šemmab̲rīn[124] *ōt̲ō, kol-hāʿām msibbīn*[125] *ʿal-hāʾắreṣ, whū mēsēb̲*[125] *ʿal-haddargāš.*

וּמוֹצִיא לְמִלְחֶמֶת הָרְשׁוּת עַל פִּי בֵּית דִּין שֶׁל שִׁבְעִים וְאֶחָד

umōṣī[126] *lmilḥémet̲-hāršūt̲ ʿal-pī*[127]*-b̲ēt̲-dīn šel-šib̲ʿīm*[128] *wʾēḥād̲.*

. . . and when they give him the funeral meal, all the people recline on the ground, but he reclines on the couch. | He leads (the people) in a voluntary war (lit. war of permission) on the decision (lit. mouth) of the Courthouse of Seventy-one. |

ad. Text as in the Kaufmann manuscript A50 (facsimile published by Georg Beer, The Hague: Nijhoff, 1929 [Jerusalem, 1968]), p. 293; this text is not identical with that used in Bergsträsser's transcription, but is an extremely valuable witness. Consulted in translating: Philip Blackman, *Mishnayoth* (New York: Judaica Press, 1963), vol. 4, pp. 242-244.

116. *dyn.* 117. *ʿwd* causative. 118. From *éšet̲*, construct state of *iššā.* 119. From *almānā.* 120. Literally 'my lord.' 121. *mṣʾ.* 122. *wṣʾ* participle. 123. *praetorium.* 124. *bry* causative. 125. *sbb* causative (Old Hebrew 'turn'). 126. *wṣʾ* causative. 127. Construct state of *pē* (monoliteral). 128. Plural of *šéb̲aʿ* 'seven.'

וּפוֹרֵץ לַעֲשׂוֹת לוֹ דֶּרֶךְ וְאֵין מְמָחִין בְּיָדוֹ דֶּרֶךְ הַמֶּלֶךְ אֵין לָהּ שִׁיעוּר	*upōrēṣ laʿśōṯ*[129] *lō ḏéreḵ, wʾēn mmaḥīn*[130] *byāḏō; déreḵ-hamméleḵ ēn lāh šiʿūr.*[131]	He breaks through to make himself a road, nor does anyone stay his hand; the king's road has no dimension. |
וְכָל הָעָם בּוֹזְזִין וְנוֹתְנִין לְפָנָיו וְהוּא נוֹטֵל חֵלֶק בָּרֹאשׁ:	*wḵol-hāʿām bōzzīn wnōṯnīn lpānāu, whū nōṭēl*[Am] *ḥéleq brōš.*	All the people take spoil and lay (it) before him, and he takes a portion first. |
לֹא יַרְבֶּה לוֹ נָשִׁים אֶלָּא שְׁמוֹנֶה עֶשְׂרֵה	*"lō-yarbē*[132] *lō nāšīm,*[133] *ellā*[Am] *šmōnē-ʿeśrē.*	"He shall not multiply wives to himself,"[134] only eighteen. |
ר׳ יְהוּדָה א׳ מַרְבֶּה הוּא לוֹ וּבִלְבַד שֶׁלֹּא יְהוּ מְסִירוֹת אֶת לִבּוֹ	*rabbī Yhūḏā ōmēr: "marbē hū lō, uḇilḇaḏ*[135] *šellō yhū*[136] *msīrōṯ*[137] *eṯ-libbō."*[138]	Rabbi Judah says: "He may multiply to himself, only that they not turn away his heart." |
ר׳ שִׁמְעוֹן א׳ אֲפִילוּ אַחַת וְהִיא מְסִירָה אֶת לִבּוֹ הֲרֵי זֶה לֹא יִשָּׂאֶינָּה:	*rabbī Šimʿōn ōmēr: "ăpillū*[Am] *aḥaṯ*[139] *whī msīrā eṯ-libbō, hrē*[Am]*-zē lō-yiśśāʾénnā."*[140]	Rabbi Simon says: "If only one and she turns away his heart, he may not marry her." |
לֹא יַרְבֶּה לוֹ סוּסִים אֶלָּא כְּדֵי מֶרְכַּבְתּוֹ וְכֶסֶף וְזָהָב לֹא יַרְבֶּה לוֹ אֶלָּא כְּדֵי שֶׁיִּתֵּן אֶפְסֶנְיָיא	. . . *"lō-yarbē lō sūsīm,"*[141] *ellā ḵḏē-merkaḇtō; wḵésep̄ wzāhāḇ lō-yarbē lō," ellā ḵḏē*[143]*-šeyyitten*[144] *apsōnyā.*[145]	. . . "He shall not multiply horses to himself,"[142] only enough for his chariot; "and silver and gold he shall not multiply to himself,"[146] only enough for giving rations. |
וְכוֹתֵב לוֹ סֵפֶר תּוֹרָה לִשְׁמוֹ:	*wḵōṯēḇ lō séper-tōrā lišmō.*[147]	He writes a Torah book for his name (i.e. for himself). |
אֵין רוֹכְבִין עַל סוּסוֹ וְאֵין יוֹשְׁבִין עַל כִּסְאוֹ וְאֵין מִשְׁתַּמְּשִׁין בְּשַׁרְבִיטוֹ	. . . *ēn rōḵḇīn ʿal-sūsō, wʾēn yōšḇīn ʿal-kisʾō,*[Ak148] *wʾēn mištammšīn*[Am] *bšarbīṭō;*[Am]	No one rides on his horse, and no one sits on his throne, and no one uses his sceptre; |
וְאֵין רוֹאִין אוֹתוֹ עָרוֹם אֶלָּא כְּשֶׁהוּא מִסְתַּפֵּר וְלֹא בְּבֵית הַמֶּרְחָץ שנ׳ שׂוֹם תָּשִׂים עָלֶיךָ מֶלֶךְ שֶׁתְּהֵא אֵימָתוֹ עָלֶיךָ	*wʾēn rōʾīn*[149] *ōṯō ʿārōm, wlō kšehū mistappēr,*[Am] *wlō-bḇēṯ hammerḥāṣ;*[150] *šenneʾmar: "śōm*[151] *tāśīm ʿāléḵā méleḵ," šetthē*[152] *ēmāṯō ʿāléḵā.*	no one sees him naked, nor while he is having his hair cut, nor in the bathhouse; as it is said, "You shall not set over you a king,"[153] that awe of him be over you.

129. *ʿśy*. 130. *mḥy* intensive. 131. Intensive. 132. *rby* causative. 133. Plural of *iššā* < **inθat-*. 134. Deuteronomy 17:17. 135. Old Hebrew *l-ḇaḏ* 'alone.' 136. *hyy*. 137. *swr* causative. 138. From *lēḇ*. 139. Feminine of *ēḥāḏ*, < **aḥḥadt*. 140. *nśʾ*. 141. Loanword of uncertain origin. 142. Deuteronomy 17:16. 143. From *dai* 'sufficiency.' 144. *ntn*. 145. *opsonium*. 146. Deuteronomy 17:17. 147. From *šēm* (biliteral). 148. For **kissʾō* from *kissē*. 149. *rʾy*. 150. Noun of place from *rāḥaṣ* 'he washed (himself).' 151. Infinitive absolute. 152. *hyy*. 153. Deuteronomy 17:15.

3. Modern Hebrew

Beginning and End of the Speech of Sir Herbert Samuel at the Opening of the Institute for the Science of Judaism in Jerusalem 22.xii.1925

[E] = European loanword

שמח אני מאוד על שהצעדים הראשונים ליסוד האוניברסיטה העברית בירושלים התקדמו במדה כזוא

עד שהנהלת המוסד יכולה לפתוח היום את־המכון למדעי היהדות נוסף למכון הביאוכימי הקים כבר.

למען נהיל את־עבודת המחקר והלמוד עלה בידי המוסד לרכוש מורים מפורסמים מארצות שונות.

הנני שבע רצון לדעת שמספר התלמידים הדורשים להכניס אל המכון גדול.

מקוי אני שלא יארכו הימים וחפץ ההנהלה ליסיד מכון לחקירת התרבות הערבית יצא לפועל.

śāmḗaḥ ănī mᵓōḏ, ᶜal-šehaṣṣᶜāḏīm[154] *hārīšōnīm lyissūḏ hāᵓūnībersīṭā*[E] *hāᶜiḇrīṯ*[155] *bĪrūšāláyim hiṯqaddmū ḇmiddā ḵāzō, ᶜaḏ-šehanhālaṯ-hammōsāḏ*[156] *yḵōlā lip̄tṓaḥ hayyōm eṯ-hammāḵōn*[157] *lmaddāᶜē*[Am] *hayyahḏūṯ, nōsāp̄*[158] *lammāḵōn habbīᵓōḵēmī*[E] *haqqayyām*[Am] *kḇār.*[Am] *lmáᶜan-nahēl*[159] *eṯ-ᶜḇōḏaṯ-hammeḥqār whallimmūḏ, ᶜālā*[160] *ḇīḏē*[161]*-hammōsāḏ lirkōš*[162] *mōrīm*[163] *mp̄ursāmīm*[Am] *mēᵓărāṣōṯ*[164] *šōnōṯ.*[165]

hinn·nī śḇaᶜ[166]*-rāṣōn*[167] *lāḏáᶜaṯ,*[168] *šemmispar-hattalmīḏīm haddōršīm lhikkānēs*[Am] *el-hammāḵōn gāḏōl. mqawwē*[169] *ănī šellō-yaᵓarḵū hayyāmīm wḥḗp̄eṣ hahanhālā lyassēḏ māḵōn laḥqīraṯ-hattarbūṯ*[Am][170] *haᶜrāḇīṯ*[171] *yēṣē*[172] *lp̄óᶜal.*

I am greatly pleased that the first steps toward the foundation of the Hebrew University in Jerusalem have progressed so far (lit. in a measure like this) | that (lit. until that) the leadership of the institution can open today the Institute of the Science of Judaism, added to the biochemical institute, already extant. | For the purpose of guiding the work of research and study, the Institute has managed (lit. it has gone up into the hands of the Institute) to acquire famous teachers from various countries. | I am satisfied to know that the number of students seeking to enter the Institute is large. | I hope that the days will not be long that the desire of the administration to found an institute for research in Arab culture will come to fruition. |

saméaḫ ani meᵓod al-šehaceᵓadim harišonim leyisud haᵓunivérsita haᵓivrit bIrušaláyim hitkadmu bemida kazo | ad-šehanhalat-hamosad yeḫola liftóaḫ hayom et-hamaḫon lemadaᵓey hayahadut, nosaf lamaḫon habiᵓoḫémi hakayam kvar. | lemaᵓan-nahel et-ᵓavodat-hameḫkar vehalimud, ala bidey-hamosad lirkoš morim mefursamim meᵓaracot šonot. | hin·ni sva-racon ladáᵓat šemispar-hatalmidim hadoršim lehikanes el-hamaḫon gadol. | mekave ani šelo-yaᵓarḫu hayamim veḫéfec hahanhala leyased maḫon laḫakirat-hatarbut haᵓaravit yece lefoᵓal. |

154. From *ṣáᶜaḏ*. 155. Nisbe. 156. From *wsd* = *ysd* 'found.' 157. Old Hebrew 'place,' noun of place from *kān* (*kwn*) 'he stood firm.' 158. *wsp* 'add.' 159. Intensive. 160. *ᶜly*. 161. From *yḏē*, construct state of *yāḏáyim*, dual of *yāḏ* (biliteral). 162. Incorrectly pronounced *lirḵōš*. 163. *wry* causative. 164. From *éreṣ*. 165. *šny*. 166. Construct state of *śāḇḗaᶜ* 'sated.' 167. From *rṣw*. 168. *ydᶜ*. 169. *qwy*. 170. *rby* 'grow up.' 171. Nisbe. 172. *wṣᵓ*.

ae. Bergsträsser's transcription is pure Biblical Hebrew. The text is here given as back-transliterated from his version, with a new transcription reflecting Israeli Hebrew pronunciation.

אין ספיק שעל האוניברסיטה הזאת יהיה להתגבר על הרבה מכשולים רוחניים לשוניים וגם כלכליים.

יוכל להיות שמוריה ותלמידיה יצטרכו להקריב קרבנות.

אך הדבר הזה הוא המבטיח לאוניברסיטה את־התפתחותה,

ויכולים אנו לומר לתהלת האנושיות כי האדם אוהב את־הדבר שבעדו הקריב עצמו יותר מן הדבר שהשיג ממנו רק תענוגות בלבד.

אני מאחיל למכון הזה ימים ארוכים של תועלת והצלחה!

. . . ēn sāp̄ēq,[Am] *šeᶜal-hāʾūnīḇersīṭā hazzōṯ yihyē lhiṯgabbēr ᶜal-harbē-mik̲šōlīm*[173] *rūḥāniyyīm,*[174] *lšōniy-yīm wḡam kalkāliyyīm.*
yūk̲al[175] *lihyōṯ, šemmōrḗhā wṯalmī-ḏḗhā yiṣṭārk̲ū*[Am] *lhaqrīḇ qorbānōṯ.*
ak̲-haddāḇār hazzē hū hammaḇ-ṭī́aḥ[176] *lāʾūnīḇersīṭā eṯ-hiṯpatḥūṯāh,*
wīk̲ōlīm[177] *ănū lōmar liṯhillaṯ-hā-ʾĕnōšiyyūṯ, kī hāʾāḏām ōhēḇ eṯ-haddāḇār šebbaᶜḏō*[178] *hiqrīḇ ᶜaṣ-mō,*[179] *yōṯēr min haddāḇār, šehiś-śīg*[180] *mimménnū raq taᶜnūḡōṯ bil-baḏ.*
ănī mʾaḥēl[181] *lammāk̲ōn hazzē yāmīm ărukkīm šel-tōᶜéleṯ*[182] *whaṣ-lāḥā!*

. . . There is no doubt that the university will have to strengthen itself against many spiritual, linguistic, and also economic stumbling-blocks. | It could be that its teachers and its students will need to make sacrifices. | But it is this circumstance that promises to the university its development, | and we can say to the praise of mankind that man loves the thing on whose account he has sacrificed himself more than the thing from which he has received only enjoyment alone. | I wish this Institute long days of prosperity and success!

eyn safek šeʾal-haʾunivérsita hazot yihye lehitgaber al-harbe-miḫšolim ruḫaniyim, lešoniyim, vegam kal-kaliyim. | *yuḫal lihyot šemoréha vetalmidéha yictarḫu lehakriv korbanot.* | *aḫ-hadavar haze hu hamavtíaḫ la-ʾunivérsita et-hitpatḫuta,* | *viḫolim anu lomar lithilat-haʾenošiyut ki haʾadam ohev et-hadavar šebaʾado hikriv acmo yoter min hadavar šehisig mimenu rak taʾanugot bilvad.* | *ani meʾaḫel lamaḫon haze yamim arukim šel-toʾélet vehaclaḫa!*

173. Noun of instrument from *kāšal* 'he stumbled.' 174. Nisbe with the Aramaic ending *-ānī*. 175. *wkl* (perfect *yāk̲ol*). 176. Causative of *bāṭaḥ* 'he trusted.' 177. From *yāk̲ōl, yk̲ōlīm*. 178. From *báᶜaḏ*. 179. Literally 'his bones' (*ᶜéṣem*), already the reflexive in Old Hebrew. 180. *yśg*. 181. From Old Hebrew *aḥlē* 'O, would that!' 182. *wᶜl*.

Chapter 4

Aramaic

I. Old Aramaic

§ 4/1.0

Of the many dialects of Old Aramaic[1] that achieved literary status, three are chosen here as representative: 1. the oldest known,[a] Biblical Aramaic, which approximately represents the Aramaic imperial language of the western half of the Achaemenian Empire; 2. the one with the most richly developed literature, Syriac, the language of the Syrian church, developed from the dialect of Edessa; and 3. Mandaic, which presents a particularly individual variant development, the language of the gnostic sect of Mandeans, spoken in southern Babylonia. The latter two dialects belong to the eastern branch of Aramaic (East Aramaic).

a. At least one strictly literary text is known from the fifth-century B.C. Egyptian Aramaic documents, and Aramaic monuments go back to the tenth or eleventh century; Biblical Aramaic is the oldest vocalized Aramaic dialect, but its vowels were not notated until the ninth century A.D. or so; there is reason to suspect contamination from Hebrew in the vocalizations.

Like that of Hebrew, the vocalization of Biblical Aramaic has been transmitted in several recensions; as with Hebrew, the Tiberian and Babylonian are considered here. — The pronunciation of Syriac shows dialectal differences between the West Syrian Jacobites and the East Syrian Nestorians, and older pronunciations sometimes underlie this difference. — Mandaic is the only Semitic language for which a more or less complete and consistent notation of the vowels using only the old consonantal alphabet has been realized. The system is far from exact. It distinguishes only four vowel qualities *a e i u*

1. In the widest sense; that is, in contrast to the living Aramaic dialects. By Old Aramaic in a narrower sense is meant the language of the time up to about the last century B.C., by Old Aramaic in the narrowest sense the language of the inscriptions and papyri through about 400 B.C.

(medially and finally *i* also stands for *e*), does not indicate quantity, and leaves spirantization unmarked; nonetheless, so that it may fully achieve its due, it is transliterated unaltered in the transcription.[2]

Phonologically, Aramaic shares a set of peculiarities with Hebrew, most sweepingly the loss of final vowels caused by the strong stress accent and medial vowel reduction, as well as the spirantization of stops.[3] Reduction and spirantization go further in Aramaic,[4] and probably had their origin here and only later were adopted in Hebrew. The consonant system is simplified to the same degree as in Hebrew, though the simplification proceeds to some extent in a different direction. In contrast to the Hebrew situation, the article is suffixed. In overall character of sentence structure and expression, the oldest Aramaic is close to Hebrew; later a tendency, already emerging to some extent in proto-Semitic, to analysis and isolated expression of individual elements of thought and to sentence conjunction takes hold, and hand in hand with that a great love of variety in means of expression, so that Classical Syriac — in sharp contrast to the concise and exact Classical Arabic — is an outspokenly analytic language with a tendency toward prolixity. As a result Syriac is not successful in differentiating and specifying its means of expression; it could not overcome a certain vagueness and haziness in expression of thought. —

b. Macuch □4/1h:2 reports that these two letters are more than orthographic variants; he records pronunciations of $\bar{h}$ and $\bar{d}$ as $\bar{\imath}$ and (*a*)*d*.

2. Only vowels in the most common words and in the third person singular pronominal suffixes are supplied — in parentheses. The special signs that Mandaic uses for the (probably already lost) final *h* of these suffixes and for the *d* of the relative pronoun are not distinguished from ordinary *h* and *d*, since they have no phonetic meaning.[b]

3. Some points of contact can probably be explained by the fact that the Jewish tradition of the pronunciation of Hebrew is affected by Aramaic.

4. Spirantization goes so far as to affect the $d < \delta$ and $t < \theta$, which in Hebrew become sibilants.

§ 4/1.1.1

The dental spirants are, in contrast to Akkadian and Hebrew, shifted to stops,[c] and specifically *δ* > *d*, *θ* > *t*, and *θ̣* > *ṭ* regularly; but the peculiarity of *δ̣* results in a remarkable phonetic odyssey that ends in ᶜ, but passes through a sound written *q* in the oldest Aramaic and still in Mandaic: e.g., **arδ̣* 'earth' > Md (with article) *arqa*, Common Aramaic *ar*ᶜ*ā*; *ᶜ*āδ̣* 'wood' > *ᶜ*ā*ᶜ*ā* > *ā*ᶜ*ā* (with dissimilation). Isolated exceptions with *z* for *d* < *δ* are found in old inscriptions influenced by Phoenician through Mandaic, particularly in the demonstrative.[d] *ś* and *ḫ* share the Hebrew development to *s* and *ḥ*; in older Aramaic *ś* is still retained. The laryngeals appear in Biblical Aramaic at exactly the same stage as in Hebrew. Later the dialects differ noticeably; Classical Syriac shows hardly any weakening, but Mandaic comes very close to Akkadian, in whose old territory it is settled: ᵓ and ᶜ have merged and mostly disappeared, *ḥ* has become *h* and like it occasionally also disappeared. E.g., *tira* 'door' from *tr*ᶜ; *bin* 'we have sought,' *bayin* 'seeking,' *buta* 'to seek' from *b*ᶜ*y*; *ištmanin* 'we have been heard,' *mištimi* 'being heard' from *šm*ᶜ; — *aškanin* 'we have found,' *maški* 'finding' from *škḥ*. ᵓ disappears in other dialects also, especially syllable- and word-finally, e.g., *rēšā* 'head' < **ra*ᵓ*š-*, *kēḇā* 'sorrow, pain' < **ka*ᵓ*b-*, also *bāṯar* 'after, behind' < **ba*ᵓ*tar* (*aṯar* 'trace'), BA *bēḏáyin* (Ba *b*ᵓ*ēḏáyin* instead) 'then, thereupon' < **bi-* + *ĕḏáyin*, and in III ᵓ words; further, e.g., *ḥaḏ*, feminine *ḥḏā* 'one' < **aḥad-*, Sy *nāšā* 'man' < BA *ĕnāšā*, Sy *baṯrā* 'at the place' < *b* + ᵓ*aṯrā* (in Biblical Aramaic in this environment — after prefix before full vowel — ᵓ is retained, e.g., *w*ᵓ*āmar* 'and saying').

The semivowels have the same fate as in Hebrew; with initial *y* whose vowel is lost, the change to *i-* found in the Babylonian vocalization prevails generally in Aramaic: *iḏa*ᶜ 'he recognized' against Ti *yḏa*ᶜ, *Irūšlem* 'Jerusalem' (in Syriac differently formed *Ōrišlem*). The *y* is entirely replaced by ᵓ in

c. This shift may have been triggered by post-vocalic spirantization: the situation of contrast between stops and spirants initially and after consonants, versus no contrast after vowels, was inimical to the principle of unchangeable roots (cf. §1/1.2.0.2), and was resolved by eliminating the contrast (in the direction of the less marked stops in the unmarked environment, leaving the more marked spirants in the marked environment "postvocalic").

d. Or else the written *z* represents the historical *δ* before it changed to *d* (this is the situation in the earliest monuments); cf. note c.

Sy *īḏā* = BA *yḏā* (construct state in Syriac still *yaḏ* beside *īḏ*) and in *īṯ(ai)* 'there exists' = H *yēš*; with prefix it is even in Ti *bīrūšlem* 'in Jerusalem,' etc.

The non-emphatic stops *b d g p t k*, including those developed from spirants, are spirantized under the same conditions as in Hebrew; e.g., after a vowel that later disappears, in BA *libḇeh* 'his heart' < **libab*-, Common Aramaic *dahḇā* 'gold' < **δahab*-. Occasionally, though, in such cases the stop is secondarily restored, particularly in Syriac, as in the feminine ending, where *-tā* is making progress against *-ṯā*; in the perfect of the basic stem (Sy *keṯbeṯ* 'I wrote' against BA *taqp̄aṯ* 'she became strong'); and in the participle of the basic stem (Sy *rāḏpīn* 'persecuting' against BA *ᶜāḇḏīn* 'serving'). Sporadically *ḇ* further becomes *w*: BA *raḇrḇā* 'big' > Sy *raurḇā*. An important dialectal distinction is that after a diphthong spirantization occurs in Biblical Aramaic but not in Syriac: BA *baiṯā* 'house' against Sy *baitā*. Reminiscent of Akkadian, beside consonant assimilation "geminate" dissimilation is found, e.g., Md *manda* 'knowledge' < **maddaᶜ*, BA *korsē* 'throne' < Ak *kussū*.

§ 4/1.1.3 Position of accent is in general the same as in Hebrew[5] (the variations of pausal accent are not found);[6] the effects of the accent, however, are limited to disappearance[7] of vowels, without any lengthenings to correspond to those of Hebrew. Lost are final short vowels as well as those in medial open syllables, with the same limitation as in Hebrew, that in sequences of such syllables alternate ones retain the vowel. The result differs only in that it is the pretonic syllable that is first

5. Just as for Hebrew, here all words not finally accented are provided with accent marks.

6. Syriac later moved the accent back one syllable.

7. Or reduction. Biblical Aramaic writes reduced vowels just like Hebrew; Syriac (and likewise Mandaic) leaves them unindicated.

to disappear; thus **qataláhū* 'he killed him,' H *qṭālō*, but Am *qaṭleh*. Here and there short vowels in other open syllables are also retained, e.g., Md *qudam* 'before' against BA and Sy *qḏām*. In Syriac and Mandaic, furthermore, most unaccented final long vowels are lost,[8] among others the old plural ending on the verb *-ū* and the first person pronominal suffix *-ī*; thus Sy *qṭal* both 'he killed' and 'they killed'; 'my king' *malk*; further, e.g., *mār* 'lord!' < **mā́rē* (with stress retraction in the vocative) (then from that *mārāḵ* 'your lord,' etc.).

§ 4/1.1.2 The laryngeals and *r* influence the vowels in Biblical Aramaic exactly as in Hebrew, plus a bit more: a short vowel before a syllable-closing laryngeal or *r* becomes *a* (e.g., Sy *mašmaᶜ* 'causing to hear' for paradigmatic *maqṭel*, *āmar* 'saying' for *qāṭel*), and the vowel is also retained in an open syllable after initial ᵓ, e.g., Sy *emar* 'he said' or 'say,' *aḥīḏ* 'possessing'; BA Ba *elāhā* 'God' (Ti *ĕlāhā*;[9] Syriac correspondance with secondary lengthening *allāhā*).

In the diphthongs, everywhere simplifications are found beside retentions; thus the plural ending with the article is *-ayyā* in Biblical Aramaic, *-ē* in Syriac (*-i* in Mandaic), but vice versa before a suffix, BA *-ē-* (Md *-i-*), Sy *-ai-*. The replacement rampant in Hebrew of *a* in closed unstressed syllables by *i* (*e*) is in Aramaic significantly more restricted, Syriac e.g. in *qeṭlaṯ* 'she killed' < **qaṭalat*, as opposed to *bašnaṯ* 'in the year . . .,' etc. (prefixed particle before double consonant), versus BA *bišnaṯ* as in Hebrew (here no vowel is written in Mandaic).

i ī and *u ū* are frequently replaced by *e ē* and *o ō*, in a distribution that sharply differentiates the dialects; and in fact the long vowels *ē ō* in such cases are mostly already proto-Aramaic, even if they were not retained in all dialects. Syriac is the dialect that goes furthest in replacing *i* by *e*.

8. These vowels are preserved in Syriac orthography.

9. Cf. § 3 n. 9.

West Syriac has distanced itself in various points from the older phonological situation: it has given up consonant length and changed long *ā ē* (medially) *ō* to *ō ī ū* (only *ē* < *a*ʾ in certain cases is retained, e.g., *tēḵul* 'thou eatest' < **taʾkul*). East Syriac in general preserves the older sounds; it has only replaced *ḥ* with *ẖ* and *u* in unstressed syllables with *o*. —

§ 4/1.2.1.1 'We' is in Biblical Aramaic *ănáḥnā*, with the beginning of *ănā* (Sy *enā*) 'I,' as in Hebrew; Syriac and Mandaic drop the first *n* and reinforce the end with an *-n* (*ḥnan anin*), which recurs to strengthen the verb suffixes that end in vowels and also in the pronoun 'they,' Sy *hennōn hennēn* (Biblical Aramaic still *himmō* without strengthening and with *m*). Simultaneously these forms have been influenced by those of the second person Sy *attōn attēn* 'you,' which likewise have *n* for both genders, but unlengthened and hence with lengthening of the preceding vowel instead. To them correspond the suffixes *-ḵōn -ḵēn* 'your, you,' *-hōn -hēn* 'their, them' (Biblical Aramaic still *-ḵōm -hōm*) and the second person plural perfect suffixes *-tōn -tēn*. For the second person Mandaic uses the idiosyncratic extension *anat* 'thou,' *anatun* 'you.' — There are enclitic short forms of the personal pronouns, with which nominal clauses are formed that are exactly the same kind as those that constituted the basis of the proto-Semitic suffix conjugation, so that the same process recurs in widely separated eras. The most important combination is with a participle to form a new present-future (in the sense of the tense-meaning of the participle described in § 1/2.2.2): Sy *sāleq-nā* 'I am getting up, am in the process of getting up,' Md *šabqat* 'thou lettest,' *qaiminin* 'we stand.' This new present is distinct from the old suffix conjugation, where the prior nominal predicate is uninflected, in that the first part must be declined for gender and number (though in, e.g., Mandaic, in which overall the feminine tends to disappear in the verb, the gender distinction is almost entirely given up); the distinction between masculine and feminine has thereby also spread to the first person, where elsewhere in Semitic it is not found. Thus in Syriac against *sāleq-nā* 'I (masculine) get up': *sālqā-nā* 'I (feminine) get up.'

After a word-final consonant, the suffixes take a linking vowel as in Hebrew; it is *a*, and the suffix 'his, him' is *-eh*. Here, as in *-āh* 'her' and *-āk̲* 'thy, thee' (masculine) and others, the final vowel of the suffix fell away early, leaving behind the *h*. Elsewhere in Aramaic there are vowel contractions in the suffix 'his, him'; these have given rise to suffix proliferation. Thus already in Biblical Aramaic *-ṓhī* from **-ai-hū* > **-ō* (so, *-au*, in Syriac) plus an again-appended **-hū* dissimilated to *-hī*; this *-hī* has then been taken over into other combinations. Furthest developed are suffix proliferations and extensions in the imperative and in III weak verbs, especially in Syriac. The two series of suffixes, which occur after a stem-final consonant and after final **-ai*, are used in Mandaic without any difference, while they are sharply distinguished in Syriac; in Biblical Aramaic the simple forms penetrate into the *ai*-series. *n*-suffixes on the verb are retained in Biblical Aramaic, as in Hebrew; in Mandaic they are common in the plural and there only, e.g., *-(i)nan* 'us.' The third person plural accusative suffixes are replaced by the independent pronouns.

§ 4/1.2.1.2 For the demonstrative 'this' Biblical Aramaic, just like Hebrew, uses the simple stem *δ-* in the singular and *l-* in the plural, strengthened, in the masculine only, by *n*: *dnā*, *dā*, *el*. Syriac extends these forms with *hā-* and strengthens the plural as well with *n*: *hānā* < **hāδnā*, *hād̲ā*, *hālēn*; similarly Md *hazin*, *haza*, *halin*. 'That' is expressed in Biblical Aramaic by the combination of the *δ*/*l*-demonstrative with *k* (*dēk̲*, *dāk̲*, *illēk̲*), in Syriac by the third person personal pronoun with *hā* (*hau* <

$h\bar{a}h\bar{u}$); Mandaic has *hak*, or else an innovation taking the personal suffixes *hanat*(*e*)*h*. When used adjectivally, the demonstratives may either precede or follow the substantive.

For the relative the demonstrative stem *δ*- is used in the forms BA *dī*, Sy Md *d* (Syriac in the possessive still *dīl*-). The relative is also used as a particle with a very wide range: from the introduction of a genitive (whence with the preposition *l*- + pronominal suffix is formed a possessive pronoun *dīlī* > Sy *dīl* 'my,' etc.) to the most diverse adnominal complements, including even the adjectival attribute itself (Md *atra dnpiš* 'a sacred place'); and for the introduction of subordinate clauses, alone (= 'that') or after prepositions (e.g., Sy *kaḏ* 'when, since, while'). This prevalence of *d*(*ī*) is one of the features that lends Aramaic its analytic character. Gradually the genitive periphrasis with *d*(*ī*) has almost entirely supplanted both the construct phrase and the old periphrasis for the indefinite genitive with *l*- (see § 1/2.2.3), which both persist in Biblical Aramaic.

The interrogatives are *man* (*mān*) 'who?,' *mā* 'what?' (and various expansions), Sy *ainā* (formed and further inflected like *hānā*) 'which?'; as generalizing relatives they are concatenated, conforming to the analytic tendency, with a following *d*(*ī*) (*ainā d*- in Syriac also simply 'which?'). A characteristically Aramaic indefinite is Sy *meddem* 'something' < *minda*ᶜ ('thing,' literally infinitive of *yd*ᶜ 'know' = Md *manda*) *mā*. —

§ 4/1.2.2 The verbal suffixes consisting of only a long vowel have vanished in Syriac and Mandaic or are retained in a form extended by -*n*; thus *qṭal* and *qṭálūn* 'they killed' occur side by side in Syriac. Correspondingly, the suffix 'we' in the perfect in Syriac is -*n* or -*nan* (Md -*n* or -*nin*, BA still -*nā*). For the perfect suffix 'I' Biblical Aramaic already has the general Aramaic innovation -*eṯ*. The imperfect prefix of the third person in all of East Aramaic (thus including Syriac and

Mandaic) is *n-* instead of *y-*; in addition, especially in Mandaic and the Jewish dialects, *l-* occurs, which already in Biblical Aramaic is found uniquely in *lehwē* 'he is, will be.'

§ 4/1.2.2.1

The imperfect distinguishes no moods; on the other hand, the tense system is enriched with the new participial tense. A phenomenon distantly related to the Hebrew consecutive tenses is that the perfect can be continued by the participle, especially with verbs of speaking: BA *ʿnā wʾāmar*[e] 'he answered and said.' The passive participle has also been dragged into the verbal conjugation, and is even used for creating active forms. In Syriac, although in only a few verbs, this participle in combination with enclitic personal pronouns tends toward innovating a new active tense for the state resulting from completed action (English perfect, pluperfect, or present, as the case may be), e.g., *aḥīḏ-nā* 'I have taken and now have.' And on the other hand (likewise in Syriac) it combines with the preposition *l-* + pronominal suffix marking the logical agent to form the beginnings of an object conjugation — a transitive verb in concord with the patient — in perfective sense: *šmīʿ-lan* 'we have heard it,' literally 'is heard to us,' with feminine object *qṭīlā-lan* 'we have killed her,' with plural *qṭīlīn-*, *qṭīlān-lan*. Both offshoots have further unfolded in Modern Aramaic.

e. But on the basis of plural forms (where perfect and participle are not homographic), such phrases should perhaps be revocalized to both be perfects or both participles.

§ 4/1.2.2.2

Verb stem formation is about as ramified as in Hebrew: besides the basic stem there is a *t*-reflexive for it (in place of the *n*-reflexive that is completely absent from Aramaic), as well as an intensive with *t*-reflexive, and a causative with, moreover, its own *t*-reflexive. Here and there, the causative prefix is *š-* (e.g., *šaḵlel* 'he completed'),[f] but usually *ʾ-*, which disappears after a prefix (Syriac perfect *aqṭel*, imperfect *naqṭel*); in Biblical Aramaic usually *h-* instead (but, e.g., *aḥeṯ* 'he caused to get up' from *nḥt*), which as a rule also disappears, but now and then remains (*yhāqīm* 'he places'). As in

f. Many causative *š*'s can be attributed to Akkadian loanwords.

Hebrew, the reflexive prefix has no vowel of its own and therefore in non-prefixed forms takes a prothesis: BA *hiṯ-* (as in Hebrew), or *iṯ-*, Md *it-*, Sy *eṯ-*. The causative-reflexive replaces *tʾ* (causative prefix + reflexive prefix) with *tt*: Sy *ettaqṭal*. For the *t* of the other two reflexives, about the same rules hold as in Hebrew. The passives[g] occur nearly exclusively in the participles; otherwise they are replaced by the *t*-reflexives. In Biblical Aramaic there are still finite passive forms, e.g. of the causative *hunḥaṯ* 'he was caused to get up'; nevertheless in the basic stem they too are assimilated to the participle: *yhī́ḇū* 'they were given' with *ī* instead of *i* following the participle *yhīḇ* 'given.'

g. Recall § 1 note x.

§ 4/1.2.2.3 In the basic stem the *u*-perfect is lost,[h] the *i*-imperfect is in decline. The vowel alternations in the perfect are shown by the Syriac forms discussed above *qṭal* 'he killed, they killed,' *qṭálūn* 'they killed,' *qeṭlaṯ* 'she killed,' along with *qṭalt* 'thou killedst.' In the imperative of all forms the vowel occurs between the last two radicals: *qṭul* 'kill' (singular or plural), *qṭúlūn* 'kill' (plural). The passive participle has the form *qṭīl*, as already mentioned several times. The infinitive is formed with *m* as in Sy *meᶜmar* 'to dwell,' and also with feminine ending as in BA *miḇnyā* 'to build.' — The vocalization of the derived stems is completely homogenized: the reflexives of the intensive and causative (and their passive participles) have *a* in the last syllable of the stem (Sy *eṯqaṭṭal neṯqaṭṭal*, etc.), the other forms *i/e* (*eṯqṭel neṯqṭel, qaṭṭel nqaṭṭel, aqṭel naqṭel*). The infinitives of the derived stems within each dialect also follow a unified pattern: BA *šaḵlālā* 'to complete,' beside *hōḏāᶜū* 'to cause to know'; likewise Syriac, but with prefix *m-*: *mqaṭṭālū*, etc.; Md *ištapuye* 'to overflow.'

h. But not entirely (Nyberg □ 1:6R4,109f).

§ 4/1.2.2.5.1 Among I *n* verbs, a weak imperative of the basic stem is found, e.g., BA *śē* 'carry.' Among I *w* verbs as well, only this imperative is weak, e.g., BA *haḇ* 'give'; in the other forms they are constructed partly like Sy *nīzep̄* 'he will borrow,' partly like BA *yiddaᶜ* 'he knows,' following the I *n* pattern. Individual I ᵓ verbs also have weak imperatives in the basic stem, e.g., Sy *zel* 'go'; but *emar* 'say,' and in Biblical Aramaic also *ĕzel* 'go.' Prefix vowel + syllable-final ᵓ gives *ē*, e.g., *mēmar* 'to say' < **maᵓmar* (but causative like I *w* Sy *aukel* 'he causes to eat'); after a consonant the ᵓ disappears in Syriac, thus *massē* < **mᵓassē* 'healing.' — *slq* 'go up' assimilates *sl* to *ss*: Sy imperfect *nessaq*, Md *masiqta* 'ascension,' and forms a weak imperative: Sy *saq*.

§ 4/1.2.2.5.2 The II geminate verbs are completely weak in the perfect of the basic stem: Sy *baz* 'he plundered,' second person *bazt*; otherwise they follow the I *n* verbs, e.g., imperfect *nebbuz*.

The II weak verbs in the basic stem are divided into the same series as in Hebrew: Sy active-mode *qām* 'he stood up' *nqūm*, *sām* 'he placed' *nsīm*; neutral-mode *mīṯ* 'he died' (in Biblical Aramaic in the Babylonian vocalization still with *ē*: *rēm* 'he was high') *nmūṯ*. In the derived stems *ī* is found, e.g., *t*-reflexive (for the basic stem as well as the causative) Sy *mittsīm* 'being placed' (but BA *mittśām*). The participle of the basic stem is strong, with ᵓ in second place: *qāᵓem*, plural *qāymīn* (*y* < ᵓ). In Biblical Aramaic as in Hebrew in the causative the prefix vowel is sometimes kept long: *yhāqīm* 'he places,' here with the prefix *h* retained also (Sy *nqīm*); *mārīm* 'raising' (Sy *mrīm*); — and the intensive and its reflexive are reduplicated: BA *hiṯrōmámtā* 'you raised yourself.'

§ 4/1.2.2.5.3 In the III weak verbs, with which the III ᵓ verbs have almost entirely merged, the perfect of the basic stem ends in *-ā*, e.g., *ᶜnā* 'he answered'; the imperative of the basic stem ends in *-ī*, e.g., *rmī* 'throw' (in III ᵓ verbs in Biblical Aramaic still *ē*: *śē* 'carry'), and so does the perfect of the derived stems, e.g., *haḡlī* 'he deported'; all the other forms end in *-ē*, e.g., imperfect in BA *lehwē* 'he will be,' active participle *ṣāḇē* 'wanting,' passive participle *bnē* 'built.' *-ā* + *-aṯ* gives *-āṯ*, e.g., *hwāṯ* 'she was' from *hwā*; but *-ī* + *-aṯ* gives *-yaṯ*, e.g., Sy *eṯqaryaṯ* 'she was named' from *eṯqrī*; likewise *āsyā* 'doctor' (with article) from the participle *āsē* 'healing.' *-ā* + *-ū* gives in Sy *-au*, in BA *-ō*, e.g., *hwau hwō* 'they were'; *-ī* + *ū* gives *-īu*, e.g., BA *haiṯīu* 'they brought' (but imperative Sy *rmau* 'throw'); *-ē* + *-ū* gives *-ō*, e.g., *termōn* 'you will throw.' The *-ē* of the participle combines with the *-īn* of the plural ending to make BA *-áyin*, Sy *-ēn*; e.g., 'seeing' *ḥāzáyin ḥāzēn*. Before a consonantal suffix *ī* remains unchanged; in the first person singular of the perfect *ē* replaces *ā*, elsewhere *ai* does. Thus 'I saw' *ḥzēṯ*, 'thou sawest' BA *ḥzáiṯā*, Sy *ḥzait*; and the other conjugations have then conformed to this distinction between *ṯ* and *t*, e.g., intensive first person *rammīṯ*, second person *rammīt*.[i] — There are in Syriac enclitic forms of the auxiliary verb *hwā* 'he was' without the *h-*, which serve for the formation of periphrastic tenses, especially with the perfect, e.g., *qabbel-wā* 'he had received, he received,' but also with the imperfect and participle (including the passive, e.g., *kṯīḇ-wā* 'it was written'). This use of *wā* is a further analytic feature of Syriac.

i. A situation reminiscent of that which brought about the devising of generative phonology, where a single class of counterexamples renders a phonemic system inadequate.

Besides *hwā* there is another way to say 'be,' BA *īṯai*, Sy *īṯ* 'exists,' negated Sy *lait*, Md *layit*. —

§ 4/1.2.3 Characteristically Aramaic nominal patterns are *qāṭōl*, which especially in Syriac can make an agent noun of nearly any verb, and then the adjectives with long middle radical, like *šallīṭ* 'powerful,' *ukkām* 'black.' Highly favored is the abstract ending *-ūṯ*, also found in Akkadian and Hebrew, perhaps of Akkadian origin, which has spread from Aramaic to other Semitic languages; as in the case of the feminine ending it loses its *-ṯ* (thus *-ū*) in the absolute state, and forms the plural with *-āwāṯā*.[j] (In III weak roots it occurs sometimes with loss of the last radical, as in *rḇūṯā* 'greatness,' *r*ᶜ*ūṯā* 'will,' sometimes with

j. *-ĕwāṯā* (Nyberg).

retention of it, as in Sy *āsyūṯā* 'healing' [but plural Md *asawata*]). The usual nisbe ending is *-āi*, with article in the Tiberian vocalization of Biblical Aramaic *-āʾā*, elsewhere *-āyā*.[k]

Nominal inflection is affected by the fact that the postposed article **-hā* (identical with the preposed Hebrew article)[l] has fused with the substantive and become an ending *-ā*. Thus in addition to the two states absolute and construct there exists a third, the definite or emphatic. It has gradually lost its definitizing sense; in Syriac and Mandaic it is the usual form of the noun, and the absolute state is limited to a few cases, e.g., the exclamation *šlām* 'hail!,' and, especially, the noun used predicatively. As a new means of definitizing, an anticipatory pronominal suffix anticipating the substantive is attached to its head substantive, governing verb, or governing preposition; the substantive itself is then introduced after substantive by *d*(*ī*), after verb by *l*-, or after preposition by the preposition repeated. E.g., Sy *breh dallāhā* 'God's son,' *qabblāh leggartā* 'he received the letter,' *bāh bmellṯāḵ* 'by your word.' There is no corresponding construction for the nominative.[m] Anticipation by pronominal suffix is one of the analytic features of Aramaic. — The declension endings are masculine plural absolute *-īn*, Md *-i*(*n*); construct Sy *-ai*, BA *-ē*; emphatic BA *-ayyā*, Sy *-ē* (but *šmayyā* 'heaven,' etc.), Md *-i* (absolute and emphatic are thus generally the same); — feminine absolute *-ā*, construct *-āṯ*, emphatic *-ṯ*/*tā*; plural absolute *-ān* (innovation modeled on *-īn*), construct *-āṯ*, emphatic *-āṯā*. Especially in Syriac, extended forms of the feminine plural ending *-wāṯā* *-yāṯā* (already BA *nḇazbyān* 'gifts' for *nḇazbā*); *-hāṯā* is Common Aramaic for several biliteral substantives: *šmāhāṯā* 'names' from *šmā* (Sy *ešmā*, Md *šuma*), absolute *šum*; *aḇāhāṯā* 'fathers' from *aḇā*. As in Hebrew the monosyllabic substantives form the plural on a disyllabic subsidiary stem: Sy *malḵē*

k. The following schema is available for further deriving nouns in Syriac: (*m*/*t*/*š* +) base (+ *t*) (+ *ān*) (+ *āy*) (+ *ū*/*īṯ*) + *ā*. The prefixes and *-ū*/*īṯ* both form abstract nouns; the suffixes *-ān* and *-āy* both form adjectives. Seemingly any nominal pattern may serve as the base for noun formation. This is another analytic trait of Aramaic.

l. This assertion is not proven.

m. Nyberg points to constructions with a resumptive independent pronoun as the nominative parallel.

'kings,' BA *ᶜab̲d̲ṓhī* 'his servants' (thus also derivatives like *malk̲ūtā* 'kingdom'), where the *k̲ d̲* instead of *k d* demonstrates the earlier presence of a second stem vowel. In unsuffixed forms the singular has its vowel between the last two radicals: Sy *mlek̲ ᶜb̲ed̲*, BA *ṭᶜem* 'command'; in our recension of Biblical Aramaic, forms in the Hebrew manner are also found: *mélek̲*, *éb̲en* 'stone.'

§ 4/1.2.4 Among the monoliteral prepositions, *k*- 'like' in Syriac is altered by addition of an *a*: *ak̲*. *l*- has attained an extraordinary diffusion, partly as a result of fondness for the ethical dative (Sy *sāleq-nā-lī* 'I get up,' *eṯṭallaq-leh* 'it is finished') — yet another analytic trait in Aramaic, but especially because *l*- has taken over the greatest part of the expression of the accusative and nearly entirely replaced the old accusative particle *yāṯ* = H *eṯ*. Since the ethical dative is necessarily pronominal, and the definite accusative is usually so (see § 4/1.2.3), there results a frequency of attachment of *l*- + pronominal suffix on the verb that practically amounts to the creation of a new series of *l*-suffixes. In Mandaic *l*- has merged with *ᶜal* to *el l*-. — From the prepositions that always ended with *-ai* (among which **ilai* 'to' is not found in genuine Aramaic) the pronominal suffixes of the *-ai* series have been transferred to others, as in Hebrew; e.g., BA *qd̲āmṓhī* 'before him,' Sy *ṣēd̲ai* 'to me.' There are feminine and plural forms of *bain*- 'between, under' before suffix (similarly also in Hebrew); in Mandaic also before a substantive *bini*. The *n* of *min*, as in Hebrew, lengthens before a vocalic pronominal suffix: BA *minneh*.

The negation is *lā*.[n] —

n. Adverbs with the suffix *-īṯ* are very common.

§ 4/1.3 Word order, in accord with the general slackness of sentence structure, is rather free; a certain preference for postposing the verb prevails, which resembles all the more the state of things in Akkadian, as may be seen exactly with the infinitive: BA *bēṯ ĕlāhā ḏnā lmiḇnē* 'to build this house of God.' — Aramaic, particularly Syriac, is exceptionally rich in conjunctions and modal adverbs; the sentence structure is lively and subtle. The syntax and phrasing of Syriac are often molded to a Greek pattern. —

§ 4/1.4 The lexicon of Aramaic among the old Semitic languages is the one most strongly permeated with foreign materials. From Akkadian, whose old territory Aramaic usurped, it has inherited a large number of culture words, many of which it has in turn passed on to Arabic. From Achaemenian times it has taken in Persian words, especially in the realm of administration; they occur in considerable number already in Biblical Aramaic. This latter stands, like the other Jewish dialects, under the shadow of Old Testament Hebrew as well. But at the same time Jewish Aramaic could not escape the influence of the Hellenistic and Roman environment; from it it has taken in masses of Greek and, mediated by Greek, Latin material. Even more extensive are borrowings of this sort into Syriac, which came into the closest contact with Greek in church, science, and literature. It has even, if not simply taken over, at least adapted the characteristic Greek particles *δέ* and *γάρ* to its own materials as *dēn* and *gēr*. Mandaic is independent from Hebrew, and from Greek; it thus represents in many particulars the Aramaic language type at its purest.

Text Specimens

^{A} after a word = Akkadian, ^{P} = Persian.

1. Biblical Aramaic[10, o]

a) Report to Darius on Construction of the Temple in Jerusalem (Ezra 5:7-17)

לְדָרְיָוֶשׁ מַלְכָּא שְׁלָמָא כֹלָּא: יְדִיעַ לֶהֱוֵא
לְמַלְכָּא דִּי־אֲזַלְנָא לִיהוּד מְדִינְתָּא לְבֵית
אֱלָהָא רַבָּא

lD̲ārya̋weš malkā šlāmā kóllā![11] *yd̲ī́aᶜ lehwē lmalkā, dī-ăzálnā lĪhūd̲ md̲īntā lb̲ēt̲-ĕlāhā rabbā,*

To Darius the king, all hail! Be it known to the king that we went to the province of Judah, to the house of the great God, |

וְהוּא מִתְבְּנֵא אֶבֶן גְּלָל וְאָע מִתְּשָׂם
בְּכֻתְלַיָּא וַעֲבִידְתָּא דָךְ אָסְפַּרְנָא מִתְעַבְדָא
וּמַצְלַח בְּיֶדְהֹם:

whū mit̲bnē éb̲en glāl, wᵓāᶜ mittśām[12] *bk̲ut̲layyā,*[13] *waᶜb̲īd̲tā d̲āk̲ ospárnā*^{P} *mit̲ᶜab̲d̲ā umaṣlḥā byed̲hōm.*

and this is being built with huge stones, and timber is laid in the walls, and this work is being diligently carried out and prospers in their hands. |

אֱדַיִן שְׁאֵלְנָא לְשָׂבַיָּא אִלֵּךְ כְּנֵמָא אֲמַרְנָא
לְהֹם מַן־שָׂם לְכֹם טְעֵם בַּיְתָא דְנָה לְמִבְנְיָה
וְאֻשַּׁרְנָא דְנָה לְשַׁכְלָלָה:

ĕd̲áyin šᵓélnā lśāb̲aiyā illēk̲, knḗmā ămárnā-lhōm: "man śām[14]*-lk̲ōm t̲ᶜem bait̲ā d̲nā lmib̲nyā wᵓuššarnā*^{P} *d̲nā lšak̲lālā?"*

Then we asked those elders, we spoke to them thus: "Who gave you a decree to build this house and to finish this structure(?)?" |

וְאַף שְׁמָהָתְהֹם שְׁאֵלְנָא לְהֹם לְהוֹדָעוּתָךְ דִּי
נִכְתֻּב שֻׁם־גֻּבְרַיָּא דִּי בְרָאשֵׁיהֹם: וּכְנֵמָא
פִתְגָמָא הֲתִיבוּנָא לְמֵמַר

wᵓap̄ šmāhāt̲hōm[15] *šᵓélnā-lhōm lhōd̲āᶜūt̲āk̲,*[16] *dīnik̲tub̲ šum-gub̲raiyā*[17] *dī-b̲rāšēhōm.*[18] *u-k̲nḗmā pit̲gāmā*^{P} *ht̲īb̲ū́nā*[19] *lmēmar:*[20]

And we also asked them their names, for your information, that we might write down the names of the men at their head (lit. heads). And this was the reply they returned to us, in the words: |

אֲנַחְנָא הִמּוֹ עַבְדוֹהִי דִי־אֱלָהּ שְׁמַיָּא וְאַרְעָא
וּבָנַיִן בַּיְתָא דִּי־הֲוָא בְנֵה מִקַּדְמַת דְּנָה
שְׁנִין שַׂגִּיאָן וּמֶלֶךְ לְיִשְׂרָאֵל רַב בְּנָהִי
וְשַׁכְלְלֵהּ:

"ănáḥnā himmō[21] *ᶜab̲d̲ṓhī d̲ī-ĕlāh-šmayyā wᵓarᶜā, ub̲ānáyin bait̲ā, dī-hwā-b̲nē miqqad̲mat̲*[22]*-dnā šnīn*[23] *śaggīᵓān, umélek̲ lYiśrāᵓēl rab̲ bnā́hī wšak̲lleh.*

"We are the servants of the God of heaven and earth, and we are building the house that was built many years earlier (lit. before this), and a great king of Israel built and finished it. |

o. See § 3 note ac.

10. See § 3 n. 14. 11. Accent irregular. 12. *śym.* 13. From *kt̲al.* 14. *śym.* 15. From *šum šmā* (biliteral). 16. *wdᶜ* (*ydᶜ*). 17. From *gb̲ar.* 18. Plural (originally disyllablic) of *rēš* (monosyllabic). 19. *twb.* 20. *ᵓmr.* 21. Personal pronoun as copula 'be.' 22. *min.* 23. From *šnā*, emphatic state *šattā*, construct state *šnat̲* (biliteral).

לָהֵן מִן־דִּי הַרְגִּזוּ אֲבָהָתַנָא לֶאֱלָהּ שְׁמַיָּא יְהַב הִמּוֹ בְּיַד נְבוּכַדְנֶצַּר מֶלֶךְ־בָּבֶל כַּסְדָּיאָ וּבַיְתָה דְנָה סַתְרֵהּ וְעַמָּה הַגְלִי לְבָבֶל׃	*lāhen min-dī-hargízū ăḇāhāṯánā le⁾ĕlāh-šmayyā, yhaḇ-himmō byaḏ-Nbūkdnṣr*[24, p] *méleḵ-Bāḇel Kaśdā⁾ā, uḇaiṯā ḏnā saṯreh*[25] *wᶜammā haḡlī lḆāḇel.*	But because our fathers have angered the God of heaven, he gave them into the hand of Nebuchadnezzar king of Babylon, the Chaldean, and he destroyed this house and deported the people to Babylon. |
בְּרַם בִּשְׁנַת חֲדָה לְכוֹרֶשׁ מַלְכָּא דִּי בָבֶל כּוֹרֶשׁ מַלְכָּא שָׂם טְעֵם בֵּית־אֱלָהָא דְנָה לִבְּנֵא׃	*bram bišnaṯ-ḥḏā lḴṓreš malkā dī-Ḇāḇel Kṓreš malkā śām ṭᶜem bēṯ-ĕlāhā ḏnā lmiḇnē,*	However in year one of Cyrus king of Babylon, Cyrus the king gave a decree to (re)build this house of God, |
וְאַף מָאנַיָּא דִּי־בֵית־אֱלָהָא דִּי דַהֲבָה וְכַסְפָּא דִּי נְבוּכַדְנֶצַּר הַנְפֵּק מִן־הֵיכְלָא דִּי בִירוּשְׁלֶם וְהֵיבֵל הִמּוֹ לְהֵיכְלָא דִּי בָבֶל	*w⁾ap̄ mānaiyā*[P, q] *ḏī-ḇēṯ-ĕlāhā dī-ḏahḇā*[26] *wḵaspā,*[27] *dī-Nbūkdnṣr hanpeq min-hēḵlā*[A] *dī-ḇĪrūšlem whēḇel*[28]*-himmō lhēḵlā dī-Ḇāḇel,*	and also the gold and silver vessels of the house of God, which Nebuchadnezzar had taken out of the temple that was in Jerusalem and brought into the temple of Babylon, |
הַנְפֵּק הִמּוֹ כּוֹרֶשׁ מַלְכָּא מִן־הֵיכְלָא דִּי בָבֶל וִיהִיבוּ לְשֵׁשְׁבַּצַּר שְׁמֵהּ דִּי פֶחָה שָׂמֵהּ׃ וַאֲמַר־לֵהּ	*hanpeq-himmō Kṓreš malkā min-hēḵlā dī Ḇāḇel wīhíḇū lŠšbṣr*[29, r] *šmeh,*[30] *dī-p̄ēḥā*[A] *śāmeh, wa⁾ămar-leh:*	these Cyrus the king took out of the temple of Babylon, and they were delivered to (one) whose name is Sheshbazzar, whom he had made governor, and he said to him: |
אֵלֶה מָאנַיָּא שֵׂא אֵזֶל־אֲחֵת הִמּוֹ בְּהֵיכְלָא דִּי בִירוּשְׁלֶם וּבֵית אֱלָהָא יִתְבְּנֵא עַל־אַתְרֵהּ׃	*'el mānaiyā śē,*[31] *ezel*[32]*-aḥeṯ*[33]*-himmō bhēḵlā dī-ḇĪrūšlem, uḇēṯ-ĕlāhā yiṯbnē ᶜal-aṯreh.'*[34]	'Take these vessels, go (and) put them in the temple which is in Jerusalem, and let the house of God be (re)built on its site.' |
אֱדַיִן שֵׁשְׁבַּצַּר דֵּךְ אֲתָא יְהַב אֻשַּׁיָּא דִּי־בֵית אֱלָהָא דִּי בִירוּשְׁלֶם וּמִן־אֱדַיִן וְעַד־כְּעַן מִתְבְּנֵא וְלָא שְׁלִם׃	*ĕḏáyin Ššbṣr dēḵ ăṯā yhaḇ uššayyā dī-ḇēṯ-ĕlāhā dī-ḇĪrūšlem, umin-ĕḏáyin wᶜaḏ-kᶜan miṯbnē wlā šlīm."*	Then this Sheshbazzar came (and) laid (lit. gave) the foundations of the house of God which is in Jerusalem, and from then until now it has been being built, and is not (yet) finished." |
וּכְעַן הֵן עַל־מַלְכָּא טָב יִתְבַּקַּר בְּבֵית גִּנְזַיָּא דִּי־מַלְכָּא תַמָּה דִּי בְּבָבֶל	*uḵᶜan hen ᶜal-malkā ṭāḇ, yiṯbaqqar bḇēṯ-ginzayyā*[P] *dī-malkā ṯammā dī-bḆāḇel,*[35]	And now, if it seem good to the king, let search be made in the royal archives (lit. house of treasures of the king) there in Babylon, |

p. The Akkadian name is *Nabū-kudurrī-uṣur* 'Nabū, protect my offspring.'

q. Nyberg denies this word is Persian, pointing out that Bergsträsser himself includes it in his Appendix on Common Semitic vocabulary.

r. The Akkadian name is probably *Šamaš-apal-uṣur* 'Shamash, protect the son.'

24. Vowels unknown. 25. Conjoined nominal clause. 26. From *dhaḇ*. 27. From *ksap̄*. 28. *wbl*, but formed like I *y*. 29. Vowels unknown. 30. See § 1/1.2.1.2. 31. *nś⁾*. 32. For *ĕzel*. 33. < **aḥḥeṯ*, from *nḥt*. 34. From *ăṯar*. 35. *b* for *ḇ* because of the following *Ḇ* (dissimilation).

הֵן אִיתַי דִּי־מִן־כּוֹרֶשׁ מַלְכָּא שִׂים טְעֵם לְמִבְנֵא בֵּית־אֱלָהָא דֵךְ בִּירוּשְׁלֶם וּרְעוּת מַלְכָּא עַל־דְּנָה יִשְׁלַח עֲלֶינָא׃	*hen-īṯai, dī-min-Kōreš malkā śīm ṭ^{c}em lmiḇnē bēṯ-ĕlāhā dī-ḇĪrūšlem; ur^{c}ūṯ*[36]*-malkā ^{c}al-dnā yišlaḥ ^{c}lēnā.*	(to see) whether it be (so) that a decree was given by Cyrus the king to (re)build the house of God in Jerusalem; and let someone send us the will of the king concerning this.

b) Daniel's Rebuke of Belshazzar
(Dan. 5:17-23, in the Babylonian vocalization)[37]

[באדין ענה] דניאל ואמר קדם מלכא מתנתך לך להוין ונבזביתך [לאחרן ה]ב ברם כתבא אקרה למלכא ופשרא אהודענה׃	*b^{ɔ}eḏáyin ^{c}nā Ḏānī^{ɔ}ēl w^{ɔ}āmar qḏām malkā: "mattnāṯāḵ*[38] *lāḵ lihwyān, winḇazbyāṯāḵ*[P] *l^{ɔ}uḥrān haḇ;*[39] *bram kṯāḇā iqrē lmalkā wpišrā ehōḏ^{c}ínneh.*[40]	Then Daniel answered and said before the king: "Let your gifts be for yourself, and give your rewards to another; nevertheless I will read the writing to the king and make known to him the interpretation. |
אנתה מלכא [אלהא] עליא מלכותא ורבותא ויקרא והדרא יהב לנבוכדנצר אבוך׃	*ántā, malkā, elāhā ^{c}illāyā malkūṯā wirḇūṯā*[41] *wīqārā whaḏrā*[42] *ihaḇ lNbūkdnṣr aḇūḵ,*	You, O King — the Most High God gave Nebuchadnezzar your father kingship and greatness and glory and majesty, |
ומן רבותא די יהב לה כל עממיא אמיא ולישניא הוו זאעין ודהלין מן קדמוהי	*wmin-rḇūṯā, dī-ihaḇ-leh, kol-^{c}am-mayyā, ummayyā wliššānayyā hwō zāy^{c}īn*[43] *wḏāḥlīn min-qḏāmōhī.*	and before the greatness that he gave him, all peoples, nations, and languages trembled and they feared before him. |
די הוה צבא הוה קטל ודי הוה צבא הוה מחא ודי הוה צבא הוה מרים ודי הוה צבא הוה משפל׃	*dī-hwā-ṣāḇē, hwā-qāṭel, wḏī-hwā-ṣāḇē, hwā-māḥē, wḏī-hwā-ṣāḇē, hwā-mārīm,*[44] *wḏī-hwā-ṣāḇē, hwā-mašpil,*	Whom he would he slew, and whom he would he smote, and whom he would he raised up, and whom he would he put down. |
וכדי רם לבבה ורוחה תקפת להזדה הנחת מן כרסא מלכותיה ויקרה העדיו מנה׃	*wiḵdī rēm*[45] *liḇḇeh wrūḥeh taqpaṯ lahzāḏā,*[46] *hunḥaṯ min-kursē*[A]*-malḵūṯeh, wīqārā ha^{c}dīu minneh.*	But when his heart was lifted up and his spirit was hardened to wantonness, he was deposed from his kingly throne (lit. the throne of his kingship), and the honor was taken from him (lit. someone distanced from him). |

36. *r^{c}y.* 37. After P. Kahle in H. L. Strack, *Gramm. d. Bibl.-Aramäischen*[4] 1921, pp. 36*-37*. 38. From *ntn.* 39. *whb.* 40. *wd^{c}.* 41. *rby.* 42. From *hḏar.* 43. *zw^{c}.* 44. *rwm* causative. 45. Ti *rīm.* 46. *zyd.*

ומן בני אינשא טריד ולבבה עם חיותא שוי ועם ערדיא מדרה עשבא כתורין יטעמונה ומטל שמיא גשמה יצטבע	*wmin-bnē*[47]*-enāšā ṭrīḏ wliḇḇeh ᶜim-ḥēwṯā šawwīu wᶜim-ᶜrāḏayyā mḏōreh;*[48] *ᶜiśbā ḵṯōrīn iṭaᶜmúnneh*[49] *wmiṭṭal*[50] *šmayyā gišmeh*[51] *yiṣṭḇaᶜ —*	He was driven from among men (lit. the sons of men), and his heart was (lit. someone made) with the beasts, and his dwelling with the wild asses; and he was fed (lit. someone fed him) with grass like the oxen, and his body was wet with the dew of heaven —
עד די ידע די שליט אלהא עליא במלכות אנשא ולמן די יצבא יהקים עליה׃	*ᶜaḏ-dī-yiddaᶜ,*[52] *dī-šallīṭ elāhā ᶜillāyā bmalḵūṯ-enāšā, wilman-dī-yiṣbē, ihāqīm*[53] *ᶜlah.*	| until he knew that the Most High God rules over the kingdom of men, and whom he will he sets over it.
ואנתה ברה בלשאצר לא השפלת לבבך כל קבל די כל דנה ידעת׃ ועל מרא שמיא התרוממת	*wʾántā breh Blšʾṣr*[54, s] *lā hašpéltā liḇḇāḵ, kol-qḇel-dī ḵol-dnā iḏáᶜtā; wᶜal-mārē-šmayyā hiṯrōmámtā*	| But you, his son Belshazzar, have not humbled (lit. lowered) your heart, though you knew all this; and you have lifted yourself up against the Lord of heaven
ולמניא די ביתיה היתיו קדמיך ואנ[תה ורב]רבניך שגלתך ולחנתך חמרא שתין בהון	*wilmānayyā ḏī-ḇaiṯeh haiṯīu*[55] *qḏā-māḵ; wʾántā wraḇrḇānāḵ, šēg̱lāṯāḵ wilḥēnāṯāḵ ḥamrā šāṯáyin bhōn,*	| and the vessels of his house have been brought before you; and you and your lords, your wives, and your concubines have drunk wine from (lit. in) them,
ולאלהי כספא ודהבא [נחשא] פרזלא אעא ואבנא די לא חזין ולא שמעין ולא ידעין שבח[ת] ולאלהא די נשמתך בידה וכל ארחתך לה לא הדרת׃	*wilʾelāhē-ḵaspā wḏahḇā nḥāšā p̄arzlā^ āᶜā wʾaḇnā,*[56] *dī-lā ḥāzáyin wlā šāmᶜīn wlā yāḏᶜīn, šabbáḥtā wilʾelāhā, dī-nišmṯāḵ bīḏeh wḵol-orḥāṯāḵ leh, lā haddártā."*	| and the gods of silver and gold, bronze, iron, wood, and stone, which do not see and do not hear and do not know, you have praised, but the God in whose hand is your breath and whose are all your ways (lit. all your ways are his) you have not honored."

s. The Akkadian name is *Bēl-šarra-uṣur* 'Bēl, protect the king.'

47. From *bnīn*, singular in Aramaic with *r*: *bar*, emphatic state *brā*, Sy *eḇrā*. 48. Noun of place from *dwr*. 49. Intensive. 50. *min*. 51. From *gšem*. 52. *ydᶜ*. 53. *qwm*. 54. Vowels unknown. 55. *ʾty*. 56. From *éḇen*.

2. Syriac

Abgar's Letter[t]

ܘܐܬܩܪܝܬ ܗܘܬ ܐܓܪܬܐ ܩܕܡܘܗܝ ܐܝܕܐ ܕܟܬܝܒܐ ܗܘܬ ܗܟܢܐ: ܐܒܓܪ ܐܘܟܡܐ ܠܝܫܘܥ ܐܣܝܐ ܛܒܐ ܕܐܬܚܙܝ ܒܐܬܪܐ ܕܐܘܪܫܠܡ. ܡܪܝ ܫܠܡ.

ܫܡܥܬ ܥܠܝܟ ܘܥܠ ܐܣܝܘܬܟ ܕܠܐ ܗܘܐ ܒܣܡܡܢܐ ܘܒܥܩܪܐ ܡܣܐ ܐܢܬ: ܐܠܐ ܒܡܠܬܟ ܡܥܘܪܐ ܡܦܬܚ ܐܢܬ. ܘܚܓܝܪܐ ܡܗܠܟ ܐܢܬ. ܘܠܓܪܒܐ ܡܕܟܐ ܐܢܬ.

ܘܠܚܪܫܐ ܡܫܡܥ ܐܢܬ. ܘܠܪܘܚܐ ܘܒܪ ܐܓܪܐ ܡܦܩ ܐܢܬ. ܘܡܫܢܩܐ ܒܗ ܒܡܠܬܟ ܡܣܐ ܐܢܬ. ܐܦ ܡܝܬܐ ܡܩܝܡ ܐܢܬ.

ܘܟܕ ܗܠܝܢ ܬܡܝܗܬܐ ܪܘܪܒܬܐ ܫܡܥܬ ܕܥܒܕ ܐܢܬ. ܣܡܬ ܒܪܥܝܢܝ: ܕܐܘ ܐܠܗܐ ܐܢܬ ܕܢܚܬܬ ܡܢ ܫܡܝܐ ܘܥܒܕܬ ܗܠܝܢ. ܐܘ ܒܪܗ ܐܢܬ ܕܐܠܗܐ: ܕܗܠܝܢ ܟܠܗܝܢ ܥܒܕ ܐܢܬ.

ܡܛܠ ܗܢܐ ܟܬܒܬ ܒܥܬ ܡܢܟ: ܕܬܐܬܐ ܠܘܬܝ ܟܕ ܣܓܕ ܐܢܐ ܠܟ. ܘܟܐܒܐ ܡܕܡ ܕܐܝܬ ܠܝ ܬܐܣܐ. ܐܟ ܕܗܝܡܢܬ ܒܟ.

wetqaryat-wāt[57] *eggartā*[A] *qdāmau, aidā-daktībā-wāt hākannā: "Abgar ukkāmā lYeššū*ᶜ *āsyā ṭābā dethzī batrā dŌrišlem. mār,*[58] *šlām!*

šemᶜet ᶜlaik wᶜal-āsyūtāk, dlā-wā bsammānē wabᶜeqqārē massē[59]*-att, ellā bmelltāk mᶜauwrē*[60] *mpattaḥ-att wlaḥgīrē mhallek-att walgarbē mdakkē-att*

walḥaršē mašmaᶜ-att, walrūḥē walbar-eggārē[61] *mappeq*[62]*-att, wamšannqē*[63] *bāh bmelltāk massē-att, āp mītē mqīm*[64]*-att.*

wkad hālēn tmīhātā raurbātā šemᶜet dᶜābed-att, sāmet[65] *breᶜyān,*[66] *dau allāhā-att danhett men-šmayyā waᶜbatt*[67] *hālēn, au breh-att dallāhā, dhālēn kullhēn, ᶜābed-att.*

mettul-hānā ketbet bᶜēt mennāk, dtētē[68] *lwāt,*[66] *kad-sāged-nā-lāk, wkēbā meddem dīt-lī tassē, akdhaimnet*[69] *bāk.*

And the letter was read before him (Jesus), in which the following was written: "Abgar the Black to Jesus, the good physician, who has appeared at the place of Jerusalem. Lord, hail! | I have heard of you and of your healing, that you do not heal by medicines and by drugs, but by your word you make blind men see (lit. open) and you make lame men walk and you make lepers clean | and you make deaf men hear and you cast out spirits and night-wandering demons (lit. roof-sons), and you heal the miserable by your word, and also raise dead men. | When I heard these great wonders that you do, I came to the conclusion (lit. put in my mind) that either you are God who came down from heaven and did these, or you are God's son, that you do all these. | Therefore I write (and) ask you (lit. wrote, asked) that you come to me, that I may prostrate myself before you, and you heal a certain pain that I have, since I believe in you. |

t. Text as in Carl Brockelmann, *Syrische Grammatik* (Berlin: Reuther & Reichard, 1905²) pp. 14*f.

57. *hwy*. 58. < *mārē*, from *mr*ᵓ. 59. ᵓ*sy*. 60. Passive participle. 61. For **bnai eggārā*: the construct phrase is treated as a single word with the plural ending at the end instead of on the noun in the construct state. 62. *npq*. 63. Passive participle. 64. *qwm* causative. 65. *sym*. 66. *-ī* of the pronominal suffix lost. 67. ᶜ*bd*. 68. ᵓ*ty*. 69. Isolated causative with *h-* of ᵓ*mn* like I *y*.

ܐܦ ܗܕܐ ܛܒ ܫܡܥܬ. ܕܝܗܘܕܝܐ ܪܛܢܝܢ ܥܠܝܟ ܘܪܕܦܝܢ ܠܟ: ܘܐܦ ܕܢܙܩܦܘܢܟ ܒܥܝܢ. ܘܠܡܣܪܚ ܒܟ ܚܝܪܝܢ.

āp̄ hāḏē ṭūḇ šemᶜeṯ, dĪhūḏāyē rāṭnīn ᶜlaik wrāḏpīn-lāḵ, wāp̄ dnezqp̄ūnāḵ bāᶜēn walmesraḥ bāḵ ḥāyrīn.[70]

Also, I have further heard this, that the Jews are murmuring against you and persecuting you, and even wish to crucify you and intend to do away with you. |

ܡܕܝܬܐ ܚܕܐ ܙܥܘܪܬܐ ܐܚܝܕ ܐܢܐ. ܘܫܦܝܪܐ ܘܠܬܪܝܢ ܣܦܩܐ ܠܡܥܡܪ ܒܗ ܒܫܠܝܐ.

mḏīttā[71] *ḥḏā zᶜōrtā aḥīḏ-nā, wšap̄pīrā wlaṯrēn*[72] *sāp̄qā lmeᶜmar bāh bšelyā."*

I have but one small province, but (it is) beautiful and for two sufficient to inhabit in peace." |

ܘܟܕ ܩܒܠܗ ܗܘܐ ܝܫܘܥ ܠܐܓܪܬܐ ܒܒܝܬ ܪܒ ܟܗܢܐ ܕܝܗܘܕܝܐ: ܐܡܪ ܠܗ ܠܚܢܢ ܛܒܘܠܪܐ:

wḵaḏ-qabblāh-wā Yeššūᶜ leggarṯā bēṯ[73]*-raḇ-kāhnē ḏĪhūḏāyē, emar-leh lḤannān ṭabbūlārā:*[74]

When Jesus received the letter in the house of the high priest of the Jews, he said to the courier Hannan: |

ܙܠ ܘܐܡܪ ܠܗ ܠܡܪܟ ܕܫܕܪܟ ܨܝܕܝ: ܛܘܒܝܟ ܕܟܕ ܠܐ ܚܙܝܬܢܝ ܗܝܡܢܬ ܒܝ. ܟܬܝܒ ܓܝܪ ܥܠܝ: ܕܐܝܠܝܢ ܕܚܙܝܢ ܠܝ ܠܐ ܢܗܝܡܢܘܢ ܒܝ:

"zel[75] *wemar-leh lmārāḵ dšaddrāḵ ṣēḏai:*[76] *'ṭūḇaik, dḵaḏ-lā ḥzaitān,*[66] *haiment bī! kṯīḇ gēr ᶜlai,*[77] *dailēn dḥāzēn-lī, lā nhaimnūn bī.*

"Go and say to your lord, who sent you to me: "Blessed are you, that when you have not seen me you believe in me![78] For it is written concerning me that those who see me will not believe in me. |

ܘܕܟܬܒܬ ܠܝ ܕܐܬܐ ܠܘܬܟ: ܗܘ ܡܕܡ ܕܐܫܬܕܪܬ ܥܠܘܗܝ ܠܗܪܟܐ. ܡܟܝܠ ܐܬܬܠܩ ܠܗ. ܘܣܠܩ ܐܢܐ ܠܝ ܠܘܬ ܐܒܐ ܕܫܕܪܢܝ:

wḏaḵtaḇt lī dēṯē lwāṯāḵ, hau meddem deštaddreṯ ᶜlau lhārḵā, mekkēl eṭṭallaq-leh, wsāleq-nā-lī lwāṯ-āḇ[66] *dšaddran;*[66]

And that you have written to me that I should come to you — that for which I have been sent here is now fulfilled, and I am about to ascend to my Father who sent me; |

ܘܡܐ ܕܣܠܩܬ ܠܘܬܗ: ܡܫܕܪ ܐܢܐ ܠܟ ܠܚܕ ܡܢ ܬܠܡܝܕܝ: ܕܟܐܒܐ ܡܕܡ ܕܐܝܬ ܠܟ ܢܣܐ ܘܢܚܠܡ. ܘܠܟܠܡܢ ܕܐܝܬ ܠܘܬܟ. ܢܦܢܐ ܐܢܘܢ ܠܚܝܐ ܕܠܥܠܡ. ܘܟܪܟܟ ܢܗܘܐ ܒܪܝܟ. ܘܒܥܠܕܒܒܐ ܬܘܒ ܠܐ ܢܫܬܠܛ ܒܗ ܠܥܠܡ.

wmā-ḏselqeṯ lwāṯeh, mšaddar-nā-lāḵ lḥaḏ men talmīḏai, dḵēḇā meddem dīṯ-lāḵ nassē wnaḥlem, walḵul-man-dīṯ lwāṯāḵ, nep̄nē-ennōn lḥayyē ḏalᶜālam. wḵarḵāḵ nehwē ḇrīḵ, waḇᶜeldḇāḇā[A] *ṯūḇ lā neštallaṭ beh lᶜālam.'"*

and when I have ascended to him, I will send you one of my disciples, who will heal and cure whatever pain you have, and all who are with you he will lead to eternal life. | And your city will be blessed, and no enemy in the future will ever take it over.'"

70. *ḥwr.* 71. < **mḏīntā.* 72. Thus Aramaic with *r* for *n.* 73. = **bḇēṯ*, cf. n. 35. 74. *tabellarius, tabularius.*
75. *ʾzl.* 76. Cf. n. 77. 77. < **ᶜalai-ya* 78. Syriac simple perfect 'believed,' but in ingressive sense.

3. Mandaic

a) From the Baptismal Liturgy[79]

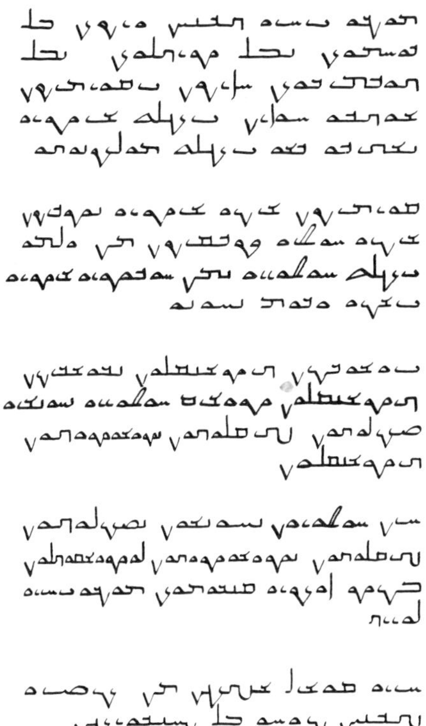

manda[80] dh(a)yi! truṣ inak[81] el rahmak wel šitlak wel tarmidak![82] hzinan[83] dqaiminin[84, 85] batra[86] hazin, dkul(e)h biši,[87] wbtira[88] r(a)ba, dkul(a)h malkawata!

qaiminin[84] bini[89] biši wšrinin[84, 90] bini haṭi.[91] parqinan m(i)n alma,[92] dkul(e)h haṭayi, wm(i)n harši biši dbni adam whawa!

dabadnin[93] tišbuqlan, wdabdinin tišbuqlan. šabiq[94] haṭayi whaubi, skilatan wtiqlatan wšabašatan tišbuqlan.

hin haṭayan whauban wskilatan wtiqlatan wšabašatan la šabqatlan, eniš zakaya qudamak, manda dh(a)yi, layit.

h(a)yi, qabil[95] butkun[P, v] m(i)n kisya wtruṣ nyaha[97] el nhuraikun.

Knowledge of Life![u] Direct your eyes to your friends and to your offspring and to your disciples! Look on us who stand in this place, which is all (full of) evil, and at the great portal, which is all (full of) (earthly) kingdoms. | We stand between evils and dwell between sins. Deliver us from the world, which is all (full of) sinners, and from the evil sorceries of the sons of Adam and Eve. | For what we have done may you pardon us, and for what we do may you pardon us. Pardoner of sins and transgressions, our follies and our blunders and our errors may you pardon for us. | If you do not pardon our sins and our transgressions and our follies and our blunders and our errors, there is no man clean before you, Knowledge of Life. | Life, accept your[96] prayer (that one that comes to you) from concealment and establish blessedness on your light.

a) מאנדא ד̄הייא תרוץ אינאך על ראהמאך ועל שיתלאך ועל תארמידאך הזינאן ד̄קאימינאן באתרא האזין ד̄כולה̄ בישיא ובתירא רבא ד̄כולה̄ מאלכאואתא | קאימינאן ביניא בישיא ושרינאן ביניא האטיא פארקינאן מן אלמא ד̄כולה̄ האטאייא ומן הארשיא בישיא ד̄בניא אדאם והאוא | ד̄אבאדנין תישבוקלאן ודאבדינין תישבוקלאן שאביק האטאייא והאוביא סכילאתאן ותיקלאתאן ושאבאשאתאן תישבוקלאן | הין האטאיאן והאובאן וסכילאתאן ותיקלאתאן ושאבאשאתאן לאשאבקאתלאן עניש זאכאיא קודאמאך מאנדא ד̄הייא לאיית | הייא קאביל בותכון מן כיסיא ותרוץ ניאהא על נהוראיכון

u. Or a two-word proper name for the spirit addressed.

v. Nyberg derives this from *$b^{c}\bar{u}\underline{t}$-, comparing Sy *$b\bar{a}^{c}\bar{u}\underline{t}\bar{a}$* ‘petition.’

79. M. Lidzbarski, *Mand. Liturgien*, pp. 42-43. 80. *jd*ᶜ. 81. **ᶜainā*. 82. < **talmīḏā*. 83. *ḥzy*. 84. Text *-an*. 85. *qwm*. 86. *aṯrā*. 87. **bīšā* from *b*ʾ*š*. 88. *tr*ᶜ. 89. **bain*. 90. *šry*. 91. The words for ‘sin’ (*haṭa* < **ḥaṭʾā*) and ‘sinner’ (*haṭaya* < **ḥaṭṭāʾā*) are often confused. 92. **ᶜālmā*. 93. ᶜ*bd*. 94. Participle in construct state. 95. Intensive imperative. 96. Mandaic plural, attracted to the plural *hayi* ‘life.’ 97. *nwḥ*.

b) From the Service for the Dead[98]

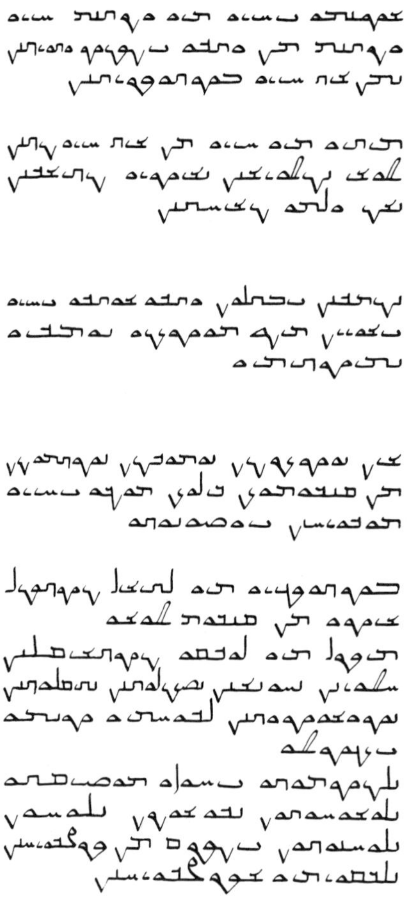

bšuma dh(a)yi! m(a)ya anatum h(a)yi, anatum m(i)n atra dnpiš ataitun wm(i)n bit h(a)yi eštapaitun.[100]

miti[101] *m(a)ya h(a)yi m(i)n bit h(a)yi, nitun*[102] *ṭabi wniṭaibun; wbiši nitibrun*[103] *wbni alma nibihtun.*[103]

wnimrun[104] *detlan atra batra dh(a)yi, dbayi*[105, 106] *min(e)h maški,*[107] *wamri wmištimi.*[108]

bin[109] *waškanin,*[110] *wamarnin wštmanin*[111] *m(i)n qudamak dilak,*[112] *manda dh(a)yi, maraihun dasawata.*[113]

eštapuyi[114] *m(a)ya ltibil ništpil biša m(i)n qudam ṭaba!*

mipal[115] *m(a)ya larqa*[116] *ništbiqlun haṭayun whaubun wskilatun wtiqlatun wšabašatun lrahmi šuma dkušṭa*

wlnišmata dhaza masiqta[117] *wlabahatan*[118] *wrabanan wlahan*[119] *wlahwatan dnpaq m(i)n pagraihun wldqaimi bpagraihun.*

In the name of Life! You[99] are living water, from an exalted place you have come and from the house of life you have overflowed. |

As the living water comes from the house of life, so will good things come and maintain the good; but evil things will be broken and the children of the world will be ashamed! | And they (the good things) will speak: "We have a place in the place of life, in which those who seek find (lit. seekers from it are finders), and those who speak are heard. | We have sought and found, we have spoken and been heard before you, Knowledge of Life, lord of healings. |

As the water overflows to Tibil (the material world), may evil sink before good! | As the water falls to the earth, so may the sins and transgressions and follies and blunders and errors of the friends of the name of righteousness | and of the souls of this ascension and of our ancestors and of our teachers and of our brothers and of our sisters be pardoned, of those who have gone out of their bodies and of those who (still) tarry in their bodies."

b) בשומא ד̄הייא מיא אנאתון הייא אנאתון מן אתרא ד̄נפיש אתאיתון ומן בית הייא עשתאפאיתון | מיתיא מיא הייא מן בית הייא ניתון טאביא וניטאיבון ובישיא ניתיברון ובניא אלמא ניביהתון | ונימרון ד̄עתלאן אתרא באתרא ד̄הייא ד̄באיין מינה̄ מאשכיא ואמריא ומישתימיא | בין ואשכאנין ואמארנין ושתמאנין מן קודאמאך דילאך מאנדא ד̄הייא מאראיהון ד̄אסאואתא | עשתאפוייא מיא לתיביל נישתפיל בישא מן קודאם טאבא | מיפאל מיא לארקא נישתביקלון האטאיון והאובון וסכילאתון ותיקלאתון ושאבאשאתון לראהמיא שומא ד̄כושטא | ולנישמאתא ד̄האזא מאסיקתא ולאבאהאתאן וראבאנאן ולאהאן ולאהואתאן ד̄נפאק מן פאגראיהון ולדקאימיא בפאגראיהון

98. Op. cit. pp. 62-63. 99. Mandaic plural, attracted to the plural *maya* 'water.' 100. *špᶜ*. 101. *ᵓty* infinitive. 102. *ᵓty*. 103. The second *i* epenthetic vowel. 104. *ᵓmr*. 105. Text *dbayin*. 106. *bᶜy*. 107. *škḥ*. 108. *šmᶜ*. 109. *bᶜy*. 110. *škḥ*. 111. *šmᶜ*. 112. Possessive strengthening the preceding suffix. 113. *ᵓsy*. 114. *špᶜ*. 115. *npl* infinitive. 116. *arqa* = Sy *arᶜā*. 117. *slq*. 118. Plural of *aba*. 119. Sy *aḥā*.

II. Modern Aramaic

1. Dialect of Maᶜlūla

§ 4/2/1.0 The Modern Aramaic dialect of Maᶜlūla in the Antilebanon, which belongs to West Aramaic, has undergone numerous changes but few phonological mergers, and retains the old inflections without loss, as well as the old sentence structure without fundamental alteration; thus it has, in spite of the alien-seeming shell, a kernel of genuine Aramaic stuff.[a] The very profound influence of Arabic has altered the vocabularly considerably and the forms and sounds in isolated cases, but it has not effaced the overall character. —

a. This dialect was the subject of fieldwork — and phonograph recordings, among the first ever used in linguistic research — by Bergsträsser himself. Since he died before he could write the grammar he had planned, this sketch is especially valuable as reflecting the impressions of one intimately familiar with the material.

§ 4/2/1.1.1 Under the influence of the Arabic model, the laryngeals are retained intact, though occasionally ᵓ is strengthened to ᶜ: *émᶜa* 'hundred' < *mᵓā*, *šᶜl* 'ask' < *šᵓl*; *ížreᶜ* 'courageous' < Ab *aǰraᵓ*. The opposition stop : spirant in the sounds *b d g p t k* generally persists, though with alterations: the spirants *δ γ*, *f θ ḫ* are unaltered, but the voiced stops *b d g* have become voiceless, and the voiceless palatalized: *t* > *t′* > *č*, *k* > *k′* (in isolated cases further > *č*, thus *íščaḥ* 'he found' < *aškeḥ*). Only *ḇ*, which has merged with *b*, and *p*, which with *p̄* = *f*, are lost — both under the influence of Arabic, which has neither *v* nor *p*. The alternation operative in Old Aramaic between stop and spirant within different forms of the same word (the same root) or even in the same word according to its position in the sentence is, however, only very rarely still found: the relative *dī* is *ti*, but *-δ* in the combination *miδ* < **mi(n) d-*; 'he halved' is *fálleγ*, but 'the half' *félk′a*; and, above all, the one case where the alternation is still really productive: the ending of the third person singular feminine of the perfect is *-aθ* (unaccented), but with pronominal suffix, etc., *-áčč-* < **-att-* (with lengthening caused in part by assimilation, in part by the effect of accent). As a rule, in each root one of the two, stop or spirant, has settled in once for all; and in fact in most cases the spirant has won out, while the stop has prevailed only when it occurred in crucial derivations of the root where it was protected by lengthening, position after a consonant (not after a diphthong, *e.g.*, *paiθa* 'house'), or to some extent initial position as well. The Arabic loanwords have also been subject to the changes *d* > *t*, *t* > *č*, and *k* > *k'*; these substitutions are still productive and are carried out with complete regularity on new borrowings from Arabic. Occasionally, especially when long, Arabic *b* also becomes *p*: thus *ᶜáppi* 'he filled (the pipe)' < *ᶜabbā*. — The *ǰ* of Arabic is borrowed with the pronunciation of the nearby metropolis of Damascus, namely as *ž* (without the initial *d* of *ǰ*), the Arabic *ḍ* contrariwise in the non-urban pronunciation *ḍ̣*.

Assimilations of consonants are numerous, especially between voiced and voiceless; further, e.g., *mmísti* 'in the middle of' < **bmísti*.

§ 4/2/1.1.2 The vocalism exhibits a change that in the Syro-Palestinian region already occurred in Hebrew and is found in Arabic: accented *ā* becomes *ō*, while unaccented *ā*, like all unaccented long vowels, is shortened; e.g., 'that' (plural) *haθínn* : (singular) *hṓθe*; 'we stood up' *qamínnaḥ* : 'they stood up' *qṓmaθ*; also in Arabic words, 'yards (measure)' *δraᶜṓ* : 'yard' *δrṓᶜa*, Ab *δirāᶜ*. Since *u* can also be the short counterpart of *ō* — when the *ō* is actually not developed from *ā*, but is original (as in *yṓma* 'day,' plural *yumṓ*) — occasionally short *u* instead of *a* will occur for *ō* < *ā*: *ḫčṓrča* 'the old (woman)' = Ab (originally Turkish) *iḫtiyāra*, but masculine plural *ḫčurṓ*. The change *ā* >

ō is also still productive and takes place in new borrowings from Arabic.

Umlaut phenomena are rather widespread, e.g., 'dumb' feminine singular *ḫrṓsa*, but masculine plural *ḫrū́sin*.

§ 4/2/1.1.3 The accent is retracted to the penultimate syllable. This shift is carried out so enthusiastically that monosyllabic words with initial consonant clusters take on an accented prothetic vowel: thus the perfect of the basic stem *ísleq* 'he got up' < *sleq*, *íqṭaᶜ* 'he cut' < *qṭaᶜ* (feminine *sílqaθ qáṭᶜaθ*), then taken over by forms with simple initial, like II geminate *áfak'* 'he loosened' < **fakk* (feminine *fákk'aθ*), II weak *áqam* 'he stood up' < *qām* (feminine *qṓmaθ*); or the passive participle of the basic stem *íqṭer* 'bound' < *qṭīr* (feminine *qṭī́ra*); further, e.g., *áᶜlaḫ* 'on you' < *ᶜlāḵ*, and even *úḫḫul* 'each' < *kul*. The accent is strongly expiratory;[b] as a result, as already mentioned, unaccented long vowels are shortened. Final *-ī*(*n*) *-ē* has often even disappeared, e.g., *ṓlef γabrū́n* 'a thousand men' for **γabrū́nin* (absolute state plural; singular *γabrṓna*), *maiθ*(*i*) 'bringing' < *maiθē*. Probably even earlier, as in Syriac and Mandaic, vowels disappeared that before the accent shift were unaccented final vowels: *íqṭaᶜ* 'he cut' and 'they cut' = *qṭaᶜū*, etc. The accent also brings about secondary consonant lengthening now and then: *áḥḥaδ* 'one,' *ḥámmeš* 'five,' *úḫḫul* 'each.'[1] —

b. Cf. § 3 note e.

§ 4/2/1.2.1 The second person personal pronouns begin with *h*: *hač* 'thou' (masculine). For the suffix 'our, us' a new formation *-ḥ* has developed out of the independent pronoun: *čaiθḗḥ* 'you will bring to us.' The third person suffixes have mostly lost their *h*. — The demonstratives *hánna* 'this,' feminine *hṓδ*(*i*), plural *hann* lose their *h-* after the preposition *l-*; in unaccented

1. Place of accent is indicated throughout.

position — they precede the substantive to which they belong — they can be shortened, as a result of which often only *ho-* (after *l-* just *-o-*) remains of *hṓδ(i)*. —

§ 4/2/1.2.2.1 Besides the old genuine verbal forms perfect, imperfect, and imperative, the verb has two extra participial tenses. These are not, however, formed as in Syriac by suffixing enclitic forms of the personal pronouns, but by prefixing the imperfect prefixes, with *n* used even for the singular of the first person (the third person masculine, and for the most part the feminine also, has no prefix). These prefixes also occur on other nominal predicates, beside verbs: *čšáuwil ḥṓlaẖ čížre*ᶜ 'you make yourself (lit. your state, Arabic) courageous.' One of these participial tenses is the ordinary present, the other a "pluperfect": as occasionally in Syriac (*aḥīḏ-nā* 'I have'), so regularly in the dialect of Maᶜlūla the passive participle is used to express completion, particularly the pre-past with an active sense. This semantic development originated in the passive participle of the basic stem *qṭīl*; the meaning inheres in the *ī* between the last two radicals (even if in some circumstances it is deaccented and shortened), and this is thence taken over into the derived verb stems. As *ṭᶜī́na* 'she had loaded herself up' (with pronominal suffix *ṭᶜinṓle* 'she had loaded it up on herself') is formed from the basic stem, so from the intensive stem *(č)šauwī́ya* 'she had made,' from *aiθ(i)* 'he brought, fetched' (causative) *aiyī́θa* 'she had brought, fetched'; the conjugation is accomplished with the prefixes and the nominal feminine and plural endings. The form can also be used attributively, as perfect participle *ṭᶜī́na* 'having loaded oneself up.' In the basic stem a third participial conjugation joins these two, where the nominal form *qattīl* is used directly as a second participle of the basic stem: *allī́ẖa* 'she goes.' The participial present is also used occasionally for the past outside a past context, especially — like Old Aramaic *āmar* 'he spoke' — in verbs of speaking: *mḥakyílle* 'they spoke to him.'

§ 4/2/1.2.2.3 In the perfect of the basic stem there occur two still-distinct vocalizations, but no longer a clear division into active-mode and neutral-mode. Thus it happens that, e.g., *ífθaḥ* (feminine *fáθḥaθ*) can mean both 'he opened' and 'he opened himself,' *áfak'* (feminine *fákk'aθ*) both 'he loosed' and 'he loosed himself.'

§ 4/2/1.2.2.4 The number of derived stems is increased by several forms that were at first borrowed from Arabic only in Arabic loanwords, but have been transferred at least in part to genuine Aramaic roots. Thus the *ā*-stem is found, as in *ḥōk*(*i*) 'he spoke to' = Ab *ḥākā* (participle with pronominal suffix the *mḥakyílle* cited above); the *n*-reflexive as in *nwáhmiθ* 'I feared' = Ab *inwahamtu*, also of Aramaic roots like *ínqṭar* 'he was bound'; the *t*-reflexive with infixed *t* as in *miž̌čám^{c}in* 'collecting themselves' = Ab *muǰtami^{c}īna*; the *st*-stem as in *ísčfeq* 'he woke up' = Ab *istafāqa*.

§ 4/2/1.2.2.5 As in the case of the strong verb forms, the weak verb forms too are altered by accent shifts and their consequences. The perfect of the basic stem *áfak'* of II geminate and *áqam* of II weak have already been cited. The related causatives, which already before the accent shift had a vowel before the first radical (Ab *atamma* 'he completed'; Am *aqēm*, Ab *aqāma*), have lengthened this vowel (then further *ā* > *ō*): *ṓčem* 'he remained,' *ṓqem*. The III weak verbs have largely lost their final vowels; they are more strongly altered by the fact that the old *n*-forms of the pronominal suffixes have spread, including into the perfect: *eḥm*(*i*) 'he saw' < *ḥmā* (the formation of the basic stem ending in -*ā* is lost): *ḥímna* 'he saw her,' and even with substantival object *ḥimn-lánna ḥmṓra*[c] 'he saw the donkey.' Common verbs are drastically shortened: *áqam* 'he

c. for the *lánna* see § 4/2/1.2.3 on the expression of definiteness.

stood up' becomes as auxiliary verb *áqa*, from *yhab̲* 'he gave' comes — proceeding from forms like *yahbat̲* > **yabbaθ* — a new verb *app*(*i*), which inflects as if it were the causative of a root **npy* (transference to the causative is anyhow not rare); 'I do not know' is *čínya* < *či*/*u* **n-yādaᶜ*; and still others. The old auxiliary verb *hwā* 'he was' is retained only in a few fixed combinations; above all it forms a component of the two new auxiliary verbs (*w*)*ōb* 'he was,' further inflected nominally: (*w*)*aíba* 'she was' (negative *čū́ba*), with *yīb* 'he is,' further inflected as imperfect: *čīb* 'she is'; and (*w*)*ōθ* 'it is, was in existence.' The second component here is the old *īθ* 'to exist'; it is also present in *ī́le* < *īθ leh* 'he has.' —

§ 4/2/1.2.3 Some common designators of persons are replaced by diminutives: *yabrṓna* 'man' for *gab̲rā*, *šunī́θa* < **nšūnīt̲ā* 'woman' from the root *nš* found in the Syriac plural *neššē*, *psṓna* 'boy' and *bisnī́θa* 'girl' from *bāb̲ōsa*.

As elsewhere in later Aramaic, the emphatic state has lost the definite meaning and become the ordinary form of the substantive. The absolute state is used nearly exclusively as predicate and — with the above-mentioned loss of the masculine plural ending *-īn* — after numbers. The construct state is nearly gone as a result of the prevalence of the periphrastic genitive. — The lost expression of definiteness is recovered not, as elsewhere in Aramaic, by the use of anticipatory pronominal suffixes, but with the help of the demonstratives; these have in many cases acquired a weakened meaning approaching that of our article. The emphatic state of the masculine plural does not have the Old West Aramaic ending *-ayyā*, but rather **-āyā* > *-ṓya*, often shortened to *-ṓi -ṓ*. —

§ 4/2/1.2.4 The prepositions *ᶜal* 'on, to' and *min* 'from, out of' are shortened before a consonant to *ᶜa* (yet still with lengthening of the following consonant) and *m-* (before vowel *ᶜal- mn-*). Among the most strongly characteristic features in the portrait of the language is the extraordinary spread of the preposition *l*-. *l*- has completely replaced the relative as genitive particle, and is beginning, from that point of departure, to oust the relative as conjunction: beside the aforementioned *miδ* stands a synonymous *mil*. But above all *l*- has become obligatory in introducing at least the definite object. As a result of that, as seen in embryo already in Syriac, beside the old pronominal suffixes on the verb a new series of *l*-suffixes has developed; both series are used indifferently. Sometimes the *l* is even inserted INTO the stem: *applálle* 'she gave to him' < **app-l-aθ-le* from *áppaθ* 'she gave' (the assimilation of the endings -*θ* and likewise -*n* to the *l* always happens). These *l*-suffixes serve also as ethical dative, as already in Old Aramaic, especially with the verbs 'go' and 'come'; here the simple forms are almost completely superseded by the *l*-forms. Thus we have (root ᵓ*ty*) *θṓle* 'he came,' *θálla* 'she came'; (root ᵓ*zl*) *zálle* 'he went,' *zlálla* 'she went,' *zlill* 'I went'; and also *zīš* 'go' (feminine), where, as usually in the second person and the first person plural, the simple suffix replaces the *l*-suffix (without suffix, e.g., *ōz*[*i*] 'going,' formed as if it came from a root ᵓ*zy* corresponding to ᵓ*ty*). The *l*- is attached to the preceding word not only when it is connected to a pronominal suffix, but also when a substantive follows it; e.g., *ṭaᶜnáčč·l ᶜirpṓla* 'she lifted up the sieve,' where the word boundary thus falls between the *l* and the substantive dependent on it. Aside from the numerous cases in which as a result of assimilation the *l* is lengthened, a lengthened *l* can also occur before substantive (with the accent then on the preceding syllable): *čhuzzél-lḥiṭṭō* 'she will sift the wheat.'

The negation *či*/*u* remains unexplained. —

§ 4/2/1.4 The vocabularly is deeply permeated with borrowings from Arabic, among which again numerous words of non-Arabic origin — especially Persian, Turkish, and European —

are included; also, the meaning of the Arabic equivalent has often been substituted even where the phonetic shape is Aramaic. The ease with which any Arabic word whatever, often just to supply a moment's need, can be adopted is extraordinary. The substitution of sounds and forms necessarily proceeds by productively operating equivalences. So it sometimes happens that Arabic words and phrases are even used unaltered in Arabic shape.

Text Specimens

[A] after a word indicates Arabic origin.

a) The Disappearing Treasure[2]

ōθ éḥδa, yumṓy·l muδrṓẖč·l ḥiṭṭṓ[3] *θálla*[4] *hošunī́θa mpaiθa wᵓaiyī́θa*[5] *ᶜémma ᶜirpṓla, ḥétta*[A] *čhuzzél*[A]*-lḥiṭṭṓ bē.*

whī allī́ẖa[6] *ᶜatárba,*[A] *bṓθar mil qaṭᶜáčč·l*[A] *mār Žúryes, ímṭaθ lγapp·l*[8] *šīr·l K'aᶜk'ᶜṓθa ṭᶜinṓl-lᶜirpṓla.*

áqam[9] *íṣqaṭ hánna ᶜirpṓla mnī́δa wtáḥk'al*[A] *ᶜabisčanṓ*[A] *lérraᶜ*[10] *mšīr·l K'aᶜk'ᶜṓθa.*
. . . ṓčem[A11] *ṓzi,*[12] *fáθḥaθ mᶜárθa érraᶜ mnánna šī́ra, éᶜber hánna ᶜirpṓla lélγul*[13] *lmísti mᶜárθa.*
qṓmaθ[14] *hošunī́θa laḥqáčče wᶜíbraθ róḥle;*[15] *wδukk'·l*[16] *ᶜíbraθ lélγul, íḥmaθ*[17] *mmísti*[18] *hṓδi mᶜárθa δahbṓya wmṓla.*[A]
qṓmaθ zṓᶜaθ,[19] *ṭaᶜnáčč·l ᶜirpṓla wnífqaθ, w·zlálla*[20] *ᶜattrṓya*[21] *aḥk'ál-lun.*[A]
amrúlla: "zīš[22] *tullánnaḥ!"*[A23] *zlálla hṓδi šunī́θa lᶜalṓδi*[24] *mᶜárθa hī wbéᶜla, ščḥaččíl*[25]*-lmᶜárθa čū́ba.*

There was a (woman), in the days of wheat threshing this woman went out of her house and had taken with her a sieve, in order to sift (lit. shake) the wheat in it. | As she went on the way,[7] after she had passed by (the monastery of) St. George (lit. had cut St. George), she reached the Kyakyᵓotha cliffs, while carrying (lit. had loaded herself with) the sieve. | Then the sieve fell out of her hand and rolled into the irrigated field (lit. garden) below the Kyakyᵓotha cliffs. | . . . It kept going further, then a cave opened under the cliffs, (and) the sieve ran into the cave. | The woman followed it and went in after it, and when she had gone in, she saw in this cave gold and money. |
She took fright, picked up the sieve, and went out; and she went to the threshing-floor and told them (i.e. the people). | They said to her: "Go, show us the way!" The woman went toward the cave, she and her husband, (but) she found (that) the cave was not there.

2. *Neuaramäische Märchen und andere Texte aus Maᶜlūla*, ed. G. Bergsträsser 1915, p. 90. 3. *ḥnṭ.* 4. *ᵓty.* 5. *ᵓty* causative. 6. *hlk.* 7. Meant as introductory clause to "then it happened that . . .," but the sentence is not correspondingly continued. 8. From *gabbā* 'side' (*gnb*). 9. *qwm.* 10. From *arᶜā* 'earth.' 11. *tmm.* 12. *ᵓzl.* 13. *l-* + *élγul* 'within' (< *l-* + *gō* [*gww*] 'interior'). 14. *qwm.* 15. < **loḥr-* < *l-* + **uḥr-* 'back.' 16. From *dukkθā* 'place.' 17. *ḥmy.* 18. *b* + *misti.* 19. *zwᶜ.* 20. *ᵓzl.* 21. From *eddrā.* 22. *ᵓzl.* 23. *dll.* 24. *l-* + *ᶜal.* 25. *škḥ.*

b) Terrification[26, d]

d. This text was reedited by A. Spitaler, □4:2v2/1,64-5. Notes e-g record his differing interpretations.

ōθ šahrṓiθ[27] *l·ẖčurṓ:*[A28] *mižčám-ᶜin*[A] *bōδ šáhrθa, mᶜáppyin*[A] *γalyu-nṓ*[A] *wθṓqnin šṓθyin;*[29] *úẖẖul qáṣ-pθa*[A] *mṣatr·l*[A] *páiθa*[30] *lᶜáčpθa.*[A]

There is an evening's amusement for the old: they gather in the evening, fill their pipes, and begin to smoke; each pipestem (reaches) from the inner end of the room to the threshold.[31] | And they have each a turban so big, the turban (i.e. the strips of cloth it is made of) (is) five hundred yards (long). They sit and converse with each other. There was a brave one among them. | There came an old woman. One said to them: "Who of you is brave (enough) to go down to the graveyard (and) bring us a sign (that he had been there)?" | One (i.e. the brave one) answered and said to them: "I; what will you give me as condition (i.e. how much will we wager)?" Those who were sitting said to him: "We will give you a medjidie (a Turkish coin). | The old woman got up, put on a white cloth, and went to a grave, wrapped herself in the white cloth, and reached out and covered herself with the shroud and lay down (lit. slept) like a dead man. | The man went there (and) found a dead man on a grave. When he saw her, he began to tremble like a leaf. |

e. *qal-ẖann*, < *qatt* < Ab *qadd* 'size' + *l-ẖann* < *(ha)k̲an(nā)*.

wī́lun úẖẖul láffθa[A] *k'alẖánn,*[32, e] *láffθa ḥámmeš émᶜa δrōᶜ.*[A] *qáᶜyin mičḥaddī́sin*[A] *bbaᶜδ̣ínnun.*[A33] *ōθ áḥḥaδ ižreᶜ*[A] *bbainṓθun.*[34]

θálla šunī́θa ẖčōr. améllun áḥḥaδ: "mōn ižreᶜ minnaiẖun yéḥḥuč[35] *ᶜasáhlθa*[A] *yaiθḗḥ*[36] *ᶜlṓmča?"*[A]

f. *čmappyill.*

áḥref[A] *áḥḥaδ améllun: "ána; mō čmappīl*[37, f] *šárṭa?"*[A] *amrúlle ti qáᶜyin: "nmappyíllaẖ mažī́tai."*[A38]

qṓmaθ hošunī́θa ẖčṓrča, ẖássaθ[39] *manšáfθa*[A] *w·zlálla lḥaṣṣ·l qábra, laffáčč·l*[A40] *ḥṓla*[A] *bmánšaf*[41] *wmáṭ-mṭaθ*[A] *k'affnáčč·l*[A] *báᶜδ̣a wδímẖaθ eẖt*[42] *mī́θa.*

zálle[43] *hánna γabrṓna, íščaḥ*[44] *mī́θa pḥaṣṣ·l qábra. lémmat*[45] *ḥímna,*[46] *íθqen mírčžaf*[A] *eẖt wárqθa.*[A]

26. G. Bergsträsser, *Neue Texte im aramäischen Dialekt von Maᶜlūla* (*ZA* 32 1918/1919), pp. 150, 152. 27. Half Aramaic: formed on the pattern of Ab *sahrīya* with the Aramaic nisbe ending *-āy-* > *-ōy-* from Am *šhr*. 28. From *ẖčōra*, feminine absolute state *ẖčōr(i)*, emphatic state *ẖčōrča*. 29. 'Drink' > 'smoke' like Ab *šariba*. 30. In the Arabic sense 'room.' 31. More precisely, the lower-lying part of the room beginning at the door. 32. < *kailā* 'extent' + *ẖann* 'such,' this < OAm *hāk̲annā*. 33. *n*-suffix, as on several particles. 34. *b* + **bain*- in feminine plural. 35. *nḥt*. 36. *ᵓty* causative. 37. *whb*. 38. With replacement of the Arabic nisbe ending *-ī* by the Aramaic *-āy-*. 39. *ksy*. 40. *lff*. 41. The unaltered Arabic form (masculine). 42. *k-* + *d-*. 43. *ᵓzl*. 44. *škḥ*. 45. < *l-* + *emmat* 'when?' + *d-*. 46. *ḥmy*.

ísleq lγapp lann γabrnṓ íqṭer liššṓna. mḥakyílle,[A] *ču máḥref ᶜlai,*[47] *eḫt ·ḫrūsin. lθēn*[48] *yṓma ᶜaṣófra lḥétta iščfeq,*[A] *áfak'*[A49] *liššṓne.*

He ascended to the men tongue-tied (lit. bound tongue). They spoke to him, (but) he did not answer them, as if they were dumb. The next day in the morning, when (lit. until) he woke up, his tongue loosed. |

θálla hōδ šunīθa, amrṓle: "ya ḥēf[A] *áᶜlaḫ, čšáuwil*[50] *ḥṓlaḫ čižreᶜ!" íθqen mšaᶜlílle hann ·ḫčurṓ, mō čšauwīya*[g] *ᶜémme.*

g. *šauwīya.*

The woman came (and) said to him: "O woe to you, you call (lit. make) yourself brave!" The old ones began to ask him what she had done with him. |

áḥref améllun hū: "zlill ᶜa-qábra, ščáḥyiθ[51] *mīθa mṣáṭṭaḥ,*[A] *nwáhmiθ*[A] *ménne, ínqṭar liššṓn." amrūlle: "ya ḥēf áᶜlaḫ, čšauwil ḥṓlaḫ čižreᶜ! ínfeq léppaḫ qṭṓᶜča."*[A]

He answered (and) said to them: "I went to a grave and found a dead man stretched out flat, I was afraid of him, and my tongue became tied." They said to him: "O woe to you, you call yourself brave! Your heart has proved cowardly (lit. come out broken)."

47. -*(h)un* lost, like -*in* in the masculine plural absolute state. 48. Like Ab *θānī*. 49. *fkk*. 50. *šwy* intensive. 51. Several forms of *škḥ* are formed as if the word were the *t*-stem of *šḥy*.

2. Dialect of Urmia

§ 4/2/2.0 The Urmia dialect, which with a group of related dialects is spoken in large parts of Kurdistan and Azerbaijan, represents Modern East Aramaic and within that East Syriac, though it does not stem directly from the old literary dialect. Phonologically it has suffered noticeable losses, especially as regards laryngeals and spirants; the old verbal inflection is largely abandoned and replaced by numerous innovations; and the vocabulary is strongly influenced by neighboring non-Semitic languages, Iranian (Kurdish and Modern Persian) and Turkic (Azerbaijani): thus the dialect is considerably distanced from its Old Aramaic forbears. The Arabic elements in the vocabulary are probably incorporated exclusively through Iranian or Turkic,[a] the Modern Persian through Turkic. —

a. This is doubtless no longer the case in present-day Iraq.

§ 4/2/2.1.1 The laryngeals, all but *h* and traces of ᵓ, are lost; *ḥ* has become *ḫ* and thus forfeited its laryngeal character. ᶜ has become ᵓ and both of them have largely disappeared. The results are, e.g., from *zd*ᶜ 'fear' the participle *zādi*, feminine *zadya*, and the substantive *zdūta*. As already in the Old Aramaic *ḥaḏ* 'one' < **aḥaḏ*, *nāšā* 'man' < *enāšā*, initial ᵓ with short (reduced) vowel is lost: *sirri* 'he bound' < *asīr-leh*, *zilli* 'he went' < **azīl-leh*, *tīli* 'he came' < **aṯē-leh*; and so are initial ᶜ: *wud* 'do' < ᶜ*ḇuḏ*, and *y* as well: *dīla* 'she knew' < *yḏī*ᶜ*-lāh*.

The spirantized pronunciation of the sounds *b d g p t k* is being lost. *d t* are always stops; the spirantized pronunciation has an after-effect only in that old *ḏ ṯ* sometimes disappear: *ḫa* 'one' < *ḥaḏ*, *qam* 'before' < *qḏām*; *bar* 'after, behind' < *bāṯar*. With the other four consonants the spirant is indeed retained, but has become rarer. Most common is still *ḇ* > *w*, then *ḵ* = *ḫ*, which remains in the second person pronominal suffixes; rarer is *ḡ* = *γ*,[b] and sporadically *p̄* > *w*. *γ* and *ḫ* have received significant input from foreign words, but foreign *f*, because of

b. The usual reflex of *ḡ* is ᶜ > ᵓ > *y*/∅, with the effect of lengthening an adjacent consonant, e.g., *narra* < *narḡā* (and consonant length is not phonemic). R. D. Hoberman has contributed these notes deriving from his familiarity with the spoken language.

the advance of the stops at the expense of the spirants, is besieged and supplanted by *p*. *w* < *ḇ* or *p̄* syllable-finally generally contracts with the preceding vowel, e.g., *gōra* 'man' < *gaḇrā*, *nōši*[c] 'he himself' < *nap̄šeh*. Also, regardless of the extent of spirant retention, the old productive alternation between stop and spirant has been abandoned; in each root one of them has become fixed. Exceptions are rare, e.g., *sāiw* 'becoming old,' but *sēbūta* 'age.' — Enriching the consonant inventory are the sounds, common in foreign words, *č* and especially *ǰ*; *č* has occasionally also developed in native roots, as from *šk* in *škḥ* 'find,' which also has *č* in the Maʿlūla dialect: *māčiḫ* 'finding.'

c. Actually *nōšu*; *nōši* is a hybrid form favored by the missionaries who devised the standard orthography.

Final *-n* of endings, as in the Maʿlūla dialect, has disappeared; e.g., *nāšiy* 'men' (absolute state) < *-īn*; third person plural pronominal suffix *-ḗ* < **-aihōn* **-aihēn*.

Old consonant lengthening has been given up; it is developed anew through word conjunction, especially the attachment of the preposition *l-* + pronominal suffix to the verb: *zilli* 'he went' < **azīl-leh*; and through assimilation, like the assimilation in precisely these circumstances of the *l* to final *r n* of the verb stem: *sirri* 'he bound' < **asīr-leh*, *tuḫminna* 'she bent over' < *-n-lāh*.[d]

d. An entire word that has an etymological emphatic consonant in it is pronounced "flat," i.e., with velarized articulation, throughout.

§ 4/2/2.1.2

Since short vowels disappear in open syllables while long vowels shorten finally and in closed syllables, the rule holds loosely that the vowels in medial open syllables are long, and all others are short. Thus most syllables originally followed by long consonants still count as closed. — With few exceptions the accent falls on the penultimate syllable, for which enclitics count within the single word.

Vowel qualities are by and large unaltered. The old diphthongs are simplified, *ai* to *ē*, as in *sēpa* 'sword,' but *au* through *ō* all the way to *ū*, as in *yūma* 'day.' Final *-ē* has become *-i*, especially in the pronominal suffix = *-eh* > *-i* 'his, him' and the plural ending *-ē* (emphatic state) > *-i*, from which the suffix 'my,' the absolute state of the plural ending *-ī(n)*, and a few other forms are distinguished by a very close vowel ending with a weak spirant, here represented by *-iy*. —

§ 4/2/2.2.1 The pronominal suffixes — *-iy* 'my'; *-uḫ* 'thou, thy' masculine, feminine *-aḫ*; *-u* 'his,' feminine *-o*; *-ḗ* 'they, their,' etc. — resemble most closely the forms which in Old Aramaic are usual with the plural, and there contain *-ai-*. In the third person singular the old singular suffixes *-i* < *-eh* and *-a* are still retained on the verb and on the preposition *l-*. — The innovation *āha* (placed before the substantive it goes with) is used for the demonstrative, and *māniy* 'who?,' *mū* or *mūdiy* (before a substantive *mud*) 'what?' for the interrogative. —

§ 4/2/2.2.2.1 Of the forms of the old finite verb only the imperative still exists; the other tenses are replaced by innovations. Already represented in Old Syriac is the present from active participle + personal pronoun — *gāniw* 'he steals,' feminine *ganwa*, *ganwit* 'thou stealest' masculine, feminine *-at*, first person masculine *-in*, feminine *-an*, plural *ganwiy* '. . . steal' without person or gender distinction[e] — and likewise the preterite from passive participle + *l-* + pronominal suffix. This represents a genuine object conjugation, in which the verb form agrees with the patient occurring in the nominative; and this construction is also genuinely found in the Urmia dialect: 'he left the woman' *šwīqāli baḫta*, literally 'the woman was left (*šḇīqā* feminine) to him (*leh*)'; with pronominal object *ḫzīdīli* 'he mowed them down,' literally 'they were mowed down to him.' But commonly the construction is already assimilated to the ordinary subject conjugation, so that the verb form no longer agrees with the object (*lwišla ǰūli* 'she put clothes on,' for *lwīšīla*) and this, if definite, is introduced by *l-* (*lwišli lǰūlu* 'he put his garment on'). As a result of this development the form can then be made from intransitive verbs; *mṭīli* 'he reached.'

e. The plural is first person *ganwaḫ*, second person *ganwiytun*, third person *ganwiy*.

The present participle has taken over most of the tense meaning of the old imperfect, and also its use as prohibitive; *la tanyat* 'do not tell' (feminine). Nonetheless, the imperative can be negated also: *la zdi* 'fear not.' — The present participle can be displaced to the past by preposing *qam* 'beforehand' or by attaching *-wa* < *hwā* 'he was': *bāyīwa* 'he wanted,' *zadyāwa* 'she was afraid.'

Entirely new forms result from compounding with a new copula. This copula is *īli* 'he is' from **īṯ-leh* (literally 'he exists to himself'), feminine *īla*, also *īwit* 'thou art' (masculine) (etc. like the present participle), from **īṯ hāwē att*; preterite *īwa* 'he, she was' from **īṯ-(h)wā*, and *īwitwa* 'thou wast,' etc. With preceding negation it is e.g. *lēwat* 'thou art not' (feminine). In addition to these forms the old *īṯ* 'exists,' as *it* (past *itwa*), is retained with its full meaning.

This auxiliary verb (in the present) now forms with preposed *b-* + infinitive a durative present (*biqṭā́lēli* 'he kills,' *bīdā́yēwat* 'thou knowest'), and with preceding passive participle a perfect (*qṭī́lēwin* 'I have killed'); the last form stems from occasional Old Syriac forms like *aḥīḏ-nā* 'I have taken' and resembles the pluperfect of the Ma^{c}lūla dialect. Further tenses result from the use of the preterite of the auxiliary verb.[f]

f. The present participle also enters into a simple present *ki gāniw* and a future *bit gāniw*; the bare participle is a subjunctive. The old passive participle used alone in the emphatic state has become a perfect; and each of these tenses, not just the durative and perfect, can be anteriorized with *-wa*. See Polotsky □4/2/2:6,20-3.

§ 4/2/2.2.2.4

Besides the basic stem (infinitive like *rḫāqa* 'to flee'), only intensive and causative are still current. The intensive has lost the participle prefix *m-*, and mostly gave up the lengthening of the middle radical so early that compensatory lengthening of the preceding vowel has taken place: *šāliḫ* 'taking off (clothes)' (the same as the participle of the basic stem), passive *šūliḫ*. The causative contrariwise has extended the *m-* to the imperative: from *škḥ māčiḫ* 'finding' and 'find,' passive *mūčiḫ*.[g] —

g. The *ma-* of the causative participle (and, in those dialects that have not lost it instead, the *m-* of the intensive) has generalized to every form of the paradigm.

§ 4/2/2.2.3

In this dialect as well the emphatic state has forfeited its definitizing meaning and become the normal form of the noun.

The absolute state exists almost exclusively in the predicatively used participle; of the construct state, traces are found. —

§ 4/2/2.2.4 The particles display many new formations, e.g., *lkis* 'at, to' from a substantive **gessā* 'side'; *min giba* 'instead of,' from **gebbā* 'side'; and still unexplained *qa*(*t*) 'to,' which largely replaces the old *l-* in its original locative uses and even as dative particle. Furthermore, foreign influences reach into the realm of the particles; thus Kurdish *but* 'because of, with regard to' (where the *-t* is the Aramaic relative particle), *īna* 'but,' *yän* 'in order to'; Turkish-Persian *hič* 'any,' Turkish-Arabic *halbát* 'however' (from *al-batta* 'unconditional'), *hāla* 'actually' (from *ḥālan*), etc. —

§ 4/2/2.3 The appearance of the clause differs markedly from that in Syriac: the anticipation of a definite substantive by pronominal suffix is no longer found, and anyway would hardly be possible on the new verb forms any more;[h] the word order diverges still more strongly from the Old Semitic style, in that the adjective (and *kul* 'all, entire' with pronominal suffix) can precede, and the verb can be placed at the end of the clause; and the prevailing syndesis and hypotaxis of Syriac are infringed by new forms of asyndesis and asyndetic subordination, e.g., *bāyīwa maẖzīwāli* 'he wanted to show it,' *gārag parqiy* 'they have to stop,' *la mṣīli mazdīwa* 'he could not frighten.'

h. Not so: *šāwiqla baẖta* (subjunctive) 'that he leave the woman,' *šwuqla baẖta* (imperative), *bišwāqoli baẖta* (durative), *šwīqoli baẖta* (perfect). The last two forms incorporate the pronominal suffixes (§ 4/2/2.2.1) before the copula (add to the inventory *-an̮* 'us, our' inclusive, exclusive *-ēniy*, *-ṓẖun* 'you, your'); the first two are in fact analogous to the forms with *-l-* described in § 4/2/2.2.2.1.

Text Specimen

The Thorn Killer[1, i]

[K] after a word indicates Kurdish (Iranian) origin, [T] Turkish, [A] Arabic.

[illegible]

ḫa nāša bāyīwa[2] *ḫēlu umardūtu*[K] *maḫzīwāli*[3] *qa baḫtu,*[K] *yän*[K] *zadyāwa*[4] *minu. kul yūma, īman*[5] *dšimša gnīli, lwišli ljūlu*[K, j] *usirri*[6] *lqēmu,*[T] *zilli*[7] *ldišta;*[K] *kul dukta dmūčiḫli*[8] *kitwi,*[k] *ḫzīdīli bqēmu.*

ādīya tīli[9] *lbēta: "baḫta, bīdáyēwat*[10] *mud ḫabra? bāha lēli raba nāši qtílēwin. ḫzi, āna tūnīliy qātaḫ, īna*[K] *at qa hič*[K] *<ḫa> nāša la tanyat!"*

hāda[11] *kul yūma zilli ldišta utīli lbēta, ḫqirri qa baḫtu: "ḫa uḫča*[T] *nāši qtílē<win>."*

ḫa yūma mṭīla lgāna[K] *dbaḫtu, tuḫminna*[A12] *lkis gāno: "in mijjid*[A] *gōriy kul yūma ḫa uḫča nāši biqṭálēli, gārag*[K] *kulé*[13] *nāši parqiy min gu*[14] *dāha dunyi;*[A] *mūdiy līwāda?"*[15]

A man wanted to exhibit his strength and manliness to his wife, that she might fear him. Each day when the sun set he put on his clothes and strapped on his dagger and went to the field; everywhere he found thorns he cut them down with his dagger. | Then he came home: "Wife, do you know what happened (lit. the news)? Tonight I have killed many men. Look, I have told you, but you are to tell no one!" | Thus every day he went to the field and came home and boasted before his wife: "I have killed several men." | One day it came into his wife's head, she pondered in her mind: "If indeed every day my husband kills several men, all men must disappear (lit. stop) from this world; what to do?" |

ḫā naša bᶜayīwa ḫelū mardītū mahzīwāli qa baḫtū yänn zadᶜyāwā mínnu. kúl yuma ī́man dšimša gnili lwišli ljullu ᶜusirri lqemu zılli ldištā kul dukta dmučiḫli kitwi ḫzī́deli bqemu, | *adī́a tili lbeta baḫta bidᶜayäwat mudḫabrā? bāhā lḗli raba nāši qtī́läwin, ḫzī́ ana tunilī́li qataḫ ī́na āt qa hič ḫā naša llatanyat.* | *hada kúl juma zilli ldišta utili lbeta ḫqirri ḳa baḫtū ḫā uḫča nā́še qṭī́lle win.* | *ḫā yúma mṭīla lgā́na dbaḫtū tuḫminna lkis gā́nō in mijjid gōrili kul yū́ma ḫā ūḫča nā́ši biqṭaläli gā́rag kúlle naši parqiḫ min gu daha dunyi mudī́li liwāda?* |

i. Schahbaz' orthography has been somewhat classicized and entirely vocalized by the printer, a native speaker of the language. Bergsträsser himself revised phoneme length to conform with his view of etymology and syllable structure. Schahbaz's version is added below.

j. The *l*-prefix is a pseudo-classical hypercorrection.

k. Text *dkitwi mūčiḫli.*

1. After *MSOS* 22 1919, *Westas. Studien* pp. 115-116, 119. 2. *bᶜy.* 3. Conflated nominal clause. 4. *zdᶜ.* 5. From Sy *emmaṯ* 'when?.' 6. *ᵓsr.* 7. *ᵓzl.* 8. *škḥ.* 9. *ᵓty.* 10. *ydᶜ.* 11. From the feminine *hāḏā* 'this.' 12. Quadriliteral, inflected on the intensive pattern (Arabic infinitive of the intensive of *ḥmn*). 13. With third person plural pronominal suffix referring to *nāši.* 14. = Sy *gō* (*gww*) 'interior.' 15. *ᶜbd.*

[illegible]

min bar gōro, har[K] *aḫ dítwāli ādat,*[A] *zilli ldišta, up āha lwišla ǰūli durzi,*[K] *zilla bāra bar gōro, halbát*[A] *braba hišyārūta,*[K] *yän la ḫazīwāla.*

[illegible]

ādīya gōro mṭīli lḫa dukta, ēka draba kitwi itwa, grišli lqadāru, šūrīli liḫzāda <*l*>*kitwi. ādīya dīla*[16] *baḫta hōna*[K, 1] *uḫēla dgōro.*

[illegible]

up āha grišla lqēma, npilla bar gōro. āha šūrīli braba zdūta[17] *lirḫāqa min qam dāha nāša zarbāna.*[A] *ādīya min qam* <*dāha*> *māṭīwa lbēta, tīla baḫta šūliḫla ǰūlo.*

[illegible]

ādīya tīli gōro milya[m] *min zdūta uratrāta: "baḫta, bīdā́yēwat mud ḫabra?" "lā, nāša." "pah, hič la wud*[18] *qāla, alāha qam pāriqliy*[19] *bāha lēli."*

[illegible]

"qamūdiy?[20] *ḫa hāqi,*[A?] *ḫazyan!" "yāṭat,*[21] *bāha lēli npilla ḫa dāwi,*[A] *āna grišliy lqēmiy umḫīliy ḫakma*[22] *rīšāni. min nāgistan*[K] *ḫzīliy, īna mū?*

After her husband, as was his custom, had gone to the field, she also put on men's clothes (and) followed behind her husband, though with great care that he did not see her. | Then her husband reached a place where there were many thorns, took his dagger, (and) began to cut down the thorns. So the woman recognized the wits and power of her husband. | She too took the dagger (and) fell upon (lit. behind) her husband. He began to flee with great fear before this strong man. Then the woman came, before he arrived home, (home and) took off her clothes. | Then came her husband filled with fear and trembling: "Wife, do you know what happened?" "No, man." "Ah, don't make a sound, God delivered me this night."| "How, tell me once, I'll see!" "You know, tonight a battle took place (lit. fell), I took my dagger and struck (dead) some ringleaders. Suddenly I saw, but what?|

min bár gorō har aḫ ďitwāli ᶜadat zillī ldišta: up-aha lwišla ǧū́lli dᶜurzi zilla bára bár gōrŏ: hălbā́t brābā hišyāruta yänn lā ḫaziwala. | *adī́a gorō mṭili lḫā dukta ē̆ka draba kitwi ī́twa grišli lqā́ddarū šurᶜili liḫzada lkitwi. adī́a dila baḫta hō̆nă uḫela dgoro.* | *up aha grišla lqḗma npilla bár goro. aha šurili braba zduᶜta lirḫaqa min qam daha naša zarbā́na. adī́a min qam aha māṭiwa lbeta tila baḫta šuliḫla ǰullo.* | *adī́a tili goro miliya min zduta uratratta: baḫta bidayäwat mud ḫabra? lā nā́ša. pah hič lā ᶜwud qala alā́hă qam pariqlili baha leli.* | *qamudiḥ ḫā ḫāqī́ ḫᶜazyān. yᶜaṭat baha leli npila ḫā dᶜawī́li ana grišlī́li lqemiliḥ umḫiliḥ ḫaqma rišani. min nagistan ḫziliḥ ī́na mu* |

1. Nyberg □ 1:6R4,111 compares Sy *haunā* 'intelligence.'

m. Bergsträsser writes *mlīya.*

16. *ydᶜ*. 17. *zdᶜ*. 18. *ᶜbd*. 19. Intensive. 20. Literally 'to what?.'
21. *ydᶜ* with *ṭ* < *d*. 22. Literally 'a how many' (*kmā* literally 'like what?").

ḫa ǰwanqa[K] *raba zarbāna, sēpa bīdu, binpāla bāriy. duz*[T] *tānīnaḫ,*[23] *īna at qa hič nāša la tanyat: la mṣīliy liklāya qāmu, šūrīliy*[24] *lirḫāqa. o zālim*[A] *qam ǰāniwliy hal*[25] *lāḫa."*[26]

baḫta šūrīla likḫāka[27] *bīyu. "pah, hatḫa*[28] *hatḫa wīta!*[29] *āna min zdūtiy libiy pqīli,*[30] *at min giba dpašmat,*[K] *but*[K] *dāha qiṣat*[A] *hāla*[A] *bikḫăkēwat?"*

ǰuwibla[A] *baḫta: "nāša, puš*[31] *libāna, la zdi!*[32] *o ǰwanqa danpilli bāruḫ, hič lēwa zarbāna miniy." "nābaḫta,*[K] *ḫu lēwat sarṣay?"*[T]

ǰuwibla: "āna lēwan sarṣay, īna at hōnuḫ qalŭlēli. ānanwa o ǰwanqa dqam ǰāniwluḫ hal lāḫa." min do yūma lbāri la mṣīli ḫīna[33] *qaṭlāna dkitwi mazdīwa lbaḫtu.*

A great strong youth, sword in his hand, fell upon me. I'm telling you pure and simple, but you are to tell no one at all: I could not resist him (lit. stand before him) (and) began to flee. This brute pursued me all the way here." | The woman began to laugh at him. "Ah, so and so are you! I — from my fear my heart has burst, (and) you, instead of sympathizing, rather laugh at this tale?" | The woman answered: "Man, take heart, fear not! This youth who fell upon you was none stronger than me." "Unfortunate, aren't you crazy?" |

She answered: "I'm not crazy, but you, your mind is weak. I was this youth who pursued you here." From this day on (lit. until later) the thornkiller could no longer frighten his wife.

ḫā ǰwanqa raba zarbana sēpa bĭdu binpala barĭḫ. duz taninnaḫ ĭna at qa hič naša lā tanyat lā mṣilĭḫ liklaiya qāmu rupililiḫ lirḫaqa ō zālim qam ǰaniwliḫ hal lāḫa: | *baḫta šurila likḫaka bĭyu. páh hátḫa hátḫa wĭta ana min zduᶜtĭḫ libbĭḫ piqili at min giba d·pašmat but daha qissat hala bikḫakäwet?* | *ǰuwibla baḫta nāša puš libbana lā zdᶜĭ ō ǰwanqa d·npilli bāruḫ hič lēwa zarbana minĭḫ. na baḫta ḫu lēwat ṣarṣay?* | *ǰuwibla ana lēwan sarsay ĭna at honuḫ qaluläli. anenwa ō ǰwanqa dqam ǰaniwluḫ hal laḫa. min dō yūma lbári lā mṣili ḫina qaṭlāna dkitwimazdiwa lbaḫtu.*

23. From *tāni*, intensive. 24. Text *rūpīliy*, which is hardly appropriate. 25. Originally = 'furthermore,' with *l-* = 'until.' 26. = *l* + Sy *hārḵā* 'here.' 27. Sy *gḫk* < *δḥk* (with *g* instead of ᶜ, dissimilation from the *ḥ*). 28. < *hāda* 'thus' + *ḫa* = H *kō* 'thus.' 29. *hwy*, < **hwītā*, feminine of the passive participle = 'being.' 30. *pq*ᶜ. 31. *pwš*. 32. *zd*ᶜ. 33. < *ḥrēnā* 'another.'

Chapter 5

South Arabic — Ethiopic

I. Ethiopic (Ge^{c}ez)

§ 5/1.0 While the proto-Semitic inventory of consonants is fully preserved in the languages of the South Arabic inscriptions, the closely related old Semitic literary language of Ethiopia, Ge^{c}ez (also called Ethiopic),[a] has undergone simplifications to a somewhat greater degree than Hebrew. It is especially archaic, though, in other phonological points, particularly in that the semivowels almost never disappear — or rather, have occasionally been reintroduced where they had disappeared. The paradigms, as a result, exhibit a transparency and regularity surpassing that of North Arabic. The influence of Amharic, which affects even the oldest preserved inscriptions, asserts itself in the plethora of stressed suffixes and postposed particles, in the tendency to gerundive verbal constructions, and in a general disintegration of the older syntax which often leads to phenomena that recur analogously in Aramaic.[b] But in Ge^{c}ez sentence structure is even vaguer and more ambiguous than in late Aramaic; for, generally speaking, among the old Semitic literary languages Ge^{c}ez is the one that least possesses refined means of expression.

a. "Ethiopic" is here used for the Ethiopian branch of Semitic and "Ge^{c}ez" for the old literary language.

b. Rather than Amharic influence on Ge^{c}ez, we might look to the common influence of Cushitic — little known in Bergsträsser's time — on both Semitic languages.

§ 5/1.1 At the time the orthography became stable, the replacement of proto-Semitic consonants was exactly as in Hebrew, with few exceptions: Ge^{c}ez participated in the mutation, characteristic of South Semitic generally, of *p* to *f* and of *ś* to *š*, and likewise that of *š* to *s*, whereby both original *š* and the one developed from *θ* merged with original *s*; contrariwise, original *δ̣*[1] had not merged with *ṣ*, nor *ḫ* with *ḥ* (though *γ* had merged

1. The Ge^{c}ez sound, like the corresponding Arabic one, is transcribed *ḍ*; but this is purely conventional, and implies nothing about the true pronunciation in ancient times, of which nothing is known. Now it is pronounced *ṣ*.

with [c]). Later, and actually in part not until the extinction of Ge[c]ez as a living language, its sounds grew even closer to those of Amharic.[2] The emphatic sounds are pronounced in what may be the original way, with following glottal stop (thus *ṣa* = something like *ṣ*ᵓ*a*).[c] Semivowels that close a syllable combine with the preceding vowel[d] to give a long vowel (*ew* > *ū*, *ey* > *ī*) or a diphthong (occasionally *au* further > *ō*); elsewhere they are retained. The laryngeals[3] show the beginnings of weakening insofar as they influence the vocalization: before a syllable-final laryngeal *a* is lengthened,[e] e.g., *Yā*ᶜ*qṓb* 'Jacob' (except that after ᵓ, *a* predominates, e.g., ᵓ*aḥzā́b* 'people');[4] and across a laryngeal, vowel harmony occurs in the sequences *e* - *a* and (within a morpheme) *a* - *e ī ū*, by which the first vowel assumes the quality of the second: *yaḥázen* 'he mourns' for **yeḥázen*, *lehī́q* 'old' for **lahī́q*. The most distinctive peculiarity of Ethiopic vocalization is that *i* and *u* merge and then sometimes (particularly finally) disappear. This recalls the conjectured proto-Semitic two-quality system, with *a* on the one hand and *i*/*u* on the other, but cannot stem directly from it, as a trace of *u* often remains in the labialization of neighboring velars: *k°ell* 'all' < **kull* (however, labialization is not confined to this case). The transformation of *u* and *i* into *e* also holds in combinations of *ū ī* with a following vowel, when with the development of a glide *w y* the vowel is shortened: e.g., -*ū* + -*ō* > -*ewō*, -*ī* + -*ān* > -*eyān*.

c. A *p* and a glottalized *ṗ* have entered the consonant inventory; they are used in loanwords.

d. Bergsträsser's transcription of Ethiopic vowels, intended to conform with his usage in the rest of the book, is at variance with the system in general use among Ethiopists: Bergsträsser's *ī ē ā ō ū e a* correspond to the more common *i e a o u ə ä*.

e. The lengthening might better be ascribed to compensatory lengthening upon actual loss of the laryngeal.

§ 5/1.1.3

Accent is fairly complicated.[f] The accent regularly falls on one of the two last syllables, generally on the one with greater

f. Nyberg □1:6R4,111-2 reports his teacher Kolmodin's assertion that the accentual system of Ge[c]ez and Tigrinya (at least) involves both pitch and stress in each word — which as a speaker of Swedish he was more apt to detect than most European researchers.

2. Whereupon many secondary consonant lengthenings were introduced, while on the other hand original ones were occasionally given up (especially in final position).

3. The later change of *ḫ* to *h* makes it clear that *ḫ* also counts as a laryngeal.

4. The manuscripts vacillate, frequently interchanging ᵓ*a*- and ᵓ*ā*-, ᶜ*a*- and ᶜ*ā*-, etc., because early on *a* was lengthened POST-laryngeally as well, although not until after the orthography had been standardized.

sonority. Prepositions, conjunctions, and other words as well, mostly ones in the construct state, cliticize to the following word.[5] The accent is not so strongly expiratory[g] that vowels would disappear; and final vowels are, as in all of South Semitic, largely retained, though with long vowels often shortened (*ána* 'I' < **ʾanʾā*, along with loss of the sound ʾ; suffix *-ka*, though with pronominal suffix still *-kāhū́*). —

g. Cf. § 3 note e.

§ 5/1.2.1.1 The third person personal pronouns (which are simultaneously the demonstrative 'this,' etc.) are considerably altered: *weʾétū* 'he,' *weʾétā* 'him'; *yeʾétī* 'she,' *yeʾétā* 'her'; masculine plural *emūntū́*, feminine plural *emāntū́*. The same extension *-tū*, feminine *-tī*, accusative throughout *-ta* is found in the true demonstratives: *zentū́* 'this' (accusative *zánta*), feminine *zātī́*, plural *ellōntū́ ellāntū́*; *zektū́* 'that,' feminine *entāktī́*, plural *ellektū́* (the simple *ze* 'this,' accusative *za*, feminine *zā*, plural *ellū́ ellā́* is rare except for *ze* 'this'); and also in isolated forms of the personal suffixes: *lōtū́* 'to him,' *lātī́* 'to her,' and others; and finally in the numbers: *arbāᶜtū́* 'four' (more rarely the simple *arbā́ᶜ*). Similar material is also found elsewhere, e.g., *em-aitḗ* 'whither?.' This *-tū* etc. appears to be the remnant of a definitizing element; a true article is not found in Ethiopic.

'My' is *-éya* (for all cases), 'me' *-nī*, as in other languages. The suffixes of the third person retain their *h* after a long vowel (e.g., *afūhū́* 'his mouth,' accusative *afāhū́*), while **-ahū* contracts to *-ō*, **-ehū* to *-ū*, and **-ahā *-ehā* to *-ā*. Then the forms *-ō -ā* are carried over into combinations where they do not originally belong, e.g., after *-kū*: *-kéwō*. In the plurals *-hṓmū -hṓn* the vowel of the contracted form *-ṓmū -ṓn* has infiltrated (while for 'your, you,' *-kémmū -kén* is retained). The accusative particle *kīyā-* with pronominal suffix forms an accusative for the personal pronouns.

5. Indicated in the texts with a grave accent ` on the accented syllable.

§ 5/1.2.1.2 The relative pronoun is *za*, feminine *énta* (which has already been mentioned in the form *entākti̇́*), plural *élla*; but already *za* occurs for all forms as well. *za* is to a great extent a particle occurring not just alone or after prepositions like the usual Semitic relative, but also in constructions like *za-enbála* 'before' (*enbála* = 'unless, except, before'). The relative also introduces the genitive and other adnominal expansions, like *kīdā́n za-la-*^{c}*ālám* 'an eternal bond,' and a much-favored construction, topicalizing sentence clefting; e.g., *ai-nū́ ḥézb za-* . . . 'which people is it that has . . .?' for 'which people has . . .?.'

The interrogatives *mannū́* 'who?,' *ment* 'what?,' *ai* 'which?' (also in *aitḗ* 'where?,' *efṓ* < **ēfṓ* < **ai-fṓ* 'how?'), usually strengthened with an attached particle, are also used as indefinites, particularly in the negative: *wa-ī-mannū-hī́* 'no one,' *wa-ī-ment-nī́* 'nothing.' —

§ 5/1.2.2.1 In South Semitic, the perfect forms without suffixes end in *-a*. The *t* of the second person suffix is replaced in Ethiopic by the *k* of the first person singular: *-ka* etc. The imperfect is conjugated in the indicative and the subjunctive; in the basic stem they are differentiated, like the Akkadian present and preterite, in that the indicative has an accented *a* after the first radical, and the subjunctive has no vowel. The vowel of the prefixes in the imperfect is *e*, as long as no contraction has taken place. The infinitive has the ending *-ṓ* or *-ṓt* (and *e* in the last syllable of the stem), e.g., for the causative *ankerṓ*(*t*) 'to be surprised.' A verbal noun in the accusative and provided with pronominal suffixes, characterized by *ī* in the last syllable of the stem, constitutes the gerundive: *qatīláka* 'while you are, were killing,' *re*$^{\supset}$*īyéya* 'while I was seeing.' This form, often with a following nominal subject, supersedes the old circumstantial clause, and the attaching of pronominal suffixes to a simple nominal descriptive term (itself an adjective) has been modeled on it: *bāḥtītáka azzázka* 'you alone commanded';

rakabkewṓmū feššūḥānī-hṓmū 'I found them content.' The old participles are in retreat, in part squeezed out by the gerundive; the participle of the basic stem survives, at least in the ordinal numbers — a usage common to South Semitic: *kālé*ᵓ 'second' (from *kel*ᵓ*ḗ* 'two').

§ 5/1.2.2.2

Verb stem formation in Ethiopic is rich, though in general already fixed.[h] As generally in South Semitic, the wealth of possible combinations of prefixes and infixes is reduced, with the result that the internal modifications are rather richly developed in the unextended stems as well as in the ones with prefixes; besides the lengthening of the second radical, Ethiopic can insert an *ā, ē*, or *ō* after the first radical. As in Arabic the causative prefix is ᵓ- but in the *t*-reflexive (and occasionally elsewhere) it is *s*-, so that an *st*-form develops. There are no passives.[i]

h. I.e., lexicalized; the productive stems are the causative, reflexive, and causative-reflexive, as opposed to the basic, intensive, and goal stems, which are non-contrastive.

i. Cf. § 1 note x.

§ 5/1.2.2.3

In the basic stem the *e* < *i*/*u* of the neutral-mode perfect has disappeared; e.g., *gábra* 'he made' (but *gabárka* etc.). In the imperfect the indicative is always like *yeqátel*,[j] so that the imperfect vowel differentiation appears only in the subjunctive: *yégbar* for *gábra*, but *yégdef* 'that he discard' for *gadáfa*. The imperative has two vowels: *néger* 'say' (before the pronominal suffixes of the first person the second *e* disappears: *negránī* 'tell me'), plural *negérū*.

j. Actually with long middle radical *yeqattel*.

§ 5/1.2.2.4

All the derived stems have *a* in the perfect, *e* in the imperfect etc. Only the *t*-reflexives (except for the *st*-form) have *a* in the imperfect etc., and furthermore, the *t*-reflexive of the basic stem usually has a neutral-mode formation in the perfect: *tawálda* 'he was born.' In the causative and the *st*-stem the indicative is related to the subjunctive as in the basic stem; e.g., *yāgábe*ᵓ 'he will cause to return,' *yā́gbe*ᵓ 'may he cause to return.' Elsewhere the two moods are distinguished in the intensive stem, which in the indicative has *ē* and not *a* in the first syllable of the stem: *yāšēnnéyū* (causative-intensive) 'they will make good,' subjunctive *yāšannéyū*. The causative formative is here and always contracted with the vowel of the prefix to *ā*; the *st*-form has the same vowel: *yāstaréᵓī* (with *e* < *a*) 'he will show himself.' The vowel of the reflexive formative *ta-* is lost following a prefix: *tanāgára* 'he spoke,' imperfect *yetnā́gar*.

§ 5/1.2.2.5 The laryngeal verbs exhibit a few divergences from the sound laws already given concerning vowel alternations. In II laryngeals, the perfect of the basic stem and its *t*-reflexive have *e* in both syllables of the stem (and the vowel of the second syllable sometimes disappears when it is an open syllable), e.g., *reᵓéya* 'he saw,' *kéḥda* 'he lied, became disloyal,' second person *reᵓī́ka* (< **reᵓeyka*) *keḥédka*, *seᵓénkū* 'I could not.' In the imperfect indicative of the basic stem, the *e* < *a* sometimes lengthens: *yerḗᵓī* 'he will see' (= the intensive). The verb *behéla* 'he said' loses its *h* in many forms: imperfect indicative *yebl*, subjunctive *yébal*; and it even loses its *l* in *yebḗ* with the past meaning 'he said.' — III laryngeals have *e* in the last stem syllable in the perfect, which however disappears after an open syllable: *nášᵓa* 'he bore, conquered,' causative *anšéᵓa* the same.

§ 5/1.2.2.5.1 In the I *w* verbs the forms without the *w* are preserved in the subjunctive and imperative of the basic stem, though with *a* for stem vowel: *télad* '(that) she may bear,' *yáhab* '(that) he may forgive,' *hab* 'forgive.'

§ 5/1.2.2.5.2 The II weak verbs are inflected weakly in the perfect, subjunctive, and imperative of the basic stem and the causative. The perfect of the basic stem does not have *ā* as in the other Semitic languages, but rather *ō* or *ē*, and even before a suffix: from II *w* *qṓma* 'he stood up,' *qṓmka*; *ḥṓra* 'he went,' *ḥṓrka*; *bṓᵓa* 'he went in,' *bṓᵓka*; — from II *y* *šēṭa* 'he sold,' *šēṭka*. In the subjunctive of II *w* verbs, the vowel can differ: usually as in *yéqūm*, but also *yéḥōr yébāᵓ*; II *y* *yéšīṭ*. The causative either adopts the stem vowel of the basic stem or is formed with a short vowel, as in *aqáma yắqem*. — From *kṓna* 'it happened' comes *akkṓ* 'is not, not' < **al-kō*.

II geminate verbs are in general strong.

§ 5/1.2.2.5.3 III weak verbs are conjugated strong throughout, e.g., *faráya* 'he bore fruit.' They merely undergo the above-mentioned sound changes, e.g., *délū* 'weigh' < **délew, yāstaréʾī* 'he will show himself' < **yāstareʾey*; *hallṓkū* 'I was' beside *halláukū*. —

§ 5/1.2.3 As for noun-stem formations, the forms *qetū́l* (with vowel harmony < *qatūl*) and *qettū́l*, which are created from various verb stems in a more or less passive sense, like *kešū́t* 'uncovered' from *kašáta, feṣṣūm* 'finished' from *faṣṣáma* (corresponding: *būrū́k* 'blessed' from *bāráka*, *mūqū́ḥ* 'caught' from *mōqáḥa*, and quadriliteral *dengū́ḍ* 'confounded' from *dangáḍa*) are especially popular; and then a series of formations with suffixes: abstracts with *-nā*, like *mūsenā́* 'devastation' from *māsána* (quadriliteral), also *ḫellīnā́* 'thought' from *ḫalláya*; similarly, abstracts with *-ē*, e.g., *fekkārḗ* 'meaning' from *fakkára*; agent nouns of the form *qat(t)ālī́* (accusative *-ḗ*), e.g., *kaḥādī́* 'faithless,' *mawātī́* 'dead, mortal'; etc. The nisbe-ending is extended to *-āwī́*, e.g., *qadāmāwī́* 'first.'

As a result of the merger and subsequent disappearance of the nominative ending *u* and the genitive ending *i*, Ethiopic has only two cases, an unmarked nominative-genitive and an accusative with *-a*. The bi- (or mono)literal substantives with final long vowels retain the length before a pronominal suffix only; thus *af* 'mouth,' construct state and accusative *afa*, but 'his mouth' *afūhū́* (nominative and genitive), accusative *afāhū́*. While uncertainties in the use of cases are creeping in, the syntax of the cases is basically the inherited system; e.g., beside a verb (at least *kṓna*), a predicate is in the accusative: *kṓna ḥeyā́wa* 'he became living.' — To the Arabic adverbial ending *-u* corresponds *-ú̄*: *qadīmú̄* 'earlier,' *bāḥtú̄* 'alone, however,' *dāᶜmú̄* 'rather.' There are a few remnants of a vocative: *egzīᵓṓ* 'O Lord!.'

The feminine ending is *-at* or very often *-t*; in the latter case a preceding long vowel is reduced so the word becomes virtually unrecognizable: *ekkú̄y* 'evil,' feminine *ekkī́t* < **ekkeyt* < **ekkuyt*. Only traces remain of the dual, e.g., *keleᵓḗ* 'two' (replacing CS **θinā*), literally 'both,' *edēhú̄* 'his hands' from *ed*.

The plural ending of the masculine is *-ān*, of the feminine (and numerous masculines) *-āt*. Over and above these, however, South Semitic generally makes use of the so-called internal or broken plural, which, for the most part developed from old collectives, is formed by alteration of the stem itself. The forms of this type of plural are legion; some are particularly common in Ethiopic: *qetál*, e.g., *edáu* 'hands' from *ed* (with secondary third radical *w*): *aqtā́l*, e.g., *aḥzā́b* 'people' from *ḥezb*, *amsā́l* 'pictures' from *mesl*, *afḥā́m* 'coals' from *feḥm*; and above all *qatālél*(*t*) from quadriliteral singulars: *kanāfér* 'lips' from *kanfár*, *ᵓanāqéṣ* 'fools' from *ᵓanqáṣ*; or from triliteral singulars with a long vowel, which is replaced by an intrusive consonant: *mawāgéd* 'waves' from *mōgád*, *mawāᶜél* 'days' from *mōᶜált* (the feminine ending does not count), *ṣalāᵓét* 'enemies' from *ṣalāᵓī́*, *ḫaṭāwéᵓ* 'sins' from *ḫaṭīᵓát*, *madāléu* 'scales' from *madlṓt* 'weight,' *baḥāwért* 'lands' from *beḥḗr*. All the plurals have *-ī*, a former independent plural ending, before a pronominal suffix.

The forms of the numerals for the units have already been mentioned; the tens have the old dual ending: *šalāsā́* 'thirty.' —

§ 5/1.2.4 Turning to the monoconsonantal prepositions, *k-* 'like' has been completely superseded by its expansion *káma*. *b-* 'in, with, by' has taken over the *a*-vowel of *la*-; with the pronominal suffix of the third person masculine singular *bō* or *bōtū́* (negated *albṓ*) it means 'is, has' (cf. CoAb *fīh*), with the complement in the nominative or accusative. For a distributive sense it, like *la*-, is doubled: *lala-geᶜzṓmū* 'each according to its own way.' *la*- absorbs the accusative and genitive functions as well as the dative, the first two cases requiring an anticipatory suffix, which serves to express definiteness: *mūsenāhā́ la-Ṣeyṓn* 'the desolation of Zion,' *auḍāʾkāhū́ la-Adā́m* 'you caused Adam to precede,' also *azzazkāhū́ lōtū́* 'you commanded him.' This construction most closely resembles that of Aramaic, except that there it is the ordinary relativizing genitive particle that introduces the definite genitive. As in Aramaic, the construction developed because the earlier direct expression of definiteness no longer sufficed. — The original prepositions that ended in *-ai* have not survived, but leave traces in the ending *-ē* common to most prepositions before a pronominal suffix. The gap is filled by various new prepositions. Some prepositions have altered meanings, e.g., *em* (*eménna*) = PS **min*, besides 'from, out of' also the temporal 'after,' *baina* more often 'on account of' than 'between.' Greatly favored, corresponding to a tendency to multiplication recognizable elsewhere, are amalgamations of prepositions, especially with *ba*- and *em*-. An example of African influence, clearer in Amharic, is that prepositions can be used as conjunctions as well; e.g., *káma* 'like': 'as, that, thus'; *áma* 'to, in' and of time: 'when'; *ḫába* 'at': 'when'; cf. also *eménna* 'than,' after a comparative: 'than.'

The usual negation is *ī*-, after which the causative prefix *a*- becomes *y-ā*-;[6] the few combinations in which *al*- serves as the negation have already been mentioned. The interrogative

6. The long vowel is explained in n. 4.

particle is *-nū́* (more rarely *-hū́*) (even appended to interrogative pronouns: *ai-nū́* 'which?'); it is one of the accented postposed particles, which together with the pronominal and noun-forming suffixes, the endings, etc. give Geᶜez the appearance of a strongly suffixing language — a foreshadowing of the development that really did occur in Amharic. Other such particles are *-ā́* as the sign of direct quotation, *-má* for emphasis, *-hī́* and *-nī́* 'also,' *-sá* 'but,' and even a postposition in the narrower sense: *-hā́*, which in certain cases indicates the accusative. —

§ 5/1.3 Word order is very free; in Amharic fashion the adjective (but not the genitive) and *k°ell-* 'all' provided with pronominal suffix precede: *ekkū́y lébb* 'the evil heart,' *kālé*ᵓ *ḥézb* 'a second people'; *k°ellṓmū ṣādeqā́n* 'all the righteous.' The demonstratives, serving as adjectives, go before the substantive: *ye*ᵓ*étī dawḗ* 'this illness.'

Notwithstanding all tendencies to polysyndesis, which besides in the predominance of *za-*, e.g., also appears in the fact that the consequent clause can still be introduced by *wa-*, Ethiopic retains several characteristically asyndetic constructions; e.g., *erḗ*ᵓ*ī yāwáḍe*ᵓ 'I see the leading out,' *re*ᵓ*īkéwō waráda* 'I saw him come down'; *ḫašáškū ā́*ᵓ*mer* (subjunctive!) 'I sought to recognize,' *aḫázkū etnā́gar* 'I began to speak,' *tebēlṓ yéḥneṣ* 'you said to him, he should build.' —

§ 5/1.4 Like Arabic, though to a lesser degree, Ethiopic has borrowed the Aramaic terms for cultural artifacts. Christianity has introduced occasional Hebrew, Greek, and Coptic expressions. There is a rather large number of words that have no correspondences in Semitic and must thus go back to an African origin, though this is not always demonstrable.

Text Specimens[7, k]

1. Ezra's First Vision: Whence Comes Sin, Why Was Zion Punished? (2 Esdras 3)

አመ ፡ ፴ዓመት ፡ እምዘ ፡ ወድቀት ፡ ሀገርነ ፡ ጽዮን ፡ ወሀሎኩ ፡ ውስተ ፡ ባቢሎን ፡ አነ ፡ ሱታ ኤል ፡ ዘተሰመይኩ ፡ ዕዝራ ፡	*àma šalāsā́ ᶜāmát em-zà wádqat hagaréna Ṣeyṓn, wa-hallṓkū wèsta*[8] *Bābī́lōn, ána Sūtāᵓḗl, za-tasamáikū ᶜEzrā́,*	In the thirtieth year after our city of Zion fell, I was in Babylon, I, Sutael, who am called Ezra, |
ወሀሎኩ ፡ ድንጉፅየ ፡ አነ ፡ በውስተ ፡ ምስካብየ፡ ወክሡት ፡ ገጽየ ፡ ወየዐርግ ፡ ኅሊናየ ፡ ውስተ ፡ ልብየ ።	*wa-hallṓkū dengūḍéya*[9] *ána ba-wèsta meskābéya,*[10] *wa-kešū́t*[11] *gaṣṣéya,*[11] *wa-yaᶜáreg ḫellīnā́ya*[12] *wèsta lebbéya:*	and I was disturbed on my bed, and with uncovered countenance, and my thought(s) rose in my heart: |
እስመ ፡ ርኢኩ ፡ ሙስናሃ ፡ ለጽዮን ፡ ወትፍሥ ሕቶሙ ፡ ለእለ ፡ ይነብሩ ፡ ውስተ ፡ ባቢሎን ።	*èsma reᵓī́kū mūsenāhā́*[13] *la-Ṣeyṓn wa-tefšeḥtṓmū*[14] *la-èlla yenabérū wèsta Bābī́lōn.*	for I saw the desolation of Zion and the well-being of those who live in Babylon. |
ወተሀውከት ፡ ነፍስየ ፡ ጥቀ ። ወአኀዝኩ ፡ እት ናገር ፡ ምስለ ፡ ልዑል ፡ ነገረ ፡ ግሩመ ፡ ወእቤ ፡ እንዘ ፡ እብል ፡	*wa-taháukat nafséya ṭéqqa wa-aḫázkū etnā́gar mèsla leᶜū́l nagára gerū́ma wa-ebḗ*[15] *ènza ébl:*[15]	And my heart was greatly stirred, and I began to address fearful words to the Most High, and (lit. while) I said: |
እግዚኦ ፡ አኮኑ ፡ አንተ ፡ ትቤ ፡ ቀዲሙ ፡ አመ፡ ፈጠርካሃ ፡ ለምድር ። ወዘንተኒ ፡ ባሕቲተከ ፡ አዘዝካሁ፡ ለመሬት ፡ ወአውፃእካሁ ፡ ለአዳም ፡ በሥጋ ፡ መዋቲ ፡	*"egzīᵓṓ, akkō-nū́ ánta tebḗ qadīmū́, àma faṭarkāhā́ la-médr, wa-zanta-nī́ bāḥtītáka*[16] *azzazkāhū́ la-marḗt, wa-auḍāᵓkāhū́ la-Adā́m ba-šegā́ mawātī́*	"O Lord, did you not speak in the beginning, when you created the earth, and alone commanded the dust and brought forth Adam in mortal flesh |
ወውእቱኒ ፡ ግብረ ፡ እደዊከ ፡ ውእቱ ። ወነፋ ኅከ ፡ ላዕሌሁ ፡ መንፈሰ ፡ ሕይወት ፡ ወኮነ ፡ ሕያ ወ ፡ በቅድሜከ ።	*— wa-weᵓetū-nī́ gèbra edawī́ka*[17] *weᵓétū*[18] *— wa-nafā́ḫka lāᶜelēhū́ manfàsa ḥeiwát? wa-kṓna ḥeyā́wa ba-qedmḗka;*	— and (also) he is the work of your hands — and breathed into him the breath of life? And (thus) he was made living before you; |

k. Consulted in translating: G. H. Box in R. H. Charles, *the Apocrypha and Pseudepigrapha of the Old Testament* (Oxford: Clarendon, 1913), vol. 2, pp. 561ff. and 616ff.; R. J. Coggins and M. A. Knibb, *The First and Second Books of Esdras* (Cambridge: Cambridge Univ. Press, 1979), pp. 111ff. and 256ff. (Cambridge Bible Commentary on the New English Bible).

7. Taking into account the transcription in E. Mittwoch, *Die traditionelle Aussprache des Äthiopischen* 1926, pp. 100-107. 8. From Ab *wasaṭun* 'middle.' 9. Predicate with pronominal suffix. 10. Noun of place from *skb* 'lie.' 11. Construction ἀπὸ κοινοῦ: *gaṣṣéya*, as more closely defining second subject, is joined to *kešū́t*, which is the predicate of *hallṓkū*. 12. From *ḫly* intensive. 13. From the quadriliteral *māsána* 'spoil' (intransitive). 14. From *fšḥ* intensive-reflexive. 15. *bhl*. 16. Circumstantial phrase in the accusative with pronominal suffix. 17. Plural of *ed* < **yad*-. 18. Personal pronoun as copula 'is.'

ወአባእከሁ ፡ ውስተ ፡ ገነት ፡ እንተ ፡ ተከለት ፡ የማንከ ፡ ዘእንበለ ፡ ትቁም ፡ ምድር ። ወአዘዝከሁ ፡ ሎቱ ፡ ትእዛዘ ፡ ጽድቅ ፡ ወዐለወከ ።	*wa-abāʾkāhū́*[19] *wèsta gannát ènta takálat yamānéka, za-enbàla téqūm médr, wa-azzazkāhū́ lōtū́ teʾzà̄za*[20] *ṣédq, wa-ʿalawáka;*	and you led him into the garden which your right hand had planted before the earth arose, and imposed on (lit. commanded) him one command of righteousness, but he transgressed against you; |
ወእምዝ ፡ ፈጠርከ ፡ ላዕሌሁ ፡ ሞተ ፡ ወላዕለ ፡ ውሉዱ ። ወተወልዱ ፡ እምኔሁ ፡ አሕዛብ ፡ ወሕዝብኒ ፡ ወነገድኒ ፡ ወበሓውርትኒ ፡ ዘአልቦ ፡ ኍልቈ ።	*wa-em-zé faṭárka lāʿelēhū́ mṓta wa-lāʿèla welūdū́.*[21] *wa-tawáldū emennēhū́ aḥzā́b*[22] *wa-ḥezb-nī́ wa-nagad-nī́ wa-baḥāwert*[23]*-nī́ za-albṓ ḫ°élq°a;*	and thereupon you established death for him and for his children. And from him were born men and people and tribes and lands that have no number; |
ወሖሩ ፡ አሕዛብ ፡ ኵሎሙ ፡ ለለግዕዞሙ ፡ ወአበሱ ፡ በቅድሜከ ፡ ወክሕዱከ ፡ ወአንተሰ ፡ ኢከላእኮሙ ።	*wa-ḥṓrū aḥzā́b k°ellṓmū lala-geʿzṓmū wa-abbásū ba-qedmḗka wa-keḥedū́ka; wa-anta-sá ī-kalāʾkṓmū.*	and all men went each their own way and blasphemed before you and rebelled against you; but you did not hinder them. |
ወካዕበ ፡ በዕድሜሁ ፡ አምጻእከ ፡ ማየ ፡ አይኅ ፡ ላዕለ ፡ ምድር ፡ ወላዕለ ፡ እለ ፡ ይነብሩ ፡ ውስተ ፡ ዓለም ፡ ወአጥፋእኮሙ ፡ ወኮነ ፡ ዕሩየ ፡ ኵነኔሆሙ ፡ በከመ ፡ አምጻእከ ፡ ሞተ ፡ ላዕለ ፡ አዳም ፡ ከማሁ ፡ አምጻእከ ፡ ማየ ፡ አይኅ ፡ ላዕለ ፡ እሉሂ ።	*wa-kāʿéba ba-ʿedmēhū́ amṣā́ʾka mà̄ya áiḫ lāʿèla médr wa-lāʿèla èlla yenabérū wèsta ʿālám wa-aṭfāʾkṓmū; wa-kṓna ʿerū́ya k°ennanēhṓmū:*[24] *ba-kàma amṣā́ʾka mṓta lāʿèla Adā́m, kamāhū́ amṣā́ʾka mà̄ya áiḫ lāʿèla ellū-hī́.*	And again in its time you brought the flood upon the earth and upon those who lived in the world, and destroyed them; and the judgment on them was the same: as you brought death upon Adam, so you brought the water of the flood over these. |
ወአትረፍከ ፡ ፩እምውስቴቶሙ ፡ ምስለ ፡ ቤቱ ፡ ዘስሙ ፡ ኖኅ ፡ ወእምኔሁ ፡ ተወልዱ ፡ ኵሎሙ ፡ ጻድቃን ።	*wa-atráfka aḥadá em-westētṓmū*[25] *mèsla bētū́ za-semū́ Nṓḫ; wa-emennēhū́ tawáldū k°ellṓmū ṣādeqā́n.*	And you rescued one of them with his house, whose name is Noah; and from him were born all the righteous. |
ወእምዝ ፡ ሶበ ፡ አኀዙ ፡ ይትባዝኁ ፡ ወይምልኡ ፡ እለ ፡ ይነብሩ ፡ ዲበ ፡ ምድር ፡ ወበዝኁ ፡ ውሉዶሙ ፡ ወተወልዱ ፡ እምኔሆሙ ፡ አሕዛብ ፡ ወሕዝብኒ ፡ ብዙኅ ። ወአኀዙ ፡ ካዕበ ፡ የአብሱ ፡ ፈድፋደ ፡ እምዘ ፡ ቀዲሙ ።	*wa-em-zé, sṑba aḫázū yetbāzéḫū wa-yemléʾū èlla yenabéru dī̀ba médr wa-bázḫū welūdṓmū wa-tawáldū emennēhṓmū aḥzā́b wa-ḥezb-nī́ bezū́ḫ, wa-aḫázū kāʿéba yaʾabbésū*[26] *fadfā́da em-zà qadīmū́.*	And thereafter, when those who lived on earth began to increase and to multiply, and their children became numerous | and from them were born peoples and many men, then they began again to blaspheme more than in the beginning. |
ወእምዝ ፡ ሶበ ፡ አበሱ ፡ በቅድሜከ ፡ ኀረይከ ፡ እምውስቴቶሙ ፡ አሐደ ፡ ዘስሙ ፡ አብርሃም ፡ ወአፍቀርከሁ ፡ ወአርአይኮ ፡ ማኅለቅተ ፡ ዓለም ፡ ባሕቲትከ ፡ ለባሕቲቱ ፡ ሌሊተ ።	*wa-em-zé sṑba abbásū ba-qedmḗka, ḫaráika em-westētṓmū aḥadá za-semū́ Abrehā́m, wa-afqarkāhū́*[27] *wa-arʾaikṓ*[27] *māḫlàqta ʿālám bāḥtītéka la-bāḥtītū́ lēlī́ta,*	And thereafter, when they blasphemed before you, you chose one from them whose name is Abraham, and you loved him and showed him the end of the world, you alone to him alone, by night, |

19. *bwʾ*. 20. From *ʾzz* intensive. 21. Passive participle substantivized. 22. Plural of *ḥezb*. 23. Plural of *beḥḗr*. 24. From *k°nn* intensive. 25. *westēt-* byform of *wésta* before pronominal suffix. 26. *abbása* < **ʾabʾasa* from Ab *biʾsa* 'he is wicked.' 27. Both possibilities, contracted and uncontracted.

ወአቀምከ ፡ ሎቱ ፡ ኪዳነ ፡ ዘለዓለም ፡ ከመ ፡ ለ ግሙራ ፡ ኢትግድፎሙ ፡ ለዘርኡ ፡ እለ ፡ ወፅ ኡ ፡ እምግብጽ ።
ወወሰድኮሙ ፡ ውስተ ፡ ደብረ ፡ ሲና ። ወአጽነ ንከ ፡ ሰማያተ ፡ ወአድለቅለቃ ፡ ለምድር ፡ ወሆ ካ ፡ ለዓለም ፡ ወአርዐድካ ፡ ለቀላይ ፡ ወአኮስካ ፡ ለባሕር ።

ወኀለፈ ፡ ፬አናቅጸ ፡ ስብሐቲከ ፡ ዘእሳትኒ ፡ ወ ዘድልቅልቅኒ ፡ ወዘመንፈስኒ ፡ ወዘበረድኒ ፡ ከ መ ፡ ተሀቦሙ ፡ ለዘርአ ፡ ያዕቆብ ፡ ሕገ ፡ ወለዘ መደ ፡ እስራኤል ፡ ትእዛዘ ፡

ወባሕቱ ፡ ኢያእተትከ ፡ እምኔሆሙ ፡ ልበ ፡ እ ኩየ ፡ ከመ ፡ ይግበሩ ፡ ፍሬ ፡ ሕግከ ፡ በላዕሌሆ ሙ ፤
እስመ ፡ ልበ ፡ እኩየ ፡ ለብሰ ፡ አዳም ፡ ቀዳማዊ ፡ ወተመውአ ። ወአኮ ፡ ውእቱ ፡ ባሕቲቱ ፡ አላ ፡ ኵሎሙ ፡ እለ ፡ ተወልዱ ፡ እምኔሁ ።

ወእምዝ ፡ ነበረት ፡ ይእቲ ፡ ደዌ ፡ ምስለ ፡ ሕግ ከ ፡ ውስተ ፡ ልበ ፡ ሕዝብ ፡ ምስለ ፡ ሥርው ፡ እ ኩይ ። ወ ጠፍአት ፡ ሠናይት ፡ ወተርፈት ፡ እኪ ት ፡

ወኀለፈ ፡ መዋዕል ፡ ወተፈጸማ ፡ ዓመታት ። ወ አቀምከ ፡ ለከ ፡ ገብረከ ፡ ዘስሙ ፡ ዳዊት ፡ ወት ቤሎ ፡ ይሕንጽ ፡ ሀገረ ፡ ለስምከ ፡

wa-aqámka[28] *lōtū́ kīdā̀na za-la-ᶜālám, kàma la-gemūrā́*[29] *ī-tegde-fṓmū la-zarʾū́ èlla wáḍʾū em-Gebṣ. wa-wasadkṓmū wèsta dàbra Sīnā́ wa-aṣnánka samāyā́ta wa-adlaqlaq-qā́*[31] *la-médr wa-hōkkā́ la-ᶜālám wa-arᶜadkā́ la-qalā́y wa-akōskā́ la-bā́ḥr;*

wa-ḫaláfa arbāᶜtá anāqèṣa[32] *sebḥa-tī́ka*[33] *za-esāt-nī́ wa-za-deleqleq-nī́ wa-za-manfas-nī́ wa-za-barad-nī́, kàma tahabṓmū*[34] *la-zàrʾa Yāᶜqṓb ḥégga*[35] *wa-la-zamàda Esrāʾḗl teʾzā́za.*
wa-bāḥtū́ ī-y-āʾtátka[36] *emennēhṓmū lébba ekkū́ya, kàma yegbárū ferḕ ḥeggéka ba-lāᶜelehṓmū.*
èsma lébba ekkū́ya lábsa Adā́m qadāmāwī́ wa-tamáuʾa; wa-akkṓ weʾétū bāḥtītū́, alā̀ k°ellṓmū èlla tawáldū emennēhū́.
wa-em-zé nabárat yeʾétī dawḗ: mèsla ḥeggéka wèsta lèbba ḥézb mèsla šérw ekkū́y; wa-ṭáfʾat šannā́it watár-fat ekkī́t.

wa-ḫaláfa mawāᶜél[37] *wa-tafaṣṣáma ᶜāmatā́t, wa-aqámka láka gabráka za-semū́ Dāwī́t; wa-tebēlṓ yéḥneṣ hagára la-seméka*

and established for him a covenant forever, that you would never destroy his descendants (lit. seed),[30] who departed from Egypt. | And you led them to Mount Sinai and made the heavens bow and the earth shake and convulsed the world and made the ground tremble and stirred the sea; | and your glory went through the four gates, that of fire, that of earthquake, that of wind, and that of hail, then you gave the descendants of Jacob a law and the race of Israel a commandment. | Nonetheless you did not banish the evil heart from them, so that they could cultivate (lit. make) the fruit of your law in themselves. | For the first Adam was clothed with an evil heart and he was overcome; and not he alone, but all who were born from him. | And then this sickness endured: in the heart of men (were) simultaneously your law and the evil root (lit. with your law . . . with the evil root); and the good perished and the evil was left over. | And the days went by and the years were finished, and you awoke (lit. put up) for yourself your servant, whose name is David; and you said to him, he should build a city for your name |

28. *qwm.* 29. Passive participle of *gmr* 'finish' with third person feminine singular pronominal suffix, as adverb. 30. At this point there is a lacuna. 31. *-qā* < *-kā.* 32. Plural of *anqáṣ.* 33. Because of the pronunciation *-ḥā-* for *-ḥa-*, treated as plural. 34. *whb.* 35. From *ḥqq*, H *ḥōq* 'law.' 36. = *ī* + *aʾtátka.* 37. Plural of *mōᶜált* (< **mōᶜadt*, from *wᶜd* 'set a date.'

ወያብእ ፡ በውስቴታ ፡ እምነ ፡ መባእከ ። ወኮነ ፡ ብዙኀ ፡ ዓመተ ፡

wa-yā́beʾ[38] *ba-westētā́ emènna ma-bāʾéka; wa-kṓna bezū́ḫa ʿāmáta.*

and bring you offerings in it (lit. offer of your offerings); and (so) it was for many years. |

ወአበሱ ፡ እለ ፡ ይነብሩ ፡ ውስተ ፡ ምድር ፡ እንዘ ፡ አልቦ ፡ ዘያሤንዩ ፡ ወኢምንትኒ ፡ በከመ ፡ ገብረ ፡ አዳም ፡ ወኵሉ ፡ ትውልዱ ፡

wa-abbásū èlla yenabérū wèsta médr, ènza albṓ za-yāšēnnéyū wa-ī-mentnī́ ba-kàma gábra Adā́m wa-kʷellū́ teweldū́;[39]

But those who lived on the earth blasphemed, while they did nothing good (lit. there was nothing that . . .), (just) as Adam and all his children had done; |

እስመ ፡ እሙንቱሂ ፡ ለብስዎ ፡ ለእኩይ ፡ ልብ ። ወመጠውከ ፡ ሀገረከ ፡ ውስተ ፡ እደ ፡ ጸላእትከ ።

èsma emūntū-hī́ labséwō la-ekkū́i lébb. wa-maṭṭáuka hagaráka wèsta èda ṣalāʾetéka.[40]

for these also were clothed with an evil heart. And you delivered your city into the hands of your enemies. |

ወእቤ ፡ አነ ፡ በልብየ ፡ ይእተ ፡ አሚረ ፡ ቦኑ ፡ ዘይኄይሱ ፡ እምኔነ ፡ በገቢረ ፡ ጽድቅ ፡ እለ ፡ ይነብሩ ፡ ውስተ ፡ ባቢሎን ፡ ከመ ፡ ይንሥእዋ ፡ ለሀገረ ፡ ጽዮን ።

wa-ebḗ ána ba-lebbéya yeʾéta amī́ra: 'bō-nū́ za-yeḫēyyésū emennḗna ba-gabī́ra[41] *ṣédq èlla yenabérū wèsta Bābī́lōn, kàma yenšeʾéwā la-hagàra Ṣeyṓn?'*

And I spoke in my heart on this day: 'Is it true (lit. really) that those who live in Babylon are better than we in doing righteousness, that they should conquer the city of Zion?' |

ወእምዝ ፡ ሶበ ፡ በጻሕኩ ፡ ዝየ ፡ ርኢኩ ፡ ኀጢአተ ፡ ዘአልቦ ፡ ኍልቍ ፡ ወብዙኃነ ፡ ከሓድያነ ፡ ርእየት ፡ ነፍስየ ። ናሁ ፡ ፴ዓመተ ፡

wa-em-zé sṑba baṣā́ḥkū zéya, reʾī́kū ḫaṭīʾáta za-albṓ ḫʷélqʷ, wa-bezūḫā́na kaḥādeyā́na[42] *reʾéyat nafséya nāhū́ šalāsā́ ʿāmáta;*

And then, when I came here, I saw the sins that have no number, and my soul saw many rebels, now for thirty years; |

በዝንቱ ፡ አንክሮ ፡ አንከረት ፡ ልብየ ፡ እፎ ፡ ትትዔገሦሙ ፡ ለኃጥኣን ፡ ርኢይየ ፡ ወከመ ፡ ትምህኮሙ ፡ ለረሲዓን ፡

ba-zentū́ ankerṓ[43] *ankárat lebbéya, efṓ tetʿēggašṓmū la-ḫāṭeʾā́n reʾī-yéya, wa-kàma temehekṓmū la-rasīʿā́n*

then my heart wondered greatly, when I saw how you tolerate the sinners, and how you spare the godless |

ወገደፍከ ፡ ሕዝበከ ፡ ወዐቀብከ ፡ ጸላእተከ ። ወኢነገርከ ፡ ወኢለመኑሂ ፡ እፎ ፡ ደኃሪታ ፡ ለዛቲ ፡ ፍኖት ።

wa-gadáfka ḥezbáka wa-ʿaqábka ṣalāʾetáka; wa-ī-nagárka wa-ī-la-mannū-hī́, efṓ daḫārītā́ la-zātī́ fenṓt.

and have discarded your people and sustained your enemies; and you have told no one how the end of this path will be. |

ቦኑ ፡ ዘይኄይሱ ፡ ባቢሎን ፡ እምጽዮን ፡ ገቢረ ።

bō-nū́ za-yeḫēyyésū Bābī́lōn em-Ṣeyṓn gabī́ra?

Is it true that Babylon is better in deed than Zion?

አው ፡ ካልእኑ ፡ ሕዝብ ፡ አእመረከ ፡ እምእስራኤል ።

àu kāleʾ-nū́ ḥézb aʾmaráka em-Esrāʾél?

Or has another people (better) recognized you than Israel? |

አው ፡ አይኑ ፡ ሕዝብ ፡ አምነከ ፡ ከመ ፡ ያዕቆብ ፡ በሕግከ ፡ ዘኢያስተርኢ ፡ ዕሴቱ ፡ ወኢፈረየ ፡ ጻማሁ ።

àu ai-nū́ ḥézb amnáka kàma Yāʿqṓb ba-ḥeggéka za-ī-yāstaréʾī ʿesētū́ wa-ī-faráya ṣāmāhū́?

Or which people has believed in you like Jacob in your law, whose reward does not appear and whose labor has not borne fruit? |

38. *bwʾ* causative. 39. Collective. 40. Plural of *ṣalāʾī́*; earlier used as singular (see § 5/2/1 n. 43) and therefore with singular-type attachment of the pronominal suffix. 41. Noun of action = gerundive stem. 42. Plural of *kaḥādī́*. 43. Paronomastic strengthening by the infinitive.

ሖርኩ ፡ ውስተ ፡ አሕዛብ ፡ ወረከብክዎሙ ፡ ፍ
ሡሓኒሆሙ ፡ እንዘ ፡ ኢይዜክሩ ፡ ሕገከ ፡ ወት
እዛዘከ ።
ወይእዜኒ ፡ ድሉ ፡ በመዳልው ፡ ኀጣውኢነ ፡ ወዘ
እለ ፡ ይነብሩ ፡ ውስተ ፡ ባቢሎን ፡ ዘበ ፡ ኀቤሁ ፡
ይትረከብ ፡ ሕቀ ፡ መጠነ ፡ እንተ ፡ ታገብእ ፡ ዐይ
ነ ፡ መዳልው ።

ḥṓrkū wèsta aḥzā́b wa-rakabke-wṓmū feššūḥānīhṓmū,[44] *ènza ī-yezzēkkárū*[45] *ḥeggáka wa-te⊃zāzáka. wa-ye⊃ezē-nī́ délū ba-madāléu*[46] *ḫaṭāwe⊃ī́na*[47] *wa-za-èlla yenabérū wèsta Bābī́lōn, za-ba-ḫabēhū́ yetrákkab ḥéqqa maṭána ènta tāgábe⊃ ᶜàina madāléu!*

^cālám au ai-nú
ḥézb za-kama-zé ^caqába te^ʾzāzáka?
wa-hezb-sá za-feṣṣúm ī-yetrákkab."

I have gone among the people and found them content, although (lit. while) they did not think on your law and your command. | And now weigh with the scales our sins and those of them that live in Babylon, that one may thereby find how little (lit. the smallness of the amount that) the beam (lit. eye) of the scales tilts. |

ወማእዜኑ ፡ ኢአበሱ ፡ በቅድሜከ ፡ እለ ፡ ይነብ
ሩ ፡ ውስተ ፡ ዓለም ፡ አው ፡ አይኑ ፡ ሕዝብ ፡ ዘ
ከመዝ ፡ ዐቀበ ፡ ትእዛዘከ ፤ ወሕዝብሰ ፡ ዘፍጹ
ም ፡ ኢይትረከብ ።

wa-mā⊃ezē-nū́ ī-abbásū ba-qedmḗka èlla yenabérū wèsta ᶜālám àu ai-nū́ ḥézb za-kama-zé ᶜaqába te⊃zāzáka? wa-ḥezb-sá za-feṣṣū́m ī-yetrákkab."

And when have those who live in the world not blasphemed, or which people (lit. is it that) has so kept your command? But a perfect people will not be found.

2. Ezra's Sixth Vision: The Man, the Savior of the World (2 Esdras 13:1-26)

ወእምዝ ፡ እምድኅረ ፡ ሰቡዕ ፡ መዋዕል ፡ ሐለ
ምኩ ፡ ሕልመ ፡ በሌሊት ፡ ወናሁ ፡ እሬኢ ፡ ነ
ፋስ ፡ ዐቢይ ፡ ዘይወፅእ ፡ እምባሕር ፡ ወተሀው
ከ ፡ ኵሉ ፡ መዋግዲሃ ፡

wa-em-zé em-dèḫra sabū́ᶜ[48] *mawāᶜél ḥalámkū ḥélma ba-lēlī́t. wa-nāhū́ erḗ⊃ī, nafā́s ᶜabī́y za-yewáḍe⊃ em-bā́ḥr, wa-taháuka k°ellū́ mawā-gedīhā́.*[49]

And then after seven days I dreamed a dream at night, and see (lit. see it), I saw a great storm that came out of the sea, and all its waves were stirred. |

ወእሬኢ ፡ ይወፅእ ፡ ውእቱ ፡ ነፋስ ፡ እምባሕር ፡
ከመ ፡ አምሳለ ፡ ብእሲ ። ወእምዝ ፡ ሰረረ ፡ ው
እቱ ፡ ብእሲ ፡ ምስለ ፡ ደመናተ ፡ ሰማይ ።

wa-erḗ⊃ī yāwáḍe⊃[50] *we⊃étū nafā́s em-bā́ḥr kàma amsā̀la*[51] *be⊃esī́; wa-em-zé sarára we⊃étū be⊃esī́ mèsla dama-nā̀ta samā́y.*

And I saw (how) this storm caused (something) like the form of a man to come forth; and then this man rose up with the clouds of heaven. |

ወኀበ ፡ ሜጠ ፡ ገጾ ፡ ወነጸረ ፡ በጊዜሁ ፡ ይገብእ ፡
ኵሉ ፡ ቅድሜሁ ። ወላዕለ ፡ ዘወፅአ ፡ ቃሉ ፡ ይት
መሰው ፡ ኵሎሙ ፡ እለ ፡ ሰምዕዎ ፡ ለቃሉ ፡ ከ
መ ፡ ይትመሰው ፡ መዓረ ፡ ግራ ፡ ሶበ ፡ ይቀርብ ፡
ኀበ ፡ እሳት ።

wa-ḫàba mḗṭa gaṣṣṓ wa-naṣṣára, ba-gīzēhū́ yegábe⊃[52] *k°ellū́ qedmēhū́; wa-lāᶜèla za-wáḍ⊃a qālū́, yetmásau k°ellṓmū èlla samᶜéwō la-qālū́, kàma yetmásau maᶜā̀ra gerā́, sṑba yeqáreb ḫàba esā́t.*

And when he turned his face and looked, at this time all trembled[53] before him; and after (lit. whereupon) his voice went out, all that heard his voice melted, as wax (lit. the bee's honey) melts when it nears the fire. |

44. Circumstantial clause with pronominal suffix. 45. *t*-stem with assimilation of the *t* to the first radical. 46. Plural of *madlṓt*, noun of instrument of *dlw*. 47. Plural of *ḫaṭī⊃át*. 48. Literally 'week.' 49. Plural of *mōgád*. 50. Text *yewáḍe⊃*. 51. Plural of *mesl*. 52. Imperfect = repetition. 53. According to the parallel texts; lit. 'returned,' probably error.

ወእምዝ ፡ ርኢኩ ፡ ሰብእ ፡ ብዙኀ ፡ ተጋብኡ ፡ ዘአልቦ ፡ ኈልቈ ፡ እምነ ፡ ፬ነፋሳተ ፡ ሰማይ ፡ ከመ ፡ ይጽብእዎ ፡ ለውእቱ ፡ ብእሲ ፡ ዘወፅአ ፡ እምባሕር ።	*wa-em-zé reʾī́kū, sábʾ bezū́ḫ tagābéʾū za-albṓ ḫ°élq° emènna arbāʿtū́ nafāsàta samā́y, kàma yeṣbeʾéwō la-weʾétū beʾesī́ za-wáḍʾa em-bā́ḥr.*	And then I saw (how) many men gathered, that had no number, from the four winds of heaven, to embattle this man who had come forth from the sea.
ወእምዝ ፡ ሐነጸ ፡ ሎቱ ፡ ደብረ ፡ ዐቢየ ፡ ወሰረረ ፡ ላዕሌሁ ። ወኀሠሥኩ ፡ ኣእምር ፡ እምአይቴ ፡ ዘተሐንጸ ፡ ውእቱ ፡ ደብር ፡ ወስእንኩ ።	*wa-em-zé ḥanáṣa lōtū́ dábra ʿabī́ya wa-sarára lāʿelēhū́. wa-ḫašáškū ā́ʾmer, em-aitḗ za-taḥánṣa weʾétū dábr, wa-seʾénkū.*	And then he built himself a great mountain and climbed upon it. And I sought to determine whence it was that this mountain was built, but could not.
ወእምዝ ፡ ኵሎሙ ፡ እልክቱ ፡ እለ ፡ ተጋብኡ ፡ ላዕሌሁ ፡ ከመ ፡ ይጽብእዎ ፡ ፈርህዎ ፡ ጥቀ ። ወባሕቱ ፡ ይትኀበሉ ፡ ይጽብእዎ ፤	*wa-em-zé k°ellṓmū ellektū́ èlla tagābéʾū lāʿelēhū́ kàma yeṣbeʾéwō, farhéwō ṭéqqa; wa-bāḥtū́ yetḫabálū yeṣbeʾéwō.*	And then all those who had gathered against him to embattle him fell into great fear; but nevertheless they dared to fight him.
ወእምዝ ፡ ሶበ ፡ ሮድዎ ፡ ወመጽኡ ፡ ላዕሌሁ ፡ ኢያንሥአ ፡ እዴሁ ፡ ወኢያልዐለ ፡ ኵናቶ ፡ ወኢምንተኒ ፡ ንዋየ ፡ ሐቅል ።	*wa-em-zé sòba rōdéwō wa-máṣʾū lāʿelēhū́, ī-y-ānšéʾa*[54] *edēhū́ wa-ī-y-ālʿála*[55] *k°enātṓ wa-ī-menta-nī́ newā̀ya*[56] *ḥáql;*	And then, when they attacked him and came to him, he did not lift his hands and did not raise his lance, nor any weapon (lit. implement of the field;)
ዘእንበለ ፡ ዳእሙ ፡ እምነ ፡ አፉሁ ፡ መዋግደ ፡ እሳት ፡ ወፅአ ። ወእምነ ፡ ከናፍሪሁ ፡ ነደ ፡ እሳት ። ወእምነ ፡ ልሳኑ ፡ አፍሓመ ፡ እሳት ፡ ከመ ፡ ዐውሎ ፡ አውፅአ ። ወኵሉ ፡ ተደመረ ፡ ዝክቱ ፡ መዋግደ ፡ እሳት ፡ ወዝክቱኒ ፡ ነደ ፡ እሳት ፡ ወዝክቱኒ ፡ አፍሓመ ፡ እሳት ።	*za-enbàla dāʾmū́ emènna afūhū́ mawāgèda esā́t wáḍʾa wa-emènna kanāferīhū́*[57] *nàdda esā́t wa-emènna lesānū́ afḥàma*[58] *esā́t kàma ʿaulṓ auḍéʾa, wa-k°ellū́ tadammára: zektū́*[59] *mawāgèda esā́t wa-zektū-nī́ nàdda esā́t wa-zektū-nī́ afḥàma esā́t;*	but rather from his mouth emerged waves of fire, and from his lips he loosed a flame of fire and from his tongue, coals (i.e. sparks) of fire like a whirlwind, and all mingled, those waves of fire and that flame of fire and those coals of fire;
ወኮነ ፡ ከመ ፡ ዐውሎ ፡ ወወረደ ፡ ላዕለ ፡ እልክቱ ፡ ብዙኃን ፡ እለ ፡ ሮድዎ ፡ ከመ ፡ ይቅትልዎ ።	*wa-kṓna kàma ʿaulṓ wa-waráda lāʿèla ellektū́ bezūḫā́n èlla rōdéwō kàma yeqteléwō,*	and it was like a whirlwind, and (this) descended upon those many who attacked him to kill him,
ወአውዐዮሙ ፡ ለኵሎሙ ፡ እስከ ፡ አልቦ ፡ ዘአትረፈ ፡ እምኔሆሙ ፡ እንበለ ፡ ጸበለ ፡ ሐመዶሙ ፡ ወጢሰ ፡ ዋዕዮሙ ።	*wa-auʿayṓmū la-k°ellṓmū, èska albṓ za-atráfa emennēhṓmū enbàla ṣabàla ḥamadṓmū wa-ṭī̀sa wāʿyṓmū.*	and burnt them all, until there was nothing that he left remaining of them besides the dust of their ashes and the smoke of their burning.
ወእምዝ ፡ ነቃህኩ ፡ ወእምድኅረ ፡ ዝንቱ ፡ ርኢክዎ ፡ ለውእቱ ፡ ብእሲ ፡ ወረደ ፡ እምነ ፡ ዝክቱ ፡ ደብር ፡ ወጸውዐ ፡ ኀቤሁ ፡ ባዕዳነ ፡ ብዙኃነ ፡ ስንኣሁ ።	*wa-em-zé naqā́hkū, wa-emdèḫra zentū́ reʾīkéwō la-weʾétū beʾesī́ waráda emènna zektū́ dábr wa-ṣauwéʿa ḫabēhū́ bāʿedā́na bezūḫā́na senʾāhū́;*[60]	And then I awoke. And after this I saw the man, (how) he came down from that mountain and called to him many others, his friends,

54. = *ī + anšéʾa.* 55. = *ī + alʿála.* 56. < **niyāy* < **ināy*, Ab *ināʾun* 'vessel.' 57. Plural of *kanfár.* 58. Plural of *feḥm.* 59. Without concord with the substantive. 60. Collective.

ወመጽኡ ፡ ኀቤሁ ፡ ብዙኃን ፡ ሰብእ ። ወቦ ፡ እምውስቴቶሙ ፡ ፍሡሓን ፡ ወቦ ፡ እምውስቴቶሙ ፡ ሕዙናን ፡ ወሙቁሓን ።	*wa-máṣᵓū ḫabēhū́ bezūḫā́n sábᵓ, wa-bṓ em-westētṓmū feššūḫā́n wa-bṓ em-westētṓmū ḥezūnā́n wa-mūqūḥā́n.*	and there came to him many men, and among them were joyful, and among them were sorrowful and captives. |
ወእምዝ ፡ ሶበ ፡ በጽሐኒ ፡ ደንገፅኩ ፡ ወነቃህኩ ፡ ወጸለይኩ ፡ ኀበ ፡ ልዑል ፡ ወእቤሎ ፤	*wa-em-zé, sṑba basḥánī, dangáḍkū*[61] *wa-naqā́hkū wa-ṣalláikū ḫàba leᶜū́l wa-ebēlṓ:*[62]	And then, when he reached me, I took fright and woke and prayed to the Most High and said to him: |
ቀዲሙኒ ፡ አንተ ፡ አርአይከ ፡ ለገብርከ ፡ ዘንተ ፡ ስብሐቲከ ፡ ወረሰይከ ፡ ሊተ ፡ ከመ ፡ ትስማዕ ፡ ጸሎትየ ። ወይእዜኒ ፡ ንግረኒ ፡ ዓዲ ፡ ፍካሬሁ ፡ ለዝንቱ ፡ ሕልም ።	*"qadīmū-nī́ ánta arᵓaíka la-gabréka zánta sebḥatī́ka wa-rassaíka lī́ta, kàma tésmāᶜ ṣalōtéya; wa-yeᵓezē-nī́ negránī ᶜādī́ fekkārēhū́ la-zentū́ ḥélm.*	"In the beginning you showed this your glory to your servant and held me worthy that you hear my prayer; but now tell me the meaning of this dream! |
ወባሕቱ ፡ ከመሰ ፡ እትሐዘብ ፡ አሌ ፡ ሎሙ ፡ ለእለ ፡ ሀለዉ ፡ በእማንቱ ፡ መዋዕል ፡ ወፈድፋደሰ ፡ ለእለ ፡ ኢሀለዉ ።	*wa-bāḫtū́ kama-sá etḥázzab: allḕ lṓmū la-èlla halláwū ba-emāntū́ mawāᶜél, wa-fadfāda-sá la-èlla ī-halláwū!*	Only, it seems to me (lit. I think), woe to them who live (lit. are) in these days, but more woe to those that live not (in them)! |
እስመ ፡ የሐዝኑ ፡ በኢያእምሮ ፡ ዘጽኑሕ ፡ ሎሙ ፡ በደኃሪ ፡ መዋዕል ፡ ዘዓዲ ፡ ኢበጽሖሙ ። ወለእለሰ ፡ ሀለዉ ፡ እስመ ፡ ወድኡ ፡ አእመርዎ ።	*èsma yaḥazénū ba-ī-y-āᵓmerṓ*[63] *za-ṣenū́ḥ lṓmū ba-daḫārī̀ mawāᶜél, za-ᶜādī́ ī-baṣḥṓmū; wa-la-ella-sá halláwū, èsma waddéᵓū aᵓmaréwō,*	For they will be sorrowful that they do not know what is in store for them at the end of days, what they will no longer experience (lit. what will not reach them); but those who live (in these days), since they have known it completely, |
ወበበይኑ ፡ ዝንቱ ፡ አሌ ፡ ሎሙ ፡ እስመ ፡ ይሬእዩ ፡ ዐቢየ ፡ ጻዕረ ፡ ወብዙኀ ፡ ሥቃየ ፡ በከመ ፡ ርኢኩ ፡ በውስተ ፡ ዝንቱ ፡ ሕልም ።	*wa-ba-bàina zentū́ allḕ lṓmū, èsma yerēᵓéyū ᶜabī́ya ṣāᶜéra wa-bezū́ḫa šeqā́ya, ba-kàma reᵓī́kū ba-wèsta zentū́ ḥélm.*	and therefore woe to them, for they will see great pain and much need, as I have seen in this dream. |
ወባሕቱ ፡ ይኄይስ ፡ ሕማም ፡ ወይበጽሕዎ ፡ ለዝንቱ ፡ እምነ ፡ ይኅልፉ ፡ እምውስተ ፡ ዓለም ፡ ከመ ፡ ደመና ፡ ወኢያአምሩ ፡ እንተ ፡ ትረክቦሙ ፡ በደኃሪቶሙ ።	*wa-bāḫtū́ yeḫḗyyes ḥemā́m wa-yebaṣeḥéwō la-zentū́, emènna yeḫléfū em-wèsta ᶜālám kàma damanā́ wa-ī-yāᵓamérū, ènta terakebṓmū ba-daḫārītṓmū."*	Nonetheless pain is better and (that) they experience this rather than (that) they depart from the world like a cloud and not realize what will meet them at their end."

61. *d* < *t* (actually *t*-stem). 62. *bhl.* 63. = *ī* + *aᵓmerṓ*.

II. Modern Ethiopic

1. Amharic

§ 5/2/1.0

The second literary language of Ethiopia, Amharic, which is the native language of a large area, has, in contrast to Geᶜez, accomodated itself to a very great extent to its African surroundings. Phonologically it is so strongly reorganized that the genuine Semitic words can scarcely be recognized; a collection of half-independent prefixes and suffixes that form a single word with the stem comprises the morphology; the lexicon is in significant part African; thus Amharic is the Semitic language that least possesses the old Semitic character.[a] —

§ 5/2/1.1.1

The laryngeals, including *ḫ*, have nearly completely disappeared (retained only initially as ᵓ or *h*), and a new *ḫ* has developed out of *k* (further reduced to *h* except finally, where a weak *ḫ* remains).[b] Several sibilants are lost: *ṣ* (and with it *ḍ*) has gone to *ṭ*,[c] *š* to *s* (and *z*, at least initially, to *y*);[d] but a large number of new *š*-type sibilants has arisen by palatalization: *s* > *š*, *z* > *ž*; *t k* > *č*, *ṣ ṭ* > *č̣*; *d g* > *ǰ*; and correspondingly *l* > *y*, *n* >*n'*. These modifications affect the root only of some words in which forms with a following front vowel have become lexicalized; in inflection they occur primarily before the first person singular pronominal suffix -*'ē*[e] and before the verbal ending -*ī* (which thereupon disappears).[f] Another alteration of the original consonantal system is the postvocalic spirantization of *b* to *ḇ*: *bắllā* 'he ate,' but *ennéḇlā* '(that) we eat.'

Some assimilations apply across the board: the reflexive *t* to the first radical, when no vowel intervenes; the *l* of the negative *al* to a following *n t* of the imperfect prefix.

Secondary consonant lengthening is very common.

a. Bergsträsser thus reveals a possible prejudice, and tends to exaggerate the alien features of the language. The dialect reported here, the one studied by his adviser Mittwoch, is that of the region of Lake Tana, in Gondar province, represented by Aleke Taye, an instructor in Berlin who went on to become a major figure in Amharic literature. The standard language was very little known in Europe even as late as the date of this book. G. B. Gragg has supplied in the notes to this chapter comparative material from Standard Amharic.

b. Not in Standard.

c. In many words.

d. Only in one very common morpheme.

e. In gerundives only.

f. Not always in Standard.

§ 5/2/1.1.2 Less radical are vocalic alternations. Except after ᵓ *h*, *a* is pronounced extremely open, almost as a kind of *ä*; word-initially it is often secondarily lengthened. *e* often appears as *i* or *u*, the latter especially after a labialized segment, from which the labialization is transferred to the vowel: *húllū* 'whole, all' < *k°ellū́*; correspondingly in an open syllable *we* > *ū* and likewise *ye* > *ī*. *a* + *a* contracts to *ā*, but *a* + *e* or *e* + *a* to *a*. *ē* and *ō* have become *'ē* and *°ō*. Before initial *r* and *n* a prothetic vowel is common: *reᵓesū́* 'his head' > *ersū́*, imperfect prefix *ne-* > *enne-*.[g]

g. This is the only case before *n*.

Accent is dependent on sonority, with the first syllable of the word especially favored; in contrast with Geᶜez, the accent can occur on the antepenult. The *-ā́l* of the compound tenses and some postposed particles attract the accent to themselves (as is always the case for these in Geᶜez), but not all.[h] The position of the accent is far from fixed; word accent is most strongly influenced by sentence accent. —

h. Even this much cannot be said about Standard accent; cf. § 5/1 note f.

§ 5/2/1.2.1.1 *en'ḗ* 'I' has absorbed the ending of the pronominal suffix *-'ē*; the palatalization has been transferred to the plural *en'ā́* 'we.'[i] The third persons are replaced by secondary formations: *essū́* 'he' < *ersū́* < *reᵓesū́* 'his head,' etc. With pronominal suffixes, the differentiation of the genitive in the noun and the accusative in the verb is carried further. In the noun the singular 'his, her' is *-ū* (*-w*) *-wā*, and before the plural in all three persons the nominal plural ending *-āč-* occurs: *-āčen -āčhū* (with *h* < *k*) *-āčau*.[j] On the verb (and likewise on the prepositions *lä-* and *bä-*, which alone among prepositions, and themselves only when appended to a verb, still take pronominal suffixes) beside the old *-n'* (< *-nī*) 'me,' 'him, her' is *-w* (*-u*, after *ū* as well as *lä-* and *bä-* it is *-t* instead) *-āt*, 'us' is *-n*(*ä*), and, at least in the gerundive, the third person singular is *-ō* (as in Geᶜez) *-ā*, plural *-au*.

i. The Standard forms are *enḗ*, *-ē*, and *en'n'ā́* respectively.

j. Standard *-āččen -āččehū -āččau*.

§ 5/2/1.2.1.2

'This' is *yīḫ* (*yih*) with *y* < *z*, which is retained after a prefix, e.g., *ka-zīḫ* 'from this.' The same change has taken place in the relative *ya* < *za*. This has become as good as obligatory as genitive particle; it is omitted only after a preposition: *wàdä fiyyàl gilgàl b′ḗt* 'to the house (*b′ḗt*) of the youth (*gilgā́l*) of the goat (*fiyyā́l*).' The genitive particle forms a possessive with the personal pronoun: *ya-n′ā́* 'our';[k] after a preposition without *ya-*: *k-ā̀nč b′ḗt* 'in thy house.' — Amharic has a definite article *-ū*, feminine *-ītū*, plural *-ū*, which, however, is often not used.[l] — The interrogatives are *mān* 'who?,' *min* 'what?' (also 'what kind of?'). A particular distributive *iyyä* expresses 'each': *bä-yyä-ḇ′ēt-ā́čau hḗdū* 'they went each into his (lit. their) house.' —

k. Standard *yä-n′n′ā́*.

l. Standard masculine *-ū*, feminine *-wā* are very common.

§ 5/2/1.2.2.1

The perfect suffixes on the verb have undergone only phonological changes (*äč < -at, -ḫ < -kā, -š < -kī* — these two the same as the pronominal suffixes —, *-ḫu* < *-kū*), and the same goes for the imperfect prefixes and suffixes (especially *enne-* first person plural for *ne-*). The old tenses, perfect and imperfect indicative and subjunctive, have been retained, the imperfect indicative however occurring alone only when negated[m] and the subjunctive only partly as expansion of the imperative. Beside these, compound tenses have arisen, which are formed in part by loose concatenations with the auxiliary verbs *näbbā́r* < *nā́bbärä* 'he was,' *h°ṓn*(*ä*) 'he has been' < *kṓna*, which have partly become fixed forms; a new perfect from the gerundive: *nagrōʾā́l* 'he has said'; and a new imperfect from the old imperfect: *īnagrā́l* 'he says.'[n] The second part of each form is the perfect *állä* 'he is' < *halláwa*, which also can partly be further inflected as a perfect within the compound: *tesäṭä-n′-álläḫ* 'thou givest me' (with the personal suffix *-n′* attached to the first element). *állä* alone with pronominal suffix means 'have': *állän′* 'I have.' A further copula is *nau* 'he is' < *nāhū́* 'see him,' feminine *nāt*.[o]

m. And in subordinate clauses.

n. The Standard prefix is *ye-*.

o. This copula exists also for all the other persons.

§ 5/2/1.2.2.3 The basic stem in the perfect always has the active-mode vocalization with secondary lengthening of the second radical, e.g., *nắggarä* 'he said'; but subjunctive *yéngar*, imperative *qemắš* 'examine' (feminine, with *-š* < *-sī*). The gerundive is formed like *gádläš* 'while you (feminine) kill' (corresponding e.g. causative *ādergā́* 'while she made').

§ 5/2/1.2.2.4 Among derived stems, a causative and a *t*-reflexive (passive) of the basic stem and a frequentative with causative and reflexive are the most common; the vowels of the final syllable of the stem are still those of Ethiopic. The causative prefixes have short vowels;[p] along with *a-*, *as-* (from the *st*-stem) is also used as causative prefix. The frequentative reduplicates the second syllable of the stem: e.g., frequentative-reflexive *tänägā́ggarū* 'they conversed with each other,' *täganān'táu* gerundive 'as they met each other' (from *agán'n'ä* [causative] 'he found').

p. Long in Standard.

§ 5/2/1.2.2.5 Because of the loss of laryngeals, the number of weak verbs is greatly increased. — I laryngeal verbs show contractions (if necessary with shortening of the following vowel) like *tā́rfī* '(that) you die' (feminine) from *ā́räfä*. The II laryngeal verbs have sometimes *ā*, as in the perfect *wā́lhū* 'I spent the day,' sometimes *i*, as in the gerundive *wílau* 'while they pass the day.' — The II weak verbs retain the old vowel differentiation: perfect *hḗdä* 'he went,' imperfect indicative *īhḗd*, but subjunctive *īhī́d* and gerundive *hīdṓ*; correspondingly, *h°ṓnä* 'he was,' *īh°ṓn*, but *īhū́n hūnṓ*.[q] The III laryngeal verbs and some of the III weak verbs form their infinitives and gerundives with the addition of a *t*, like the Hebrew III weak: *sämtā́* 'while she hears' from *sā́mmā* 'he heard.' — As already in Ge^{c}ez, *bhl* 'say' is irregular; it loses not only its *h*, but in many forms the *b* as well: subjunctive *ī́ḇäl*, imperative *bäl* (feminine *bäi* with *-i* < *-lī*), gerundive *belṓ*, but perfect *ā́lä*, imperfect indicative *yil*. —

q. But the gerundive may also be *hēdṓ h°ōnṓ*.

§ 5/2/1.2.3 Nothing remains of noun declension; in its place a new accusative suffix *-n* has arisen, which when the substantive has a modifier is attached to the modifier: *ya-ennāt-wằ-n míkir* 'the advice of her mother,' and likewise *ya-lämmäná-w-en ṭerḗ* 'the grain (singular) that he had begged.' There are but traces of the feminine ending; the plural ending is *-ṓč*. —

§ 5/2/1.2.4 The negative particle is in two parts: *al-* before and *-m* after the word; though in subordinate clauses the *-m* under certain circumstances is omitted. A question can be stressed by the suffix *-ā*;[1] otherwise there is a question particle identical with the accusative suffix *-n*, which not only occurs in interrogative clauses, but also can be attached to one-word questions: *yät-abbāš-én* 'where is your father?.' 'And' is expressed by *-ennā́* on the first conjunct or by *-m* on one of the first words of the second conjunct (double *-m*: 'not only . . . but also'). Other suffixed particles are *-s* and *-gín* 'but.'

A peculiarity of the prepositions is that they can be reiterated (e.g., *ka-zī́ẖ ka-ṭeqī́t* 'from these few').[r] As in Geᶜez, many prepositions can also be used as conjunctions: *bä-* 'in, with, by' not only in combinations like *bä-säṭṭäč-éu giz'ḗ* 'at the time when she gave it to him,' but also alone for 'if'; *ka-* 'from, by, in' for 'after.' Other prefixed conjunctions are *si-* and *iyyä-* 'while.'

r. Pronominal suffixes attached to the verb with *-b-* express a "malefactive" case, where the action of the verb is done to the detriment of the oblique object: *āwwäqačebbén'* 'she found me out' (literally 'she knows on me').

§ 5/2/1.3 Entirely unSemitic is the word order: the modifier (adjective, genitive, relative clause) goes before the substantive; subject and object before the verb (which often resumes the object with a pronominal suffix) and also before a conjunction that governs the verb; subordinate clause before main clause; direct speech before the verb of speaking.

1. Now archaic.

Text Specimens[2]

[F] after a word indicates that it does not come from Ethiopic.

a) The Student and the Greedy Woman

አንድ ፡ ተማሪ ፡ የለመነውን ፡ ጥሬ ፡ ይዞ ፡ ምጣድ ፡ ከጣደች ፡ ሴት ፡ ሒዶ ፡ እባክሽ ፡ ይህን ፡ ጥሬ ፡ ቁይልኝ ፡ አላት ።	*ànde[3] tämā́rī[4] ya-lämmäná[F]-w-en ṭerḗ[5] yezṓ,[6] meṭā́d[F7] ka-ṭā́däč[7] s′ḗt[8] hīdṓ "eb̲ā́k[F]-iš, yíhin ṭerḗ quy[9]-éllen′!" āl[10]-ā́t.*	A student holding (gerundive) grains of corn that he had begged went (gerundive) to a woman who had set a frying pan on the fire, (and) said to her: "Please roast these grains of corn for me!" |
እርስዋ ፡ ግን ፡ እየቀመሰች ፡ ጨረሰችበትና ፡ ጥቂት ፡ ቀረው ።	*esswā-gín[F] iyyä[F]-qámmäsäč,[11] ç̌ärräsäč[12]-ebbät-ennā́ ṭeqī́t[F] qárrau.[F]*	But she ate them, in tasting them, (almost) all up (lit. finished them on him), and little was left for him. |
አውጥታ ፡ በሰጠችው ፡ ጊዜ ፡ ቈንጥሮ ፡ እንኪ ፡ አላት ። እርስዋም ፡ አዬ ፡ ከዚህ ፡ ከጥቂት ፡ ምን ፡ ትሰጠኛለህ ፡ አለችው ። እርሱም ፡ ቅመሽው ፡ እንጂ ፡ አላት ።	*āuṭetā́[13] bä-säṭṭäč-èu[14] giz′ḗ,[15] q°anṭerṓ[F] "énkī!"[16] āl-ā́t. esswá-m "āyḗ, ka-zī́ḫ ka-ṭeqī́t mín tesäṭä-n′-álläḫ?" āläč-éu. essū-m "qemäš[17]-èu ínǰī!"[18] āl-ā́t.*	When she, in taking it out, gave him (the pan), he said to her, while picking up (some grains) with his fingers: "Take!" But she said to him: "Ah, why do you give me of such paucity?" and he said to her: "Just taste it!"

b) The Leopard Cub and the Goat Kid

የነብር ፡ ግልገልና ፡ የፍየል ፡ ግልገል ፡ ተገናኝተው ፡ ባንድ ፡ ሲጫወቱ ፡ ውለው ፡ ማታ ፡ ሁሉም ፡ በየቤታቸው ፡ ሔዱ ።	*ya-nä̀b̲r[19] gilgäl[F]-ennā́ ya-fiyyä̀l[F] gílgäl täganān′táu,[F] b-ánd[20] s-iç̌ç̌ā́watū[F21] wílau,[22] mā́tā[23] húllu[24]-m bä-yyä-b̲′ēt-āčáu hḗdū.*	A leopard cub and a goat kid met (gerundive), passed the day (gerundive) playing together, and each evening went each to her house. |

2. E. Mittwoch, *Proben aus amharischem Volksmunde* (MSOS 10 1907, *Westas. Studien* pp. 185-241), pp. 232, 238-240. 3. *ʾḥd*; *e* prosthetic vowel. 4. From *mhr*. 5. From *ṣrḫ*. 6. *ʾḫz*. 7. Same stem. 8. From *sabʾ* 'man.' 9. *q°allā́* (*qly*); *u* < °*e* and *-y* < *lī*. 10. From *bhl*. 11. < *qsm*. 12. *ṭrs*. 13. *wṣʾ*. 14. *sṭw*; *e* linking vowel. 15. Gz *gīzḗ*. 16. From *näkkā́*, for **nékī*. 17. *š* < *-sī*. 18. Gz *endeʿī́* 'perhaps.' 19. Gz *namr*. 20. 'with one.' 21. *i* < *ī* < *e-ye*. 22. *wʿl*. 23. Time noun from Gz *atáwa* 'return home.' 24. Gz *k°ell*.

የነብር፡ግልገል፡ለእናቷ፡እኔ፡ዛሬ፡ከፍየል፡ግልገል፡ጋራ፡ስጫወት፡ዋልሁ፡ብላ፡ነገረቻት።	*ya-nä̀b̲r gílgäl lä-ennāt*[25]*-wā́ "en'ḗ zārḗ*[F] *ka-fiyyä̀l gilgä̀l gārā́*[26] *s-eč̣č̣ā́wat wā́lhū" belā́ näggaräč-ā́t.*	The leopard cub spoke to her mother, saying: "Today I passed the day playing with the goat kid."|
እናትዋም፡የታባሽ፡አንቺ፡ሞኝ፡ስለምን፡አንቀሽ፡ያልገደልሻትና፡ያላመጣሻት።	*ennāt-wá-m "yät-abbā́š!*[27] *ànč m°ṓn'!*[F] *silä*[29]*-mín ā́nqaš*[30] *y-al-gaddälš-āt-ennā́ y-āl-ālmaṭṭāš*[31]*-ā́t?*	Her mother said: "Where is your father?[28] You are stupid! Why didn't you (lit. is it that you did not) kill it by strangling it and bring it (here)?|
አምጥተሻት ፡ ቢሆን ፡ አሁን ፡ ደምዋን ፡ ጠጥተን ፡ ሥጋዋን ፡ በልተን ፡ እንጠግብ ፡ ነበርን።	*amṭetäš-ā́t b-īh°ṓn,*[32] *āhū́n*[F] *däm-wā́-n ṭäṭetä́n,*[F] *segā*[33]*-wā́-n bältä́n,*[34] *enneṭä́ggeb̲*[35] *näbbä́rnä.*	If you had brought it, we would now drink (gerundive) its blood and eat (gerundive) its flesh and satisfy ourselves.|
አሁንም ፡ ነገ ፡ ማለዳ፡ሒጅና፡ነይ፡እንጫወት፡ብለሽ ፡ አታለሽ፡አምጪትና፡እንበላታለን፡አለቻት።	*āhū́n-em nága*[36] *mālädā́*[37] *hīǰ*[38]*-ennā́ 'nài enneč̣č̣ā́wat!' belā́š*[39] *āttā́lläš*[40] *amč̣*[41]*-āt-ennā́ enneb̲älā-t-állän!" āläč-ā́t.*	But now go early in the morning and, by deceiving it by saying 'Come, let's play,' bring it (here) and we will eat it!"|
የፍየልም፡ግልገል፡ወደ፡እናቷ፡ሒዳ፡እናቴ፡እኔ፡ዛሬ፡ከነብር፡ግልገል፡ጋራ፡ስጫወት፡ዋልሁ፡ብላ፡ነገረቻት።	*ya-fiyyä̀l-em gílgäl wàdä ennāt-wā́ hīdā́, "ennāt-'ḗ, en'ḗ zārḗ ka-nä̀b̲r gìlgäl gärā́ s-eč̣č̣ā́wat wā́lhū" belā́ näggaräč-ā́t.*	And the goat kid, coming to her mother, said, "My mother, today I played with the leopard cub."|
እናቷም ፡ ደነገጠችና ፡ እወይ ፡ እወይ ፡ አንቺ ፡ ዘላ ፡ የታባሽንስ ፡ ነብሮች ፡ የኛ ፡ ጠላቶች ፡ ባለደሞቻችን ፡ እንደሆኑ ፡ አተውቂምን።	*ennāt-wá-m dänäggaṭäč*[42]*-ennā́ "ewái ewái! ànč z°ṓlā!*[F] *yät-abbāš-én-es? näb̲rṓč ya-n'ā́ ṭälātṓč*[43] *bālä*[44]*-dämōč-āčén èndä h°ṓnū at-täuqí*[45]*-m-en?*	And her mother was surprised and said; "Woe, woe! You are an idiot! So where is your father? Don't you know that leopards are our blood enemies?|
የነብር ፡ ግልገል ፡ እንቅ ፡ አድርጋ ፡ ገድላሽ ፡ በሆነ ፡ ታርፊው ፡ ነበር። አሁንም ፡ ነገ ፡ ነይ ፡ እንጫወት ፡ ያለችሽ ፡ እንደሆን ፡	*ya-nä̀b̲r gílgäl énneq ādergā́*[F] *gádläš bä-h°ṓnä, tarfī́u*[46] *näbbä́r. āhū́n-em nága 'nài enneč̣č̣ā́wat!' y-āläč-éš èndä h°ṓn,*	If the leopard cub had killed you by strangling, you would be deceased. But now, if tomorrow she says to you: 'Come, let's play,'|
አልመጣም ፡ ካንቺ ፡ ጋራ ፡ ምን ፡ ጨወታ ፡ አለኝ፡በያት፡እንጂ፡እንዳትገልሽና፡እንዳትበላሽ፡አትሒጅ፡አለቻት።	*'al-mā́ṭa*[47]*-m, k-ā̀nč gārā́ mìn č̣awatā́ állän'?' bày*[48]*-āt ínǰī, èndä t-tegall*[49]*-eš-ennā́ èndä t-te-b̲ā́la-š, at-tehī́d!" āläč-ā́t.*	then say instead to her: 'I won't come, what kind of game could (lit. do) I play with you?,' so that she won't kill you and won't eat you, don't go!"|

25. Gz *emmā́t*, plural of *emm*. 26. Literally 'in the society of.' 27. *abbā́* archaic, now *abbā́t*. 28. I.e. 'you have no father' (invective). 29. From *sʾl* 'ask.' 30. *ʿnq*. 31. *mṣʾ*. 32. *kwn*; 'if it were, while. . . .' 33. Gz *šegā́*. 34. *blʿ*. 35. *ṣgb*. 36. *ngh*. 37. From *mā́lädä* 'he awoke early,' denominative from Gz *maʿā́lt* 'day' (from *wʿl*). 38. *-ǰ* < *-dī*. 39. *bhl*. 40. Causative with secondary lengthening of the *t* of *tā́lälä* (actually *t*-stem with repetition of the last radical of Gz *ḥbl* 'behave the wrong way.' 41. *-č̣* < *-ṭī*. 42. *dngḍ*. 43. From the Gz plural *ṣalāʾét* (see § 5/1 n. 40). 44. 'Lord of' (Gz *bā́ʿla*) for the expression of concatenation. 45. *ā́wwäqa* 'he realized, knew,' Gz *ʿwq*. 46. *ʿrf*. 47. = *emā́ṭā*. 48. *bhl* (*-y* < *-lī*). 49. *tegadl-*.

የፍየል ፡ ግልገልም ፡ የእናቷን ፡ ምክር ፡ ሰምታ ፡ እሺ ፡ አልሔድም ፡ አለች ፤	*ya-fiyyȁl gilgā́l-em ya-ennāt-wā̀-n míkir sämtā́*[50] *"íšī,*[F] *al-hḗd*[51]*-em" ā́läč.*	But the goat kid said, upon hearing her mother's advice, "Okay, I won't go."
በነጋው ፡ የነብር ፡ ግልገል ፡ እናትዋ ፡ እንደ ፡ መከረቻት ፡ ወደ ፡ ፍየል ፡ ግልገል ፡ ቤት ፡ አጠገብ ፡ ሔደችና ፡ በጓሮ ፡ ሁና ፡ ፍየሉት ፡ ፍየሉት ፡ ብላ ፡ ጠራቻት ፤	*bä-nagā́-u ya-nȁb̲r gílgäl, ennāt-wā́ èndä mäkkäräč-ā́t, wàdä fiyyȁl gilgȁl b'ȅt aṭägā́b̲*[F] *hēdäč-ennā́ ba-g°ārṓ*[F] *hūnā́ "fiyyälū́t! fiyyälū́t!" belā́ ṭärrāč̌*[52]*-ā́t.*	On the following day the leopard cub went, as her mother had advised her, near the house of the goat kid and called to her, when she was in the yard: "Kiddy! Kiddy!" |
የፍየል ፡ ግልገልም ፡ አቤት ፡ ባለቻት ፡ ጊዜ ፡ እንደ ፡ ትላንቱ ፡ ነይና ፡ እንጫወት ፡ አለቻት ፤	*ya-fiyyȁl gilgā́l-em "āb̲'ḗt!"*[F] *bāläč-ȁt giz'ḗ, "èndä telā́nt*[53]*-ū näy-ennā́ enneč̣č̣ā́wat!" āläč-ā́t.*	And when the goat kid said to her "Sir," she said to her, "Come, and let's play like yesterday!" |
እርስዋ ፡ ግን ፡ አልመጣም ፡ አለች ፤ የነብር ፡ ግልገልም ፡ ምነዋ ፡ አለች ፤	*esswā-gín "al-mā́ṭa-m" ā́läč. ya-nȁb̲r gilgā́l-em "mìn naw-ā?"*[54] *ā́läč.*	But she said: "I'm not coming!" But the leopard cub said: "What's up?" |
የፍየል ፡ ግልገል ፡ ካንቺም ፡ ቤት ፡ ተመከረ ፡ ከኔም ፡ ቤት ፡ ተመከረ ፡ ብላት ፡ ወደ ፡ እናትዋ ፡ ሔደች ፤	*ya-fiyyȁl gilgā́l "k-ȁnč-im b'ḗt tämā́kkärä, k-an'ȅ-m b'ḗt tämā́kkärä" belā́t wàdä ennāt-wā́ hḗdäč.*	The goat kid, saying "Just as advice was given in your house, so also was advice given in our house," went to her mother. |
የነብር ፡ ግልገልም ፡ አወቀችብኝ ፡ ብላ ፡ አፍራ ፡ ተመለሰች ።	*ya-nȁb̲r gilgā́l-em "āwwäqačebbén' " belā́ āfrā́*[55] *tämā́lläsäč.*[F]	But the leopard cub went away ashamed, saying: "She found me out (lit. knows on me, i.e., to my disadvantage)." |

50. *smᶜ*. 51. = *ehḗd.* 52. *ṣrḫ.* 53. From Gz *temā́lem* 'yesterday.' 54. Interrogative suffix. 55. *ḫfr.*

2. Tigrē

§ 5/2/2.0 Among modern Ethiopic languages, Tigrē, a descendant not directly from Geᶜez but from a dialect closely related to it, is the one that has most faithfully preserved its Semitic character and fallen least under African influence. Nonetheless Tigrē has undergone sound losses and changes in the same direction as Amharic and incorporated elements of foreign sentence structure as well as considerable foreign vocabulary. —

§ 5/2/2.1.1 The laryngeals are retained, but where they had occurred at the end of a syllable they are transferred to the beginning of the syllable:[a] *samᶜákō* 'I heard' = Gz *samā́ᶜkū*. Initial ᵓ elides now and then; e.g., *ḥar* 'thereafter' from *ᵓḫr*, *ḥáttē* 'one' from *ᵓḥd*. The influence of laryngeals on the vowels remains strong; in particular the changes *e* > *a* (e.g., *tahayáfkō* 'I supplied myself with,' vs. the usual reflexive prefix *t*- < **te*-) and *a* > *e* are more widespread, the latter affecting even the vowels of proclitic particles (e.g., *ke-hetā́* 'and she' vs. the usual *ka*-) and extended to *ā* > *e*. Epenthesis and lengthening also occur after laryngeals. — *ḫ* has merged with *ḥ*:[b] *bezúḥ* 'much' = Gz *bezūḫ*, *ḥar* 'thereafter' from *ᵓḫr*. Foreign *ḫ* is therefore borrowed as *k*: *mašā́yik* 'sheikh' < Ab *mašāyiḫ*.

a. This is merely the normal form of the Tigrē verb.

b. As already in early Geᶜez.

Labialization is not found, e.g., *kel* 'all, entire' = Gz *k°ell*. Contrariwise, palatalization does occur, in the same way as in Amharic, though less pervasively and regularly; it is most common before the pronominal suffix 'my,' e.g., *éččē* 'to, at me' from *et*. As in Amharic, original *š* has become *s*.

Final consonant clusters are eliminated: in part by epenthetic vowels, as in *méder* 'earth, land' = Gz *medr*, *mésel* 'with' = Gz *mésla*, *dáᵓam* 'but' = Gz *dāᵓmū́*; in part by loss of one of the two consonants, as in *sab* 'people' = Gz *sabᵓ*, especially the feminine ending -*t*, e.g., in *meᶜél* 'day' = Gz *mōᶜált* (with *e* < *u* as shortening of *ō*). Initial consonant clusters were generally not possible in Ge^{c}ez, but have often arisen in Tigrē; only rarely are they simplified, e.g., *kestā́n* 'Christian' < **kr-* = Gz *kerestīyā́n*, or given a prothetic vowel, as in the prefixes *eb-* and *el-* = Gz *ba- la-*.

Consonant lengthening, as in Amharic, is widespread, e.g., *addā́m* 'men,' and especially before a pronominal suffix, as with the affix *-at* + *ō* = *-áttō*. In laryngeals and semivowels, on the other hand, it is largely abandoned.

§ 5/2/2.1.2 The indeterminate short vowel *e* is pronounced according to its environment, commonly *i*, sometimes *u*. *a* often shades toward *ä*.

§ 5/2/2.1.3 Accent is divergent from that in Ge^{c}ez and Amharic. The accent can retract to the antepenult; appended particles etc. attract it to the last syllable of the preceding word.

§ 5/2/2.2.1 The pronouns have changed but little. The third person pronouns retain the *h-* of **hū*$^{\supset}$*a* etc., which has been lost in Ge^{c}ez (*we*$^{\supset}$*étū*): *hetū́* 'he,' feminine *hetá*, plural *hetṓm* (already in Ge^{c}ez *we*$^{\supset}$*etṓmū* beside *emūntū́*) *hetán*; the second halves of these forms *tū* etc. serve as copula (also for the first and second persons) 'is,' etc., beside which there is a sort of imperfect in subordinate clauses, *éntū*. The endings *-ū* etc. are identical with the third person pronominal suffixes; they are also attached to the demonstrative pronouns in the feminine and plural: 'this' *éllī élla éllōm éllan*, 'that' *lahái lahá lahṓm lahán*. After a long vowel the third person pronominal suffixes retain their initial *h*. The suffix 'my' is *-yē* < *-ē* < *-eya*, with 'me' correspondingly *-nē*. *la-* serves as relative, and is identical with the definite article that Tigrē has developed in contrast to Ge^{c}ez but uses only sparingly. Contradicting the old Semitic rule, it can occur before a substantive with pronominal suffix: *la-bētna* 'our house.' The interrogatives are *man* 'who?,' *mī* 'what?.' —

§ 5/2/2.2.2.1 Like the pronouns, the verbal affixes are more or less the original ones: the plural ending has differentiated into *-au* (from the III weak verbs) in the perfect and *-ō* < *-ū* in the imperfect etc. Before pronominal suffixes, the perfect forms that end with *-a* exhibit a *y* likewise originating in the III weak verbs: *-ayū* etc. (in other forms the third person masculine suffix is *-ō*), and the plural suffix *-ū* is found before the last radical (epenthesis): *leqattū́lō* < **leqatelū* + *-ō*, *qetṓlō* < **qetalū* + *-ō*. The imperfect has lost the prefix *y-* of the third person; in the subjunctive, and often in the indicative, it is replaced by *le-* (causative *la-*). Thus, basic stem, e.g., indicative (*le*)*qáttel*, subjunctive *léqtal*. — Supplementing the old tenses are periphrastic formations made of finite verbs or participles with the copula *tū* etc., or the auxiliary verbs *hálla* 'he is' < *halláwa* and ^{c}*ála* 'he was' < *wa*^{c}*ála* 'he passed the day.' The gerundive constructions otherwise so widespread in Ethiopic are not found in Tigrē.

§ 5/2/2.2.2.3 In the basic stem the neutral-mode inflection has been generalized: perfect *qátla* (sometimes with epenthetic vowel *fáqeda* 'he remembered,' *báṣeḥa* 'he reached'), subjunctive *léqtal* (with epenthesis *léḥerad* '[that] he slew'). The participle *qā́tel*, no longer found in Ge^{c}ez, is still used, especially in periphrastic verb forms; besides this, *qatā́l* is a second participle of the basic stem, e.g., *talā́i* 'shepherd.' As a result of secondary lengthening of the second radical, the *t*-reflexive of the basic stem has merged with that of the intensive; this form is the usual passive. The *t-* is mostly vowelless, like *tqáṣṣaba* 'he was angry.' The *ā*-stem with its *t*-reflexive is fully productive; e.g., *ta*^{c}*ā́re* 'she makes peace,' *let*^{c}*ā́rē* 'he reconciles himself.' Beside the original causative with the prefix *a-* there are two new ones, with the prefixes *at-* (actually causative-reflexive), e.g., *atrā́dawō* 'they advised him' and *atta* < **at-a-*

(double causative). The causative prefixes of the imperfect have the vowel *a*, not, as in Geᶜez, *ā*: *támṣiʾ* '(that) she get,' *naqalléllō* 'we will make it light' (causative-intensive). Reduplication, as in Amharic, forms an iterative.

§ 5/2/2.2.2.5 The I *w* verbs exhibit weak formations only occasionally in the imperative, e.g., *de* 'do' from *wáda*, beside *wedḗ*; in the subjunctive, where there should also be weak formations, they have been reshaped by analogy with other verbs, mostly I *y* (as elsewhere *y* often replaces *w*), thus *nī́dē* 'we would do.' — The II weak verbs shorten their vowel before a consonantal suffix in the perfect, e.g., *léšnā* 'we inserted' (with *e* < *u*) from *lṓša*, *géska* 'thou wentest' from *gēsa* (against Gz *qṓma qṓmka*). — All the III *w* verbs have become III *y*; the inflection is no longer so rigorously strong as in Geᶜez. The perfect ends in *-a* (before suffixes and pronominal suffixes, in *-ē-*), the imperfect in *-ē* (before pronominal suffix indicative *-eiy-*, subjunctive *-aiy-*); thus, e.g., *hálla* 'he is,' feminine *hállēt*, first person *hallḗkō*; *taᶜárē* 'she makes peace.' *bhl* 'say' is irregular, as already in Geᶜez: *bḗla* 'he said,' *bḗlawō* 'they said to him,' but from its "past" imperfect (Gz *yebḗ*): *bḗlla* 'he said to her' (before a suffix the *l* remains), *tebḗllō* or *tḗllō* 'she said to him,' etc.; imperfect *tebél*, plural *léblō*, *lebū́la* 'they say to her' (< **lebelū* + *-ā*), subjunctive *tī́bal*, causative *ábala*. The same loss of medial *b* affects *gaʾá* 'he, it became, happened,' a shortening of Gz *gábʾa* 'he returned' (but not imperfect *tgā́bbiʾ*). —

§ 5/2/2.2.3 The accusative and construct state ending *-a* is gone. The construct phrase itself is fully productive. The plural ending is *-ām* on adjectives and participles, *-āt* or extensions thereof (*-ōtāt*, etc.) on substantives; in addition the broken plural remains common, especially in the form *qetál* and in multiliteral singulars, like *masānī́t* from *masnái* 'friend.' The nisbe ending is *-āi* (e.g., *kestēnā́i* 'Christian'), feminine *-āit*. —

§ 5/2/2.2.4 As in Geᶜez and Amharic, prepositions can also function as conjunctions: *et* 'at, after, to' and 'while'; *men* 'from' and 'if, since'; *égel* 'to' and 'therefore, so that.' *el-* (dative particle) and *eb-* 'in, by, over' are still found, *k-* in combinations like *kem* 'as, than,' *keᵓénna* 'so'; otherwise *ka-* is 'and.' The negation is *ī-*. —

§ 5/2/2.3 Word order is not quite so unSemitic as in Amharic; postposing of genitive and adjective is retained. But the verb is almost always at the end of the sentence, usually with a pronominal suffix resuming the object, and a conjunction or relative invariably comes before the verb it governs; subordinate clauses usually precede main clauses (only attributive relative clauses follow); and direct speech often precedes the verb of speaking.

Text Specimens[1]

[A] after a word indicates that it comes from Arabic, [F] that it is of foreign, i.e., non-Semitic, origin.

a) A Reluctant Convert to Islam

ዎሮት ፡ እናስ ፡ ለአመስለማ ። ገሌ ፡ ሰብ ፡ እብ ፡ ዲን ፡ እት ፡ ልትሃገው ፡ ዎሮቶም ፡ ክእና ፣ ደግማ ፤	*wṓrōt*[F] *enā́s, la-amáslama.*[A2] *gàlē*[F] *sáb*[3] *eb dī́n*[A] *et*[4] *lethā́gau, wōrṓtōm keʾénna dágma:*	A man who became a Moslem. While some people were talking about religion, one of them related the following: |
በዲር ፡ መንሰዕ ፡ ክላ ፡ ክስታን ፡ ዐለት ። ደአም ፡ ሐር ፡ መሻይክ ፡ እስላም ፡ ክም ፡ መጽኣ ፡ ገሌሃ ፡ አመስለማ ።	*badī́r Mā́nsaʿ kélla kestā́n-ʿàlät.*[5] *dáʾam*[6] *ḥar*[7] *mašā́yik*[A] *eslā́m*[A] *kem máṣa,*[8] *galḗha amáslama.*	Formerly all of the Mansa were Christian. But then, when the Moslem sheikhs came, some became Moslem. |
ወእግል ፡ ዎሮት ፡ ክስቴናይ ፤ አመስልም ፡ ዲን ፡ እስላም ፡ ሐይስ ፡ ወለፍትሕ ፡ ነቀልሎ ፡ እልካ ፡ ቤለዎ ። ወብዙሕ ፡ ክም ፡ አትራደዎ ፡ አመስለማ ።	*we-ègel*[F] *wṓrōt kestēnā́i: "amáslem, dī́n eslā́m ḥáyis,*[9] *wa-fetéḥ naqallḗllō-èlka!" bḗlawō,*[10] *wa-bezúḥ*[11] *kem atrā́dawō,*[A12] *amáslama.*	And they said to a Christian: "Become Moslem, the Moslem religion is better, and we will make the law easy for you!" and after they had talked to him a great deal, he became Moslem. |
ክሐቴ ፡ ምዕል ፡ ምስል ፡ ተላዩ ፡ እት ፡ አሓ ፡ ውዕል ፡ እት ፡ እንቱ ፤ ወአት ፡ መካን ፡ ጸድፈት ፡ ምኑ ። ወእባ ፡ እባ ፡ ትንፋሳ ፡ ፈግረት ።	*ka-ḥáttē meʿél*[13] *mèsel talā́yū*[14] *et aḥá*[F] *weʿél*[15] *et éntū, waʾát*[F] *makā́n ṣáḍfat-mènnū we-ebbā́-bba*[16] *tenfā́sa fágrät.*	And one day, while he was guarding the cows with his shepherd, a fat (lit. barren) cow fell away from him, and her spirit departed straightaway. |
ወህቱ ፡ እግል ፡ ልሕረዳ ፡ ደርባ ፡ ትከራ ። ደአም ፡ ገሌ ፡ ምን ፡ ለእስላም ፡ ለረአዎ ፡ ቤለዎ ፤ ኢትሕረዳ ፡ ሞተት ፤ ስጋሃ ፡ ሐራም ፡ እትካ ፡ ቱ ።	*we-hetū́ ègel leḥerádda, dárba*[A17] *tkárra.*[18] *dáʾam galḗ men le-eslā́m, la-ráʾawō,*[19] *bḗlawō: "ī-teḥerádda! mṓtät,*[20] *segā́ha*[21] *ḥarā́m*[A] *etkā́-tū."*	And he climbed down after her, in order to butcher her. But some of the Moslems who saw him said to him: "Don't butcher her! She died, her flesh is forbidden to you!" |
ወህቱ ፡ ቤላ ፤ ማይተት ፡ ምን ፡ ትገብእ ፡ አማንኩም ፡ ቱ ፡ እት ፡ እስላም ፡ ወእት ፡ ክስታን ፡ ሕርምት ፡ ወገአት ።	*we-hetū́ bḗla: "māität men tgā́bbiʾ, amānkúm-tū, et eslā́m we-et kestā́n ḥerremét*[22] *wa-gaʾát."*[23]	And he said: "If she were dead, you would be right (lit. your truth would be), for the Moslems and for the Christians she would be forbidden." |

1. E. Littmann, *Tigrē-Erzählungen* (*ZDMG* 65 1911, pp. 697-708), Nos. 2, 5. 2. Quadriliteral verb formed from the Ab participle *muslim*. 3. Gz *sabʾ*. 4. Gz *énta*. 5. (*w*)*ʿl*. 6. Gz *dāʾmū́*. 7. *ʾḫr*. 8. *mṣʾ*. 9. *ḫys* (imperfect). 10. *bhl*. 11. Gz *bezūḫ*. 12. Probably from *rada* 'be satisfied' < Ab *raḍiya*. 13. Gz *mōʿált*. 14. From *tlw* 'follow.' 15. Participle, with *e* < *a* < *ā* because of the laryngeal. 16. *ébba* 'in it' = 'at this moment,' repeated. 17. Probably from Ab *darb* 'way.' 18. *kry*. 19. *rʾy*. 20. *mwt*. 21. Gz *šegā́*. 22. Passive participle of the intensive. 23. *gbʾ*.

ደአም ፡ እላ ፡ መአዜ ፡ ክም ፡ ማይተት ፡ ትትዐለብ ። ወሀቶም ፡ እላዲ ፡ ሐራም ፡ ታ ፡ ቤለዎ ። ወሀቱ ፡ ሐድገያ ፤ ደአም ፡ እት ፡ ለእስላም ፡ ትቀጸባ ።

dáʾam élla máʾazē[24] kem mā́ität tetʿállab?" we-hetṓm "ellā́-dī[F] ḥarā́m-ta!" bḗlawō, we-hetū́ ḥádgaya,[25] dáʾam et le-eslā́m tqáṣṣaba.

But how (lit. when) can this be counted (lit. is counted) as dead?" And they said to him: "This is indeed forbidden." And he left her, but was angry with the Moslems. |

ወሐር ፡ አዳም ፡ አስክ ፡ ገለብ ፡ ገይስ ፡ ምን ፡ ረኣ ፤ እት ፡ ለመሳኒቱ ፡ ለክስታን ፡ ለሀለው ፡ ለአከዮም ፤ እት ፡ ምስልምና ፡ ኢትትሀየፎ ፤ እት ፡ ምስልምና ፡ ምን ፡ ተሀየፍኮ ፡ አናማ ፡ እተዐስሀሌኮ ፡ እንዶ ፡ ቤላ ።

wa-ḥar addā́m àsek[26] Gā́läb gáyis[27] men raʾá, et la-masānī́tū,[28] la-kestā́n la-hállau,[29] láʾakayōm: "et mesleménna[30] ī-tetháyafō! et mesleménna men tahayáfkō, anā́-ma ettáʿas[A]-hallḕkō." èndō[31] bḗla.

And later, when he saw people going to Galab, he sent her to his friends, who were Christians, saying: "Don't deceive yourselves about Islam! That (lit. since) I deceived myself with Islam, I now regret."

b) Reconciliation between God and the Devil

ድግም ፡ ሐቴ ፡ እሲት ፡ ላውሁት ፡ ሰመራ–እዝጊ ፡ ለልቡላ ። ሐቴ ፡ እዋን ፡ ምን ፡ መምህር ፡ አልኣዛር ፡ እሊ ፡ ድግም ፡ ሰምዐኮ ።

dégem ḥáttē[32] essī́t[33] lā́uhät,[F] Samarā-zgī́ la-lebū́la. ḥáttē uwā́n[A34] men mámher Alʾāzā́r éllī dégem samʿákō:

Story of a compassionate woman, whom they call Samara-zgi. One time I heard this story from Master Eliezer: |

እት ፡ ምድር ፡ ሐበሽ ፡ ሐቴ ፡ እሲት ፡ ጻድቀት ፡ ወላውሀት ፡ ሰመራ–እዝጊ ፡ ለትትበሀል ፡ ዐለት ።

et méder Ḥábaš ḥáttē essī́t ṣādqat wa-lā́uhät, Samarā-zgī́ la-tédbahal,[35] ʿálät.

In the land of Abyssinia was a just and compassionate woman, who was called Samara-zgi. |

ክህታ ፡ ሐስበት ፡ ረቢ ፡ ወሼጣን ፡ እግል ፡ ተዓሬ ። ወእት ፡ ረቢ ፡ እንዶ ፡ ጌሰት ፡ ቴሎ ፤ ምስል ፡ ሼጣን ፡ እግል ፡ ልትዓሬ ፤ ወብዙሕ ፡ ረምቀቶ ።

ke-hetá ḥásbät, rā́bbī[A] wa-šḗṭān[A36] ègel taʿā́rē.[37] we-et rā́bbī èndō gḗsät,[38] tḗllō,[39] mèsel šḗṭān ègel letʿā́rē. wa-bezúḥ ramqáttō.

And she thought that she would reconcile God and Satan. And when she went to God she said to him that he should reconcile himself with Satan. And she importuned him greatly. |

ወህቱ ፡ ቤላ ፤ ሰኒ ፡ እትዓሬ ፡ ምን ፡ ተመጽእዮ ፡ እቼ ። ወህታ ፡ ሰኒ ፡ ትቤ ፤ ከጌሰት ፡ ሼጣን ፡ እግል ፡ ተምጽእ ። ወእት ፡ ጀፈር ፡ ሕፍረት ፡ ጀሀነብ ፡ ክም ፡ በጽሐት ፤ ዎ ፡ ድያብሎስ ፡ እት ፡ ትብል ፡ ትላኬት ።

we-hetū́ bḗlla: "sā́nnī,[40] etʿā́rē, men taṃaṣṣʾiyṓ[41]-èččē." we-hetá "sā́nnī!" tebḗ[42] ka-gḗsät, šḗṭān, ègel támṣiʾ. we-ed[43] ǧā́fär[A] ḥéfrät[A] ǧahánnäb[A44] kem báṣeḥat, "wō diyā́blōs!"[45] et tebél, tlākḗt.[46]

And he said: "Good, I will reconcile myself, if you bring him to me." And she said "Good!" and went to fetch Satan. And when she arrived at the edge of the pit of hell, she called, saying, "O Devil!" |

24. Gz *yeʾezḗ* 'now,' *māʾezḗ* 'when?.' 25. *ḫdg.* 26. = Gz *éska* 'until.' 27. Imperfect. 28. From *šny* 'beautiful.' 29. *hlw.* 30. Abstract ending *-nā.* 31. From Gz *énza* 'while.' 32. *ʾḥd.* 33. Shortened from Gz *beʾesī́t* 'woman.' 34. Ab *awān iwān* 'time.' 35. $d < t$. 36. < Ab *šēṭān*, itself borrowed from Gz *šaiṭā́n.* 37. *ʿry.* 38. *gys.* 39. *bhl.* 40. *šny.* 41. With feminine ending *-ī.* 42. *bhl.* 43. $d < t$. 44. Ab *ǧahannam*, with $b < m$ (dissimilation). 45. *διάβολος.* 46. *lky.*

ወድያብሎስ፡ምን፡ሕፍረቱ፡ፈግራ፡ወእንዶ፡ነዝዐያ፡እት፡ለአካኑ፡ትከራ፡ባ።	*wa-diyā́blōs men ḥéfrätū fágra, we-éndō názʿaya, et la-akā́nū*[47] *tkarrā́-ba.*	And the devil came out of his pit and, seizing her, climbed down with her to his place. |
ደአም፡ረቢ፡እብ፡ለውሀታ፡ፈቅዳ፤ ከመልኣኩ፡ነድኣ፡ወምን፡ጀሀነብ፡ምን፡እዴ፡ሼጣን፡አፍገረያ፡ልብሎ።	*dáʾam rā́bbī eb láuhata fáqeda ka-malʾā́kū nádʾa wa-men ǰahánnäb men edḕ šḗṭān áfgaraya, léblō.*	But God thought of her compassion and sent his angel, and he plucked her out of the hands of Satan, they say.

47. = Gz *makān*, noun of place from *kṓna* 'he was, became.'

III. Mehri

§ 5/3.0 The group of Semitic languages to which the languages of the Old South Arabic inscriptions belong is still represented in southern Arabia and the islands south of it by several living dialects, of which the most important is Mehri.

Mehri retains traces of the greatest antiquity. It still differentiates the trio of proto-Semitic sibilants and retains practically the entire proto-Semitic consonant inventory (though with diminution of its old integrity), with the single exception of ᶜ; the pronouns are simply the old forms — most notably the leveling of the stem consonants of the third person masculine and feminine, elsewhere complete, has not taken place. The vowels display to the highest degree the Semitic peculiarity of great freedom of articulation. Verbal inflection is very complicated; with Ethiopic, Mehri shares the existence of a subjunctive differing in the stem from the indicative. The individuality of the dialect is obscured by the far-reaching influence of North Arabic, which affects especially the vocabulary but also the morphology, and which found itself welcomed so hospitably that North and South Arabic from the beginning closely resemble each other. —

§ 5/3.1.1 Proto- and North Semitic *š* is replaced by *ś* (a lateral *š*-sound), *ś* by *š*, while proto- and Common Semitic *s* is also *s* in Mehri;[a] yet the three sounds are often confused, and *h* appears in many roots for *ś* < *š*, e.g., *hṓbā* 'seven' < **šab*ᶜ, *hīma* 'he heard' from **šm*ᶜ. *ṣ* can indifferently be pronounced *ẓ* (here transcribed as *ṣ*).[b] *ḍ* still has the old lateral realization. *g*, as in the neighboring North Arabic dialects, has become *d′*. ᶜ is lost, either replaced by ᵓ or disappearing without a trace; roots containing ᶜ form a new class of weak roots. Initial ᵓ often becomes *h*, e.g., *hē* 'what?' < *ᵓ*aiy*, *hām* 'mother' < *ᵓ*imm*, or even *ḥ*, e.g., *ḥeib* 'father' < *ᵓ*ab*; *ḥ*- also occurs

a. Epigraphic South Arabic sibilants are transliterated with numerical superscripts to avoid prejudicing phonetic considerations. The regular correspondences are ESA s^1 = H (and CS) *š*, ESA s^2 = H *ś*, and ESA s^3 = H (and CS) *s*. GRAPHICALLY, however, ESA s^1 = Ph *s*, ESA s^2 = Ph *š*, and ESA s^3 < two s^2's.

b. In Mehri a dot under a letter indicates glottalized rather than emphatic articulation.

before a prothetic vowel, e.g., *ḥamū* 'water' < **māyu*, *ḥa/erē* 'head' < **raʾš*, *ḥaliy* 'at night' < **lailai.*

§ 5/3.1.2 Vowel quality exhibits the most enormous and astounding variation within a single word, let alone in the same position in different words, and not only with short vowels but even to a considerable extent with the long ones. The long vowels center around *ī* and *ē* (between which the boundary is not always firm) on one side, and *ō* and *ū* (even less clearly distinguished) on the other; the two groups undergo *i*-umlaut, by which *ī* commonly replaces *ō* before an *i* in the next syllable. In the middle *ā* occurs comparatively rarely: it is found, in certain words only, in the position of the usual *ē*. Laryngeals and emphatics diphthongize neighboring *i*'s to *ai* etc., *u*'s to *au* etc. The quantity of the vowels is completely dependent on the accent; in general, only the vowel of the accented syllable is long, if this is an open penult (*ā̆dem* 'man') or an open or simply-closed final (*hamā* 'hear,' *siyōr* 'he went'); doubly-closed syllables usually retain the short vowel when accented, even when the cluster is resolved by an epenthetic vowel (*ṣadéqak* 'you spoke the truth,' the same formation as *amérk* 'you said').[1] With the addition of pronominal suffixes, the vowel of the accented syllable is often shortened; its quality then frequently changes, due to the great variability of the short vowels. Anaptyctic vowels are common; the variations that result from their presence or absence, or (on the other hand) from the disappearance or retention of unstressed short vowels, are also noticeable. — The relation of the present vocalism to the old system is very complicated; besides spontaneous alterations (such as the changes *ā* > *ō* and *ā* > *ē*), there are assimilations to neighboring consonants and especially the effects of the accent. Placement of the accent is sure for each

1. From this follows the stress rule that if a word has one and only one long vowel (or diphthong), this bears the accent. In all other cases the accent is marked.

particular nominal or verbal pattern; it is more characteristic of the pattern than is the distribution, quantity, or quality of the vowels. —

§ 5/3.2.1

The personal pronouns are *ho/u* 'I,' *hēt* 'thou,' *he* 'he,' *si* 'she';[c] *nha* 'we,' *tem* 'you' masculine, feminine *ten*, *hem* 'they' masculine, feminine *sen*.[d] The suffixes for the singular are -(*n*)*ī* -*k* -*š* (with a shift also found elsewhere of a *k* beside original *i*) -*h* -*s* (extended after a plural by an appended -*e*); 'our, us' is -*n*, for second and third person plural the forms are those of the independent pronoun.[e] The preceding vowel is usually *e*; but after the monoliteral prepositions, etc., e.g., *šūk* 'with thee,' *šēn* 'with us,' *šīš* 'with her' (as against *šeh* 'with him'). The accusatives of the personal pronouns are supplied by the accusative particle *t*- + pronominal suffix. 'This' is *dā* (feminine *dī*, plural *lā*), strengthened *dōm*, 'that' *dāk*.[f] The relative is *d*-, plural *l*-, with both as genitive particle as well;[g] there is also a generalized relative *hal*. 'Who?' is *mōn*, 'what?' *hē* (often extended *hē/āśen*, corresponding to the Ab *ēš* < *aiyu šaiʾin* 'which thing?').[h] —

c. There are also dual personal pronouns: 'we two' *ékey*, 'you two' *étey*, 'they two' *hey*.

d. In Epigraphic South Arabic only the third person is certainly attested; there the contrast between forms with *h* and forms with *s* is dialectal (Sb *h*, Mn Qt *s*). Ḥaḍramautian, however, has masculine *š*, feminine *s*(/*θ*) (cf. Sh *š*, *s*); this seems to underlie the Mehri situation (with *h* < *š*, see § 5/3.1.1), which thus cannot be taken as evidence for the proto-Semitic state of affairs (R. Steiner).

e. Johnstone □5/3b:3,15&16 gives modern forms of the second person plural suffixes as -*kem* -*ken*.

f. Epigraphic South Arabic demonstratives are built on the stem *s*, or (in Sabean) *h*; *δ* also occurs.

g. Epigraphic South Arabic has *δ* relatives, and also *ʾl* in both singular and plural.

h. Epigraphic South Arabic has an emphatic particle *ʾy*.

§ 5/3.2.2

-*i*/*em*, etc., replaces the usual verbal plural ending -*ū*. In the perfect the feminine plural has no ending; in the imperfect it ends with the CS -*n*. The third person feminine singular of the perfect ends with accented -*ō*/*ūt*. For the rest, the perfect suffixes are the same as the pronominal suffixes, except that the first person singular is the same as the second person masculine -*k*. The plural ending -*i*/*em* and the ending -*ī* of the second person feminine singular imperfect etc. often cause umlaut in the preceding syllable. The imperfect prefixes are the old Semitic ones. In many forms the imperfect indicative differs from the subjunctive in the shape of the stem, and in the intensive and reflexive stems in the ending -*en* as well.[i]

i. In Epigraphic South Arabic, the verb is inflected for the dual number; the imperfect and infinitive can take a suffix -*n*, perhaps corresponding to a demonstrative *-*ān*.

§ 5/3.2.2.3

The perfect of the basic stem has three different formations, with in addition to (1) the active-mode and (2) the neutral-mode conjugations, (3) a special conjugation for II laryngeal roots (except for II ᶜ roots, which are inflected weakly); in the imperfect etc., the second and third series merge. Exemplifying the first series are: *amōr* 'he said,' *kafōd* 'he got up,' *ḫarōd'* 'he went, brought out,' *yalōq* 'he saw,' *qabōr* 'he buried,' *ṣadōq* 'he spoke the truth,' *ftōḥ* 'he opened,' *herō/ūd'* 'he supported himself'; feminine *amrō/ūt kafdōt*, first/second person *amérk ṣadéqak heréd'ek*, plural *amōrem herōd'em*, but *ḫarīd'em*, with pronominal suffix *qabā́rmeh* 'they buried him.'[j] The second series has initial accent: *aimel* 'he made,' *aileq* 'he burned,' *ḍaibeṭ* 'he took possession of,' but feminine *amlūt* as in the first series. The third series again has final accent, but with *ā/ē* as the vowel of the accented syllable: *saḥāṭ* 'slew,' *śhēd* 'he gave testimony'; second person *sḥā́/áṭäk*. In the imperfect only the first series distinguishes indicative and subjunctive: indicative *yifōteḥ*, subjunctive *yiftāḥ*; and thus imperative *ftāḥ*, *yalā́/ēq* 'see,' with pronominal suffix, e.g., *qabā́rmeh* 'bury him.' In the second and third series the imperfect has only one form: *yeśhōd*, plural *yeśhīdem*, imperative *śhōd*, feminine *śhīd* (irregularly *yiḍōṭ* from *ḍaibeṭ*). The participle — in Mehri the usual means of expressing the future — takes the special ending *-ōne* in the basic stem (with pronominal suffix, e.g., *-áneh*), feminine *-īte*, plural *-ā/ēye*.

j. The plural suffix can also be *-am -om*: *zāqam* 'they called,' *qoṣṣom* 'they cut.'

§ 5/3.2.2.4 The intensive no longer has lengthening: *kōteb*, etc. The causative prefix is *h*, e.g., *hālū́q* 'he kindled,' imperfect *yihālṓq*, subjunctive *yihāleq*; but this is missing in some verbs in some forms, e.g., *ḫaṣoub* 'he sent,' imperfect *yiḫaṣōb*, but subjunctive *yiháḫṣab* and imperative *háḫṣab*. The reflexive formations are idiosyncratic:[k] the *t* of the *t*-reflexive is always infixed, with various vowel relations: *ḫtiyūr* 'he chose' (imperfect *yaḫtiyīren*, subjunctive *yaḫtiyōr*, imperative *ḫtiyōr*), but *yátirī*

k. Mehri also has a passive of the basic stem with perfect in the shape VCCV̄C and imperfect *ya*CCV̄C.

'he spoke'; and in the causative-reflexive, instead of the *st*-, etc., of other languages there is a simple *š*: *šḫabōr* 'he questioned,' imperfect *yišaḫbōr*, subjunctive *yišáḫber*, imperative *šáḫber*.[1] The participles of the derived stems have the usual prefix *m*-, with the ending *-e* as well. — An example of quadriliteral formation is *tḫoulū́l* 'he sat,' plural *tḫūlī́lim* (feminine singular with divergent stem *tḫouwelṓt*).

Mehri is not so poor in weak verb forms as Ge^{c}ez. II geminate verbs have monosyllabic perfects: *qoṣṣ* 'he cut off,' *śoll* 'he took' (feminine *śällōt*, plural *śállem*), and also participles *qoṣṣōne* (plural *qaṣṣāye*); otherwise they are triliteral: imperfect *yiś(e)lūl*, subjunctive *yiśelēl* (with pronominal suffix, e.g., *neśeléleh*), imperative *qaṣāṣ* (plural *qaṣāṣem*). — The I *w* verbs lose their first radical only in the subjunctive (and imperative), not in the imperfect indicative: *yiqā* 'may he become,' *yizēm* 'may he give,' but *yiwṓqā yiwūzem*. Otherwise they exhibit only minor vagaries: *we/uqōb* 'he entered,' *we/uzōm* 'he gave' (with pronominal suffix *ūzeméh*; feminine *ūqebū́t*), participle *wuzemōne* (with pronominal suffix *ūzemének*); causative *hūqū́b* (plural *hūqī́bem*). — In the II weak verbs the strong forms gain ground: *mōt* 'he died,' *kān* 'he was' (feminine *mtūt*), imperfect *tkūn*, subjunctive *tkān*: but *siyōr* 'he went' (feminine *sīrū́t*), imperfect *yisiūr*, subjunctive *yisiēr* (imperative with contraction *sēr*). — In the II weak verbs the neutral-mode series has initial stress, just like the strong verbs: *bedú* 'he lied,' *ksu* 'he found,' *d'irú* 'he went by,' *ṭowú* 'he came in the night' (feminine *d'irūt ṭowōt*, first/second person *bōdek kusk*): but *mīle* 'he was full.'

The old classes of weak verbs are augmented by verbs containing ^{c}. An example for I ^{c} is the above-mentioned *aileq* 'he burned,' causative *hālū́q*; examples for II ^{c} *ḥām* (really

1. The Epigraphic South Arabic stems attested are the basic and causative (with formative *h* in Sabean, *s* elsewhere), each with infixed-*t* reflexive (giving *-st* in Sabean); putative intensive

and goal stems, each with prefixed-*t* reflexive; and a stem with double middle radical, presumably representing **qatātala*, perhaps with "frequentative" meaning. The only passives are internal passives.

II *w*) 'he wanted,' *zāq* 'he called,' *bār* 'he went in the night' (feminine *bārṓt*), imperfect *tḥōm naḥōm* (indicative and subjunctive alike). The III ᶜ verbs differentiate the active-mode and the neutral-mode in the basic stem: *nū́kā* 'he came' (feminine *nkōt*, first/second person *núkāk*, plural *núkām*): but *wī́qā* 'he became,' *hīma* 'he heard' (second person plural *hámākem*, first person *hámān*); imperfect the same in both series, indicative *yinṓkā*, subjunctive *yinkā*, imperative *nka*, and *yiwṓqā yiqā hamā*. An *h*-less causative that belongs here is *firā* 'he went up' (feminine *firōt*), imperfect *yifōra*, but subjunctive *yiháfera*. —

§ 5/3.2.3

The feminine ending of the noun receives the accent when the stem has no original long vowel; it is then *-ōt* or *-ēt*. The plural ending is *-īn*, feminine *-ōt*(*en*); besides this there are, as elsewhere in South Semitic, broken plurals, like *mṣoubaḥ* for *mṣabāḥ* 'lamp,' sometimes with an ending, like *ad'izōn* for *ad'ūz* 'old woman.'[m] A great number of these formations are genuinely South Arabic; others come from North Arabic influence. An article no more exists in Mehri than in Geᶜez. —

m. Epigraphic South Arabic nominal patterns include abstracts with *n*- or *t*-, and nouns of place with *m*-. Plurals include many *-t* suffixes on masculine nouns, and broken plurals with ᵓ-prefix or infixed *y* or *w*. Note the reduplicated ᵓ*l*ᵓ*lt* 'gods.'

§ 5/3.2.4

As the Mehri lexicon includes much that is peculiar to it, lacking parallels even in Ethiopic, so is particularly the case with the particles. The old preposition *b*- 'in, with, by' is unchanged; the old *l*- (dative particle), though, has been replaced by *h*-, while an existing *l*- 'on, after, to' corresponds much more closely to Ab ᶜ*alā* (partly also *ilā*).[n] Two further monoliteral prepositions are *š*- and *k*- 'with' (the first before a pronominal suffix, the second before a substantive); multiliteral ones besides the old *mi*/*en* 'from, out of' (*mänk* 'from you') are *ha*/*ä*/*el* 'at, to' (*lä-häl* 'to'), *ser* 'behind,' *ṭar* 'above'; *birék* 'in,' *tuwól* (only with pronominal suffix) 'hither,' *nḫáli* 'under,' *berék*[o] 'between, among.'

n. In Epigraphic South Arabic, Sabean and Qatabanian retain the old *l*-, and Minean the old *k*-.

o. Addition of A. Schaade □ 1:6R6,170.

Among the conjunctions, there are several that are widespread: *ū-* (*we-*, *w-*) 'and' (and *ullū* 'or'),[p] *tā̆/ē* 'until, as soon as, when,'[q] *he/än* 'if';[r] and several that are specifically Mehri, e.g., *hīs* 'as,' and the preposition *l-*, which with the subjunctive expresses 'should.' The adverb *ber* 'already' is used as a verbal particle very similarly to the Ab *qad.* The negative particle is *lā*,[s] which is, however, postposed, as the interrogatives often are.[t] —

p. ESA *ᵓw*, *fᵓw*.

q. ESA *ywm* 'when.'

r. ESA *hm*, *hn*.

s. ESA *ᵓl* before perfect and imperfect, *lm* before imperfect and jussive.

§ 5/3.4

The vocabulary is swamped with North Arabic elements; but these are in general strongly assimilated to the phonology, especially the vowel relations, and morphology of Mehri, and therefore do little to attenuate its peculiar character. It is not possible to distinguish them throughout with certainty from cognates that happen to also be present in North Arabic.

t. Epigraphic South Arabic syntax, as attested, involves simple parataxis with very rare exceptions. An action expressed by a finite verb may be continued by any number of infinitives, with or without the *-n* suffix.

Text Specimen

The Talking Head[2]

[A] after a word indicates that it also occurs in Arabic with the same consonants in the same meaning.

nṹkā[3] *ṭād faḍouli,*[A] *siyōr häl doulet*[A] *w-amōr heh: "yaid' ṭād nṹkā bä-mqahōyit,*[A] *amōr, ksū*[4] *ḥarē da-ben-ādem*[A] *ū-herūd' šeh."*

amōr doulet: "yábem[5] *yaid' l-änkā!" siyōrem, zāqam*[A6] *teh, amōrem heh: "hamā*[7] *doulet." ū-siyōr.*

tā̈ nṹkā häl doulet, amōr heh: "hēt men hō?"[8] *amōr: "ho min d'ibā̈l."*[A] *amōr: "hā̈śen kusk?"*[9]

amōr: "kusk ḥerē ū-heréd'ek šeh. amérk heh: 'a ḥarē! hā̈śen nṹkā būk būm?' amōr: 'wusāẖ[A] *dä-dunyā̈.'"*[A] *amōr heh doulet: "sēr!"*

w-ūzeméh rabōt askēr[A] *l-eśhīdem leh, w-amōr heh: "hän ṣadéqak,*[A] *ūzemének häl tḥōm,*[A10] *ū-hän bōdek,*[11] *qoṣṣṓne*[A12] *ḥerēk."*

siyōr, he w-askēr. tā̈ núkām hal ḥarē, amōr heh: "a ḥarē! hā̈śen nṹkā būk būm?" amōr: "wusāẖ dä-dunyā̈."

There came a gossip, he went to the sultan and said to him: "A man came into the coffeehouse (and) said he had found the head of a man (lit. son of Adam) and conversed with it."| The sultan said: "Let the man come here!" They went (and) called him, they said to him: "Obey the sultan!" And he went. | When he came to the sultan, he said to him: "Where are you from?" He said: "I am from the mountain." He said: "What have you found?"| He said: "I have found a head and conversed with it. I said to it: 'O head! What brought you here (lit. came here with you)?' It said: 'The filth of the world.'" The sultan said to him: "Go!"| And he gave him many soldiers to vouch for him, and said to him: "If you have told the truth, I will give you whatever you want, but if you have lied, I will cut your head off."| He went, he and the soldiers. When they came to the head, he said to it: "O head! What has brought you here?" It said: "The filth of the world."|

2. A. Jahn, *Die Mehri-Sprache in Südarabien* 1902, pp. 78-81 = M. Bittner, *Studien zur Laut- und Formenlehre der Mehri-Sprache in Südarabien* V, 2 1915, pp. 22-27. 3. III laryngeal. 4. III weak. 5. Interjection *yāb* + plural ending. 6. *z*ᶜ*q*. 7. *šm*ᶜ. 8. 'where?.' 9. From *ksū*. 10. II weak. 11. III weak. 12. *qṣṣ*.

amōr h-āskḗr: "hámākem?" amōrem: "hámān, lākén[A] *naḥōm neśeléleh*[13] *šēn hä*[14]*-rḥabḗt."*[A] *ū-śā́llemeh šēhem.*
tā̈ núkām beh häl doulet, amōr hēhem: "hámākem teh herōd′?" amōrem: "yalā̈q[15] *ḥerē, ū-šáẖberem*[A] *teh!"*
amōr heh doulet: "ho mšáẖbere ḥerē, ū-hän herōd′ lā, ḥerēk qaṣṣāyeh!"[A] *. . . ẖarīd′em*[A] *ḥarē ū-herōd′em šeh, yátirī*[16] *lā.*

amōr doulet: "qaṣāṣem ḥeréh!" qóṣṣom ḥeréh. hīs ber qóṣṣom ḥerēh, yátirī ḥerē qṓśā, amōr heh:

"yalēq, hu ber amérk hūk: 'nū́kā bī wusāẖ dä-dunyā̈.'" nū́kā dóulet, amṓr: "qabä́rmeh!"[A] *ū-qabä́rmeh. . . .*
ū-šeh ḥäbríth kafdōt här[17] *raḥbēt, nkōt häl ad′ūz,*[A] *tẖouwelṓt. hīs nehōr,*[A] *amlūt*[A18] *ḥanáfs*[19] *dára*ᵓ[A] *dä-ḥadīd*[A] *ū-kálleh*[A] *mṣoubäḥ,*[A] *ū-halqōt*[A20] *beh.*

hīs fáqaḥ[21] *dä-ḥalīy,*[22] *śällōt ais ū-bārṓt.*[23] *tā̈ ṭowōt*[A24] *häl būwṓb,*[A] *amrūt heh: "ftāḥ!"*[A] *amōr hīs: "hēt mōn?"*

*amrōt: "hu mä́l*ᵓ*ek-el-móut."*[A25] *amōr: "tḥōm l-hō?" amrōt: "ḥōm*[u] *lä-häl doulet." ū-ftōḥ hīs . . . ū-d′irūt.*[A26]

u. < *aḥom* (Schaade).

He said to the soldiers: "Have you heard?" They said: "We have heard, but we want to take it back to the city with us." And they took it with them. | When they came to the sultan with it, he said to them: "Did you hear it talk?" They said: "Look at the head, and question it (yourself)!" | The sultan said to him: "I will question the head, and if it does not speak, they'll cut your head off." . . . They brought the head out and talked to it, (but) it did not respond. | The sultan said: "Cut his head off!" They cut off his head. When they had cut off his head, the dessicated head responded (and) said to him: | "See, I already told you: 'The filth of the world brought me (here).'" The sultan came and said: "Bury it!" And they buried it. . . . | And with him was his daughter. She descended to the city (and) came to an old woman (and) stayed (lit. sat) (there). One day (lit. when a day [was]), she herself made armor out of iron and full of lamps, and she lit it. | When it was midnight she took a dagger and went out. When she came to the gatekeeper she said to him: "Open!" He said to her: "Who are you?" | She said: "I am the angel of death." He said: "Where are you going?" She said: "I want to go to the sultan." And he opened for her . . . and she passed. |

13. *śll.* 14. *hal.* 15. Text *yalä.* 16. *yry.* 17. *hal.* 18. ᶜ*ml.* 19. *ḥanāf* 'soul.' 20. ᶜ*lq.* 21. 'half.' 22. Text *ḥalī(u).* 23. *b*ᶜ*r.* 24. *ṭwy.* 25. Arabic genitival phrase with article, taken over unaltered. 26. *ǰry.*

. . . tē firōt,[27] *nkōt häl doulet, amrūt heh: "salām alēk!"*[A28] *amōr doulet: "alēk es-salām!*[A28] *mōn tkūn?"*[A29] *amrōt: "mā́lᵓek-el-móut.*
ū-núkāk tuwólke maqadē γaid′ dōm, dä-sḥāṭäk." amōr heh: "hu häl bálī mänk." amōr: "ū-ánᵓam[A30] *bā́lī!*

ū-hēt ẖtiyōr:[A] *l-äḍōṭ*[A31] *ámerek,*[A32] *ullū tezēm*[33] *ḥeib dä-γaid′ dōm, dä-sḥáṭäk, raḥbēt?" amōr: "wuzemōne ḥeib dä-γaid′ raḥbēt."*
amrūt: "háẖṣab leh!" ū-ẖaṣoub leh w-ūzeméh raḥbēt nẖáli śhūd. hūqī́bem[34] *teh doulet u-ṯoulū́l, ū-doulet dāk wī́qā*[A35] *wuzīr.*[A]

. . . When she had ascended, she came to the sultan and said to him: "Peace to you!" The sultan said: "To you peace! Who are you?" She said: "The angel of death. | And I have come to you on account of this man whom you have slain." He said to him (sic): "I am with God (i.e. under his protection) before you." He (sic) said: "And God (be) gracious! | And you choose: shall I take your life, or will you give the city to the father of the man you slew?" He said: "I will give the city to the man's father." | She said: "Send for him!" And he sent for him and gave him the city before witnesses. They installed him as sultan and (so) he remained, and the sultan became vizier.

27. III laryngeal. 28. Taken over from Arabic unaltered (only without the ᶜ of *ᶜalēk*). 29. *kwn*. 30. Ab *anᶜam* 'gracious.' 31. *ḍbṭ*. 32. Ab *ᶜamr* (*ᶜumr*). 33. *wzm*. 34. *wqb*. 35. *wqᶜ*.

Chapter 6

North Arabic

I. Classical Arabic

§ 6/1.0 Except for the language of the South Arabic inscriptions, it is Classical Arabic[1] that has best preserved the consonant inventory of old Semitic, and likewise the vocalism, so that the old inflection has not been destroyed by the loss of the endings. In spite of these very archaic features, Arabic is on the whole the most striking representative of a more recent development in the Semitic language character: older freedom, individual variation, and indefiniteness are effaced — in morphology by the pervasive influence of unifying analogies, in syntax by strict regulation of the possibilities of usage and the allocation of all syntactic means of expression to carefully demarcated spheres of meaning. A system of great precision and clarity has thus developed, which in the process has made extensive and productive use of the broad potential that was available. The preserved remains of Old Arabic dialects and occasional irregularities of the poetry give glimpses of earlier, less constrained linguistic conditions previous to and independent of the classical language.

§ 6/1.1.1 South Semitic as a whole has interchanged the sibilants *ś* and *š*; while the South Arabic inscriptions keep the resulting state of affairs, in Arabic as in Ethiopic the new *ś* < *š* has further become *s* and so merged with the original *s*. Above and beyond that, the current traditional pronunciation of Arabic alters the original proto-Semitic sounds to the extent that *θ̣* is replaced by *ẓ* and *δ̣* by *ḍ*. *θ̣* can be identified in older times,

1. The examples in this section are occasionally taken from the Colloquial Arabic specimens of the next section and back-translated into Classical Arabic.

and probably also still in modern dialects; for *ḍ* the classical pronunciation is as lateral emphatic spirant (thus a sound distantly related to *l*),[a] and this pronunciation likely comes very near to the proto-Semitic value only roughly indicated by the transcription *δ̣*. *g* is palatalized to *ǰ*; *q* was in older days voiced (*ġ*). The laryngeals are retained as full consonants, as are the semivowels in general as well. In syllable-final position these form a diphthong or long vowel with the preceding vowel (*iw* and *uy* both usually > *ī*). After short vowels they are retained when *ā* follows (*ayā*, etc.), or when *a* follows and *i* or *u* precedes (*iwa* and *uya* both > *iya*). Otherwise they are contracted, to *ī* when the preceding as well as the following vowel was *i* or *u*; but if the preceding vowel was *a*, to *ā*, for which *ē* is recognizable as the older pronunciation. In the III weak roots, except in the active basic stem of the verb and some of the nouns, *w* throughout becomes *y*.

a. See § 1 note g.

§ 6/1.1.2 Most old final long vowels are shortened.

Arabic has very elaborate sandhi rules (governing word combination within clauses); the most important is that the epenthetic vowel that intrudes before a word-initial consonant cluster (e.g., imperative *ifʿal*; in fact usually *i*) occurs only utterance-initially, but disappears after a vowel within clausal context, in which case a long vowel is shortened (*fī* 'in' + *al-baiti* 'of the house' > *filbaiti*[2] 'in the house'); but a final consonant requires an epenthetic vowel (usually *i*, but, e.g., *min* 'out of' + *al-baiti* > *minalbaiti*[3] 'out of the house'). A special treatment of utterance-final (pause) forms goes along with the sandhi rules; it is usually not taken into account in the writing of vowels and has therefore been left out of the text

2. The script preserves the length, and consequently it is transcribed in these materials.

3. *-al-* in this combination differs in the absence of the strong onset (glottal stop) from the *al-* of absolute initial position.

specimens, except for the prose rhymes of the Koran excerpt. The chief feature of the pause is the loss of short-vowel endings (including the *-un*, etc. that end with *n*). —

§ 6/1.2.1

'He' and 'she' are *huwa hiya*. The masculine plurals 'you,' 'they' generally lose their endings: *antum* (suffix *-kum*) *hum*. The feminines have taken over the *u* of the masculines: *antunna* (suffix *-kunna*) *hunna*. 'My' after a long vowel is still *-ya* (e.g., *fīya* 'in me'), elsewhere usually *-ī* (also 'me' *-nī*). The third person suffixes with *u* change it to *i* after final *-i -ī -ai*: *-hĭ̄ -him -hinna*. *-hŭ̄ -hĭ̄* retains its long vowel after a short syllable.[b] The accusative of the personal pronouns can be expressed, where direct suffixation is not possible, with the object particle *īyā-* with pronominal suffix, which is used only in that case (before a substantive it is unnecessary, since in this case the accusative is recognizable from the ending): *īyāka* 'thee.'[c]

b. This is a determination by Bergsträsser's teacher Fischer □6/1.2.1:1 that has gone largely unnoticed and unremarked; it is based on metrics and on the testimony of Arab grammarians.

c. It is possible to conjoin suffixes on a single verb form, with disambiguation between direct and indirect objects accomplished on pragmatic grounds: a first or second person suffix is taken as indirect object, and a second or third person as direct object.

The article is *al-*; its *l* is assimilated to a following dental, sibilant, or sonorant, and its *a* acts secondarily as epenthetic vowel before a double consonant. The possibility of using the definite article on a generic (*ar-rağulu* 'the man' = 'one') is realized in the syntax quite consistently. As demonstrative Arabic uses numerous forms of the stems *δ-*, *l-*, and *k-*, often strengthened by *hā*, the particle that in Hebrew constitutes the article; the most usual forms are 'this' *hāδā*, feminine *hāδihī*, plural *hāʾulāʾi* (for all cases); 'that' *δālika*, *tilka*, *ulāʾika*; also the particle *hākaδā* 'thus' containing the prefix *ka-* 'like.' The demonstratives go BEFORE the substantive they modify: *hāδā r-rağulu* 'this man.' From the stem *δ/l-* Arabic forms a declinable construct state *δū*, feminine *δātu*, plural *ulū* 'belonging to,' 'posssessing such and such,' etc.; so *δāta yaumin* 'one day.' The stem *δ-* with the article further furnishes the (generally indeclinable) relative *allaδī* 'which' (also 'he who,' 'that which'), feminine *allatī*, plural *allaδīna*, which, being definite, can only occur after a definite substantive (or as a definite substantive itself). Besides this the interrogative pronouns *man* 'who?,' *mā* 'what?' can be used as substantival, indefinite, and generalizing relatives: *man* 'who,' 'one who,' more commonly interpreted as plural (though construed as singular) 'people who.' The generalizing meaning 'whoever' shades into the conditional 'if anyone'; therefore these relatives tend to have conditional sequence of tenses (see § 6/1.3). *mā* simultaneously is a conjunction 'the fact that' and attached to prepositions forms compound conjunctions (contained also in *lammā* 'when, after'). 'Which?' is *aiyun*, constructed with genitive; *aiyu šaiʾin* 'which thing?' = 'what?.' —

§ 6/1.2.2.1 The vowels of the perfect suffixes correspond to those of the pronominal suffixes; the first person singular suffix deviates: it has the old vowel, but the *t* of the second person. The suffixless forms of the perfect end, as in Ethiopic, with *-a*. The verb — like the pronoun and noun — distinguishes the dual, though only in the second and third persons. The dual ending is *-ā* (second person perfect *-tumā*, third person feminine *-atā*). In the indicative of the imperfect this ending is extended with *-ni*, and correspondingly the plural ending *-ū* with *-na*: *-ūna*.[d] Besides the indicative, which in the suffixless forms ends with *-u*, there are a subjunctive with *-a*, an apocopate (wish form, additionally to some extent equivalent to the perfect) without a final vowel,[e] and an energic (emphatic description or command) with *-an*(*na*). For sharper definition and modification of the tense meaning the auxiliary verb *kāna* 'he was' and verbal particles, especially *qad* and *sa-*, are used. *kāna* with perfect expresses the pre-past, and with imperfect, habit in the past; *qad* with perfect, factualness, also expectedness or unexpectedness, and with imperfect, what might actually occur

d. The second person feminine singular has the suffix *-ī*(*na*).

e. Usually called the jussive.

in the present; *sa*- with imperfect, the future. But the simple tenses can also express these meaning-modifications to a certain degree, so long as no great weight is placed on them.

§ 6/1.2.2.2 The full range of possibilities of deriving verb stems with prefixes and infixes is diminished in Arabic; instead, a rich use is made of internal modifications of the stem (lengthening or diphthongization of vowels, lengthening or repetition of consonants), even though only a few of the forms thus developed achieve great frequency. The productive verb stems are: basic stem with *n*- and *t*- reflexives (the latter with infixing of the *t* after the first radical); intensive, with *ta*-reflexive; causative (with prefix *a*-) and *t*-reflexive for it (with deviant prefix, namely *st*-), and finally a so-called goal stem, characterized by lengthening of the first stem vowel, along with a *ta*-reflexive; and a passive to each of the stems. The vocalization of the derived stems, beyond the above-mentioned final vowels, follows simple rules: in the active of all the stems except the two *ta*-reflexives, the last syllable of the imperfect stem has *i*, the imperfect prefixes of the intensive, causative, and goal stems have *u*,[f] and all other syllables have *a*; in the perfect passive the last syllable of the stem has *i*, the other syllables *u*, and in the imperfect the prefix has *u*, the other syllables *a*. The participles of the derived stems have the prefix *mu*- and otherwise the vowels of the imperfect; only the two *ta*-reflexives constitute an exception, in that their active participles, following those of the other actives, have *i* in the last syllable of the stem. Most infinitives are indicated by *ā* in the last syllable of the stem and *i* earlier (e.g., *imsākun* 'holding back' from the causative, *intiṣārun* 'to help' from the *t*-reflexive of the basic stem), but those of the two *ta*-reflexives have *u* in the last syllable of the stem and *a* before (*ta*ᶜ*allumun* 'to learn'); from the intensive

f. Perhaps this reflects a dissimilation to help avoid confusion between *taqattala* and *tuqattilu*, *taqātala* and *tuqātilu*, *taqtulu* and *tuqtilu*.

stem is formed *taqlīdun* 'to mimic'; in the goal stem the feminine participle of the passive can also be used as the infinitive (*muwādaᶜatun* 'reconciliation').

§ **6/1.2.2.3**   In the basic stem all the vocalization schemes are realized: active-mode perfect *a*, imperfect *u* (*daḫala* 'he came in,' *yadḫulu*), or *i* (*ᶜarafa* 'he recognized,' *yaᶜrifu*) — *a* only in laryngeal verbs (*δahaba* 'he went out,' *yaδhabu*); neutral-mode perfect *i*, imperfect *a* (*ᶜalima* 'he knew, knows' *yaᶜlamu*; *qabila* 'he received,' *yaqbalu*) or, rarely, perfect *u*, imperfect *u*. The imperative has taken over first-radical vowellessness from the imperfect and therefore needs an epenthetic vowel: *imši* 'go,' but *uskut* 'be quiet.' The infinitive has an unusually large number of forms; among them *faᶜlatun* for a one-time action (feminine ending, as often, individualizing): *ḍarbatun* 'single blow,' hence also 'occurrence.' The passive participle is, e.g., *mauǰūdun* 'extant,' from *waǰada* 'find.'

§ **6/1.2.2.4**   The *n*- and *t*-reflexives of the basic stem differ in that the former tends more to a passive meaning, the latter to a reciprocal. E.g., *kasara* 'he broke' (transitive), *inkasara* 'it broke' (intransitive); but *iṣṭalaḫū* 'they made peace with each other,' from *ṣulḫun* 'peace' (frequently, as shown here, with assimilation of the *t* to the beginning of the stem).

The causative formative disappears after the prefixes (including the participle prefix): *alḥaqa* 'he unified,' imperfect *yulḥiqu* < **yuᵓalḥiqu*.

The *st*-form often means 'to ask something for oneself'; e.g., *nastaᶜinu* 'we ask for help,' from *ᶜaunun* 'help.'

The *ta*-reflexive of the goal stem has reciprocal meaning, e.g., *tatafānayāni* 'they two (feminine) destroy each other.' If the reflexive meaning-element contained therein is factored out, then there remains as the meaning of the goal stem itself 'to carry out an action,' or 'to find oneself in a situation, with regard to someone,' whereby the latter becomes an accusative object (but without its being the direct or indirect object of an action capable of being expressed by the basic stem). E.g., *ǰalasa* 'he sat,' *ǰālasanī* 'he sat near me,' further the *ta*-form *taǰālasā* 'the two of them sat by each other.'

§ 6/1.2.2.5.2 The II geminate verbs are strong when they have a consonantal suffix: *dalaltu* 'I indicated.' Otherwise, most forms (except in the intensive and its reflexive) have a monosyllabic stem with lengthening of the second consonant: imperfect *yadullu*, causative *aḥassa* 'he tracked'; likewise the participle of the basic stem *ḍāllun* 'going astray,' *ḥāǰǰun* 'pilgrim to Mecca' (but infinitive of the causative *iḥsāsun*, because of the *ā*).

The II weak verbs distinguish three series in the basic stem: besides the two with *ū* and *ī* a third, neutral-mode one, with *ā* in the imperfect; the characteristic vowel also appears in the perfect in the forms with consonantal suffix and consequent shortening of the stem vowel. Thus *kāna* 'he was,' imperfect *yakūnu* (apocopate with shortening in closed syllable *yakun*), 'thou wast' *kunta*; *ṣāra* 'he arrived at' *yaṣīru ṣirta*; *kāda* 'he was near to' *yakādu*, 'we were near to' *kidnā*, with *i* as the characteristic vowel of the neutral-mode perfect, likewise *nāma* 'he slept' *yanāmu nimtu*. In the derived stems the weak conjugation of these verbs alternates only the two vowels *ī* and *ā* (taking into account the shortenings of both); e.g., causative *yuḥīṭu* 'he surrounds,' *yuᶜīdu* 'he repeats' (imperative *aᶜid*, *st*-form *nastaᶜīnu* 'we ask for help'; but imperfect passive of the basic stem *yuqālu* 'it is said,' perfect of the causative *aḥāṭa aᶜāda*, *t*-reflexive of the basic stem *iṣṭāda* 'he hunted,' *yaṣṭādu*.

§ 6/1.2.2.5.3 The inflection of the III weak verbs results from the sound laws already given. E.g., with syllable-final *y*: *raᵓaitu* 'I saw,' *ruᵓītu* 'I was seen'; uncontracted *atayā* 'the two of them came,' *ya*ʾ*tiya* '(that) he come' (subjunctive), *ḥukiya* 'it has been told'; contracted *atā* 'he came,' imperfect *ya*ʾ*tī*. Correspondingly in the related nominal forms: uncontracted *muntahiyan* 'paying attention' (accusative of the active participle of the *t*-reflexive of the basic stem), but contracted *muntahin* < **-iyun* (nominative) or **-iyin* (genitive), *fatan* 'young man' < **-ayun*, **-ayin*, or **-ayan*, i.e., for all three cases (the contracted vowels are here shortened because of the closed syllable; without the *n* of "nunation":[4] *aulā* 'measured'). — Only in the active of the basic stem are *w*-forms still retained beside such *y*-forms: *γazā* (originally with dark *ā*) 'he went on campaign,' imperfect *yaγzū*, subjunctive *yaγzuwa*. —

§ 6/1.2.3 The most characteristic nominal form in Arabic is *af*ᶜ*alu*, which primarily indicates colors and defects (e.g., *aḥmaru* 'red,' *aḥmaqu* 'foolish'), and secondly serves as the comparative form ("elative") of adjectives of various patterns, e.g., *ausa*ᶜ*u* 'farther, farthest' from *wāsi*ᶜ*un*, *akθaru* 'more, most' from *kaθīrun*; likewise *aḥwaǰu* 'more needy' from *muḥtāǰun*, the participle of the *t*-reflexive of the basic stem *ḥwǰ* (feminine like *dunyā* 'this world, world,' literally feminine of *adnā* 'lowest, nearest'). In the first of the two uses, *af*ᶜ*alu* has its very own corresponding verb stem, e.g., *iḥmarra* 'it was, is red.'[g]

g. Known as the IXth Form, cf. § 1 note w.

Arabic distinguishes the three cases, nominative, genitive, and accusative, which in their usual (indefinite) form end in *-un -in -an*, whereas after the article or before the genitive the *n* is lost. Beside this full (triptotic) declension there is a defective one (diptotic); it does not have nunation, and the genitive ends in *-a* like the accusative. After the article and before the genitive the diptotic words take on the triptotic inflection. *af*ᶜ*alu* is a diptote, as are a number of broken plurals and another major category, that of proper names,

4. From the name of the letter *nūn*.

principally ones which by form or meaning are feminine or foreign, e.g., *Murratu* (male, but with feminine ending), *Zainabu* (female, but without feminine ending); *Hārūnu* (foreign, = Aaron). Proper names also lose their nunation before *(i)bnu* 'son of,' e.g., *J̌assāsu bnu Murrata*, and in the vocative, e.g., *yā γulāmu* 'O youth' (if a genitive follows, then it is much more likely to be accusative, e.g., *yā amīra l-muʾminīna* 'O prince of believers').

The dual ending is *-āni* (as in the verb), genitive and accusative *-aini*, the plural ending *-ūna* (as in the verb), genitive and accusative *-īna*; before a genitive the *-ni* or *-na* is absent, e.g., *banū Bakrin* 'the sons of Bakr' (tribe name).

Feminines with the ending *-atun* (and with the rarer ending *-tun*, e.g., *uḫtun* 'sister') inflect like the masculine; another feminine ending *-ā* (e.g., in *dunyā* 'world') is indeclinable. The plural ending is *-ātun*, genitive and accusative *-ātin* (or *-ātu -āti*). A peculiarity of Arabic is that adjectives that have to do with matters relating to the female sex do not have a feminine ending (e.g., *ḥāmilun* 'pregnant'), just as the substantives that indicate female nature also very often forego the feminine ending (e.g., *ummun* 'mother'). — The feminine ending derives names for the individual (noun of unity) from certain collectives; e.g., *samakun* 'fish,' *samakatun* 'a fish.'

While the feminine plural ending is productive without restriction, the masculine is limited to certain cases, especially participles like *ʿālimūna* 'wise men,' *muʾminūna* 'believers.' Elsewhere the masculines, and many feminines as well, by alterations in the word stem form the internal or broken plurals which are characteristic of South Semitic. The most common of the very numerous plural forms are *afʿālun* (e.g., *alfāẓun* 'words' from *lafẓun*, *aṭfalun* 'children' from *ṭiflun*; *aʿmālun* 'deeds' from *ʿamalun*, *aḫbārun* 'news' from *ḫabarun*, *aṭrāfun* 'borders' from *ṭarafun*; *aǰwādun* 'goods' from *ǰaiyidun*), *fiᶜālun* (*riǰālun* 'men' from *raǰulun*), and *fuᶜūlun* (*ᶜuyūnun* 'eyes' from *ᶜainun*); further from quadriliteral substantives *CaCāCiCu* (C = consonant), a diptote (*darāhimu* 'dirhems, drachmas' from the foreign word *dirhamun*; also *ḥawāʾiǰu* 'needs, things,' although the singular *ḥāǰatun* is not quadriliteral).

The basic rule of the genitive phrase, that a definite genitive definitizes its head word, admits of an exception in some words of inherently indefinite meaning, e.g., *baᶜḍun* 'part' (*baᶜḍuhū* 'a part of it,' *baᶜḍu l-ᶜarabi* 'one, some of the Arabs'), *γairun* 'other than' (almost always with genitive: 'another' = *γairuhū*; also as a negation: *γairu ḥasanin* 'not beautiful'), *miθlun* 'sameness' (*miθlī* 'like me, one similar to me'). In other cases where the head substantive must remain indefinite, a circumlocution is used: sometimes a paronomasia, as in 'an administrative area of Chorasan' *ᶜamalun min aᶜmāli Ḫurāsāna* (literally 'an administrative area of the administrative areas of Chorasan'), or else *l-*, also widely found beyond Arabic, as in 'a brother of mine' *aḫun lī* (literally 'belonging to me'); this is also found after an infinitive word in a gerundive sense (see below), e.g., *tarkan li-l-masʾalati* 'while one forbore from asking' (in contrast to *tarka l-masʾalati* 'the forbearing [accusative] from asking'). — An explicative genitive of a particular kind is used after elatives: *auwalu* (elative, for **aʾwalu*) *lailatin* 'the first night' (literally 'first of night'); similarly also *āḫiru* (not elative in form) *qatīlin* 'the last one killed.'

The accusative as a result of its adverbal nature is further used as the predicate of verbal copulas, like *kāna* 'he was,' but also, e.g., *aṣbaḥa* 'he was, in the morning,' etc. — Of the adverbal accusatives the most peculiar are the so-called circumstantial clauses. That is the name given first of all to indefinite adjectives that indicate the state of one of the substantives of the clause (but not adnominally; rather, corresponding to an adverb), e.g., *kaʾīban* 'filled with remorse'; and secondly to indefinite infinitives in a gerundive sense, e.g., *taqlīdan* 'while one mimics.' Even more strongly adnominal, but still basically a verbal conception, is the use of the accusative in a limitative sense: *lisānu l-ᶜarabi akθaru alfāẓan* 'the language of the Arabs is more with respect to words,' i.e., 'has more words.' — As is also the case in Hebrew, several particles that introduce nominal clauses exert verbal rection, after which the subject of the nominal clause is in the accusative: *inna* (deictic, untranslatable), *anna* 'that,' *lākinna* 'but,' *laᶜalla* 'perhaps,' and others. If the subject is a personal pronoun, then it is attached as a suffix on the particle: *innanī* (with verbal suffix!) 'I. . . .'

The number 'one' in Arabic is expressed by two different words: the older *aḥadun*, still used in the compound *aḥada ᶜašara* 'eleven' (indeclinable, like all the numbers from 11 to 19), otherwise a more pronouny 'someone,' with negation 'no one'; and *wāḥidun* 'one, single.' — In the realm of number syntax, fixed rules exist for the number and case of the counted object: after 3-10 genitive plural, after 11-99 accusative singular (in limitative sense), after 100 and 1000 genitive singular. As in South Semitic generally, the ordinals have the form of participles: *ᶜāširun* 'tenth,' literally 'making ten.' —

§ 6/1.2.4 Negation of the verb for present and future is *lā*, for present and past *mā* (originally identical with the interrogative pronoun 'what?'); the past can also be negated by *lam* with the apocopate. The apocopate with *lā* expresses prohibition, as the apocopate can also be used affirmatively in imperative sense. For the nominal clause *mā* is usual; there is also the negative copula *laisa* 'he is not' ('I am not' *lastu*), which also occurs in combination with verb forms. Non-existence is expressed by *lā* with accusative without nunation: *lā šakka* 'there is no doubt.'

All the negations including *γairu* 'different from' can be continued with *wa-lā*. — Arabic has two interrogative particles, a weaker *a-* and a stronger (often translatable with a tag question) *hal.*

The three monoliteral prepositions are *la-* (still so only before suffixes, otherwise *li-*), *bi-*, and *ka-*; *bi-* has in part been forced out of locative use by *fī* 'in, with regard to' and retains primarily the meaning 'with, by.' The spheres of use of the separate prepositions are in general sharply delimited; so they have become not just an important means of closer specification of verb meaning, but they also function syntactically. Primarily, *min* 'from' is used in such a way that like *bi-* it has been relieved of some of its original duties, by *ᶜan* 'thither, hither.' From its partitive use *min* has acquired explicative meaning. In combinations like *γairuhu mimman* (< *min man*) . . . , it means simply 'namely': 'others, namely people who. . . .' Similarly it occurs in a very frequent relative construction after the relative *mā* for the resumption of the concept on which the relative clause depends: *mā kānū fīhi min-a-l-balāʾi* 'that wherein they had been from need,' not entirely synonymous with 'the need in which they had been' or 'in which need they had been.' The old introduction by *min* of the standard of comparison after comparative (in Arabic elative) is refined, so that not just objects but also conditions and states of the same object can be compared: *antum ilā . . . aḥwaǧu minkum ilā . . .* 'you are needier for . . . than you for . . .' = 'your need for . . . is greater than that for. . . .' — The old prepositions in *-ai* have this ending only before a pronominal suffix, while the unbound ending is *-ā*: *ᶜalā* 'on, against,' but *ᶜalaika* 'on thee.' — Many accusatives of substantives serve as secondary prepositions, e.g., *fauqa* 'on, over'; beyond these most adverbs end in *-u*, like *fauqu* 'above.' —

§ 6/1.3 For sentence structure the distinction between nominal and verbal clause is fundamental, and is not vitiated by there being intermediate forms between the two, which for their part are just as carefully regulated. Much favored is the compound nominal clause (its predicate consisting of a complete clause, either nominal or verbal). This construction has particular flexibility and adaptibility to the most varied requirements of expression: e.g., *lisānu l-ᶜarabi lā yuḥīṭū bi-ǧamīᶜi ᶜilmihī illā nabīyun* 'the language of the Arabs: no (one) encompasses the full knowledge (accusative) OF IT except a prophet'; as in this example, the connection between main subject and predicate clause is usually accomplished by a genitive or accusative pronominal suffix referring to the subject.

The interplay between syndesis and asyndesis has developed into a syntactic means of expression of great fineness and sharpness, in part again helped by the fact that the old conjunctive particle *wa-*[5] has given up some of its functions to the parallel *fa-* 'and, since, then (= at this point in the story), thus, therefore,' etc. The[h] strict application of the rule that only syntactic sames can, and in general must, be coordinated makes it possible for on the one hand asyndesis, and on the other *wa-* or *fa-* between differents, both to be means of hypotaxis. "Asyndesis" designates the conjunctionless relative clause after an indefinite substantive (e.g., *γulāmun sammathu l-Hiǧrisa* 'a boy whom she named al-Hijris'), also 'in order to,' negative 'without' (e.g., *daḫala yuṣallī* 'he came in order to pray'). "Syndesis" or combination of differents by *wa-* designates the circumstantial clause (the clausal counterpart of the circumstantial accusative), English 'while' (e.g., *qatalhū* [verbal clause] *wa-hiya ḥāmilun* [nominal clause] 'he killed him while

5. Which in Arabic is also an oath particle 'by' (with genitive) and a pseudo-preposition 'from' (with accusative).

h. This obscure passage in the German resists all interpretation (this reading is based on a twofold emendation); it is here given in the original: Die strenge Durchführung des Grundsatzes, dass nur syntaktisch Gleichartiges koordiniert werden kann, im allgemeinen aber auch muss, macht einerseits die Asyndese, andrerseits *wa-* oder *fa-* zwischen Ungleichartigem dazu frei, dass beides Mittel der Hypotaxe werden kann. Asyndese bezeichnet den konjunktionslosen Relativsatz nach indeterminiertem Substantiv (z.B. *γulāmun sammathu l-Hiǧrisa* "ein Knabe, den sie al-Hiǧris nannte"), Asyndese oder Verbindung von Ungleichartigem durch *wa-* den Zustandssatz, das Satzgegenstück des Zustandsakk., deutsch "indem, während", auch "um zu . .", negativ "ohne dass, ohne zu . ." (z.B. *daḫala yuṣallī* "er trat ein, um zu beten", *qatalahū* [Verbalsatz] *wa-hiya ḥāmilun* [Nominalsatz] "er tötete ihn, während [als] sie schwanger war"), Anfügung von Ungleichartigem durch *fa-* bildet Nachsätze zu verschiedenartigen subordinierten, hauptsächlich zu konditionalen Vordersätzen (*in* ᶜ*aṣā* [Perf.], *fa-wailun lahū* (Nominalsatz) "wenn er ungehorsam ist, so wehe ihm!"). —

i. I.e., the transformation known as Raising.

[when] she was pregnant'). Connection of differents by *fa-* forms apodoses to various kinds of subordinate protases, principally conditional ones (*in* ᶜ*aṣā* [perfect], *fa-wailun lahū* [nominal clause] 'if he is disobedient, then woe to him!'). — A further means of forming hypotactic constructions is the construction ἀπὸ κοινοῦ.[i] In this case, a nominal clause can become a subordinate clause whose subject is simultaneously the object of a verb like 'know'; e.g., the above-described compound nominal clause (with replacement of the substantival subject by the third person pronoun): *lā na*ᶜ*lamuhū yuḥīṭu bi-ǧamī*ᶜ*i* ᶜ*ilmihī illā nabīyun* 'we do not know that (anyone) encompasses all knowledge of it (the Arabic language) except a prophet.' Another case of ἀπὸ κοινοῦ is when an adjectival predicate is simultaneously the modifier of a superordinate substantive; e.g., *al-kutubu l-ātī δikruhā* (accusative *al-kutuba l-ātiya δikruhā*) 'the books coming their mention,' i.e., 'the books whose mention is still to come, which are yet to be named.' It is common to both cases that the first superordinate syntactic element ('we know it [the Arabic language] not,' 'the coming books') is unspecified and is more clearly defined by the second.

Aside from these possibilities of asyndetic or (according to form) coordinating hypotaxis, Arabic also uses a whole series of hypotactic conjunctions clearly delimited in what they govern and sharply characterized as to their meanings; all these means of hypotaxis together also suit it to the most precise expression of the most complicated intellectual relations. The conditional conjunctions deserve particular attention, specifically (aside from the counterfactual *lau*) on the one hand *in* 'if' and on the other the conditional-temporal *iδā* 'when.' The periods introduced by these conjunctions, especially *in*, are characterized by a strict sequence of tenses; regularly in both subordinate and main clauses the perfect occurs, though the apocopate can substitute for it. — *in* with the negation *lā* forms the exception-particle *illā* 'except,' which in positive clauses takes the accusative but in negative ones takes no particular case ('no [one] knows the language of the Arabs except for a prophet' *illā nabīyun* in the nominative, since 'prophet' is the logical subject). —

§ 6/1.4 In richness of vocabulary Arabic ineffably transcends all other Semitic languages; not only does it derive new words from Common Semitic roots, but it also uses a host of roots peculiar to it. Above all the sharpness of observation and the eye for detail that characterize the Bedouin have created a richness of novel expressions for the phenomena of the Bedouin environment: desert and steppe with their topography, flora, and fauna on one side, camel and horse and their care on the other. While the horizon of Old Arabic may be circumscribed, yet within it the finest nuances are distinguished. — Already in pre-Islamic time a great number of terms for cultural achievements had been borrowed into Arabic from Aramaic and Persian, and also South Arabic. The influence of Persian and Aramaic (Syriac) continued into the first centuries of Islam; by way of Syriac and Middle Persian, Greek words as well were borrowed, especially in the language of science. Yet Arabic preserved itself from excessive foreignization, partly thanks to its extraordinary capacity for forming terms for new ideas by derivation, partly by its energetic assimilation of borrowed material into its own phonology and morphology. Thus the Greek *φιλόσοφος* delivered up its consonants *f l s f* for a new verb root, which was then conjugated in a thoroughly Arabic fashion and used for nominal derivations: *yatafalsafu* 'he philosophizes,' *falsafatun* 'philosophy.' —

To the traits of the old Arabic Bedouin — level-headedness, gift for observation, and explicit interest in linguistic matters — the oldest Arabic owes the fineness of its grammatical systematicity and the inexhaustibility of its vocabulary, which make it superbly adapted to vivid, richly detailed description of the environment and life of the Bedouin, even though it cannot express emotion, mood, and thought equally well. In this respect, Islam powerfully extended Arabic: for scientific expression it is almost unsurpassable in its suppleness and exactitude, in a terseness already apparent in the old desert tales, in its ability to form substantives from any verb, adjective, etc., and adjectives from substantives; it is able also to articulate the deepest religious experiences of a highly elaborated mysticism. A rationalistic strain always clings to it; it is least suited to emotional directness and poetic effulgence.

Text Specimens

[A] after a word indicates a borrowing from Aramaic.

1. The First Sura of the Koran

ٱلْحَمْدُ لِلَّهِ رَبِّ ٱلْعٰلَمِينَ
al-ḥamdu li-llāhi[6] *rabbi l-ˁālamīn,*[A]
Praise is Allah's, the Lord of the worlds,

ٱلرَّحْمٰنِ ٱلرَّحِيمِ
ar-raḥmāni[7] *r-raḥīm,*
the gracious, the merciful,

مٰلِكِ يَوْمِ ٱلدِّينِ
māliki[8] *yaumi d-dīn!*[A]
master of the day of judgment!

إِيَّاكَ نَعْبُدُ وَإِيَّاكَ نَسْتَعِينُ
īyāka naˁbudu wa-īyāka nastaˁīn![9]
Thee we serve and thee we implore for help!

ٱهْدِنَا ٱلصِّرٰطَ ٱلْمُسْتَقِيمَ
ihdinā[10] *ṣ-ṣirāṭa*[A11] *l-mustaqīm,*[12]
Guide us on the straight path,

صِرٰطَ ٱلَّذِينَ أَنْعَمْتَ عَلَيْهِمْ غَيْرِ ٱلْمَغْضُوبِ عَلَيْهِمْ وَلَا ٱلضَّآلِّينَ
ṣirāṭa llaδīna anˁamta ˁalaihim, γairi[13] *l-maγḍūbi ˁalaihim*[14] *wa-lā ḍ-ḍāllīn!*
the path of those on whom you have bestowed grace, with whom you are not displeased, and who do not go astray!

2. Blood Revenge on Uncle for Grandfather[15]

آخر من قتل فى حرب بكر وتغلب جساس بن مرّة
āḫiru man qutila fī ḥarbi Bakrin wa-Taγliba[16] *J̌assāsu bnu*[17] *Murrata . . .,*
The last of those who were killed in the war of Bakr and Taghlib was Jassas ibn Murra (of Bakr), |

وهو قاتل كليب بن ربيعة وكانت أخته تحت كليب
wa-huwa qātilu[18] *Kulaibi bni Rabīˁata; wa-kānat*[19] *uḫtuhū*[20] *<mraˀata>*[21, j] *Kulaibin.*
and he it was that had killed Kulaib ibn Rabi'a (of Taghlib); and his sister was Kulaib's wife. |

فقتله جساس وهى حامل فرجعت الى أهلها ووقعت الحرب فكان من الفريقين ما كان
fa-qatalahū J̌assāsun, wa-hiya ḥāmilun; fa-raǰaˁat ilā ahlihā; wa-waqaˁat-i-l-ḥarbu,[22] *fa-kāna min-a-l-farīqaini mā kāna.*
Jassas killed him when she was pregnant; then she returned to her family; and the war broke out (lit. fell), and it happened on both sides as it happened (i.e., these well-known occurrences need not be repeated here). |

6. From *aḻḻāhu* "the god" < *al-ilāhu*. 7. Borrowing from South Arabic. 8. Participle. 9. *ˁwn*. 10. *hdy*. 11. < Latin (*via*) *strata*, borrowed via Greek-Aramaic. 12. *qwm*. 13. lit. '(which are) different from.' 14. Participle of *γuḍiba ˁalaihim* "to them became displeased." 15. *Kitāb al-Aγānī* (Būlāq 1323) IV pp. 150-151 (= *Rannāt al-maθāliθ wa-l-maθānī fī riwāyāt al-Aγānī* [Beirut] II 1888, pp. 75-76). 16. Diptote. 17. In isolation *ibnun*. 18. The participle specified by the genitive has past meaning. 19. *kwn*. 20. *uḫtun* 'sister,' feminine of *aḫun* 'brother.' 21. In isolation *imraˀatun*. 22. Feminine.

j. Text *taḥta* 'under.'

ثم صاروا الى الموادعة بعدما كادت القبيلتان تتفانيان	*θumma ṣārū*[23] *ilā l-muwādaᶜati, baᶜda mā kādat*[24]*-i-l-qabīlatāni tatafānayāni.*	Then they approached reconciliation, after the two tribes were near to exterminating each other. |
فولدت أخت جساس غلاما سمته الهجرس رباه جساس فكان لا يعرف أبا غيره فزوجه ابنته	*fa-waladat uḫtu J̌assāsin γulāman sammathu*[25] *l-Ḥiǰrisa rabbāhu*[26] *J̌assāsun; fa-kāna lā yaᶜrifu aban γairahū, fa-zauwaǰahū*^[27] *bnatahū.*	Then Jassas' sister bore a boy, whom she named al-Hijris and whom Jassas brought up; and it was (so that) he knew no father but him, and he wedded him to his daughter. |
فوقع بين الهجرس وبين رجل من بنى بكر بن وائل كلام	*fa-waqaᶜa baina l-Hiǰrisi wa-baina raǰulin min banī Bakri bni Wāᵓilin kalāmun;*	Then occurred (lit. fell) between al-Hijris and a man of the Bani Bakr ibn Wa'il an argument (lit. conversation); |
فقال له البكرى ما أنت بمنته حتى نلحقك بأبيك	*fa-qāla*[28] *lahū l-Bakrīyu:*[29] *"mā anta bi*[30]*-muntahin,*[31] *ḥattā nulḥiqaka bi-abīka."*	then the Bakrite said to him: "You will not be finished until we make you follow your father." |
فأمسك عنه ودخل الى أمّه كئيبا فسألته عما به فأخبرها الخبر	*fa-amsaka ᶜanhu wa-daḫala ilā ummihī kaᵓīban; fa-saᵓalathu ᶜam*[32]*-mā bihī, fa-aḫbarahā l-ḫabara.*	Then he left him and went in to his mother filled with pain; then she asked him what was with him, and he reported to her the matter (lit. report). |
فلما اوى الى فراشه ونام تنفس تنفسة تنفط مابين ثديها من حرارتها	*fa-lammā awā*[33] *ilā firāšihī wa-nāma,* <. . .> *tanaffasa tanaffusatan*[34] <*aḥassat minhā mraᵓatuhū lahība nārin*>.[k]	When he now had gotten into his bed and slept, he breathed a breath in which his wife detected the burning of a fire. |
فقامت فزعة قد أقلتها رعدة حتى دخلت على أبيها فقصت عليه قصة الهجرس	*fa-qāmat*[35] <. . .> *faziᶜatan, qad aqallathā raᶜdatun, ḥattā daḫalat ᶜalā abīhā fa-qaṣṣat ᶜalaihi qiṣṣata l-Hiǰrisi.*	Then she stood up troubled, for shudders having seized her (circumstantial clause), she went (lit. until she entered) to her father and told him the story (lit. tale) of al-Hijris. |
فقال جساس ثائر وربّ الكعبة	*fa-qāla J̌assāsun: "θāᵓirun, wa-rabbi l-Kaᶜbati!"*	Then Jassas said: "An avenger, by the Lord of the Kaaba!" |
وبات جساس على مثل الرضف حتى أصبح فأرسل الى الهجرس فأتاه	*wa-bāta*[36] *J̌assāsun ᶜala miθli r-raḍfi, ḥattā aṣbaḥa; fa-arsala ilā l-Hiǰrisi fa-atāhu.*[37]	And Jassas spent the night as on (lit. on the likeness of) a glowing stone until morning (lit. until he was at morning); then he sent to al-Hijris, and he came to him. |

k. Text *tanaffaṭa mā baina θadīha min ḥarāratihā* 'he burned with emotion in her bosom.'

23. *ṣyr*. 24. *kyd*; before a feminine dual the verb must be in the feminine (but usually singular). 25. *smy*. 26. *rbw*. 27. From *zauǰun* 'pair; spouse' < ζεῦγος. 28. *qwl*. 29. Nisbe. 30. The predicate of *mā* (and *laisa*) 'not' can be introduced by *bi-*. 31. *nhy*. 32. < *ᶜan*. 33. *ᵓwy*. 34. Feminine form of the infinitive of the intensive-reflexive. 35. *qwm*. 36. *byt*. 37. *ᵓty*; the verbs of coming to someone are transitive.

فقال له انما أنت ولدى ومنى بالمكان الذى قد علمت وقد زوّجتك ابنتى وأنت معى

fa-qāla lahū: "inna-mā[38] *anta waladī wa-minnī*[39] *bi-l-makāni*[40] *llaδī qad ᶜalimta, wa-qad zauwaǰtuka bnatī, wa-anta maᶜī;*[41]

Then he said to him: "You are my child and by me (lit. from me out) in the place that you know, I married you to my daughter, and you live (lit. are) with me; |

وقد كانت الحرب فى أبيك زمانا طويلا حتى كدنا نتفانى وقد اصطلحنا وتحاجزنا

wa-qad kānat-i-l-ḥarbu fī abīka zamānan ṭawīlan, ḥattā kidnā natafānā,[42] *wa-qad-i-ṣṭalaḥnā wa-taḥāǰaznā.*

the war on account of your father lasted a long time, until we were near to exterminating each other, and we concluded peace and disengaged ourselves. |

وقد رأيت أن تدخل فيما دخل فيه الناس من الصلح وأن تنطلق حتى نأخذ عليك مثل ما أخذ علينا وعلى قومنا

wa-qad raʾaitu,[43] *an tadḫula fī-mā daḫala fīhi n-nāsu*[44] *min-a-ṣ-ṣulḥi, wa-an tanṭaliqa, ḥattā naʾḫuδa ᶜalaika miθla mā uḫiδa ᶜalainā wa-ᶜalā qauminā."*

So I feel that you should enter into the peace into which the people have entered, and you should go away, so that we deprive you of what we and our tribe have been deprived of." |

فقال الهجرس أنا فاعل ولكن مثلى لا يأتى قومه الا بلأمته وفرسه

fa-qāla l-Hiǰrisu: "ana fāᶜilun; wa-lākinna miθlī lā yaʾtī qaumahū illā bi-laʾmatihī wa-farasihī."

Then al-Hijris said: "I will do so; but one like me will not come to his tribe except with his cuirass and his horse." |

فحمله جساس على فرس وأعطاه لأمة ودرعا

fa-ḥamalahū J̌assāsun ᶜalā farasin wa-aᶜṭāhu laʾmatan wa-dirᶜan.

Then Jassas mounted him on a horse and gave him a cuirass and armor. |

فخرجا حتى أتيا جماعة من قومهما فقص عليهم جساس ما كانوا فيه من البلاء وما صاروا اليه من العافية

fa-ḫaraǰā, ḥattā atayā ǰamāᶜatan min qaumihimā; fa-qaṣṣa ᶜalaihim J̌assāsun mā kānū fīhi min-a-l-balāʾi wa-mā ṣārū ilaihi min-a-l-ᶜāfiyati;[45]

And they both went out until they came to a number of their tribe; then Jassas told them in what need they had been and to what prosperity they had turned; |

ثم قال وهذا الفتى ابن أختى قد جاء ليدخل فيما دخلتم فيه ويعقد ما عقدتم

θumma qāla: "wa-hāδā l-fatā[46] *bnu uḫtī qad ǰāʾa,*[47] *li-yadḫula fī-mā daḫaltum fīhi wa-yaᶜqida <fī->mā ᶜaqadtum."*

and then he said: "And this young man, the son of my sister, has come to enter where you have entered, and renounce what you have renounced." |

فلما قربوا الدم وقاموا الى العقد أخذ الهجرس بوسط رمحه ثم قال

fa-lammā qarrabū d-dama wa-qāmū ilā l-ᶜaqdi, aḫaδa l-Hiǰrisu bi-wasaṭi rumḥihī, θumma qāla:

When they now brought the blood close and made (lit. stood) the (act of) renunciation, al-Hijris seized the middle of his lance, then he said:

38. Topicalizing particle; the topic at the end of the clause. 39. *min* + *ī* with lengthening of the *n*. 40. Noun of place from *kwn* 'be.' 41. From *maᶜa*. 42. *fny*. 43. *rʾy*. 44. Without article *unāsun*. 45. *ᶜfw*. 46. Indefinite *fatan* < **fatawun*. 47. *ǰyʾ*.

وفرسى وأذنيه ورمحى ونصليه	*"wa-farasī wa-uδnaihi,* *wa-rumḥī wa-naṣlaihi,*	"By my horse and his two ears, by my lance and its two points (dual in singular sense),
وسيفى وغراريه لا يترك الرجل قاتل أبيه وهو ينظر اليه	*wa-saifī wa-γirāraihi:* *lā yatruku r-rajulu qātila abīhi, wa-huwa yanẓuru ilailhi!"*	by my sword and its two edges: A (lit. the) man does not leave the murderer of his father when he espies him!"
ثم طعن جساسا فقتله ثم لحق بقومه فكان آخر قتيل فى بكر بن وائل	*θumma ṭaᶜana Jassāsan fa-qatalahū; θumma laḥiqa bi-qaumihi. fa-kāna āḫira qatīlin fī Bakri bni wāᵓilin.*	Then he thrust Jassas through and killed him; thus he joined his tribe. Thus was he the last one killed of Bakr ibn Wa'il.

3. Four Anecdotes[48]

a) The Thieving Bedouin

سَرَقَ رَجُلٌ صُرَّةً مِنَ ٱلدَّرَاهِمِ وَمَضَى حَتَّى أَتَى إِلَى ٱلْمَسْجِدِ فَدَخَلَ يُصَلِّي.	*saraqa rajulun ṣurratan min-ad-darāhimi*[49] *wa-maḍā,*[50] *ḥattā atā ilā l-masjidi*[A] *fa-daḫala yuṣallī.*[A51]	A man stole a purse of dirhems and went away until (i.e., and finally) he came to the mosque and went in to pray. |
فَقَرَأَ ٱلْإِمَامُ: وَمَا تِلْكَ بِيَمِينِكَ يَا مُوسَى. وَكَانَ ٱسْمَ ٱلْأَعْرَابِيِّ.	*fa-qaraᵓa*[A] *l-imāmu: "wa-mā tilka bi-yamīnika, yā Mūsā?"; wa-kāna sma*[53] *l-aᶜrābīyi.*	Then the imam recited: "And what is this in your right hand, O Musa (Moses)?";[52] and this was the name of the Bedouin. |
فَقَالَ: لَا شَكَّ أَنَّكَ سَاحِرٌ. ثُمَّ رَمَى ٱلصُّرَّةَ وَخَرَجَ هَارِبًا	*fa-qāla: "lā šakka, annaka sāḥirun!"*[54] *θumma ramā*[55] *ṣ-ṣurrata wa-ḫaraja hāriban.*	Then he said: "No doubt, you are a sorcerer!" Then he threw away the purse and exited fleeing.

48. *Majānīl-adab* (Beirut) I Nos. 226, 254; II Nos. 230, 267. 49. Plural of *dirhamun* < *δραχμή*, borrowed via Persian. 50. *mḍy.* 51. *ṣlw.* 52. Koran 20:18; it refers to Moses' staff. 53. In isolation *ismun.* 54. Participle. 55. *rmy.*

b) Joha's Luck Almost Runs Out

حُكِيَ أَنَّ جُحَى قَالَ ذَاتَ يَوْمٍ لِرَجُلٍ وَهٰذَا ٱلرَّجُلُ جَارُهُ: هَلْ سَمِعْتَ يَا أَخِي ٱلْبَارِحَةَ صُرَاخَنَا.	*ḥukiya anna J̌uḥā qāla δāta yaumin li-rağulin, wa-hāδā r-rağulu ǧāruhū: "hal samiᶜta, yā aḫī, l-bāriḥata ṣurāḫanā?"*	It is related that Joha said one day to a man — and this man was his neighbor: "Did you hear, O my brother, our screams yesterday?" |
فَقَالَ لَهُ: نَعَمْ. وَأَيُّ شَيْءٍ نَزَلَ بِكُمْ. قَالَ لَهُ: سَقَطَ ثَوْبِي مِن أَعْلَى ٱلسَّطْحِ إِلَى ٱلْأَرْضِ.	*fa-qāla lahū: "naᶜam; wa-aiyu šaiᵓin nazala bikum?" qāla lahū: "saqaṭa θaubī min aᶜlā*[56] *s-saṭḥi ilā l-arḍi!"*	Then he said to him: "Yes; and what befell you?" He said to him: "My cloak fell from the heights of the roof to the ground!" |
فَقَالَ لَهُ: وَإِذَا سَقَطَ مَا ٱلَّذِي يَضُرُّهُ. قَالَ لَهُ: يَا أَحْمَقُ لَوْ كُنْتُ فِيهِ أَلَسْتُ كُنْتُ أَتَكَسَّرُ وَأَمُوتُ.	*fa-qāla lahū: "wa-iδā saqaṭa, mā llaδī yaḍurruhū?" qāla lahū: "yā aḥmaqu, lau kuntu*[57] *fīhi, a-lastu*[58] *kuntu atakassaru wa-amūtu?"*[59]	Then he said to him: "And if it fell, what of it, how is it harmed (lit. it hurting it)?" He said to him: "You fool, if I had been in it, wouldn't I have broken in bits and died?"

c) A Ready Answer

حُكِيَ أَنَّ هَارُونَ ٱلرَّشِيدَ لَمَّا حَضَرَ بَيْنَ يَدَيْهِ بَعْضُ أَهْلِ ٱلْمَغْرِبِ قَالَ لَهُ:	*ḥukiya anna Hārūna r-Rašīda, lammā ḥaḍara baina yadaihi baᶜḍu ahli l-Maγribi,*[60] *qāla lahū:*	It is related that Haroun al-Rashid, when one of the people of the Maghreb (northwest Africa) appeared before him (lit. was present between his hands), said to him: |
يُقَالُ إِنَّ ٱلدُّنْيَا بِمَثَابَةِ طَائِرٍ ذَنَبُهُ ٱلْمَغْرِبُ.	*"yuqālu: inna d-dunyā bi-maθābati*[61] *ṭāᵓirin*[62] *δanabuhū l-Maγribu."*	"It is said that the world is like a bird, whose 'tail' is the Maghreb." |
فَقَالَ ٱلرَّجُلُ: صَدَقُوا يَا أَمِيرَ ٱلْمُؤْمِنِينَ وَإِنَّهُ طَاوُوسٌ.	*fa-qāla r-rağulu: "ṣadaqū, yā amīra l-muᵓminīna, wa-innahū ṭāwūsun."*[A63]	Then the man said: "They have told the truth, O prince of believers, and it is a peacock." |
فَضَحِكَ ٱلرَّشِيدُ وَتَعَجَّبَ مِنْ سُرْعَةِ جَوَابِ ٱلرَّجُلِ وَٱنْتِصَارِهِ لِقُطْرِهِ	*fa-ḍaḥika r-Rašīdu wa-taᶜağğaba min surᶜati ǧawābi r-rağuli wa-ntiṣārihī li-quṭrihī.*	Then al-Rashid laughed and marveled at the quickness of the man's answer and his vindication of his homeland (lit. region).

56. Elative of *ᶜālin* 'high,' from *ᶜlw*. 57. *kwn*. 58. From *laisa*. 59. *mwt*. 60. Noun of place from *γrb* 'set' (said of the sun). 61. From *θwb*. 62. Participle of *ṭyr*. 63. Indic, borrowed via Greek (*τάως*) -Aramaic.

d) A Short Speech

كَانَ ثَابِتُ قُطْنَةَ قَدْ وُلِّيَ عَمَلاً مِنْ أَعْمَالِ خُرَاسَانَ.

kāna Θābitu Quṭnata[64] *qad wulliya ᶜamalan min aᶜmāli Ḫurāsāna.*

Thabit Qutna[65] was appointed manager of one of the administrative districts of Khorasan. |

فَلَمَّا صَعِدَ ٱلْمِنْبَرَ يَوْمَ ٱلْجُمْعَةِ رَامَ ٱلْكَلَامَ فَتَعَذَّرَ عَلَيْهِ وَحَصِرَ فَقَالَ: :

fa-lammā ṣaᶜida lminbara[66] *yauma l-ǰumᶜati, rāma*[67] *l-kalāma fa-taᶜaδδara ᶜalaihi wa-ḥaṣira fa-qāla:*

And when he now ascended to the pulpit on Friday, he wanted to speak, but it was difficult for him, he hesitated and then said: |

سَيَجْعَلُ ٱللّٰهُ بَعْدَ عُسْرٍ يُسْرًا وَبَعْدَ عِيٍّ بَيَانًا.

"sa-yaǰᶜalu l̤l̤āhu[68] *baᶜda ᶜusrin yusran wa-baᶜda ᶜīyin*[70] *bayānan!*

"Allah will set after difficulty ease[69] and after stammering clarity! |

وَأَنْتُمْ إِلَى أَمِيرٍ فَعَّالٍ أَحْوَجُ مِنْكُمْ إِلَى أَمِيرٍ قَوَّالٍ

wa-antum ilā amīrin faᶜᶜālin[71] *aḥwaǰu*[72] *minkum ilā amīrin qauwālin.*[71]

You need an effective emir more than an eloquent emir. |

وَإِلاَّ أَكُنْ فِيكُمْ خَطِيبًا فَإِنَّنِي،
بِسَيْفِي إِذَا جَدَّ ٱلْوَغَى لَخَطِيبُ

wa-illā, akun[73] *fīkum ḫaṭīban; fa-innanī*
bi-saifī, iδā ǰadda l-wayā,[74] *la*[75]*-ḫaṭību!"*[76, 77]

If not, I will be a preacher for you; for indeed,
with my sword, if the battle tumult is serious, I am a preacher!" |

فَبَلَغَتْ كَلِمَاتُهُ خَالِدَ بْنَ صَفْوَانَ. فَقَالَ: وَٱللّٰهِ مَاعَلاَ ذٰلِكَ ٱلْمِنْبَرَ أَخْطَبُ مِنْهُ

fa-balayat kalimātuhū Ḫālida bna Ṣafwāna ... fa-qāla: "wa-l̤l̤āhi, māᶜalā[78] *δālika l-minbara aḫṭabu*[79] *minhu!"*

Then his words reached Khalid ibn Safwan ... and he said: "By Allah, to that pulpit (there) has never ascended a preacher like him!" |

4. Shafi'i on Knowledge of the Arabic Language[80]

الواجب على العالمين أن لا يقولوا الا من حيث علموا
وقد تكلم فى العلم من لو أمسك عن بعض ما تكلم فيه منه

al-wāǰibu ᶜalā l-ᶜālimīna, an lā yaqūlū illā min ḥaiθu[81] *ᶜalimū; wa-qad takallama fī l-ᶜilmi man, lau amsaka ᶜan baᶜḍi mā takallama fīhi minhu,*

It is a necessity for scholars that they not speak except on that which they know; | but one has (i.e. some have) spoken about knowledge in such a way that if he had restrained himself from speaking about it, |

64. 'Piece of cotton (wool),' from *quṭnun* 'cotton'; here diptote because it is used as a proper name. 65. I.e., Thabit with the Cotton Ball (with which he covers a missing eye). 66. From Ethiopic. 67. *rwm.* 68. The name of God is pronounced with *l̤* (velar *l*) after a back vowel. 69. Koran 65:7. 70. *ᶜwy.* 71. Noun of agent with intensive meaning. 72. Elative of *muḥtāǰun.* 73. *kwn*; apodosis of the conditional clause implicit in *illā.* . 74. *wyy.* 75. Asseverative particle. 76. In the rhyme for *ḫaṭīb*(*un*). 77. Double verse of the meter ⏑–– ⏑––– ⏑–– ⏑–⏑–. 78. *ᶜlw.* 79. Elative of *ḫaṭībun.* 80. Aš-Šāfiᶜī, *Ar-Risāla* (Būlāq 1321) p. 8 ll. 15ff. 81. Lit. 'where.'

لكان الامساك أولى به وأقرب الى السلامة له ان شاء الله تعالى	*la-kāna l-imsāku*[82] *aulā*[83] *bihī wa-aqrabu ilā s-salāmati lahū; in šāᵓa*[84] *ḷḷāhu taᶜālā.*	this restraint would have been better and would have been more conducive to his integrity; if God, who is exalted, will. |
فقال لى قائل منهم ان فى القرآن عربيا وأعجميا	*fa-qāla lī qāᵓilun minhum "inna fī l-qurᵓāni ᶜarabīyan wa-aᶜǰamīyan,"*	Thus one (lit. a sayer) of them said to me: "In the Koran there is Arabic and non-Arabic," |
والقرآن يدل على أن ليس فى كتاب اللّه شىء الا بلسان العرب	<. . .> *wa-l-qurᵓānu yadullu ᶜalā an laisa fī kitābi llāhi šaiᵓun illā bi-lisāni l-ᶜarabi.*	although the Koran (itself) points out that in the book of Allah is nothing except the language of the Arabs. |
ووجد قائل هذا القول من قبل ذلك منه تقليدا له وتركا للمسئلة له عن حجته ومسئلة غيره ممن خالفه	*wa-waǰada qāᵓilu hāδā l-qauli, man qabila δālika minhu taqlīdan*[85] *lahū wa-tarkan li-l-masᵓalati lahū ᶜan ḥuǰǰatihī wa-masᵓalati γairihī mim*[86]*-man ḫālafahū. . . .*	And he who said these words had found (people) who accepted this from him uncritically and omitted to question about his authority and to question others who contradict him. . . . |
ولعل من قال ان فى القرآن غير لسان العرب وقبل ذلك منه ذهب الى أن من القرآن خاصا يجهل بعضه بعض العرب	*wa-laᶜalla man qāla "inna fī l-qurᵓāni γaira lisāni l-ᶜarabi" wa-qabila δālika minhu, δahaba ilā anna*[87] *min-a-l-qurᵓāni ḫāṣṣan yaǰhalu baᶜḍahū baᶜḍu l-ᶜarabi.*	But perhaps whoever says "In the Koran there is what is other than the Arabic language" or accepts this from him means that in (lit. belonging to) the Koran there are special things some of which some Arabs do not know. |
ولسان العرب أوسع الألسنة مذهبا وأكثرها ألفاظا ولا نعلمه يحيط بجميع علمه انسان غير نبي	*wa-lisānu l-ᶜarabi ausaᶜu*[88] *l-alsinati maδhaban wa-akθaruhā*[89] *alfāẓan;*[90] *wa-lā naᶜlamuhū yuḥīṭu*[91] *bi-ǰamīᶜi ᶜilmihī insānun γairu nabīyin.*[A]	For the language of the Arabs is the widest-spread language in extent and most abundant in words; and we do not know that any man except a prophet encompasses complete knowledge of it. |
ولكنه لا يذهب منه شىء على عامتها حتى لا يكون موجودا فيها من يعرفه	*wa-lākinnahū lā yaδhabu minhu šaiᵓun ᶜalā ᶜāmmatihā, ḥattā lā yakūna mauǰūdan*[92] *fīhā man yaᶜrifuhū.*	However, nothing of it can escape the totality of them (the Arabs) so that not one is found among them who knows it (i.e. that thing). |
والعلم به عند العرب كالعلم بالسنة عند أهل الفقه	*wa-l-ᶜilmu bihī ᶜinda l-ᶜarabi ka-l-ᶜilmi bi-s-sunnati ᶜinda ahli l-fiqhi.*	The knowledge of it among the Arabs is like the knowledge of the sunnas (exemplary acts and authoritative words of Mohammed) among the practitioners of jurisprudence. |

82. Infinitive of *amsaka*. 83. Elative of *wālin* (*wly*). 84. *šyᵓ*. 85. Infinitive of the intensive. 86. < *min*. 87. Lit. 'goes up to, that.' 88. Elative of *wāsiᶜun*. 89. Elative of *kaθīrun*. 90. Plural of *lafẓun*. 91. *ḥwṭ* causative. 92. *wǰd*.

لا نعلم رجلا جمع السنن فلم يذهب منها عليه شيء	*lā naʿlamu rağulan ğamaʿa s-sunana*[93] *fa-lam yaδhab minhā ʿalaihi šaiʾun;*	We do not know that a man has assembled the sunnas, so that none escapes him; |
فاذا جمع علم عامة أهل العلم بها أتى على السنن	*fa-iδā ğumiʿa ʿilmu ʿāmmati ahli l-ʿilmi bihā, utiya ʿalā s-sunani,*	so if the knowledge of the totality of the people of knowledge of it is collected, the sunnas are arrived at; |
واذا فرق علم كل واحد منهم ذهب عليه الشيء منها ثم كان ما ذهب عليه منها موجودا عند غيره	*wa-iδā furiqa ʿilmu kulli wāḥidin minhum, δahaba ʿalaihi š-šaiʾu*[94] *minhā, θumma kāna mā δahaba ʿalaihi minhā mauğūdan ʿinda γairihī. . . .*	but if the knowledge of each one of them is separated out, some thing of it escapes him, then what escapes him of it is found with another. . . . |
وهكذا لسان العرب عند خاصتها وعامتها لا يذهب منه شيء عليها ولا يطلب عند غيرها	*wa-hā-ka-δā lisānu l-ʿarabi ʿinda ḫāṣṣatihā wa-ʿāmmatihā; lā yaδhabu minhu šaiʾun ʿalaihā wa-lā yuṭlabu ʿinda γairihā,*	So also is the language of the Arabs in their individuality (lit. specials) and their totality; nothing of it escapes from them but can be sought from others, |
ولا يعلمه الا من قبله عنها ولا يشركها فيه الا من اتبعها فى تعلمه منها	*wa-lā yaʿlamuhū illā man qabilahū ʿanhā, wa-lā yušrikuhā fīhi illā man-i-ttabaʿahā fī taʿallumihī min-hā. . . .*	no one knows it except (him) who has received it from them, nor shares in it with them except whoever has succeeded in learning it from them. . . . |
وعلم أكثر اللسان فى أكثر العرب أعم من علم أكثر السنن فى أكثر العلماء	*wa-ʿilmu akθari l-lisāni fī akθari l-ʿarabi aʿammu*[95] *min ʿilmi akθari s-sunani fī akθari l-ʿulamāʾi.*[96]	But the knowledge of most of the language among most of the Arabs is more common than the knowledge of most of the sunnas among most of the scholars.

93. Plural of *sunnatun*. 94. Lit. 'the thing (in question).' 95. Elative of *ʿāmmun*. 96. Plural of *ʿālimun*.

II. Colloquial Arabic

§ 6/2.0 From as early as the time of Old Arabic we are aware of a full measure of dialectal variations from the Classical language, though it is not possible to reconstruct particular individual dialects as coherent wholes. The modern Arabic dialects by and large go back to a single unified basic form, which in general was close to the Classical language, but deviated from it in details. In part these deviations are only apparent; they would disappear if the old standard language lay before us not in the simplifying schematization of the orthography, but in an exact phonetic transcription. — The linguistic development that lies between Classical Arabic and the modern dialects repeats many changes that older Semitic languages had already undergone before first being fixed in writing; thus may be explained reminiscences in Colloquial Arabic of, above all, Hebrew and Aramaic.

The Arabic dialects show only traces of foreign influence — mainly in phonological matters — although Arabic spread, borne often by a thin layer of Arab conquerors, over a vast territory, and settled in place of or beside the native languages. This vitality of Arabic is explained by a sense of superiority and a never entirely severed cultural bond, both of which were the effects of Islam. To one side stands Maltese, which, spoken by Christians for centuries, has adapted itself to the language of the neighboring Christian lands, Italian (Sicilian), and, unique among Semitic languages, has adopted European script.[1] As for the rest, the strongest dialect split is not geographical but cultural; the Bedouin dialects of the entire

1. The specimen, which presents the dialect of the village of Balzan, is therefore given not only in exact phonetic transcription but also in the native conventional orthography (within which many variations are found).

Arabic-speaking territory form a relative unity among themselves that is fairly close to Classical Arabic. They are best represented by a Central Arabian dialect.[2] The strongest contrast to the Bedouin dialects is found in the language of the Arab cities of Egypt and the Near East; as the most characteristic example the dialect of Cairo has been chosen. It also represents the eastern dialects, which belong close together as against the western ones, whose idiosyncrasy is most strongly marked in Moroccan, of which a specimen is therefore given.[3] —

§ 6/2.1.1 The Classical Arabic consonant inventory is least abridged in various Bedouin dialects; our specimen, though, allows at least *ẓ* (old *θ̣*), e.g., in *ẓhr* 'show oneself, come out,' to merge with *ḍ* (old lateral *δ̣*) as *δ̣*. On the other hand, some dialects surpass Classical Arabic: the west has an emphatic *r*, which is perhaps also not entirely unknown in the east,[4] and here and there new sounds have been taken over from foreign languages, although foreign words were on the whole energetically adapted to Arabic phonology. The most widespread simplification is the loss of the dental spirants, which became stops; this includes *θ* (> *t*) and *δ* (> *d*), and also the old *δ̣* (> *ḍ*), and finally the old *θ̣*, which in Moroccan *ṭhaṛ* 'back' < **θ̣ahrun* retains its voicelessness, but otherwise is usually replaced by *ḍ* (at least to the extent that the later Classical pronunciation *ẓ* has not been transferred to the dialects).

The velars have undergone noteworthy sound changes. *ǰ* in Egypt has gone back to the old Semitic *g*; otherwise it reverses to *ž* (Mo) or further develops (by way of *g* > *g′*) to *d′* (Bd). The change, parallel to Cl *g* > *ǰ*, of *k* > *č* is widespread,

2. Of the ᶜÖtäbeh Rwugeh.
3. Dialect of Tangier.
4. It could even have been present in Classical Arabic, without being differentiated by the script.

although it is not found in our selection. *q* has retained its old voicing in Bedouin; it is "emphatic" (deeply velar) *ġ* or, under particular phonological conditions (in an environment of palatal vowels and such), following the sound change *g* > *ǰ*, changed to a sound different from and remaining distinct from old *ǰ* (in our specimen *ɟ*). In many cities and on Malta the shift of the place of articulation even farther back has led to the merger of *q* with ʾ — one of the most noteworthy phonological phenomena of Colloquial Arabic.

The laryngeals are intact nearly everywhere; only the disappearance of ʾ, starting in Classical Arabic and already widespread in Old Arabic dialects, has achieved wide distribution. Examples are Eg *ḫad* 'he took' < *aḫaδa*, Ma *māra* 'wife' < *marʾatun* (elsewhere with short vowel *mara*), cf. Eg *imrāto* 'his wife' from *imraʾatuhū*; Bd Eg *nāyim* 'sleeping' as against Cl *nāʾimun* (where the modern form could have come directly from the base form **nāwimun*). ʾ is also largely abandoned as the strong onset of initial vowels. The Classical Arabic initial epenthetic vowels have become permanent; only in extremely close combinations do they still drop, e.g., Mo *yā́-vni* ('O my son' = Cl *yā bnī*, pronounced *yabnī* (in isolation *ibnī*), but Eg already *ya ibni*. Final *h*, as long as it is not a radical and thus protected in forms where it occurs within a word, disappears after a short vowel in most dialects; it often remains in Bedouin. The most important cases are the feminine ending *-ah* (pause form for *-atun*, etc.). Bd *-a/eh* > others' *-a/e*, and the pronominal suffix 'his, him' *-uhū* (where the first *u* is originally the nominative ending), pause form *-uh* > *-u/o* (as against Bd *-eh* < *-ih*, the pause form of *-ihī*, the old genitive).

w and *y* usually become *u* and *i* when they lose their vowel; especially initially, like *wa-* 'and' > *u-* (before simple consonant) or Ma *idēya* 'my (two) hands' < *yadaiya*; and as last radical after a vowelless second radical like Bd *bedū* 'Bedouins' < *badwun*, *d'edī* 'kid' < *ǰadyun*.

Maltese exhibits much more extensive consonant shifts. The emphatic sounds have merged with the non-emphatics (except for *q* > ʾ, see above), *ḫ* has become *ḥ*, and *γ* has become ʿ — a noteworthy recurrence of a sound change characteristic of Northwest Semitic (Hebrew and Aramaic). *h* is lost, having either changed to ʾ or disappeared (thus *ū* 'he' < *huwa*, *au* 'here' < *haun* < *hāhunā*) or else strengthened to *ḥ* (thus the pronominal suffix 'his, him' after long vowel, e.g., *ʿamlōḥ* 'they made it' < *ʿamilūhu*). ʿ disappears finally, e.g., *erba* 'four' < *arbaʿun*, *ma* 'with' < *maʿa* (but *mīʿei* 'with me' < *maʿī*), *ta* genitive particle < *matāʿu* (but *tīʿou* 'his' < *matāʿuhū*). Lastly, final voiced stops become voiceless (a tendency also found elsewhere). — Moroccan (in certain dialects) shifts many *t* to affricate *c* and many *b* to spirant *v*.

Consonant assimilations exceed even the limits already known to Old Arabic pronunciation, if not orthography. Noteworthy, among others are *ln* > *nn*, as in Bd *ġāl-ɨnnā* < **ġāl-ilnā* < *qāla* + *lanā* 'he said to us,' Mo *srqu-nna* < *saraqū lanā* 'they stole from us,' Ma *yoʾtonni* < *yaqtulunī* 'he kills me,' — and oppositely *nl* > *ll*, e.g., Ma *kella* < *kāna lahā* 'it was hers'; *ḥh* > *ḥḥ*, e.g., Eg *ṭarahḥa* < *ṭaraḥahā* 'he threw it (fem.) away'; *ʿh* > *ḥḥ*, e.g., Ma *taḥḥa* 'belonging to her' < *matāʿahā*. A few common words have altered their appearance by irregular assimilations; especially *waǰhun* 'face' > Eg *wišš*, Ma *wičč*; *niṣfun* 'half' > Eg *nuṣṣ*. Assimilations at a distance occasionally lead to the change of nonemphatics into emphatics; e.g., Mo *ḍāṛ* 'house' < **dāṛ*, Cl *dārun*; *ṛāṣ* 'head' < **ṛās*, Cl *raʾsun*.

§ 6/2.1.2 The short vowels are found in an unsystematizable multiplicity of qualities; many if not most of them were probably already present in Classical Arabic and only hidden by the orthography, which is limited to the three short vowels *a i u*. This limitation is legitimate to the extent that, as in fact seems also to be the case in the modern dialects, all that matters for the meaning of the word is whether the vowel belongs to the *a*-, *i*-, or *u*-GROUP, while the gradation within the groups depends on accent, syllable structure, neighboring consonants, and also the vowels of the adjacent syllables.[a] The *a*-group stretches from *e* to *o*, thus bordering the *i*- and *u*-groups on the two sides, and has the borderline cases in common, which must be especially kept in mind in the *e* direction. Even the opposition *i* : *u*, which for us is established by the contrary natures of the two vowels and in fact appears to be thoroughly realized in Classical Arabic, holds for the dialects only with qualifications: in part they have a full-fledged scale of transitions from *i* to *u*, within which the exact placement of the vowel is influenced by accent, syllable structure, and phonetic environment; but in part they make the DISTINCTION BETWEEN *i* and *u* dependent on such features. Colloquial Arabic thus reflects the proto-Semitic situation in this regard rather accurately. — Beyond the fluctuations within the same quality group, switches from one group to the other are common. The direction is usually from the *a*-group to the *i*/*u*-group; e.g., the above-mentioned *waǧhun* 'face' > Eg *wišš*, Ma *wičč*; *auwalu* 'first' > Mo *åuwul* (assimilation to the *w*); *abūhā* 'her father' > Bd *ubūhā* (vowel harmony); the feminine ending of the perfect is often *-it* instead of Cl *-at*, the article usualy *il-* instead of Cl *al-*, the broken plural form *af*ᶜ*ālun* is replaced by *if*ᶜ*āl*. But if the imperfect preformatives have *i* for Cl *a* (e.g., Bd *yiġderūn* 'they can' = Cl *yaqdirūna*), that belongs at most only partly under this rubric, and on the whole is one of those cases where Colloquial Arabic preserves formations that the Classical language gave up.

a. Bergsträsser here applies the phonemic principle in the analysis of the minute phonetic detail recorded in his sources.

More secure are the qualities of the long vowels. The most important change is the tendency, also already present in many Old Arabic dialects, to tip *ā* toward *ǟ* - *ē* - *ī*. On the whole, this alteration only occurs in conducive phonetic environments of the vowel and only goes as far as *ǟ* or at most *ē*; Maltese, however, e.g., replaces every *ā* with *īe ī* and the like, or at least with *ē* (e.g., in part near laryngeals): *kāna* 'he was' > *kīen*, *matāᶜuhū* 'belonging to him' > *tīᶜou*, *qāᶜidatun* 'sitting' (feminine) > *ᵓēᶜeda*. — The diphthongs *au* and *ai* succumb to quality variations of their components (e.g., *zaujun* 'pair' > Ma *zeuč* 'two') and are often monophthongized, usually to *ō* and *ē*, sometimes further to *ū* and *ī*; e.g., *lau-lā* 'let it be then that' > Eg *lūla*, *ᶜalaihi* 'on him' > Mo *ᶜlīh*, *kaifa* 'how?' > Ma *kīf*, *aiwa* 'yes' > Ma *īva*.

The quantitative alterations of the vowels are likewise general. The short final vowels, which already in Classical Arabic fell away at the end of a measure of speech (in pause), are lost throughout (and with them case inflection in the noun and mood inflection in the verb); as for long vowels, most final ones, those in medial closed syllables, and many in unaccented open syllables are shortened. Especially noticeable are the shortenings in syllables that became closed only in Colloquial Arabic with the attachment of the *l*-suffixes (e.g., Mo *qål-la* 'he said to her' < *qāla lahā*) or the negation (interrogative particle) -*š* (e.g., Eg *ma tḫaf-š* 'fear not' < *tḫāf* + *š*, Ma *trič* 'do you want?' < *trīt* [Cl *turīdu*] + *š*), or with vowel loss (e.g., Mo *waḥd* 'one' < *wāḥidun*). The shortening can be connected with noticeable quality change, e.g., Ma *ziš t-itfǟl* 'two children' (treated as a single word) against isolated *zeuč*.

The loss of short vowels is most apparent in the loss of the final ones; this is the result of the fact that the Classical Arabic undifferentiated accent is replaced by a more or less strongly marked stress accent. Bedouin is the most conservative; it loses only short vowels of the most unaccented open syllables, like that of the first syllable (*wa-* 'and' before single consonant > *u-*, *rajaᶜna* 'they [feminine] returned' > *erd'aᶜén* with prothetic vowel, as also for the prefix *ya-*, in some cases *iy-*) or that which occurs between main and secondary accent (*dāḫilīna* 'entering' > *dāḫlīn* or *sāriyātun* 'pulling' [feminine] > *sāryāt*, or AFTER the main accent *mā ana* 'not I' > *mā́-nā*). Egyptian is at about the same stage; here also cases are found with vowel loss in the first syllable and prothetic vowel, like *itᶜallimt* 'I learned' < *taᶜallamtu*. Similar also Ma *ezzauweč̌t* 'I married' < *tazauwaǰtu*, *ekmānda* 'he commanded' < Italian *comandare*; on the whole Maltese goes somewhat further, e.g., *ᵓabdūwa* 'they seized her" = Cl *qabaḍūhā*, Eg *ᵓabaḍūha*. The extreme of vowel loss is Moroccan, which in this point comes under the influence of Berber. Here vowels disappear to a great degree even in closed syllables, if an easily pronounced consonant cluster results or if one of the consonants is suited to becoming syllabic; the former in cases like *qålt-lu* 'she said to him' < *qālat lahū* (also Ma *ᵓalt-lu*) or *gāls* 'sitting' < *ǰālis(un)*, the second in cases like *ckellm* 'speak' < *takallam* or *zzmān* 'the time' < *az-zamānu* (thus the article nearly always without vowel), and even with an accented consonant *cṁmet* 'she is at an end' < *tammat, Žḥḥa* < **J̌uḥḥā* (Cl *J̌uḥā*); with the disappearance of two short vowels of successive open syllables *gĺsec* 'she sat down' < *ǰalasat*. Forms like *yadḫulū* 'they came in,' *ismuhum* 'their name' (closed syllable + short-vowelled open + long-vowelled or closed) often undergo a special development. Here the short vowel can disappear and an epenthetic vowel replace it before the beginning of the second syllable: Mo *idaḫlu*, Eg *isimhum* (Ma with loss of the *h* *isémom*); similarly also Ma *aᵓabdūwa* 'seize her' < *iqbiḍūhā*.

As in these cases epenthetic vowels are also common elsewhere, especially with final consonant clusters, and there between the two consonants, as in Bd *ṣubeḥ* 'morning' < *ṣubḥ(un)*, verbal feminine ending *-en* < *-n(a)*; or after the second, like Eg *ᶜamme* 'uncle,' *ḥagge* < *ḥāǧǧ(un)* 'pilgrim,' Ma *taḥte tīna* 'under a fig tree.' The prosthetic vowel is in many cases a vestige of the old case and mood vowel; this is clearest when a pronominal suffix beginning with a consonant is attached to a word that ends with a consonant cluster: Bd *ᶜɨnduhum ᶜɨndena* 'at them, us' = Cl *ᶜindahum ᶜindanā*, Eg *baᶜḍíkum* 'of one of you' = Cl *baᶜḍikum* (genitive), cf. *baᶜḍu/akum* (nominative, accusative).

§ 6/2.1.3 The place of the word accent tends to be influenced by the sentence accent and therefore to fluctuate considerably; e.g., Ma *táᵓta* 'she cuts off,' but *taᵓtȁ ši-tīna* 'she cuts off some figs.' Aside from that, in general the stress rule in our traditional pronunciation of Classical Arabic is valid: the last long (with long vowel or closed) syllable of the word, except final long vowels, bears the accent, and if none is present, the first syllable of the word does.[5] Many dialects vary in isolated groups of cases. Contrary to the rule, Egyptian accents a short penult after a long antepenult: *yeᶜallímek* 'he will teach you' for *yuᶜállimuka*. Bedouin transfers the accent of an open syllable onto the following open syllable (wherewith the vowel of the first usually disappears): *δábaḥahū* 'he slew him' > *δbɨ́ḥeh* (similarly also Egyptian in isolated cases: **fútuwa* 'hero' > *ftíwa*). This also happens when the second vowel is epenthetic, such as Bedouin prefers to develop after a laryngeal: *áhlihī* 'his people' > *ahéleh*, *áᶜmā* 'blind' > **aᶜámā* > *ᶜámā*. Moroccan goes further in a similar direction; throughout (as long as the sentence accent does not deflect the accent)

5. The accented syllables that conform to this rule are not marked in the texts.

it accents not only disyllabic words with open first syllable on the second syllable (*mášā mášat* 'he, she went' > *mša mšäc*, *ᶜálā* 'on' > *ᶜla*, *máᶜa* 'with' > *mᶜa*/*ā*), but often also disyllabic words with closed first syllable: *áḥmaq*(*u*) 'crazy' > *ḥmåq* *márʾa* 'wife' > *mṛa*. And in line with this tendency it has reshaped many monovocalic substantives to metathesized forms: *sábᶜ*(*un*) 'lion' > *svaᶜ*. —

§ 6/2.2.1.1 The pronoun *ana* 'I' often lengthens its vowel: Mo *āna* (beside *ana*), Ma *yēna*; likewise *huwa hiya* 'he, she' > Mo *hūwa hīya*, while in other dialects these pronouns are contracted: Bd *hū hī*, Ma *ū ī*. The second person pronouns have initial *i-*: e.g., Eg *intu* 'you' (masculine plural) = *antum* (final *-m* is lost in the perfect suffix as well *-tum* > *-tu*); in Moroccan they are considerably reshaped: *ncīn* 'thou,' literally the feminine form, but used for both masculine and feminine, as both here and in Maltese the gender distinction in the second person generally is to a large extent abandoned. The third person plurals often retain in the pronoun and in the suffix the vowel difference between the genders, which is lost in Classical: Bedouin masculine pronoun and suffix *hum*, feminine *hin*.

The pronominal suffixes 'thy, thee' and 'his, him' have undergone entirely similar reshapings, rather as in Hebrew, as a result of the loss of the vocalic endings to which those beginning with a consonant could be attached: for attachment to the now consonantally-ending words specific initial vowels (linking vowels) have developed, which correspond in part to their own previous vocalic endings. Thus the basic forms are *-ak* 'thy, thee' masculine, *-ik* feminine; for 'his, him' two forms *-uh* and (Bd) *-ih*, which last calls to mind Am *-eh*. The suffix *-hā* 'her' can also be attached directly to consonants, e.g., Mo *naᶜmelha* 'I will make her'; often the *h* disappears, in some cases with lengthening of the preceding consonant: Ma *ᶜalʾetta* 'they enclosed her' = *γalaqathā*. After a preserved final vowel, the *h* drops only in Maltese: *tuᶜṭīhā* 'she gives her' > *ettēya*, *qabaḍūhā* 'they seized her' > *ᵓabdūwa*. 'His, him' in the same environment is *-h*: *fīh* 'in him,' Ma *fīḥ*. For 'my' the old *-ya* is retained after long vowels: Mo *fīyä* 'in me,' as well as after secondarily long vowels: Mo *mᶜāyä* 'with me' = Cl *maᶜī*, Eg *līye* 'to me' = Cl *lī*.

§ 6/2.2.1.2 As demonstratives the short forms that are rare in Classical Arabic have become widespread; on the one hand Eg Ma *da*, feminine *di*, on the other hand Bd *hā*. In Egyptian the demonstratives can follow, e.g., *es-semek da* 'this fish,' a phenomenon that has a parallel in the noteworthy placement of the interrogative at the end of the sentence in Egyptian: *btištaɣal fēn*[6]? 'where do you work?.' This word order rule derives from Coptic, which on the whole, however, is not much of an influence. — A shorter form has also prevailed for the relative: Bd *ellī*, Eg *elli*, Mo *lli*, Ma *li*. The interrogative 'who?' has, as in, e.g., Hebrew, the vowel *ī*: *mīn*. For 'what?' the circumlocution *aiyu šaiᵓin* 'which thing?,' already early contracted to *aiš*, has spread; Mo *ăš*, *š*, extended *šnnī* (= *aiyu šaiᵓin hiya*) is also related to this, and likewise Ma *-š*, which also acts as the interrogative particle: *trič* < *trīt* + *š* 'do you want?.' Bedouin and Egyptian use the simple *aiy*(*un*) = *ē*, also in Bd *lăh* 'why?.' —

§ 6/2.2.2.1 The feminine verbal forms with *-na* are still found only in the Bedouin and related dialects; the ending has become *-én* (*-enn*), including before a pronominal suffix: *dfenenneh* 'they buried him.' That the prefix vowel is *i* has already been mentioned; *a* occurs in Egyptian in the first person, e.g., *aḫalli* 'I will let,' and in addition as the result of the influence of the first radical, as in Mo *yaᶜmel* 'he will make.' In the western dialects, among which Maltese is also counted, a change in the first person of the imperfect has taken place which constitutes

6. < *fī aina*.

an important characteristic of these dialects: the plural has adopted the ending *-ū*, making it possible for a singular with the prefix *n-* to be formed. Mood distinctions in the imperfect have disappeared even where they were expressed by not just the short vowel endings; the modern forms correspond somewhat to the old subjunctive. Only Bedouin retains the indicative plural ending *-ūn*; the perfect ending *-ū* has here become *-ou* (before a pronominal suffix *-ō-*), so that a differentiation results similar to that in Tigrē.[b] Besides using the participle as durative present (Eg *ᶜārif* '[I] know' — with unequivocal reference even without person indication) and compounding with forms of *kāna* 'he was,' as was already popular in Classical Arabic, greater exactness of time indication is achieved by verbal particles, which are combined with the imperfect, e.g., Eg *bi-* for the punctual present, Mo *ka-* (*ca-*) for the present, Ma *sa-* (with consonant lengthening: *sannibda* 'I will begin') for the future.

b. In a few dialects of southern Arabia, the first person singular suffix is *-k* as in South Arabic and Ethiopic.

§ 6/2.2.2.3 In the basic stem the neutral-mode inflection takes the upper hand; in the perfect *faᶜila* has then become *fiᶜil* by vowel harmony, e.g., Bd *ḥilim* 'he dreamed.' The neutral vocalization with *i* in the last syllable of the stem in the perfect has penetrated into the *t*-reflexive of the intensive;[c] e.g., Eg *itᶜallimt* 'I learned' = Cl *taᶜallamtu*, and thereafter also in the imperfect *atᶜallim* 'I learn.' The same equalization between perfect and imperfect vowel is carried out in many dialects in the derived stems generally; e.g., Eg *ᶜallim* 'he taught,' imperfect *yeᶜallim*; *ištaγal* 'he worked,' imperfect *yištaγal*. The causative is usually supplanted by the intensive; also, the *n*-reflexive is in retreat in many dialects.

c. This pattern could just as well have come from pattern pressure of the other derived stems.

§ 6/2.2.2.5 The II geminate verbs have developed the same "separation vowel" before a consonantal suffix that we already found in Old Semitic; Eg *marr* 'he passed by' (Ma *mār*), first person *marrēt* (versus Cl *marartu*). In the II weak verbs the vowel shortenings of the imperative etc. have been abandoned, since in other closed syllables long vowels are not shortened either: Bd Eg *rūḥ* 'go away.' The verb *ǰāʾa* 'he came,' which as a result of the cooccurrence of *y* as second and ʾ as third radical already exhibited peculiarities in Classical, does so even more in the dialects; e.g., Ma *tīǰi* 'thou comest' = Cl *taǰīʾu* with secondary lengthening of the first syllable. Through consolidation of *ǰāʾa* with the preposition *bi-* a new verb *ǰāb yiǰīb* has come into being: 'come with' = 'bring.'

§ 6/2.2.3 Of the nunation of nouns, frozen traces are found here and there; it is still productive in Bedouin, although without case distinction, for the expression of indefiniteness: *ḓilᶜen* 'a mountain.' In other dialects the numeral 'one' is in the process of weakening into an indefinite article: Ma *darba waḥeda* 'once.' Of the dual only a little is retained; the ending *-ēn*, like the plural ending *-īn*, is that of the old oblique case. The most important innovation in the area of nominal inflection is the development of genitival locutions. The most widespread is the substantive *matāᶜun* 'property,' Eg *betāᶜ*, in Maltese shortened to *ta* (with pronominal suffix *tīᶜ-*): Eg *es-semek da betāᶜ el-baḥr* 'this river fish,' Ma *is-siǰar ta-tīn* 'the fig tree.' Often a *t* also appears in the combination of numeral with substantive: Ma *erba t-irǰīel* 'four men,' *zìš t-itfā̆l* 'two children.' But this *t* has a different origin, coming from the ending of the feminine form of the numeral that occurs in Old Arabic before a masculine substantive. Entirely different from these nominal genitive locutions is the pronominal *d-* in Moroccan, which is, strikingly, identical with that in Ethiopic and Aramaic and can be construed the same way; besides the simple specification of the governing substantive (as in the examples just presented from other dialects), anticipation of the genitive with a pronominal suffix is also possible, at least after kinship terms: *l-ᶜurs d-vencu* 'the marriage of his daughter,' but *yimmåh d-Žḥḥa* 'the (literally his) mother of Joha.' Before a pronominal suffix this genitive morpheme has an extended shape: *diāla* 'belonging to her.'

§ 6/2.2.4 As in later Aramaic and Ethiopic, in Colloquial Arabic the preposition *l-* + pronominal suffix is enclitically attached to the verb, so that a new series of *l*-suffixes comes into being; yet their meaning remains strictly dative, with the ethical dative so popular in Aramaic playing no role. Beside direct attachment as in Bd *δɨbäḥ-lɨh* 'he killed for himself,' Eg *ᶜārif-lak* '(I) know for you,' Mo *srqu-nna* < *saraqū lanā* 'they have stolen from us,' Ma *kel-la* < *kāna lahā* 'it was hers,' an epenthetic vowel *i* is found (especially after a long syllable): Bd *ġāl-ɨnna* = **ġāl-ilna* 'he said to us,' Eg *gibt-ílak* 'I brought to you,' Ma *ᵓetᶜet-íla* 'she cut for her.' In Moroccan *l-* has partly become *n-*. Maltese, at variance with most Old Arabic, can introduce the accusative with a double *l-*: *līli* 'me,' *lilmīn* 'whom?.' Part of the semantic range of *l-* has been taken over by *ᶜinda*: Mo Ma *ᶜanda* 'she has.' In general the old *ilā* 'to' has changed over to *l-*; in Bedouin it survives as *ilyā* 'until,' merged with the conjunction *iδā* > *ilyā* 'behold, if, when.'

The prepositions *b- l- k-* on one hand and *fī* on the other are assimilated to each other with regard to their endings: Bd *f-el-lēl* 'at night,' Mo *f-ḍ-ḍāṛ* 'in the house,' reversed Eg *līye* 'to me,' Ma *bīya* 'with her.' In Egyptian and elsewhere *fīh* 'in him' has become equivalent in meaning to a verb 'exists.' Other prepositions are also shortened, *ᶜalā* 'on' frequently > *ᶜa-* and *min* 'from, out of' at least before the article > *m-*: Eg *mi-l-baḥr* 'out of the river,' Ma *mi-s-safar* 'from the journey,' but also *m-baᶜt* 'afterward.' Among the numerous new prepositions the most interesting is Eg *wīya* 'with' from synonymous old *wa-* (with accusative) + accusative particle *īyā-*, which properly was only appropriate before a pronominal suffix.

The negations, among which *mā* achieves the greatest ascendancy (*lā* recedes, the others are not found), tend to be strengthened by *šai*ᵓ 'thing,' negated 'nothing': Eg *ma tḫaf-š* = *tḫāf* + *š* 'fear not,' Mo *ma qulci-lī-ši* 'you have not said to me,' Ma *ma kenič* < *kīenet* + *š* 'she was not'; and not abbreviated *ma kìm vēru šēn* (< *šai*ᵓ*an*) 'it was not true.' Somewhat parallel to the development in French, the negation proper can then be absent and the negative meaning be transferred to the *šai*ᵓ: Ma *tibza šēn* 'fear nothing.' In Maltese, as already mentioned, this particle is also used as the interrogative.

Like ᶜ*an* 'from, away from,' the specifically Arabic counterpart to *min* 'from, out of,' so also *fa*- 'and, thus,' the counterpart of *wa*- 'and,' is not widespread in the dialects. 'Or' is usually replaced by the innovation *wa-illā* 'and if not,' e.g., Bd *wellā*. Of *an*(*na*) 'that' survives the meaning, of *inna* 'behold' the shape in the modern *in* or *inn*- 'that.' Numerous conjunctions are innovated out of nouns. —

§ 6/2.4 The vocabulary of Colloquial Arabic includes many foreign components, but retains the genuine Arabic character throughout. Maltese is an exception, in which the Italian-Sicilian words constitute a clearly defined portion of the total picture of the linguistic inventory. Elsewhere, Spanish, etc., and (to a lesser extent) Berber words prevail in the west, while in the east the Italian, French, and Greek borrowings do, with in addition a number of Turkish and Persian-Turkish items.

Text Specimens[7]

1. Central Arabian Bedouin[8]

a) The Good Spirits of Mefar

Mefār δ̣ilᶜen fī Kɨšɨb meγīb[9] *šems min el-Ḥafer; u-hū fīh ed'wād*[10] *fī ɟēf fī d'ämbeh min šerġ. we-l-ġenūṣ*[11] *mā yiġderūn*[12] *yeδbeḥūn min eṣ-ṣeid ellī fī ṭerrāf*[13] *eδ̣-δ̣ileᶜ, δāllīn min el-ed'wād.*

kān fīh ġannāṣ, δɨbäḥ-lɨh δ̣abī fī Mefār.

yōm[14] *d'āh*[15] *u-lezmeh, lɨġā*[16] *ᶜalā d'ambeh el-eimen mā*[17] *w-ᶜalā d'amb el-eisar mā;*

u-baᶜdēn ɨftekar fī hā δ̣-δ̣abī u-rāḥ[18] *bɨh yemm*[19] *ahéleh.*

ṭabaẖōh w-akalōh; u-rɨġed ellī d'āb[20] *eδ̣-δ̣abī. ḥilim f-el-lēl u-hū nāyim*[21] *b-el-ed'wād.*

d'ōh u-ġālou: "lā̈h teδbaḥ rāḥletnā ellī nerwī ᶜalā̈hā?" yōm aṣbaḥ, ilyā́hū ᶜamā;[22] *seddedou ᶜiyūneh.*[23]

Mefar is a mountain in Kishib west of el-Hafer; and there there are good (spirits) in a grotto in its eastern flank. | And the hunters cannot fell any of the wildlife that is on the borders of the mountain, for they fear the good (spirits). | There was a hunter who killed himself a gazelle in Mefar. | When he went to it and picked it up, he found on its right side water and on the left side water; | and thereafter he considered this gazelle and went with it (i.e. brought it) to his people. | They cooked it and ate it; but the one who had brought the gazelle went to sleep. He dreamed in the night while he was sleeping of the good (spirits). | They came to him and said: "Why have you slain our beast of burden, on which we fetch water?" When he woke, lo, he was blind; they had blinded (lit. closed) his eyes. |

7. Classical forms are as a rule given without case vowel or nunation (the feminine ending is given as *-a*). 8. Courtesy of Prof. Dr. J. J. Hess of Zurich. 9. Noun of place from *γyb* 'set' (said of the sun). 10. Plural of Cl *ǰaiyid* (*ǰwd*) 'good.' 11. Plural of the intensive noun of agent *qannāṣ*. 12. Cl *qdr* with *an* 'that.' 13. = Cl *aṭrāf*, plural of *ṭaraf*. 14. Cl *yauma* 'on the day that,' after which the consequent effectively occurs in the genitive. 15. Cl *ǰāᵓahū* (*ǰyᵓ*). 16. *lqy*. 17. Cl *māᵓ(un)*. 18. *rwḥ*. 19. Literally substantive 'side.' 20. < *ǰāᵓa bi-* 'he came with. . . .' 21. *nwm*. 22. = Cl *aᶜmā* (*afᶜalu* for [bodily] defect). 23. Plural of *ᶜain*.

w-ed'wād Mefār meδkūrīn; ennās el-wed'ᶜānīn iyrūḥūn u-ybātūn ᶜɨnduhum f-el-ɟēf ellī hum fīh.
w-el-wed'ᶜān iyd'īb mɨᶜeh šāh u-yeδbaḥhā ᶜɨnduhum u-ynām[24] *ilya ṣ-ṣubeḥ f-el-ɟēf.*
w-ilyā bayā yemšī, ᶜálleġ ᶜaṣāh[25] *wellā ḫātimeh wellā wāḥid min hedūmeh*[26] *ᶜɨnduhum. w-akθar el-wed'ᶜānīn iyṭībūn*[27] *b-šīt*[28] *Állāh.*

And the good (spirits) of Mefar are famous; sick people go there and spend the night with them in the grotto that they are in. | And the sick one brings with him a sheep and slaughters it by them and sleeps until morning in the grotto. | And when he wants to depart, he hangs up his staff or his signet ring or one of his garments by them. And most of the sick recover by the will of Allah.

b) Star Fable

ġāl-ɨnnā[29] *ᶜAly el-Manṣūr ᶜalā sālfeh*[30] *ᶜan Banāt*[31] *naᶜaš*[32] *— u-hin ᶜɨndenā ye*[33]*-l-bedū ísimhin es-Sibbäᶜ*[34] *—,*

in kān fī mā muδ̣ā[35] *ḫaṭab ed-D'edī waḥḥedeh*[36] *min Banāt naᶜaš min ubūhā*[37] *u-lā riδ̣ī*[38] *yd'ouwizeh.*[39]

u-ġɨδ̣ubhā[40] *u-yaṣabhā, u-ḫāf*[41] *min ubūhā w-δbɨḥeh u-daḫal ᶜal el-Ḥowēd'izēn.*

Ali el-Mansur told us of a tradition about the Banat-na'ash (= Daughters of the Bier, the seven stars of the Big Dipper) — and their name among us Bedouins is es-Sibbe —, | that in the past (lit. in what is past) el-Dyedi (= Little Kid, the Pole Star) asked for one of the Banat-na'ash from her father, but he did not consent to marry (her) to him. | And he seized her and raped her, and he was afraid of her father and killed him and sought sanctuary with el-Howeydyizen (= Two Little Guardians, the stars β γ UMi). |

24. *nwm.* 25. From Cl *ᶜaṣan ᶜaṣā* (*ᶜṣw*). 26. Plural of *hidm.* 27. *ṭyb.* 28. *šyʾ* (Cl *mašīʾa*). 29. = **ġāl* + **ilnā.* 30. Feminine participle. 31. Plural of *bint.* 32. Cl *naᶜš.* 33. Cl *yā*, literally vocative particle. 34. From Cl *as-sabᶜ* 'the Seven.' 35. *mḍy.* 36. Cl *wāḥida.* 37. Cl *abūhā.* 38. *rḍw.* 39. Cl *rḍw* with *an* 'that.' 40. Cl *qbḍ.* 41. *ḫwf.*

u-šālén[42] *ubūhin b-én-naᶜaš u-dfenenneh, u-d'en*[43] *bi-nᶜašhin yebén*[44] *yeδbɨḥɨnneh bi-θār*[45] *ubūhin u-yaṣab ɨẖthin.*

And they carried out their father on the bier and buried him, and they came with their bier since they wanted to kill him in revenge for their father and for the rape of their sister. |

w-ilyā δ̣harén yebenneh, ġāl:
"yā sāryāt[46] *el-lēl, heilen heil, terā*[47] *má-nā b-el-yerīm,*[48] *el-yerīm-e*[49]*-Sheil."*

And when they came and wanted him, he said: | "O circlers of the night, heylen heyl (rhyming nonsense words), you see, not I am the guilty one, the guilty one is Suheyl (the star Canopus)." |

θim[50] *nuṣā́n*[51]*-e*[49]*-Sheil u-ġābäl-hin min beᶜīd u-ġāl:*

Then they sought Suheyl, and he approached them from afar and said: |

"yā sāryāt el-lēl, hed'in hedī, terā mā́-nā b-el-yerīm, el-yerīm el-D'edī."
erd'aᶜén[52] *ᶜal el-D'edī, u-d'ou*[53] *el-Ḥowēd'izēn min dūneh u-fakkōh, ḥeiδ*[54] *inneh dāẖlin ᶜalāhum. u-hāδä suwāthum*[55] *dāyim.*[56]

"O circlers of the night, hedyin hedi (nonsense), you see, not I am the guilty one, the guilty one is el-Dyedi." | They returned to el-Dyedi, but el-Howeydyizen came before him (lit. on this side of him) and protected him, since he was a refugee of theirs. And this they do perpetually.

2. Egyptian

The Fellah Learns to Fish (from a shadow play)[57]

Meʾeddim: *inte b-tištayal di-l-waʾte*[59] *fēn, ya Zibriʾāš?*
Zibriʾāš: *itᶜallimt eṣ-ṣēd. . . .*
Me.: *lākin ᶜārif-lak, ḥatta tiṣṭād*[61] *fīha, kwaiyisa ẖāliṣ, baḥr kebīr!*

Me'eddim:[58] Where do you work at this time, Zibriash?[60]
Zibriash: I have learned fishing. . . .
Me.: But I know (a place) that you can fish in, very (lit. pure) beautiful, a great river (lit. sea)!

42. *šyl.* 43. Cl *jiʾna* (*jʾy*). 44. *yebā* irregular imperfect of *bayā.* 45. Cl *θaʾr.* 46. Feminine plural participle. 47. *rʾy* (already Cl *tarā*). 48. *bi-* introducing a predicate noun after negation. 49. Helping vowel. 50. Cl *θumma.* 51. *nsy.* 52. = Cl *rajaᶜna*, with prothetic vowel. 53. Cl *jāʾū* (*jyʾ*). 54. Cl *ḥaiθu.* 55. From *swy* 'make.' 56. *dwm.* 57. P. Kahle, *Das Krokodilspiel (Liᶜb et-Timsâḥ), ein egyptisches Schattenspiel, Nachtrag (Nachrichten d. Ges. d. Wiss. zu Göttingen, Philol.-hist. Kl.*, 1920, pp. 277-284), pp. 278-281. 58. 'The introducer,' who speaks the prefatory poem; a stock figure. 59. *-e* helping vowel. 60. A fellah. 61. *ṣyd.*

Z.: *ṭaiyib, ya ᶜamm, urih*[62]*-li, we-nibʾa*[63] *širka.*

Z.: Truly, uncle, show it to me, and we will be a partnership (i.e. set up a business together).

Me.: *ahu l-baḥr elli ʾuddāmak da.*

Me.: The river there, which is in front of you.

(Z. *ṭallaᶜ el-yābe*[64] *we-ṭarraḥḥa*[65] *fi-l-moiye*[66] *we-ʾāl:) maḥmaḥīm! (ṭilᶜit semeke*[68] *kebīre u-ḫaṭafit eš-šebeke u-waʾʾeᶜto ᶜala wiššo,*[69] *ḥatta inno beʾa nuṣṣo*[70] *fi-l-moiye we-nuṣṣo ᶜala l-barr, u-yeʾūl:) ilḥaʾni, ya Meʾeddim!*

Z. (takes [lit. took, and so in the past as description throughout] *out the pole, throws it into the water, and says):* mahmahim![67] *(A big fish comes out, grabs at the net, and throws it* [lit. makes it fall] *on his face, so that he is half in the water and half on land, and he says):* Save (lit. reach) me, Me'eddim!

(Me. *giri*[71] *le-ᶜando we-rafaᶜo min el-moiye we-ʾāl:) mā-lak?*

Me. (runs to him, lifts him out of the water, and says): What's with you?

Z.: *iskut, ya aḫi, es-semek da betāᶜ el-baḥr ftiwa, ḫad*[72] *minni l-yāb we-kafāni*[73] *ᶜala wišši.*

Z.: Quiet, brother, this fish from the river is an athlete, it has taken my pole and thrown me onto my face.

Me.: *la*[74]*-ašuf*[75]*-lak ᶜamm yeᶜallímak eṣ-ṣēd.*

Me.: I will look for a man (lit. uncle) who will teach you fishing.

Z.: *aᶜmil maᶜrūf,*[76] *ya Meʾeddim, we-šuf-li ᶜamm yeᶜallimni!*

Z.: Be so good, Me'edim, as to (lit. do good) look for a man to teach me!

Me.: *ṭaiyib, ḫallīk*[77] *wāʾif, we-ana agib*[78]*-lak wāḥid yeᶜallímak eṣ-ṣanᶜa. (meši*[79] *l-Meʾeddim, daḫal gūwa*[80] *we-ʾāl:) ya ḥagge*[81] *Manṣūr! ya šēḫ el-maᶜās!*[82]

Me.: Good, stay here, and I will bring you someone who will teach you the craft. *(Me. goes off, comes on, and says:)* Mr. (lit. [Mecca] pilgrim) Mansur! Master of ship passengers!

Manṣūr: *mīn dah, elli be-yindah?*

Mansur: Who is it that calls?

Me.: *taᶜāla, gibt-ílak walad teᶜallímu ṣ-ṣēd.*

Me.: Come here, I'm bringing you a young man for you to teach fishing.

62. *wry* causative, imperative with pronominal suffix. 63. *bqy*, literally 'stay.' 64. Noun of unity. 65. *ḥḥ* < *ḥh.* 66. Diminutive of *māʾ*, after a root *mwy.* 67. Comical pious euphemism for the formula *bi-smi llāhi r-raḥmāni r-raḥīm* 'in the name of God, the gracious, the merciful.' 68. Noun of unity. 69. Cl *waǰh.* 70. Cl *niṣf.* 71. *ǰry.* 72. *ʾḫδ.* 73. *kfy.* 74. 'Thus that.' 75. *šwf.* 76. Passive participle of *ᶜrf* 'recognize.' 77. *ḫly.* 78. *ǰyb.* 79. *mšy.* 80. From Cl *ǰauw* 'interior.' 81. Cl *ḥāǰǰ*, participle; *-e* helping vowel. 82. 'People who travel down the Nile in a boat.'

Ma.: *ḥāḍir, ya ibni! (we-ḫarag ᵓuddām Zibriᵓāš we-ᵓāl:) . . . ya Zibriᵓāš,*
in gibt-ílak el-ᶜaṣabīye,
tiṣṭād elli tiṣṭādo līye? . . .

Ma.: Ready, my son! *(And he goes out to* [lit. before] *Zibriash and says)* . . . Zibriash, if I bring you the fishing rod, will you fish what you fish for ME?[83]. . .

Z.: *ya ᶜamme,*[84] *ma tḫaf*[85]*-š; elli aṣṭādo lik. w-igri, hat*[86]*-li l-ᶜaṣabīye! . . .*

Z.: Uncle, fear not; what I fish is yours. And run, give me the fishing rod! . . .

Ma.: *ḫud,*[87] *ya ibni, w-ittékel*[88] *ᶜal-áḷḷah! (rāḥ.)*

Ma.: Take, my son, and trust in Allah! *(Exit.)*

(Z.: *ḫad el-ᶜaṣabīye we-deldilha fi-l-baḥr u-b-iᵓūl:) maḥmaḥīm! (ṭiliᶜ et-timsāḥ mi-l-baḥr we-rāḥ belaᶜo huwa w-il-ᶜaṣabīye, wa-la beᵓā*[89]*-š bāyin min buᵓᵓ et-timsāḥ illa rāso.*[90]

Z. (takes the fishing rod, lowers it into the river, and says): mahmahim! *(The crocodile rises out of the river, goes* [and] *swallows him, him and the fishing rod, and nothing remains visible outside the mouth of the crocodile except his head.)*

daḫal er-Riḫim, laᵓa[92] *t-timsāḥ nāyim, ᵓāl:) . . . mīn da?*

Rikhim[91] *(enters, finds the crocodile sleeping,* [and] *says):* . . . Who is that?

Z.: *ana Zibriᵓāš.*

Z.: I am Zibriash.

R.: *mā-lak, ya Zibriᵓāš?*

R.: What's with you, Zibriash?

Z.: *iskut, ya Riḫim, aḥsan*[93] *et-timsāḥ balaᶜni, we-ḫallīk beᶜīd, l-aḥsan*[94] *yiblaᶜak inte rāḫar.*[95]. . .
(Ma. enters again).

Z.: Quiet, Rikhim, since the crocodile has swallowed me, and keep away, lest it swallow you too. . . .
(Ma. enters again).

R.: *aḷḷāh aḷḷāh, ya šeḫ Manṣūr, la-mā tegīb et-timsāḥ teḫallīh yiblaᶜ er-rāgil?*[96]

R.: Allah, Allah, Sheikh Mansur, why do you bring the crocodile and have it swallow the man?

Ma.: *ana, ya rāgil, ḫallēto yiblaᶜ er-rāgil?*

Ma.: I, man, had it swallow the man?

R.: *ummāl; ana šuft it-timsāḥ ᵓāᶜid wīyāk ᶜala l-ᵓahwa, we-intu ᵓāᶜdīn wīya baᶜḍíkum we-yilᶜab wīyāk ed-dōmana.*[97] *w-aḷḷāh el-ᶜaẓīm illa arūḥ aᵓul*[98]*-l-imrāto w-ibno w-aḫallīhum yigū*[99]*-lak hine*[100] *fi-l-ḥāl.*

R.: Sure; I saw the crocodile sitting with you at coffee, you were sitting together and it was playing dominoes with you. By Allah the mighty, if I don't go tell it to his wife and his son and have them come here in a moment (lit. circumstance)!

83. Rhymed. 84. *-e* helping vowel. 85. *ḫwf.* 86. Interjection, Cl *hāti* 'here with . . !" 87. Already Cl *ḫuδ* imperative of *ᵓḫδ*. 88. *wkl* (*tt* < *wt*). 89. *bqy.* 90. Cl *raᵓs.* 91. Stock figure, the "cat father." 92. *lqy.* 93. Elative of *ḥasan*, 'better, more beautiful.' 94. = Cl *al-aḥsan.* 95. = Cl *al-āḫar.* 96. For Cl *rajul.* 97. Italian, etc., *domino.* 98. *qwl* imperfect, Cl *aqūlu.* 99. *jyᵓ.* 100. = Cl *hunā.*

3. Moroccan[101]

Joha Guards the Door

kān f-å̀uwul z-zmā̈n ṛāžl smā̈h[102] *Žḥ́ḥa. u-kā̈nec ᶜandu yimmā̈h,*[103] *smā̈ha Ḥlīmä. u-kā̈nc yimmā̈̀h d-Žḥ́ḥa ᶜanda*[104] *ẖāha*[105] *smā̈h ᶜlī.*[106]

u-kān ᶜàndu l-ᶜùrs d-vencu. žā̈̀c[107] *yimmā̈̀h d-Žḥ́ḥa mšäc*[108] *n-l-ᶜùrs d-ẖāha, u-ᶜaiyṭǻc ᶜlà Žḥ́ḥa qålt-lu: "yǻ-vni, ḥḍì*[109] *l-bā̈̀v ḍ-ḍ-ḍāṛ!"*

qål-la: "ẖyā̈r,[110] *a-yimmä!" wú-mšäc hī̀ya l-l-ᶜurs u-ẖallcu*[111] *kä-yàḥḍi l-bā̈v. žā̈̀c hī̀ya immā̈h glísec*[112] *f-ḍ-ḍā̈̀ṛ d-l-ᶜurs.*

žā̈̀ hūwa qṇåṭ gā̈ls f-ḍ-ḍāṛ v-weḥdīcu.[113] *žā̈̀ hūwa ẖammem, šǹni yaᶜmel. qā̊̄l: "āna yimmä qålt-li: 'àḥḍi l-bā̈v!';*
w-āna vā̈̀š[114] *nqå̀llaᶜ l-bā̈v u-naᶜmèlha ᶜlà ṛāṣi u-neddī̀ha*[115] *mᶜāyä u-nimši wu-nᶜàiyåṭ ᶜlà immä džì*[116] *n-ḍ-ḍā̈̀ṛ diā̈la."*
žā̈̀ hūwa mšà n-ḍ-ḍā̈̀ṛ d-l-ᶜurs, wòqqof l-bā̈v mᶜà l-ḥaiṭ[117] *u-då̀qq f-l-bā̈̀v ḍ-ḍ-ḍā̈̀ṛ d-l-ᶜurs.*

There was once upon a time (lit. at the beginning of time) a man whose name was Joha. And he had a (lit. his) mother whose name was Halima. And Joha's mother had a brother whose name was Ali. | And he celebrated (lit. had) his daughter's wedding. Joha's mother went to her brother's wedding (i.e. that her brother had) and she called to Joha and said to him: "O my son, guard the door of the house!" | He said to her: "Yes, O mother!" And she went to the wedding and left him while he guarded the door. She, his mother, sat down in the wedding-house. | He got bored sitting in the house alone (lit. in his solitude). He considered what he should do. He said: "My mother said to me: 'Guard the door'; | and I will therefore pick up the door and set it on my head and take it with me and go and call to my mother (that) she come to her house." | He went to the wedding-house, placed the door by the wall, and knocked on the door of the wedding-house. |

101. Courtesy of Prof. Dr. A. Fischer of Leipzig. 102. *smā-* byform of *ism-*. 103. Cl *umm* (*imm*), reshaped after Berber *imma*. 104. Conflated nominal clause. 105. Cl *aẖāhā*. 106. Cl *ᶜAlīy*(*un*). 107. 'She came' (*ǰy*ᵓ), strengthens the ingressive meaning of the following perfect. 108. *mšy*. 109. *ḥḍy*. 110. = Cl *ẖair* 'good thing.' 111. *ẖly*. 112. Cl *ǰls* (dissimilation). 113. Abstract in *-īyat-* (nisbe ending) from Cl *waḥda*(*hū*) 'alone.' 114. *b* + *ā̈š*, literally 'where-with,' then conjunction 'therefore.' 115. ᵓ*dy*. 116. *ğy*ᵓ. 117. Cl *ḥā*ᵓ*iṭ*.

ḫàržec ʿandu wàḥd l-mṛa[118] *mǹ ḍ-ḍā̀ṛ d-l-ʿurs u-qålt-lu: "ā̀š ca-cqūl, a-Žḥ́ḥa?" qål-la: "ʿaiyåṭ-li ʿlà immä!" qålt-lu: "mlīḥ."*
daḥlec ᶜànd immä̀h d-Žḥḥa, qål̀t-la:
ckèllm n-ebnek!" ḥàržec n-ᶜandu ka-

A woman came to him from the wedding-house and said to him: "What do you say, O Joha?" He said to her: "Call my mother for me!" She said to him: "Fine." |

daḫlec ʿànd immā̀h d-Žḥ́ḥa, qålt-la: ckèllm n-ebnek!" ḫàržec n-ʿandu ka-cγōwuc,[119] *qålt-lu: "yå-wùld l-ḥrām, škū̀n*[120] *ḫallī̀ci f-ḍ-ḍāṛ, yå-wùld l-ḥrām?"*

She went in to Joha's mother (and) she said to her: "Talk with your son!" She went out to him, whereupon she cried out (and) said to him: "O good-for-nothing (lit. child of the forbidden, bastard), whom did you leave in the house, O good-for-nothing?" |

qål-la: "ya-immä, ʿlā̀š[121] *ka-dzèbbl fīyä? qulcī-li: 'ḥḍì l-bā̄v!'; mā̀ qulci-lī-ši: 'àḥḍi ḍ-ḍāṛ!'*

He said to her: "O mother, why do you insult me? You said to me: 'Guard the door!'; you didn't say to me: 'Guard the house!' |

žī̀c ana qållàʿt l-bā̄v wu-rftcà[122] *ʿlà ṛāṣi. rā̀hi*[123] *mwòqqfa mʿà l-ḥait."*

I picked up the door and brought it here on my head. See, it is placed by the wall." |

žā̀c hīya qålt-lu: "kā̄n ncīn ḥmåq[124] *àu š-ʿandek? dā̀va*[125] *idàḫlu s-surrāq*[126] *n-ḍ-ḍāṛ, srqù-nna l-ḥwāiž."*[127]

She said to him: "Are you a fool, or what's with you? Now the thieves will enter the house and steal our belongings." |

žà hūwa qål-la: "āna mà ʿàndi ḫvāṛ.[128] *ncīn mà qulcī-li ḥḍī γè̄r l-bā̄v. ṛā́nī*[129] *žìvca*[130] *ʿlà ṭáḥri." žā̀c yimmā̄h ka-caʿrf vna ṛāžel vūhāli.*

He said to her: "I have no information (i.e. am not guilty). You did not tell me to guard anything but the door. Look at me, I brought it here on my back." (So) his mother realized (that) her son (was) a simpleton. |

vdā̀c[131] *kå̀-ṭṭhåk*[132] *ʿlīh u-qā̄lc: "hāda hū̀wa l-ḥåqq llì qulci, yå-Žḥ́ḥa, wu-s-sā̄lā̄m.*[133] *ḥàtc*[134] *āna ḥamqå*[135] *llì ka-nsā̀ʿaf l-ḥmåq." cm̀met l-ḫrā̀fa d-Žḥ́ḥa.*

She began to laugh at him and said: "That is the truth, what you said, O Joha, and there's an end to it (lit. hail, the parting greeting)! I too am foolish, that I encourage a fool." So ends the story of Joha.

118. Cl *imraʾa*. 119. *γwθ* intensive. 120. = *š* + *yakūn* 'what is it?' 121. < *ʿalā aiyi šaiʾin*. 122. *rfd*. 123. *rā* (imperative of *rʾy* 'see') + *hī* 'she.' 124. Cl *aḥmaqu* (*afʿalu* for [bodily] defect). 125. < Cl *daʾban* (accusative) 'usually.' 126. Plural of *sāriq*. 127. Cl *ḥawāʾiǰu*, plural of *ḥāǰatun*. 128. Cl *aḫbār*, plural of *ḫabar*. 129. *rā* 'see' + pronominal suffix *-nī*. 130. *ǰyb*. 131. *bdʾ*. 132. *ḍḥk*. 133. Instead of *slā̄m*, borrowed from literary *salām*. 134. Cl *ḥattā* 'likewise, also.' 135. Cl *ḥamqāʾu* (form *faʿlāʾu* as feminine of *afʿalu* for [bodily] defects).

4. Maltese[136, d]

[I] after a word indicates Italian origin.

The Wicked Mother-in-Law

Darba icun hemm rè, u dan ir-rè siefer. U il mara tighou chienet ma ommu.
Chella zeuġ t'itfal, chien isemhom ix-xemx u il kamar. U omm ir-rè chitbitlu, li ghanda kattus u kattusa.

U il leil ghalketa giò il cantina, u chienet tatiha biccia hobz u ftit ilma.

U ir-rè, meta kalitlu, li ghanda kattus u kattusa, ikattagh wicciu; u dan li chitbitlu ommu, ma chien veru xein.

darba[137] *íkon*[138]*-èm*[139] *re,*[I] *u-då-r-ré sīefer. wi-l-māra*[140] *tīᶜou kīenet m-ommu.*
kel-la[141] *zìš*[142] *t-itfå̄l,*[143] *kīen isémom iš-šemš wi-l-ᵓamar. uw-omm ir-ré kidbit*[144]*-lu, li-ᶜanda ᵓattōs*[145] *uᵓattōsa.*
wi-l-lēl ᶜalᵓetta ǰò[146] *l-kantīna,*[I] *u-kīenet ettēya*[147] *bičča*[I] *ḥops*[148] *wì-ftit íl-ma.*
w-ir-ré, metta[149] *ᵓalt-lu, li-ᶜanda ᵓattōs u-ᵓattōsa, yaᵓatta*[150] *wičču;*[151] *u-då̄n li-kidbit-lu ommu, mā kìm*[152] *vēru*[I] *šēn.*

Once there was a king, and this king went on a journey, and his wife was with his mother. |
She bore (lit. had) two children, their names were Sun and Moon. And the king's mother wrote him that she had (borne) a tomcat and a queencat. | And in the night she locked her in the cellar, and she gave her always (just) a piece of bread and some water. | But the king, when she wrote (lit. said) to him that she had (borne) a tomcat and a queencat, raked (lit. cut up) his face; but what his mother had written to him was not true at all.

U darba wahda kalet: "Chif seira nibda naghmel biha, din il mara? Ghax issa yigi minn is-safar u lili joktolni!"

u-darba waḥeda[153] *ᵓå̄let: "kīf sannibda*[154] *naᶜmel bīya, di-l-māra? ᶜaš ís-sa*[155] *yīǰi*[156] *mi-s-safar u-līli yoᵓtonni!"*[157]

And one time she (the king's mother) said: "How shall I begin to deal with her, this woman? For he will now return from the trip, and he will kill me!" |

Darba ikun hemm rè, u dar-rè siefer. U il-mara tiegħu kienet ma' ommu. | Kellha żweġt itfal, kien jisimhom ix-xemx u il-qamar. U omm ir-rè kitbitlu li għanda qattus u qattusa. | U il-lejl għalqeta ġol-kantina, u kienet tagħtiha biċċa ħobż u ftit il-ma. | U ir-rè, meta qalitlu, li għanda qattus u qattusa, iqatta' wiċċu; u dan li kitbitlu ommu, ma kien veru xejn.

U darba waħda qalet: "Kif sejra nibdaq nagħmel biha, dil-mara? Għax issa jiġi mis-safar u lili joqtolni!" |

d. Stumme's text was published in 1905; Maltese orthography was standardized in 1924. A transcription into modern standard spelling is here appended, based on □6/2f:1.

136. H. Stumme, *Maltesische Studien* 1904 (LSS 1/4), pp. 47, 76. 137. Noun of unity from infinitive *ḍarb* 'strike,' literally 'a blow.' 138. *kwn.* 139. = Cl *θamma.* 140. = Cl *marᵓa* (byform of *imraᵓa*). 141. = *kān* + *lahā.* 142. Cl *zauǰ* 'pair.' 143. Plural of *ṭifl.* 144. *ktb.* 145. *qṭs.* 146. Cl *ǰauw* 'interior.' 147. Cl *tuᶜṭīhā* (ᶜ*ṭy*). 148. *ḫbz.* 149. Cl *matā.* 150. *qṭᶜ.* 151. Cl *waǰh.* 152. = *kīen* (destressing, assimilation of *n* to *v*). 153. Cl *wāḥida.* 154. *bdᵓ.* 155. < Cl *as-sāᶜata* 'the/this hour.' 156. *ǰyᵓ.* 157. *qtl.*

X'ghamlet? Hargita minn giò il cantina u marret tellketa giò il ghalka u katghetila ideiha.
Din il mara mbaghd ma chieniċ tistagh tiecol. Chien hemm is-sigiar ta tin; chienet tkum tmur taht tina, taktagh xi tina b'halka.

Giè zeugia minn is-safar. Mar ghand ommu, kalla: "Il mara tighei feina?" Kalitlu: "Checceita il-barra: chella kattus u kattusa!"

Darba wahda hareġ il caccia u mar idur giò din il ghalka, u rà xebba kieghda bil kaghda.
Kalla: "Binti, haun x'inti taghmel?" Kalitlu: "Fein tridni immur?" Kalla: "Triċ tigi mighei?"

Kalitlu: "Iva!" Kalla: "Kabelma tigi mighei, gheidli il fatt, chif in hù!"

š-ʿamlet? ḥarǰitta[158] *min-ǰò l-kantīna u-marret telleʾetta*[159] *ǰò l-ʿalʾa*[160] *o-ʾetʿet*[161]*-íla idēya.*[162]
di-l-mā̀ra m-baʿt[163] *mā keníč tista*[164] *tīekol.*[165] *kèn ém is-siǰar*[166] *ta-tīn; kīenet tʾōm*[167] *tmūr*[168] *tàḥte*[169] *tīna, taʾtā̀*[170] *ši-tīna p-ḥalʾa.*

ǰīe zeuǰa mi-s-safar. mā̊r ʿànt ommu, ʾal-íla: "il-māra tīʿei fēna?"[171] *ʾalt-lu: "keččèita*[1] *l-barra: kel-la ʾattōs u-ʾattōsa!"*

darba waḥeda ḥareč[172] *il-kačča*[1] *u-mā̊r idūr*[173] *ǰō di-l-ʿalʾa, u-rā̊̄*[174] *šebba*[175] *ʾēʿeda bi-l-ʾeʿda.*[176]
ʾal-íla: "binti, au[177] *š-inti taʿmel?" ʾalt-lu: "fēn trī̀dni*[178] *mmūr?"*[179] *ʾal-íla: "trìš*[180] *tīǰi mīʿei?"*

ʾalt-lu: "īvá!" ʾal-la: "ʾábel-ma tīǰi mīʿei, ʿèid-li[181] *l-fat,*[1] *kīf-enn-ū́!"*

What did she do? She took her out of the cellar and went (and) brought her out to the field and cut her hands off. | This woman could not eat any more. There were fig trees there; she proceeded to get up (and) go under a fig tree (and) cut off a few figs with her mouth.

Her spouse returned from the journey. He went to his mother (and) said to her: "Where is my wife?" She said to him: "I threw her out: she had a tomcat and a queen-cat!"

One time he went out hunting and went around on this field, and saw a young woman sitting there. | He said to her: "My daughter, what are you doing here?" She said to him: "Where would you like me to go?" He said to her: "Would you like to come with me?" | She said to him "Yes!" He said to her: "Before you come with me, tell me what happened (lit. the story, what it is)!" |

X'għamlet? Ħarġetha minn ġol-kantina u marret tellqetha ġol-għalqa u qatgħetilha idejha. | Dil-mara mbagħad ma kienetx tista' tiekol. Kien hemm is-siġar ta' tin; kienet tqum tmur taħt tina, taqta' xi tina b'ħalqa.

Ġie żewġha mis-safar. Mar għand ommu, qalilha: "Il-mara tiegħi fejna?" Qaletlu: "Keċċejtha l-barra: kellha qattus u qattusa!"

Darba waħda ħareġ il-kaċċa u mar idur ġo dil-għalqa, u ra xebba qiegħda bil-qagħda. | Qalilha: "Binti, hawn x'inti tagħmel?" Qaletlu: "Fejn tridni immur?" Qalilha: "Tridx tiġi miegħi?" | Qaletlu: "Iva!" Qallha: "Qabelma tiġi miegħi, għidli l-fatt, kif in hu!" |

158. *ḫrǰ* (basic stem < causative). 159. *ṭlq.* 160. Cl *ḥaqla.* 161. *qṭʿ.* 162. Cl *yadaihā* (dual). 163. Cl *min baʿdu* '(from) later (on).' 164. Cl *tastaṭīʿu* (*ṭwʿ*). 165. *ʾkl.* 166. Cl *šaǰar* (dissimilation). 167. *qwm.* 168. *mrr.* 169. *-e* helping vowel. 170. *qṭʿ.* 171. = *fī* + *aina* + *-hā.* 172. *ḫrǰ.* 173. *dwr.* 174. *rʾy.* 175. Cl *šābba.* 176. Noun of unity from infinitive *qaʿd*; paronomastic. 177. < *haun* < Cl *hāhunā.* 178. *rwd* causative. 179. < **nmūr.* 180. =*trīt* (*ŕwd* causative) + *š.* 181. *ʿwd* causative (Cl *aʿīdī*) + *lī.*

Kalitlu: "Jena izzewweġt rè, u ir-rè siefer u hallieni ma ommu —"; issa ir-rè jaf lil mara tighou,

Kalla: "Imxi mighei id-dar mela!" Marret id-dar mighou b'daun izzeuġ t'itfal f'ideiha. Kalla: "Tibzagh xein!

Issa nhallsuha ta li ghamlet mighak; ghax li chitbitli ommi ma chien minnu xein; ghax kalitli, li inti ghandec kattus u kattusa!"

Meta wasal id-dar, iccmanda erbgha t'irgiel, kallom: "Akbduha!" Kalulu: "Lil min?" Kallom: "L'ommi!"
Kabduha u selhuha, u il gild tahha ghamluh pagliett, biex coll min ighaddi, jimsah sakeih fih.

ᵓalt-lu: "yēna ezzàuwečt re, w-ir-re sīefer o-ḥallīeni[182] m-ommu —"; ìs-sa r-re yā̊f[183] li-l-māra tīᶜou,

al-íla: "emši mīᶜei id-dā̊r mella!"[184] marret id-dā̊r mīᶜou b-da-zìš ti-iṭfā̊l f-idēḥ. ᵓal-íla: "tibza[185] šēn!

ís-sa nḥalsōwa[186] ta-lle-ᶜamlet mīᶜak; ᶜaš[187] li-kidbit-li ommi mā kìm minnu šēn, ᶜaš ᵓalt-li, li-yinti ᶜandek ᵓattōs u-ᵓattōsa."

metta wasal[188] id-dā̊r, ekmānda[1] erba[189] t-irǰīel,[190] ᵓal-ílom: "aᵓabdūwa!"[191] ᵓalū-lu: "lil-mīn?" ᵓal-ílom: "l-ommi!"
ᵓabdūwa u-selḥōwa,[192] w-il-j̣elt[193] taḥḥa ᶜamlōḥ palyét,[1] biš[194] kol mìn yᶜaddi, yimsaḥ saᵓēḥ[195] fīḥ.

She said to him: "I was married to a king, and the king went on a journey and left me with his mother —"; then the king recognized his wife | (and) said to her: "Then come with me into the house!" She went into the house with him with those two children at her hands. He said to her: "Fear not! | Now we will make her repent for what she did with you; for what my mother wrote to me was nothing of it (true), for she said to me that you had a tomcat and a queencat."

When he arrived at the house, he commanded four men (and) said to them: "Seize her!" They said to him: "Whom?" He said to them: "My mother!" | They seized and flayed her, and made her skin into a doormat, on which everyone who entered wiped his feet.

Qaletlu: "Jiena iżżeweġt rè, u ir-rè siefer u ħallieni ma' ommu —"; issa r-rè jaf lil mara tiegħu, | qalilha: "Imxi miegħi d-dar mela!" Marret id-dar miegħu bi dawż-żweġt itfal f'idejha. Qalilha: "Tibża' xejn!" | Issa nhallsuha talli għamlet miegħek; għax li kitbitli ommi ma kien minnu xejn, għax qaletli, li inti għandek qattus u qattusa.

Meta wasal id-dar, ikkmanda erbat irġiel, qalilhom: "Aqbduha!" Qalulu: "Lil min?" Qalilhom: "'L ommi!" Qabduha u selħuha, u il-ġild tagħha għamluh paljett, biex kull min igħaddi, jimsaħ saqajh fih.

182. *ḫly*. 183. Cl *yaᶜrifu*. 184. Cl *ammā* 'as concerns' + *lā*. 185. *bzᶜ*. 186. *ḫlṣ*. 187. = *ᶜalā* + *šaiᵓ* 'for (the) thing (that).' 188. *wṣl*. 189. Cl *arbaᶜ*. 190. Plural of *raǰul*. 191. *qbḍ*. 192. *slḫ*. 193. *ǰld*. 194. = *bi-* + *šaiᵓ* 'with (the) thing (that).' 195. Cl *sāq*.

Appendix

Common-Semitic Words

The following list includes the more or less certain correspondences among the five principal branches of the Semitic languages, with the exception of such as occur because of the borrowing of words from one branch into another. The proto-Semitic vocabulary is naturally far from exhausted here; all words are omitted that in some or all of the five branches are completely lost or altered beyond recognition.

In general only one word form of each root, the most characteristic and usually the putatively oldest, is given; the weak verbs are exhibited in the preterite for Akkadian, in the perfect and imperfect[1] for West Semitic; for strong verbs the vowels of these tenses are added in parentheses. Forms that differ greatly in phonology or stem formation from the cognates are given in parentheses; more serious divergences in meaning are indicted by the addition of a gloss to the individual language in parentheses.

As a representative of Aramaic, Syriac is given in the first place, and as representative of South Arabic-Ethiopic, Ge^{c}ez; the words not found in Syriac are placed in angle brackets and, for the words not found in Ge^{c}ez, it is stated which dialect the correspondence is taken from.

1. In Ethiopic the subjunctive.

	Akkadian	**Hebrew**
man(kind)	(*nišū*)	*ĕnōš*
man, male	*zikaru*	*zāḵār*
woman[2]	*aššatu* (wife)	*iššā*
father[3]	*abu*	*āḇ*
mother	*ummu*	*ēm*
father-in-law[3]	*emu*	*ḥām*
son[3]	*bīnu*	*bēn*
daughter[3]	*bintu*	*baṯ*
firstborn	*bukru*	*bḵōr*
bear	*ūlid*	*yālaḏ tēleḏ*
brother[3]	*aḫu*	*āḥ*
lord, husband	*bēlu*	*báʿal*
slavegirl	*amtu*	*āmā*
rival wife[4]	*ṣerretu*	*ṣārā*
love	*wdd*	(*yāḏīḏ* beloved)
king	*malku*	*méleḵ*
foreign	*nakru* (enemy)	*noḵrī*

	arwū (gazelle)	*ărī aryē* (lion)
panther, leopard	*nimru*	*nāmēr*
wolf	*zību*	*zʾēḇ*
dog	*kalbu*	*kéleḇ*
bark	(*nbḫ* [*u*])	*nbḥ* (*a, a*)
(wild) boar	*ḫuzīru*	*ḥzīr*
stag	*ayalu*	*ayyāl*
ox	*šūru*	*šōr*
ass	*imēru*	*ḥmōr*
eagle, hawk	*našru*	*néšer*
scorpion	*aqrabu*	*ʿaqrāḇ*

2. Root *ʾnθ*. 3. Biliteral. 4. Root *δ̣rr*.

Aramaic	South Arabic-Ethiopic	Arabic
nāšā	ESA *ʾnś*	(*u*)*nāsun*
deḵrā	ESA *δkr*	*δakarun*
attā	*anést*	*unθa*
aḇā	*ab*	*abun*
emmā	*emm*	*ummun*
ḥmā	*ḥam*	*ḥamun*
(*brā*)	ESA *bn*	*ibnun*
(*barṯa*)	*bent* (orphan)	*bintun*
buḵrā	*bak°ér*	*bikrun*
īleḏ nēlaḏ	*waláda yélad*	*walada yalidu*
aḥā	*eḫ°*	*aḫun*
baʿlā	*bāʿl*	*baʿlun*
amṯā	*amát*	*amatun*
ʿarrṯā	(*ḍar* enemy)	*ḍarratun*
ydd intensive	ESA *wdd*	*wadda yawaddu*
malkā	(*malākī́* lord)	*malikun*
nuḵrāyā	(*nakī́r*)	*nukurun* (unknown)
aryā (lion)	*arwḗ* (wild animal)	*arwā* (mountain goat)
nemrā	*namr*	*namirun*
dēḇā	*zeʾb* (hyena)	*δiʾbun*
kalbā	*kalb*	*kalbun*
nbḥ (*a, u*)	*nbḥ* (-, *ā*)	*nbḥ* (*a, i/a*)
ḥzīrā	(*ḥanzī́r*)	*ḫinzīrun*
ailā	(*hayál*)	*īyalun*
taurā	*sōr*	*θaurun*
ḥmārā	ESA *ḥmr*	*ḥimārun*
nešrā	*nesr*	*nasrun*
ʿeqarḇā	*ʿaqráb*	*ʿaqrabun*

	Akkadian	Hebrew
fly(s), horsefly(s)	(*zubbu*)	*zḇūḇ*
wine grape(s)	*inbu* (tree fruit)	*ᶜēnāḇ*
garlic	*šūmu*	*šūm*
cucumber(s)	*qiššū*	*qiššūᵓā*
cumin	*kamūnu*	*kammōn*
seed	*zēru*	*zéraᶜ*
ear of grain	*šubultu*	*šibbóleṯ*
head	*rēšu*	*rōš*
eye	*ēnu*	*ᶜáyin*
ear	*uznu*	*ózen*
hear	*išmē*	*šmᶜ* (*e*,[5] *a*)
nose	*appu*	*ap̄*
mouth[6]	*pū*	*pē*
tongue	*lišānu*	*lāšōn*
flavor	*ṭēmu* (understanding)	*ṭáᶜam*
bitter	*marru*	*mar*
tooth	*šinnu*	*šēn*
hair	*šārtu*	*śēᶜār*
gray hair	*šību*	*śēḇ*
hand, arm, side[3]	*īdu*	*yāḏ*
right, right side	(*imnu*)	*yāmīn*
palm, handful	*upnu*	*ḥop̄náyim*
fingernail, claw[7]	*ṣupru*	(*ṣippóren*)
knee	*birku*	*béreḵ*
wing	*kappu*	*kānāp̄*
tail	(*zibbatu*)	*zānāḇ*

5. Usually *a* instead, as in several other Hebrew verbs. 6. Monoliteral. 7. Root *θ̣pr*.

Aramaic	South Arabic-Ethiopic	Arabic
dabbāḇā	Mh (*δebēb*)	*δubābun*
ᶜenbṯā	ESA *ᶜnb* (vine)	*ᶜinabun*
tūmā	*sōmát*	*θūmun*
(*qaṭṭūṯā*)	*q°esseyắt*	*qiθθāᵓun*
kammūnā	*kamǘn*	*kammūnun*
zarᶜā	(*zarᵓ*)	*zarᶜun*
šebbeltā	(*sabl*)	*sunbulatun*
rēšā	*reᵓs*	*raᵓsun*
ᶜainā	*ᶜain*	*ᶜainun*
udnā	*ezn*	*uδnun*
šmᶜ (*a*, *a*)	*smᶜ* (-, *ā*)	*smᶜ* (*i*, *a*)
appayyā	*anf*	*anfun*
(*pummā*)	*af*	(*famun*), construct state *fū*
leššānā	*lesắn*	*lisānun*
ṭáᶜmā	*ṭāᶜm*	*ṭaᶜmun*
(*mar nemmar* verb)	(*márra yémra/er* verb)	*murrun*
šennā	*senn*	*sinnun*
saᶜrā	*šeᶜért*	*šaᶜrun*
saibāṯā	*šībát*	*šaibun*
īḏā	*ed*	*yadun*
yammīnā	(*yamắn*)	*yamīnun*
ḥup̄nā	*ḥefn* (fist)	*ḥufnatun*
ṭep̄rā	*ṣefr*	*ẓufrun*
burka	*berk*	(*rukbatun*)
kenp̄ā	*kenf*	*kanafun*
dunḇā	*zanáb*	*δanabun*

	Akkadian	Hebrew
horn	*qarnu*	*qéren*
bone, skeleton[8]	*eṣemtu*	*ᶜéṣem*
heart	*libbu*	*lēḇ*
belly	*karšu*	*kārēš*
liver	*kabittu*	*kāḇēḏ*
kidney	*kalītu*	*kilyā*
soul (throat)	*napištu*	*nép̄eš*
death	*mūtu*	*máweṯ*
strangle	*ḫnq* (*i*)	*ḥnq* intensive
bury	*qbr* (*i*)	*qbr* (*a, o*)
blood[3]	*damu*	*dām*
urine	*šīnāti*	*šáyin*
heaven	*šamū*	*šāmáyim*
star	*kakkabu*	*kōḵāḇ*
sun[9]	*šamšu*	*šémeš*
set	*īrub*	*ᶜrb*
shadow[10]	*ṣillu*	*ṣēl*
day	*ūmu*	*yōm*
night[11]	*līlātu* (evening)	*láylā*
land	*erṣetu*	*éreṣ*
field	*eqlu*	(*ḥéleq*)
water[6]	*mū*	*máyim*
lightning	*birqu*	*bārāq*
spring[12]	*nambaᵓu*	*mabbṓaᶜ*
well, cistern	*būru*	*bōr bᵓēr*
lower a bucket, ladle	*idlū*	*dālā yiḏlē*
flame	*laᵓbu*	*láhaḇ*

8. Root *ᶜθm*. 9. Root probably *śmš*. 10. Root *θll*. 11. Basic form **lailai*. 12. With prefix *m-*.

Aramaic	**South Arabic-Ethiopic**	**Arabic**
qarnā	*qarn*	*qarnun*
^{c}*aṭmā* (hip)	(^{c}*aḍm*)	^{c}*aẓmun*
lebbā	*lebb*	*lubbun*
karsā	*karš*	*karišun* (second stomach of a ruminant)
kab̲dā	*kabd*	*kabidun*
kolīṯā	*k°elī́t*	*kulyatun*
nap̄šā	*nafs*	*nafsun*
mautā	*mōt*	*mautun*
ḥnq (*a*, *u*)	*ḫnq* (*a*, *e*)	*ḫnq* (*a*, *u*)
qbr (*a*, *u*)	*qbr* (*a*, *e*)	*qbr* (*a*, *u*/*i*)
dmā	*dam*	*damun*
tīnā	*šent*	(*maθānatun* bladder)
šmaiyā	*samā́y*	*samā*$^{\supset}$*un*
kaukb̲ā	*kōkáb* (Mh *kebkīb*)	*kaukabun*
šemšā	ESA *šmś*	*šamsun*
^{c}*rb* (a, u)	^{c}*rb* (-, *a*)	*ɣrb* (*a*, *u*)
<*ṭullā*>	(*ṣelālṓt*)	*ẓillun*
yaumā	*yōm* (today)	*yaumun*
lelyā	*lēlī́t*	*lailatun*
ar^{c}*ā*	ESA $^{\supset}$*rḍ*	*arḍun*
ḥaqlā	*ḥaql*	*ḥaqlun*
maiyā	*māi*	*mā*$^{\supset}$*un*
barqā	(*mabráq*)	*barqun*
mabbō^{c}*ā*	(*nb*^{c} weep)	*manba*^{c}*un*
bērā	ESA *b*$^{\supset}$*r*	*bi*$^{\supset}$*run*
dlā ned̲lē	*daláwa yédlū* (weigh)	*dalā yadlū*
(*šalheb̲* kindle)	*lāhb*	*lahabun*

	Akkadian	Hebrew
smoke[13]	*qutru*	*qṭóreṯ* (incense)
track	*ašru* (place)	(*āšūr* step)
wood[14]	*iṣu*	*ᶜēṣ*
house	*bītu*	*báyiṯ*
doorposts	(*imdu* stanchion)	*ᶜammūḏ*
bed	*eršu*	*ᶜéreś*
bow[3]	*qaštu*	*qéšeṯ*
arrow[15]	*uṣṣu*	*ḥēṣ*
shoot, throw	*irmī*	*rāmā* **yirmē*
cord	*eblu*	*ḥéḇel*
vessel	*unūtu*	*ŏnī* (ship)
flour	*qēmu*	*qémaḥ*
grind	*iṭēn*	*ṭḥn* (*a, a*)
honey	(*dišpu*)	*dḇaš*
poison[3]	*imtu*	*ḥēmā*
slaughter	*ṭbḫ* (*u*)	*ṭbḥ* (*a, o*)
ripe, cooked	*bašlu*	*bāšēl*
roast	*iqlū* (burn)	*qālā* **yiqlē*
intoxicant	*šikaru*	*šēḵār*
1. fixed, straight, 2. become, be set	*kīnu* 1.	*kēn* 1.
set	*išīm*	*śām* *yāśīm*
lift, carry	*iššī*	*nāśā* *yiśśā*
rest	*inūḫ*	*nāḥ* *yānúaḥ*

13. Root probably *qtr*. 14. Biliteral, root *ᶜδ̣*. 15. Root *ḥθθ*.

Aramaic	South Arabic-Ethiopic	Arabic
<*qiṭrā*>	*qetārḗ* (incense)	(*qutārun* aloe wood)
aṯrā	(*ašár*)	*aθarun*
<*āʿā*>	*ʿeḍ*	*ʿiḍatun*
baitā	*bēt*	*baitun*
ʿammūḏā	(*ʿamd*)	*ʿamūdun*
ʿarsā	(*ʿarī́s* arbor)	*ʿaršun* (throne, nest, bier)
qeštā	*qast*	(*qausun*)
<EgAm *ḥṭ*>	*ḥaṣṣ*	*ḥaẓẓun* (allotment of luck)
rmā nermē	*ramáya yérmī*	*ramā yarmī*
ḥaḇlā	*ḥabl*	*ḥablun*
(*mānā*)	(*newā́y*)	*ināʾun*
qamḥā	*qamḥ* (fruit)	*qamḥun* (wheat)
ṭḥn (*e*, *a*)	(*ṭeḥn* barley flour)	*ṭḥn* (*a*, *a*)
deḇšā	ESA *dbś*	*dibsun*
ḥemṯā	(*ḥamṓt* gall)	*ḥumatun*
ṭbḥ (*a*, *a*)	(*ṭbḥ* [-, *ā*])	*ṭbḫ* (*a*, *u*) (cook)
(*bšl* [*e*, *a*] ripen)	*bsl* (*a*, *e*)	*bsl* (*a*, *u*) (sour)
qlā neqlē	*qaláwa yéqlū*	*qalā yaqlū*
šeḵrā	*sekā́r*	*sakarun*
kēnā 1.	*kṓna yékūn* 2.	*kāna yakūnu* 2.
sām nsīm	*šḗma yéšīm*	*šāma yašīmu* (insert)
<*nśā* **yiśśā*>	*nšʾ* (-, *ā*)	*nšʾ* (*a*, *a*) (get up)
nāḥ nnūḥ	*nṓḫa yénūḫ*	(causative *anāḫa* make camels sit)

	Akkadian	Hebrew
go out[16]	*ūṣī*	*yāṣā yēṣē*
go up	*ēlī*	*ʿālā yaʿlē*
go forward, precede	(*qudmu* past time)	*qdm* intensive
go near	*qrb* (*i*/*u*)	*qrb* (*e, a*)
weep	*ibkī*	*bāḵā yiḇkē*
shout	*ṣrḫ* (*u*)	*ṣrḥ*
blow	*npḫ* (*u*) (blow on a fire)	*npḥ* (*a, a*)
seize	*īḫuz*	*āḥaz yōḥez*
remember, think	*zkr* (*u*) (name)	*zkr* (*a, o*)
name[3]	*šumu*	*šēm*
ask	*išʾal*	*šʾl* (*e, a*)
(as intensive) bring good news	(*bsr*)	*bśr*
like	*irām*	*rḥm* intensive
count, allot	*imnū*	*mānā yimnē*
put on (clothes)	*lbš* (*i*)	*lbš* (*e, a*)
wash[17]	(*rḫṣ* [*i*])	*rḥṣ* (*a, a*)
steep, mix	*bll* (*u*)	*bālal yāḇol*
	īgir (twist)	*ḥgr* (*a, o*) (gird)
twist, weave	*ptl* (*i*)	(*pāṯīl* string)
bore	*nqb* (*u*) (deflower)	*nqb* (*a, o*)
dig	(*ḫpr* [*i*])	*ḥpr* (*a, o*)
winnow, strew	*izrū*	**zārā yizre*
pasture	*irʾī*	*rāʿā yirʿē*
water	*išqī*	(causative *hišqā*)
harness[18]	*ṣmd* (*i*)	(*ṣémeḏ* team)
ride	*rkb* (*a*)	*rkb* (*a, a*)

16. Root *wδʾ*. 17. Root *rḥδ*. 18. Root *δmd*.

Aramaic	South Arabic-Ethiopic	Arabic
īʿā/ī nēʿē (grow)	*wáṣʾa yéḍāʾ*	*wḍʾ* (*u*, *u*) (be shining, pure)
(intensive *ʿallī* elevate)	*ʿaláwa yéʿlū* (surpass)	*ʿalā yaʿlū*
qdm (*a*, *u*)	*qdm* (*a*, *e*)	*qdm* (*a*, *u*)
qrb (*e*, *u*)	*qrb* (-, *a*)	*qrb* (*i*, *a*)
bḵā neḇkē	*bakáya yébkī*	*bakā yabkī*
(*ṣrḥ* causative)	*ṣrḫ* (-, *ā*)	*ṣrḫ* (*a*, *u*)
npḥ (*a*, *u*)	*nfḫ* (-, *ā*)	*nfḫ* (*a*, *u*)
eḥaḏ nēḥuḏ	*áḫza yéʾḫez*	*ʾḫδ* (*a*, *u*)
dkr t-stem	*zkr* (*a*, *e*)	*δkr* (*a*, *u*)
šmā	*sem*	*ismun*
šel nešal	*sʾl* (*a*, *a*)	*sʾl* (*a*, *a*)
(*sbr*)	(*bsr* causative)	*bšr*
rḥm (*e*, *a*) (love)	(*mḥr* [-, *a*])	*rḥm* (*i*, *a*)
mnā nemnē	ESA *mnw*	*manā yamnī*
lbš (*e*, *a*)	*lbs* (-, *a*)	*lbs* (*i*, *a*)
<EgAm *rḥʿ*>	*rḥḍ* (-/*a*, *a*) (sweat)	*rḥḍ* (*a*, *a*)
balbel (entangle)	Te *balla*	*balla yabullu*
ḥgr (*a*, *u*) (obstruct)	(*ḥagl* fetter)	*ḥǰr* (*a*, *u*) (lock out, lock in)
ptl (*a*, *u*)	*ftl* (*a*, *e*)	*ftl* (*a*, *i*)
nqb (*a*, *u*)	ESA *nqb*	*nqb* (*a*, *u*)
ḥpr (*a*, *u*)	ESA *ḥfr*	*ḥfr* (*a*, *i*)
drā neḏrē	*zaráwa yézrū*	*δarā yaδrī*
rʿā nerʿē	*réʿya yérʿai*	*raʿā yarʿā*
(causative *ašqī*)	*saqáya yésqī* (irrigate)	*saqā yasqī*
(*ṣmd* bind)	*ḍmd* (*a*, *e*)	*ḍmd* (*a*, *i*) (bind wounds)
rkb (*e*, *a*)	(ESA *rkb* rider)	*rkb* (*i*, *a*)

	Akkadian	Hebrew
guard[19]	*nṣr* (*u*)	*nṣr* (*a*, *o*)
1. pay attention to, 2. miss, seek	*pqd* (*i*) 1.	*pqd* (*a*, *o*) 1.
hold back	*iklā*	*kālā yiḵlā*
	pṭr (*u*) (loosen)	*pṭr* (*a*, *a*) (free)
peace	*šalāmu*	*šālōm*
1. sweet-smelling, 2. good	*ṭābu* 1.	*ṭōḇ* 1., 2.
1. bad-smelling, 2. be bad	*ibʾiš* 1.	*bʾš* (*a*, *a*) 1.
destroy	*ḫbl* (*i*)	*ḥbl* intensive
get lost	(*iʾbut* destroy)	*āḇaḏ yōḇeḏ*
break	*šbr* (*i*)	*šbr* (*a*, *o*)
pulverized, fine	*daqqu*	*daq*
pinch	(*krṣ* [*i*])	*qrṣ*
(as intensive) cultically purify, hallow	*qdš*	*qdš*
fail, sin	*iḫṭī*	*ḥāṭā yeḥṭā*
offering	*zību*	*zéḇaḥ*
bless	(*krb* [*u*])	*brk* intensive
entire, all	*kalu*	*kōl*
full	*malū*	*mālē*
be the same	*mšl* (*i*)	*mšl* *n*-stem
light, small, quick	*qallu*	*qal*
1. costly, 2. difficult	*waqru* 1.	*yāqār* 1.
strong, powerful	*ezzu* (fierce)	*ʿaz*
new	*eššu*	*ḥāḏāš*

19. Root *nθ̣r*.

Aramaic	South Arabic-Ethiopic	Arabic
nṭr (*a*, *u*/*a*)	*nṣr* (*a*, *e*) (consider)	*nẓr* (*a*, *u*) (consider)
pqd (*a*, *u*) 1., 2.	*fqd* (*a*, *e*) 1., 2.	*fqd* (*a*, *i*) 2.
klā neḵlē	*klᵓ* (-, *ā*)	*klᵓ* (*a*, *a*) (protect)
pṭr (*a*, *a*) (distance oneself)	*fṭr* (*a*, *e*) (produce)	*fṭr* (*a*, *u*) (split, create)
šlāmā	*salā́m*	*salāmun*
ṭāḇā 2.	(ESA *ṭyb* incense)	(*ṭaiyibun* 1., 2.)
beš neḇaš 2.	*bᵓs* (-, *a*) 2.	*biᵓsa* (defective verb) 2.
ḥbl intensive	ESA *ḫbl*	*ḫbl* (*a*, *u*)
eḇaḏ nēḇaḏ	*ᵓbd* (-, *a*) (be insane)	*abada* (*a*, *u*/*i*) (be skittish, said of cattle)
tbr (*a*, *u*)	*sbr* (*a*, *e*)	*θbr* (*a*, *u*) (annihilate)
daq neddaq (verb)	(*daqī́q*)	*diqqun*
(*qrṣānē* frost)	*qrṣ* (*a*, *e*) (incise)	*qrṣ* (*a*, *u*)
qdš	*qds*	*qds*
ḥṭā neḥṭē	*ḫṭᵓ* (-, *ā*) (not find, have)	*ḫṭᵓ* (*i*, *a*)
deḇḥā	*zebḥ*	*δibḥun*
brk intensive	*brk* *ā*-form	*brk* *ā*-form
kul	*k°ell*	*kullun*
mlē	(*mlᵓ* [-, *a*] verb)	(*mlᵓ* [*i*, *a*] verb)
mtl (*a*, *u*) (compare)	*msl* (-/*a*, *a*)	*mθl* (*a*, *u*)
(*qal neqqal* verb)	(*qalī́l*)	(*qalla yaqillu* verb)
(*īqar nēqar* verb 2.)	(ESA *wqr* honor [noun])	*waqurun* (discreet)
(*ᶜaz neᶜᶜaz* verb)	(*ᶜazī́z*)	(*ᶜazza yaᶜizzu* verb)
ḥattā	(*ḥadī́s*)	*ḥadaθun* (youth)

	Akkadian	**Hebrew**
low	*šaplu*	*šāp̄āl*
open	*iptē*	*ptḥ* (*a*, *a*)
1. yellow green, 2. vegetables	*warqu* 1., 2.	*yéreq* 1., *yārāq* 2.
one	*ēdu* (single, alone)	*ēḥāḏ*
two[3]	*šinā*	*šnáyim*
three	*šalāš*	*šālōš*
four	*erbe*	*arbaʿ*
five	*ḫamiš*	*ḥāmēš*
six[20]	*šeššet*	*šēš*
seven	*sebe*	*šéḇaʿ*
eight	*samāne*	*šmōnē*
nine	*tiše*	*téšaʿ*
ten	*ešer*	*ʿéśer*
hundred[3]	*meat*	*mēʾā*
when?	*matī*	*māṯai*
in, through, with	*ba* (in *bašū* 'be')[a]	*b*
like	(*kī*)	*k*
	kīma	*kmō*
on	*eli*	*ʿal*
and	*u*	*w*

a. Unlikely, as the monoconsonantal prepositions are not found in Akkadian (§ 2.2.4).

20. Root *šdθ*.

Aramaic	South Arabic-Ethiopic	Arabic
šap̄lā	ESA *śfl*	(*sfl* [*a*/*u*, *u* or *i*, *a*] verb)
ptḥ (*a*, *a*)	*ftḥ* (-, *ā*)	*ftḥ* (*a*, *a*)
yarqā 2.	*warq* (gold)	*war*(*i*)*qun* (silver money), *waraqun* (leaves)
ḥad	*aḥadū́*	*aḥadun*
(*trēn*)	(*sānī́t* following day)	*iθnāni*
tlāṯ	(*šallā́s*)	*θalāθun*
arbaᶜ	*arbā́ᶜ*	*arbaᶜun*
ḥammeš	*ḫams*	*ḫamsun*
šeṯ	*sessū́* (ESA *śdθ*)	*sittun*
šḇaᶜ	*sabᶜū́*	*sabᶜun*
tmānē	*samānī́*	*θamānin*
tšaᶜ	*tesᶜū́*	*tisᶜun*
ᶜsar	*ᶜašrū́*	*ᶜašrun*
mā	*meᵓét*	*miᵓatun*
emmaṯ	ESA *mt*(*y*)	*matā*
b	*ba*	*bi*
k	*ka*	*ka*
kmā	*káma*	*kamā*
ᶜal	ESA *ᶜly*	*ᶜalā*
w	*wa*	*wa*

Appendix A

Paradigms

These paradigms present the regular verbs and the pronouns (left-hand page) and "principal parts" of the weak verbs (right-hand page) of each of the five literary languages. A nonexistent root **pdk* has been chosen in order to maximize comparability among the paradigms without prejudicing the data in the direction of any one language, and so that spirantization of stops may be fully displayed in Hebrew and Syriac. The vertical and to some extent the horizontal spacing of the paradigms is such as to make possible easy comparisons among formal (not necessarily semantic) correspondents. Because these charts are both artificial and idealized, they must not be used without reference to grammars of the individual languages.

Akkadian

		stative	preterite	present	perfect	coh/imv/prec	participle	infinitive
G	sg. 1	*padkāku*	*apduk*	*apaddak*	*aptadak*	*lupduk*		
	2m	*padkāta*	*tapduk*	*tapaddak*	*taptadak*	*puduk*		
	f	*padkāti*	*tapdukī*	*tapaddakī*	*taptadkī*	*pudkī*		
	3m	*padik*	*ipduk*	*ipaddak*	*iptadak*	*lipduk*	*pādikum*	*padākum*
	f	*padkat*	*tapduk*	*tapaddak*	*taptadak*	*lū tapduk*		
	du. 3	*padkā*	*ipdukā*	*ipaddakā*	*iptadkā*			
	pl. 1	*padkānu*	*nipduk*	*nipaddak*	*niptadak*	*i nipduk*		
	2m	*padkātunu*	*tapdukā*	*tapaddakā*	*taptadkā*	*pudkā*		
	2f	*padkātina*						
	3m	*padkū*	*ipdukū*	*ipaddakū*	*iptadkū*	*lipdukū*		
	f	*padkā*	*ipdukā*	*ipaddakā*	*iptadkā*	*lipdukā*		
Gt		*pitduk*	*iptadak*	*iptaddak*	*iptatdak*	*pitdak*	*muptadkum*	*pitdukum*
Gtn		*pitadduk*	*iptaddak*	*iptanaddak*	*iptataddak*	*pitaddak*	*muptaddikum*	*pitaddukum*
D		*pudduk*	*upaddik*	*upaddak*	*uptaddik*	*puddik*	*mupaddikum*	*puddukum*
Dt		—	*uptaddik*	*uptaddak*	*uptataddik*	*putaddik*	*muptaddikum*	*putaddukum*
Dtn		*putadduk*	*uptaddik*	*uptanaddak*	*uptataddik*	*putaddik*	*muptaddikum*	*putaddukum*
Š		*šupduk*	*ušapdik*	*ušapdak*	*uštapdik*	*šupdik*	*mušapdikum*	*šupdukum*
Št		*šutapduk*	*uštapdik*	*uštapaddak*	*uštatapdik*	*šutapdik*	*muštapdikum*	*šutapdukum*
Štn		*šutapduk*	*uštapdik*	*uštanapdak*	*uštatapdik*	*šutapdik*	*muštapdikum*	*šutapdukum*
N		*napduk*	*ippadik*	*ippaddak*	*ittapdak*	*napdik*	*muppadkum*	*napdukum*
Ntn		*itapduk*	*ittapdak*	*ittanapdak*	*ittatapdak*	*itapdak*	*muttapdikum*	*itapdukum*

subjunctive *padku*, *ipduku*, etc.; ventive *padkam* (plural *padkunim*), *ipdukam* (plural *ipdukūnim*), etc.

pronoun	1	*anāku*	*nīnu*	*-ī*, *-nī*	*-ni*
	2m	*attā*	*attunu*	*-ka*	*-kunu*
	f	*attī*	*attina*	*-ki*	*-kina*
	3m	*šū*	*šunu*	*-šu*	*-šunu*
	f	*šī*	*šina*	*-ša*	*-šina*

Akkadian

		stative	preterite	present	perfect	imperative	participle	infinitive
I ʾ	G	*adik*	*īduk*	*iddak*	*ītadak*	*aduk*	*ādikum*	*adākum*
	D	*udduk*	*uddik*	*uddak*	*ūtaddik*	*uddik*	*muddikum*	*uddukum*
	Š	*šūduk*	*ušādik*	*ušaddak*	*uštādik*	*šūdik*	*mušādikum*	*šūdukum*
	N	*nanduk*	*innadik*	*innaddak*	*ittandak*	*nandik*	*munnadkum*	*nandukum*
I *n*	G	*nadik*	*idduk*	*inaddak*	*ittadak*	*uduk*	*nādikum*	*nadākum*
I *w*	G	*wadik*	*ūdik*	*uddak*	*ittadak*	*dik*	*wādikum*	*wadākum*
	Š	*šūduk*	*ušādik*	*ušaddak*	*uštādik*	*šūdik*	*mušādikum*	*šūdukum*
	N	?	*iwwadik*	*iwwaddak*	?	?	?	?
I *y*	G	*idik*	*īdik*	*iddik*	*ītadik*	*adik*	*ādikum*	*adākum*
	D	*udduk*	*uddik*	*uddak*	*ūteddik*	*uddik*	*muddikum*	*uddukum*
	N	*nīduk*	*innedik*	*inneddak*	?	?	?	?
II ʾ	G	*paʾik*	*ipāk*	*ipāk*	*iptāk*	*pāk*	*pāʾikum*	*pākum*
	D	*pūk*	*upaʾʾik*	*upāk*	*uptaʾʾik*	?	*mupaʾʾikum*	*pūkum*
	N	?	*ippāk*	*ippāk*	?	?	?	?
II weak	G **w*	*pīk*	*ipūk*	*ipāk*	*iptūk*	*pūk*	*pāʾikum*	*pākum*
	**y*	*pā/īk*	*ipīk*	*ipīak*	*iptīk*	*pīk*	*pāʾikum*	*piākum*
	D	*pūk*	*upīk*	*upāk*	*uptīk*	*pīk*	*mupikkum*	*pukkum*
	Š	*šupūk*	*ušpīk*	*uspāk*	*uštapīk*	*šupīk*	?	*šupūkum*
	N	?	?	*ippāk*	?	—	?	?
III ʾ	G	*padi*	*ipdi*	*ipaddi*	*iptadi*	*pidi*	*pādūm*	*padūm*
	D	*puddu*	*upaddi*	*upadda*	*uptaddi*	*puddi*	*mupaddūm*	*puddūm*
	Š	*šupdu*	*ušapdi*	*ušapda*	*uštapdi*	*šupdi*	*mušapdūm*	*šupdūm*
	N	*napdi*	*ippadi*	*ippaddi*	*ittapdi*	—	?	*napdūm*

Hebrew

	perfect	imperfect	coh./imv.	act. part.	pass. part.	inf. abs.	inf. cst.
G (qal) sg. 1	*pāḏáḵtī*	*ep̄doḵ*	*ep̄dḵā*				
2m	*pāḏáḵtā*	*tip̄doḵ*	*pḏoḵ*				
f	*pāḏaḵt*	*tip̄dḵī*	*piḏḵī*				
3m	*pāḏaḵ*	*yip̄doḵ*		*pōḏēḵ*	*pāḏūḵ*	*pāḏōḵ*	*pḏōḵ*
f	*pāḏḵā*	*tip̄doḵ*					
pl. 1	*pāḏáḵnū*	*nip̄doḵ*	*nip̄dḵā*				
2m	*pḏaḵtem*	*tip̄dḵū*	*piḏḵū*				
f	*pḏaḵten*	*tip̄dóḵnā*	*pḏóḵnā*				
3m	*pāḏḵū*	*yip̄dḵū*					
3f		*tip̄dóḵnā*					
D (piel)	*piddeḵ*	*yp̄addeḵ*	*paddeḵ*	*mp̄addēḵ*		*paddē/ōḵ*	*paddēḵ*
Dp (pual)	*puddaḵ*	*yp̄uddaḵ*	—		*mp̄uddāḵ*	*puddōḵ*	*puddāḵ*
tD (hitpael)	*hiṯpaddeḵ*	*yiṯpaddeḵ*	*hiṯpaddeḵ*	*miṯpaddēḵ*		*hiṯpaddēḵ*	*hiṯpaddēḵ*
Š (hifil)	*hip̄dīḵ*	*yap̄dīḵ*	*hap̄deḵ*	*map̄dīḵ*		*hap̄dēḵ*	*hap̄dīḵ*
Šp (hofal)	*hop̄daḵ*	*yop̄daḵ*	—		*mop̄dāḵ*	*hop̄dēḵ*	*hop̄dāḵ*
N (nifal)	*nip̄daḵ*	*yippāḏeḵ*	*hippāḏeḵ*		*nip̄dāḵ*	*nip̄dōḵ/ hippāḏōḵ*	*hippāḏēḵ*

consecutive *wayyíp̄doḵ*, *wp̄āḏaḵtī*; jussive = imperfect except G II weak *yāp̄ōḵ yāp̄ēḵ* (*wayyā́p̄oḵ wayyā́p̄eḵ*), III weak *yíp̄eḏ/yip̄d/yep̄d*, Š *yap̄deḵ*, II weak — both modes — *yāp̄ēḵ* (*wayyā́p̄eḵ*)

pronoun 1	*ānōḵī*	*ănáḥnū*	*-ī, -nī*	*-nū*
2m	*attā*	*attem*	*-ḵā*	*-ḵem*
f	*attī*	*atten*	*-ēḵ*	*-ḵen*
3m	*hū*	*hem*	*-hū̆*	*-hem*
f	*hī*	*hénna*	*-hā̆*	*-hen*

Hebrew

	perfect	imperfect	imperative	act. part.	pass. part.	inf. abs.	inf. cst.
I lar. G	ḥāḏeḵ	yeḥḏoḵ	ḥḏoḵ	ḥoḏēḵ	ḥāḏūḵ	ḥāḏōḵ	ḥḏōḵ
Š	heḥḏīḵ	yaḥḏīḵ	haḥḏēḵ	maḥḏīḵ		haḥḏēḵ	haḥḏīḵ
Šp	hoḥḏaḵ	yoḥḏaḵ	—		moḥḏāḵ	hoḥḏēḵ	hoḥḏāḵ
N	neḥḏaḵ	yēḥāḏeḵ	hēḥāḏeḵ		neḥḏāḵ	hēḥāḏōḵ	hēḥāḏēḵ
I n G	nāḏaḵ	yiddaḵ	daḵ	nōḏēḵ	nāḏūḵ	nāḏōḵ	déḵeṯ
I weak G *w	yāḏaḵ	yēḏeḵ	deḵ	yōḏēḵ	yāḏūḵ	yāḏōḵ	déḵeṯ
*y	yāḏaḵ	yīḏaḵ	yḏaḵ	yōḏēḵ	yāḏūḵ	yāḏōḵ	yḏōḵ
Š	hōḏīḵ	yōḏīḵ	hūḏeḵ	mōḏīḵ		hōḏēḵ	hōḏīḵ
Šp	hūḏaḵ	yūḏaḵ	—		mūḏāḵ	hūḏēḵ	hūḏāḵ
N	nōḏaḵ	yiwwāḏeḵ	hiwwāḏeḵ		nōḏāḵ	hōḏōḵ	hōḏēḵ
II lar. D	piḥaḵ	yp̄aḥeḵ	paḥeḵ	mp̄aḥēḵ		paḥē/ōḵ	paḥēḵ
II ʾ D	pēʾeḵ	yp̄āʾeḵ	pāʾeḵ	mp̄āʾēḵ		pāʾēḵ	pāʾēḵ
II gem. G	pāḏaḏ	yāp̄oḏ	poḏ	pōḏēḏ	pāḏūḏ	pāḏōḏ	pōḏ
D	pōḏeḏ	yp̄ōḏeḏ	pōḏeḏ	mp̄ōḏeḏ		pōḏeḏ	pōḏeḏ
Š	hēp̄eḏ	yāp̄eḏ	hāp̄eḏ	mēp̄ēḏ		hāp̄ēḏ	hāp̄ēḏ
Šp	hūp̄aḏ	yūp̄aḏ	—		mūp̄aḏ	—	—
N	nāp̄aḏ	yippaḏ	hippaḏ		nāp̄āḏ	hippōḏ	hippēḏ
II weak G	pāḵ	yāp̄ūḵ	pūḵ	pāḵ	pūḵ	pōḵ	pūḵ
D	pōḵeḵ	yp̄ōḵeḵ	pōḵeḵ	mp̄ōḵēḵ		pōḵēḵ	pōḵēḵ
Š	hēp̄īḵ	yāp̄īḵ	hāp̄eḵ	mēp̄īḵ		hāp̄ēḵ	hāp̄īḵ
Šp	hūp̄aḵ	yūp̄aḵ	—		mūp̄āḵ	hūp̄ēḵ	hūp̄āḵ
N	nāp̄ōḵ	yippōḵ	hippōḵ		nāp̄ōḵ	hippōḵ	hippōḵ
III ʾ G	pāḏā	yip̄ḏā	pḏā	pōḏē	pāḏū	pāḏō	pḏō
D	piddē	yp̄addē	paddē	mp̄addē		paddō	paddē
Š	hip̄dī	yap̄dī	hap̄dē	map̄dī		hap̄dē	hap̄dī
N	nip̄dā	yippāḏē	hippāḏē		nip̄dā	nip̄dō	hippāḏē
III weak G	pāḏā	yip̄dē	pḏē	pōḏē	pāḏūy	pāḏō	pḏōṯ
D	piddā	yp̄addē	paddē	mp̄addē		paddē	paddōṯ
Š	hip̄dā	yap̄dē	hap̄dē	map̄dē		hap̄dē	hap̄dōṯ
N	nip̄dā	yipāḏē	hippādē		nip̄dē	nip̄dō	hippāḏōṯ

Syriac

	perfect	imperfect	imperative	act. part.	pass. part.	infinitive
G (peal) sg. 1	*peḏkeṯ*	*ep̄duḵ*				
2m	*pḏaḵt*	*tep̄duḵ*	*pḏuḵ*			
f	*pḏaḵt*	*tep̄dḵīn*	*pḏuḵ*			
3m	*pḏaḵ*	*nep̄duḵ*		*pāḏeḵ*	*pḏīḵ*	*mep̄daḵ*
f	*peḏkaṯ*	*tep̄duḵ*		*paḏḵā*	*pḏīḵā*	
pl. 1	*pḏaḵn(an)*	*nep̄duḵ*				
2m	*pḏaḵtōn*	*tep̄dḵūn*	*pḏuḵ(ūn)*			
f	*pḏaḵtēn*	*tep̄dḵān*	*pḏuḵ(ān)*			
3m	*pḏaḵ(ūn)*	*nep̄dḵūn*		*pāḏḵīn*	*pḏīḵīn*	
f	*pḏaḵ(ūn)*	*nep̄dḵān*		*paḏḵān*	*pḏīḵān*	
tG (ethpeel)	*eṯpḏeḵ*	*neṯpḏeḵ*	*eṯpaḏk*		*meṯpḏeḵ*	*meṯpḏāḵū*
D (pael)	*paddeḵ*	*np̄addeḵ*	*paddeḵ*	*mp̄addeḵ*	*mp̄addaḵ*	*mp̄addāḵū*
tD (ethpaal)	*eṯpaddaḵ*	*neṯpaddaḵ*	*eṯpaddaḵ*		*meṯpaddaḵ*	*meṯpaddāḵū*
Š (afel)	*ap̄deḵ*	*nap̄deḵ*	*ap̄deḵ*	*map̄deḵ*	*map̄daḵ*	*map̄dāḵū*
tŠ (ettafal)	*ettap̄daḵ*	*nettap̄daḵ*	*ettap̄daḵ*		*mettap̄daḵ*	*mettap̄dāḵū*
pronoun 1	*enā*	*ḥnan*		—	*-an*	
2m	*at*	*attōn*		*-āḵ*	*-ḵōn*	
f	*at*	*attēn*		*-eḵ*	*-ḵēn*	
3m	*hū*	*hennōn*		*-eh*	*-hōn*	
f	*hī*	*hennēn*		*-āh*	*-hēn*	

Syriac

		perfect	imperfect	imperative	act. part.	pass. part.	infinitive
I ʾ	G	*eḏaḵ*	*neḏuḵ*	*aḏuḵ*	*āḏeḵ*	*aḏīḵ*	*meḏaḵ*
	tG	*eṯeḏeḵ*	*neṯeḏeḵ*	*eṯaḏk*		*meṯeḏeḵ*	*meṯeḏāḵū*
	D	*addeḵ*	*naddeḵ*	*addeḵ*	*maddeḵ*	*maddaḵ*	*maddāḵū*
	tD	*eṯaddaḵ*	*neṯaddaḵ*	*eṯaddaḵ*		*meṯaddaḵ*	*meṯaddāḵū*
	Š	*awdeḵ*	*nawdeḵ*	*awdeḵ*	*mawdeḵ*	*mawdaḵ*	*mawdāḵū*
	tŠ	*ettawdaḵ*	*nettawdaḵ*	*ettawdaḵ*		*mettawdaḵ*	*mettawdāḵū*
I *n*	G	*nḏaḵ*	*nedduḵ*	*duḵ*	*nāḏeḵ*	*nḏīḵ*	*meddaḵ*
	Š	*addeḵ*	*naddeḵ*	*addeḵ*	*maddeḵ*	*maddaḵ*	*maddāḵū*
	tŠ	*ettaddaḵ*	*nettaddaḵ*	*ettaddaḵ*		*mettaddaḵ*	*mettaddāḵū*
I weak	G	*īḏeḵ*	*nīḏaḵ*	*īḏaḵ*	*yāḏeḵ*	*īḏīḵ*	*mīḏaḵ*
	tG	*eṯīḏeḵ*	*neṯīḏeḵ*	*eṯīḏk*		*meṯīḏeḵ*	*meṯīḏāḵū*
	Š	*awdeḵ*	*nawdeḵ*	*awdeḵ*	*mawdeḵ*	*mawdaḵ*	*mawdāḵū*
	tŠ	*ettawdaḵ*	*nettawdaḵ*	*ettawdaḵ*		*mettawdaḵ*	*mettawdāḵū*
II ʾ	G	*peḵ*	*nep̄aḵ*	*paḵ*	*pāʾeḵ*	*pīḵ*	*mep̄aḵ*
	tG	*eṯpeḵ*	*neṯpeḵ*	*eṯpaḵ*		*meṯpeḵ*	*meṯpāḵū*
	Š	*ap̄eḵ*	*nap̄eḵ*	*ap̄eḵ*	*map̄eḵ*	*map̄aḵ*	*map̄āḵū*
	tŠ	*ettap̄aḵ*	*nettap̄aḵ*	*ettap̄aḵ*		*mettap̄aḵ*	*mettap̄āḵū*
II gem.	G	*paḏ*	*neppuḏ*	*puḏ*	*pāʾeḏ*	*pḏīḏ*	*meppaḏ*
	Š	*appeḏ*	*nappeḏ*	*appeḏ*	*mappeḏ*	*mappaḏ*	*mappāḏū*
	tŠ	*ettappaḏ*	*nettappaḏ*	*ettappaḏ*		*mettappaḏ*	*mettappāḏū*
II weak	G	*pāḵ*	*np̄ūḵ*	*pūḵ*	*pāʾeḵ*	*pīḵ*	*mp̄āḵ*
	D	*payyeḵ*	*np̄ayyeḵ*	*payyeḵ*	*mp̄ayyeḵ*	*mp̄ayyaḵ*	*mp̄ayyāḵū*
	tD	*eṯpayyaḵ*	*neṯpayyaḵ*	*eṯpayyaḵ*		*meṯpayyaḵ*	*meṯpayyāḵū*
	Š	*ap̄īḵ*	*np̄īḵ*	*ap̄īḵ*	*map̄īḵ*	*mp̄āḵ*	*mp̄āḵū*
	(tG =) tŠ	*ettp̄īḵ*	*nettp̄īḵ*	*ettp̄īḵ*		*mettp̄īḵ*	*mettp̄āḵū*
III weak	G	*pḏā*	*nep̄dē*	*pḏī*	*pāḏē*	*pḏē*	*mep̄dā*
	tG	*eṯpḏī*	*neṯpḏē*	*eṯpday*		*meṯpḏē*	*meṯpḏāyū*
	D	*paddī*	*np̄addē*	*paddā*	*mp̄addē*	*mp̄adday*	*mp̄addāyū*
	tD	*eṯpaddī*	*neṯpaddē*	*eṯpaddē*		*meṯpaddē*	*meṯpaddāyū*
	Š	*ap̄dī*	*nap̄dē*	*ap̄dā*	*map̄dē*	*map̄day*	*map̄dāyū*
	tŠ	*ettap̄dī*	*nettap̄dī*	*ettap̄dā*		*mettap̄dē*	*mettap̄dāyū*

Geʿez

	perfect	subjunctive	imperfect	imperative	gerundive	infinitive
G sg. 1	*fadakkū*	*efdek*	*efaddek*		*fadīkēya*	
2m	*fadakka*	*tefdek*	*tefaddek*	*fedek*	*fadīkaka*	
f	*fadakkī*	*tefdekī*	*tefaddekī*	*fedekī*	*fadīkakī*	
3m	*fadaka*	*yefdek*	*yefaddek*		*fadīkō*	*fadīkōt*
f	*fadakat*	*tefdek*	*tefaddek*		*fadīkā*	
pl. 1	*fadakna*	*nefdek*	*nefaddek*		*fadīkana*	
2m	*fadakkemmū*	*tefdekū*	*tefaddekū*	*fedekū*	*fadīkakemmū*	
f	*fadakken*	*tefdekā*	*tefaddekā*	*fedekā*	*fadīkaken*	
3m	*fadakū*	*yefdekū*	*yefaddekū*		*fadīkōmū*	
f	*fadakā*	*yefdekā*	*yefaddekā*		*fadīkōn*	
šG	*afdaka*	*yāfdek*	*yāfaddek*	*afdek*	*afdīk-*	*afdekō*
tG	*tafadka*	*yetfadak*	*yetfaddak*	*tafadak*	*tafadīk-*	*tafadekō*
štG	*astafadaka*	*yāstafdek*	*yāstafaddek*	*astafdek*	*astafdīk-*	*astafdekō*
D	*faddaka*	*yefaddek*	*yefēddek*	*faddek*	*faddīk-*	*faddekō*
šD	*afaddaka*	*yāfaddek*	*yāfēddek*	*afaddek*	*afaddīk-*	*afaddekō*
tD	*tafaddaka*	*yetfaddak*	*yetfēddak*	*tafaddak*	*tafaddīk-*	*tafaddekō*
štD	*astafaddaka*	*yāstafaddek*	*yāstafēddek*	*astafaddek*	*astafaddīk-*	*astafaddekō*
L	*fādaka*	*yefādek*	*yefāddek*	*fādek*	*fādīk-*	*fādekō*
šL	*afādaka*	*yāfādek*	*yāfāddek*	*afādek*	*afādīk-*	*afādekō*
tL	*tafādaka*	*yetfādak*	*yetfāddak*	*tafādak*	*tafādīk-*	*tafādekō*
štL	*astafādaka*	*yāstafādek*	*yāstafāddek*	*astafādek*	*astafādīk-*	*astafādikō*

pronoun 1	*ana*	*neḥna*	*-ya, -nī*	*-na*
2m	*anta*	*antemmū*	*-ka*	*-kemmū*
f	*antī*	*anten*	*-kī*	*-ken*
3m	*weʾetū*	*emūntū/weʾetōmū*	*-hū*	*-hōmū*
f	*yeʾetī*	*emāntū/weʾetōn*	*-hā*	*-hōn*

Ge^{c}ez

		perfect	subjunctive	imperfect	imperative	gerundive	infinitive
I lar.	G	*ḥadaka*	*yeḥdek*	*yaḥaddek*	*ḥedek*	*ḥadīk-*	*ḥadīkōt*
	štG	*asteḥdaka*	*yāsteḥdek*	*yāstaḥaddek*	*asteḥdek*	*asteḥdīk-*	*asteḥdekō*
I *w*	G	*wadka*	*yedak*	*yewaddek*	*dak*	*wadīk-*	*wadīkōt*
II lar.	G	*feḥka*	*yefḥak*	*yefeḥḥek*	*faḥak*	*feḥīk-*	*feḥīkōt*
II *w*	G	*fōka*	*yefūk*	*yefawwek*	*fūk*	*fawīk-*	*fawīkōt*
	šG	*afaka*	*yāfek*	*yāfawwek*	*afek*	*afwīk-*	*afwekō*
II *y*	G	*fēka*	*yefīk*	*yefayyek*	*fīk*	*fayek-*	*fayī/ekōt*
	šG	*afēka*	*yāfīk*	*yāfayyek*	*afīk*	*afīk-*	*afīkō*
III lar.	G	*fadḥa*	*yefdāḥ*	*yefaddeḥ*	*fedāḥ*	*fadīḥ-*	*fadīḥōt*
	L	*fādeḥa*	*yefādeḥ*	*yefāddeḥ*	*fādeḥ*	*fādīḥ-*	*fādeḥō*
	tL	*tafādeḥa*	*yetfādāḥ*	*yetfāddāḥ*	*tafādāḥ*	*tafādīḥ-*	*tafādeḥō*
III *w*	G	*fadawa*	*yefdū*	*yefaddō*	*fedū*	*fadīw-*	*fadewōt*
	D	*faddawa*	*yefaddū*	*yefēddū*	*faddū*	*faddīw-*	*faddewō*
III *y*	G	*fadaya*	*yefdī*	*yefaddī*	*fedī*	*fadeyye*	*fadeyōt*
	D	*faddaya*	*yefaddī*	*yefēddī*	*faddī*	*faddeyye*	*faddeyō*

Arabic

	perfect	imperfect	imperative	participle	infinitive
G (I) sg. 1	*fadaktu*	*afduku*			
2m	*fadakta*	*tafduku*	*ufduk*		
f	*fadakti*	*tafdukīna*	*ufdukī*		
3m	*fadaka*	*yafduku*		*fādikun*	*fadkun*, etc.
f	*fadakat*	*tafduku*			
du. 2	*fadaktumā*	*tafdukāni*	*ufdukā*		
3m	*fadakā*	*yafdukāni*			
f	*fadakatā*	*tafdukāni*			
pl. 1	*fadaknā*	*nafduku*			
2m	*fadaktum*	*tafdukūna*	*ufdukū*		
f	*fadaktunna*	*tafdukna*	*ufdukna*		
3m	*fadakū*	*yafdukūna*			
f	*fadakna*	*tafdukna*			
Gp	*fudika*	*yufdaku*		*mafdūkun*	
Gt (VIII)	*iftadaka*	*yaftadiku*	*iftadik*	*muftadikun*	*iftidākun*
Gtp	*uftudika*	*yuftadaku*		*muftadakun*	
D (II)	*faddaka*	*yufaddiku*	*faddik*	*mufaddikun*	*tafdīkun*
Dp	*fuddika*	*yufaddaku*		*mufaddakun*	
tD (V)	*tafaddaka*	*yatafaddaku*	*tafaddak*	*mutafaddikun*	*tafaddukun*
tDp	*tufuddika*	*yutafaddaku*		*mutafaddakun*	
Š (IV)	*afdaka*	*yufdiku*	*afdik*	*mufdikun*	*ifdākun*
Šp	*ufdika*	*yufdaku*		*mufdakun*	
Št (X)	*istafdaka*	*yastafdiku*	*istafdik*	*mustafdikun*	*istifdākun*
Štp	*ustufdika*	*yustafdaku*		*mustafdakun*	
N (VII)	*infadaka*	*yanfadiku*	*infadik*	*munfadikun*	*infidākun*
(Np	*unfudika*	*yunfadaka*		*munfadakun*)	
L (III)	*fādaka*	*yufādiku*	*fādik*	*mufādikun*	*fidākun* or *mufādakatun*
Lp	*fūdika*	*yufādaka*		*mufādakun*	
tL (VI)	*tafādaka*	*yatafādaku*	*tafādak*	*mutafādikun*	*tafādukun*
tLp	*tufūdika*	*yutafādaku*		*mutafādakun*	

subjunctive *yafduka*, etc.; apocopate *yafduk*, etc.; energic *yafdukan(na)*, etc.

pronoun 1	*ana*		*naḥnu*	*-ī, -nī*		*-nā*
2m	*anta*	*antumā*	*antum*	*-ka*	*-kumā*	*-kum*
f	*anti*		*antunna*	*-ki*		*-kunna*
3m	*huwa*	*humā*	*hum*	*-hŭ*	*-humā*	*-hum*
f	*hiya*		*hunna*	*-hā*		*-hunna*

Arabic

	perfect	imperfect	imperative	participle	infinitive
I weak G	*wadaka*	*yadiku*	*dik*	*wādikun*	*dikatun*
Gt	*ittadaka*	*yattadiku*	*ittadik*	*muttadikun*	*ittidākun*
Š	*awdaka*	*yūdiku*	*awdik*	*mūdikun*	*īdākun*
Št	*istawdaka*	*yastawdiku*	*istawdik*	*mustawdikun*	*istīdākun*
II gem. G	*fadda*	*yafuddu*	*fudd*V / *ufdud*	*fāddun*	*faddun*
Š	*afadda*	*yufiddu*	*afdid*	*mufiddun*	*ifdādun*
L	*fādda*	*yufāddu*	*fādid*	*mufāddun*	*fidādun*
II weak G	*fāka*	*yafūku*	*fuk*	*fāʾikun*	*fawkun*
Gp	*fīka*	*yufāku*		*mafūkun*	
Gt	*iftāka*	*yuftāku*	*iftak*	*muftākun*	*iftiyākun*
Š	*afāka*	*yufīku*	*afik*	*mufīkun*	*ifākatun*
Št	*istafāka*	*yastafīku*	*istafik*	*mustafīkun*	*istifākatun*
N	*infāka*	*yanfāku*	*infak*	*munfākun*	*infiyākun*
III weak G	*fādā*	*yafdū*	*ufdu*	*fādun*	*fadwun*
Gp	*fudiya*	*fudā*		*mafdūwun*	
Gt	*iftadā*	*yaftadī*	*iftadi*	*muftadun*	*iftidāʾun*
Gtp	*uftudiya*	*yuftadā*		*muftadun*	
D	*faddā*	*yufaddī*	*faddi*	*mufaddun*	*taftiyatun*
tD	*tafaddā*	*yutafaddā*	*tafadda*	*mutafaddun*	*tafaddun*
Š	*afdā*	*yufdī*	*afdi*	*mufdun*	*ifdāʾun*
L	*fādā*	*yufādī*	*fādi*	*mufādun*	*fidāʾun / mufādātun*
tL	*tafādā*	*yatafādā*	*tafāda*	*mutafādun*	*tafādun*

Appendix B

Semitic Scripts

§ **B.0** The writing systems used by the Semitic languages encompass all three principal kinds: alphabetic, syllabic, and logographic-syllabic.

§ **B.1** The alphabets in which the Semitic literary languages are written, and in fact all alphabets everywhere, are descended from a common ancestor, earliest attested in the graffiti of Canaanite mine workers in the Sinai from about the 16th century B.C. While the interpretation of this proto-Sinaitic is far from certain, the next stages of the script, found in Phoenician and Aramaic inscriptions from about 1300 B.C. on, are well understood and the principal difficulties in interpretation stem from poor preservation of the materials and from the fact that at various eras various pairs of characters came to resemble each other more than is optimal for differentiating them. By the sixth century B.C. there could be distinguished a Canaanite and an Aramaic script. The former died out almost entirely, surviving only in Samaritan, to be replaced by the latter, which by the time of the Qumran documents (as early as 200 B.C.), if not the Egyptian Aramaic ones (up to 400 B.C.), had nearly achieved the shape of today's square Hebrew letters. A striving for ease and speed in writing led, in separate developments, to cursive Syriac (by A.D. 400), Arabic (by 500), and Mandaic writing.

Puzzling is the relationship between the main stream of alphabetic systems and the Ugaritic alphabet (14th c. B.C.):

Table 4

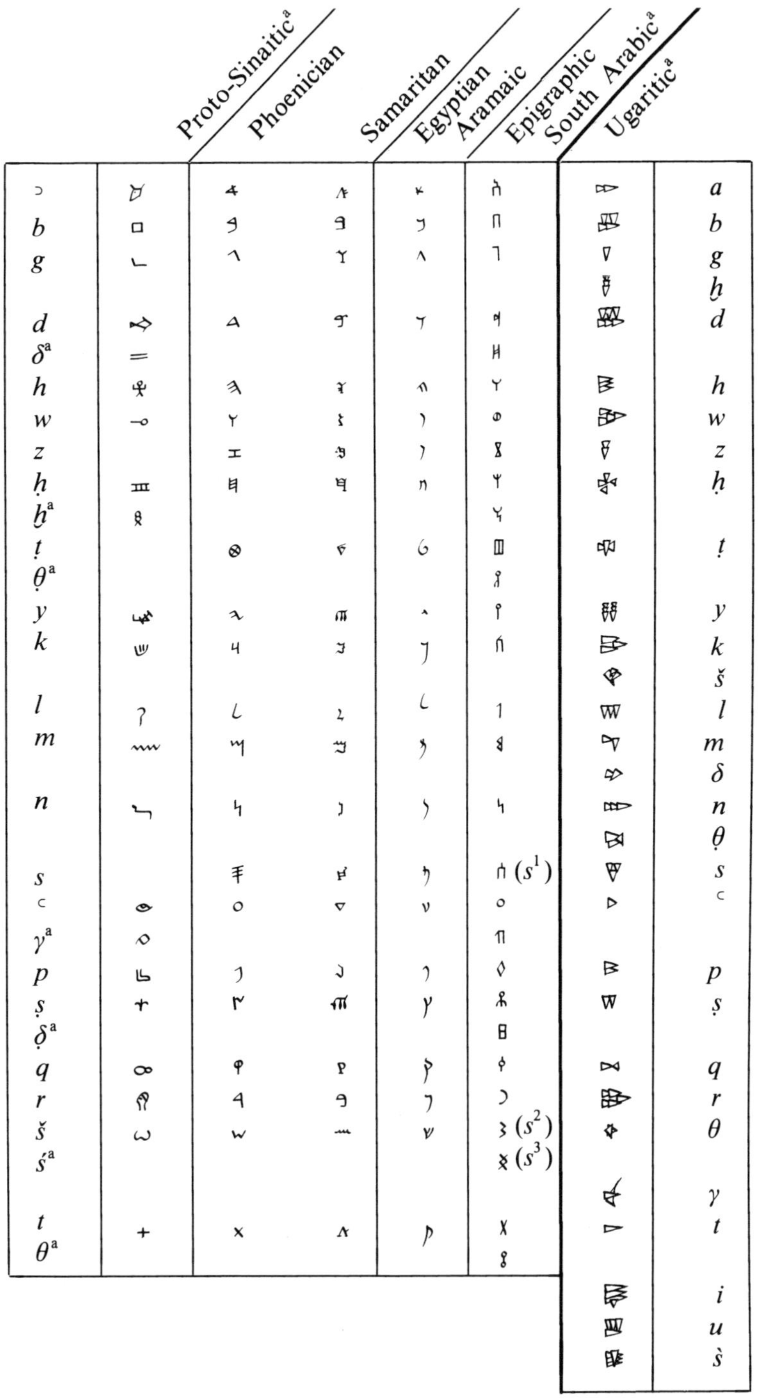

a. The Epigraphic South Arabic letters that have no correspondences in the Phoenician alphabet are inserted in the order conventionally used for them (and, incidentally, for Ugaritic) in glossaries. The attested apparent order is h l h m q w s^2 r γ t s^1 b k n h ... s^3 f $\jmath$ ς ... (compare the Ethiopic order, Table 11). The attested Ugaritic order is given here. The Proto-Sinaitic forms follow Albright's conjectural decipherment.

The table columns, from left to right, are: (transliteration), Proto-Sinaitic[a], Phoenician, Samaritan, Egyptian Aramaic, Epigraphic South Arabic, Ugaritic[a].

	Proto-Sinaitic[a]	Phoenician	Samaritan	Egyptian Aramaic	Epigraphic South Arabic	Ugaritic[a]
$\jmath$						a
b						b
g						$\dot{g}$
						$\underline{h}$
d						d
δ[a]						
h						h
w						w
z						z
$\dot{h}$						$\dot{h}$
$\underline{h}$[a]						
$\underline{t}$						t
θ[a]						
y						y
k						k
						$\check{s}$
l						l
m						m
						δ
n						n
						θ
s					$\dot{h}\,(s^1)$	s
ς						ς
γ[a]						
p						p
$\dot{s}$						$\dot{s}$
$\dot{\delta}$[a]						
q						q
r						r
$\check{s}$					(s^2)	θ
$\acute{s}$[a]					(s^3)	
						γ
t						t
θ[a]						
						i
						u
						$\dot{s}$

some of its letters, which are cuneiform signs (see § B.3), resemble the Phoenician counterparts, while a connection is difficult to perceive for others; but the alphabet of the South Arabic inscriptions (from at least 500 B.C.) is closest in letterforms to the Ugaritic. The earliest Arabic graffiti (Safaitic, 1st c. B.C. - 3rd c. A.D.; Thamudic, perhaps 5th c. B.C. - 5th c. A.D.) are in a South Arabic script. The Ethiopic syllabary is derived from the South Arabic alphabet.

The order of the alphabet is fundamentally the same for all the systems in use today (except the Ethiopic syllabary). Extra letters as required by individual languages are inserted here and there acording to resemblance now of sound, now of shape. The order of the South Arabic alphabet is not certainly known.

In the shapes of the original signs that became the letters may be recognized the working of an acrographic principle, by which the first sound (always a consonant) of the name of the item depicted in the pictogram becomes the sound for which the picture stands, e.g., □ *bayt-* 'house' > *b*. The fact that the letters represent only consonants leads some scholars to deny that these sets of signs are alphabets (in which each sign stands for approximately one phoneme — the qualification is necessary because no sytem ideally fits its language); they are rather syllabaries, in which every sign represents a consonant plus some indeterminate vowel. In this view the first alphabet, according signs to vowels as well as consonants, is the Greek, whose letterforms are borrowed from the Phoenician or Aramaic. Nevertheless, with the devising of marks to indicate vowels, complete and adequate alphabets have been achieved for each of the literary languages (Ge^{c}ez excepted). Actually, only in Phoenician and South Arabic is there absolutely no indication of vowel quality.[b] Ugaritic, otherwise vowelless, has three separate characters for ᵓ*a*, ᵓ*i*, and ᵓ*u* (the treatment of

b. Fortunately, at a late stage some Phoenician texts were written in the Greek alphabet and careful study allows the determination of some of the vowels; the South Arabic pattern *qtlw* may represent **qatalaw* or possibly **qatalu*.

V$^{\supset}$C is less clear), which makes possible considerable confidence in reconstructing the vocalism, particularly conjugation patterns, when roots containing $^{\supset}$ are studied. Early in the history of recorded Aramaic, the letters for the semivowels *w* and *y* in effect stood for the diphthongs *aw* and *ay*, and later were retained to mark *ō* and *ē* as contractions of the diphthongs, and then also *ū* and *ī*. Perhaps by analogy $^{\supset}$ was used for *ā*, and *h* (particularly finally) also entered the system. Mandaic (see § 4/1 n. 2) adjoins ^{c} as well (the rules for reading Mandaic vowels are given in Table 9).

The other scripts have adopted versions of this system. Arabic, not surprisingly the most regular, indicates all long vowels with *w*, *y*, or *alif*. Hebrew shows considerable freedom in using vowel letters or not; Syriac employs an intermediate system.

Hebrew, Syriac, and Arabic can all add signs indicating vowel quality, and other phonological features, to the basic consonantal text; the vowel sign denotes the vowel following the consonant to which it is appended. The three scripts have different systems, Syriac and Hebrew more than one.

All three read from right to left. In books where they are combined with a western language (grammars, dictionaries, commentaries, etc.), the individual words in a series of examples are usually to be taken one at a time from left to right. If a sentence or other long example does not fit on a single line in a primarily left-to-right text, the quotation begins at the right end of the first line, occupies the space to the middle of that line, and continues from as far to the right of the next line as necessary, reading to the left margin. The English, etc., text then resumes at the middle of the line in which the quotation ends.[c] E.g.:

These words from the Palestinian Talmud summarize the Rabbis' attitude toward their languages: ארבע לשונות נאה לעולם שישתמשו בהם לעז לזמר רומי לקרב סורסי לאילייא עברי לדיבור: "There are four tongues

c. One reason for including the script specimens and this discussion is to facilitate the use of older grammars and dictionaries, where citation of parallels, cognates, etc., in languages other than the principal one was often done in original orthography. One advantage in this system was the obviation of a language label on every form; another was the necessity for the reader to become familiar with all the Semitic scripts. The principal disadvantages were purely technological: the need for typesetters familiar with the scripts, and the difficulty and expense of inserting out-of-sorts type into the main text. The advent of electronic photocomposition has alleviated at least the latter burden, so we may hope that the practice will return. As an aid to the user of such materials, the letters of each alphabet are here presented rearranged according to similarity of shape, so that the more easily confused ones may be more easily compared.

worthy of common use: Greek for song, Latin for war, Syriac for lamentation, and Hebrew for ordinary speech" (Megilloth iv 4).

The letters of the alphabets can also be used as numerals. Arabic normally uses its own decimal notation; the digits of a number are then read from left to right.

§ B.1.1 Certain letters of the Hebrew alphabet (Table 5) have distinctive forms word-finally.

The vowel signs are placed above, below, and beside the letters (Table 6).

A dot inside *b d g p t k* indicates non-spirantized pronunciation; inside final *h* it marks it as consonantal rather than a vowel letter; in other letters it indicates a long consonant. Long *b d g p t k* are never spirantized. A dash above a letter verifies the absence of the dot.

A "hyphen" joins particles to their head words, and other closely connected items. A "colon" marks the end of a verse of the Bible.

§ B.1.2 Three forms of the Syriac alphabet are in common use, the Serto (Sy *serṭā* [*pšīṭā*] '[simple] stroke'), the Estrangelo (*στρογγύλη* 'round,' or perhaps Ab *saṭr angīliyya* 'gospel writing'), and the Nestorian. The last is primarily found in Modern Aramaic texts; both the first two are used in scholarly works. Because the script is a cursive one, many letters are joined with those that precede and follow. Some may not join on one side or the other, so there are up to three different forms of each letter. Only final *k* and *n* differ greatly from the basic form, though. There are ligatures for *l*ʾ ܠܐ and ʾ*l* ܐܠ; *k* and *n* standing alone (as when being cited qua letters) are doubled: ܟܟ, ܢܢ. Nestorian can substitute ܬܐ for final ܬܐ and ܗܝ for ܗܝ, as space dictates; a diacritic produces ܓ̰ and ܟ̰ for modern *ǰ* and *č* respectively.

Table 5

transliteration	Hebrew	Hebrew name	numerical value	Syriac name	Syriac: Serto final	Serto medial	Serto initial	Serto alone	Estrangelo	Nestorian	Mandaic	Md transliteration
ʾ	א	ắlep̄	1	ālap̄	ܐ	—	—	ܐ	ܐ	ܐ	ࡀ	—[d]
b	ב	bēṯ	2	bēṯ	ܒ	ܒ	ܒ	ܒ	ܒ	ܒ	ࡁ	b
g	ג	gī́mel	3	gāmal	ܓ	ܓ	ܓ	ܓ	ܓ	ܓ	ࡂ	g
d	ד	dā́leṯ	4	dālaṯ/ḏ	ܕ	—	—	ܕ	ܕ	ܕ	ࡃ	d
h	ה	hē	5	hē	ܗ	—	—	ܗ	ܗ	ܗ	ࡄ	—[e]
w	ו	wāw	6	waw	ܘ	—	—	ܘ	ܘ	ܘ	ࡅ	w[d]
z	ז	záyin	7	zay(n)	ܙ	—	—	ܙ	ܙ	ܙ	ࡆ	z
ḥ	ח	ḥēṯ	8	ḥēṯ	ܚ	ܚ	ܚ	ܚ	ܚ	ܚ	ࡇ	h
ṭ	ט	ṭēṯ	9	ṭēṯ	ܛ	ܛ	ܛ	ܛ	ܛ	ܛ	ࡈ	ṭ
y	י	yōḏ	10	yō/ūḏ	ܝ	ܝ	ܝ	ܝ	ܝ	ܝ	ࡉ	y[d]
k	כ ך	kāp̄	20	kāp̄	ܟ	ܟ	ܟ	ܟ	ܟ ܟ	ܟ ܟ	ࡊ	k
l	ל	lā́meḏ	30	lāmaḏ	ܠ	ܠ	ܠ	ܠ	ܠ	ܠ	ࡋ	l
m	מ ם	mēm	40	mīm	ܡ	ܡ	ܡ	ܡ	ܡ ܡ	ܡ ܡ	ࡌ	m
n	נ ן	nūn	50	nūn	ܢ	ܢ	ܢ	ܢ	ܢ ܢ	ܢ ܢ	ࡍ	n
s	ס	sā́mek̲	60	semkaṯ	ܣ	ܣ	ܣ	ܣ	ܣ	ܣ	ࡎ	s
ʿ	ע	ʿáyin	70	ʿē	ܥ	ܥ	ܥ	ܥ	ܥ	ܥ	ࡏ	—[d]
p	פ ף	pē	80	pē	ܦ	ܦ	ܦ	ܦ	ܦ	ܦ	ࡐ	p
ṣ	צ ץ	ṣāḏē	90	ṣāḏē	ܨ	—	—	ܨ	ܨ	ܨ	ࡑ	ṣ
q	ק	qōp̄	100	qōp̄	ܩ	ܩ	ܩ	ܩ	ܩ	ܩ	ࡒ	q
r	ר	rēš	200	rēš	ܪ	—	—	ܪ	ܪ	ܪ	ࡓ	r
ś	שׂ	śīn										
š	שׁ	šīn	300	šīn	ܫ	ܫ	ܫ	ܫ	ܫ	ܫ	ࡔ	š
t	ת	tāw	400	taw	ܬ	—	—	ܬ	ܬ	ܬ	ࡕ	t
											ࡖ	—[e]

d. See Table 8.
e. See § 4/1 n. 2.

י ו ן נ ז ג ב כ ד ר ך ל ק ף פ ט מ ה ח ת ם ס שׂ שׁ ע צ ץ א

ʾ ṣ# ṣ ʿ š ś s m# t ḥ h m ṭ p p# q l k# r d k b g z n n# w y

ܠ ܐ ܥ ܚ ܓ ܨ ܛ ܦ ܡ ܩ ܣ ܘ ܫ ܕ ܪ ܟ ܒ ܗ ܠ ܛ ܬ ܐ ܙ ܢ ܝ ܠܐ ܬ

t lʾ y n z ʾ t ṭ l h b k r d š w s q m p ṭ ṣ g ḥ ʿ ʾl

f. The transliterations used in the standard grammars differ considerably; the table collects those in the most-often-cited ones (listed in □3b). The systems in the last two columns are those most likely to be found in articles. A dot under a letter signifies a higher (close) vowel, a hook (sometimes pointing the other way) lower (open). Numerous systems for indicating vowel length and/or vowel letters exist, some etymological, some transliterational, involving macrons, circumflexes, and *w y* etc.

g. In closed unaccented syllables or before ◌ֳ. Manuscripts with Babylonian vowel signs differ in their treatment of this vowel.

h. The dot of the *ḥṓlem* coalesces with that of a preceding *ś* or a following *š*.

Table 6[f]

Tiberian	Babylonian	name	this volume	Kautzsch	Bergsträsser	Bauer-Leander	Lambdin	Blau
◌ִ	◌̇	*ḥī́req*	*i*	*i*	*i*	*i*	*i*	*i*
◌ֵ	◌̈	*ṣērē*	*e*	*e*	*e*	*e*	*ē*	*ẹ*
◌ֶ	◌ٚ	*sḡōl*		*è, ä*	*ę*	*æ*	*e*	*ę*
◌ַ		*páṯaḥ*	*a*	*a*	*ạ*	*a*	*a*	*a*
◌ָ	◌˂	*qā́meṣ*			*a*	*å*	*ā*	*å*
		qā́meṣ ḥaṭūp̄[g]	*o*	*å, ŏ*	*ǫ*		*o*	
◌ֹ	◌̈	*ḥṓlem*[h]		*o*	*o*	*o*	*ō*	*o*
וּ, ◌ֻ	◌ٝ	*qibbūṣ*	*u*	*u*	*u*	*u*	*u*	*u*
◌ְ		*šwā*	∅	*e*	*e*	*e*	*ə*	*ə*
◌ֱ		*ḥāṭēp̄ sḡōl*	∅/*ĕ*	*ĕ*	*ę*		*ĕ*	*ĕ*
◌ֲ		*ḥāṭēp̄ páṯaḥ*	∅/*ă*	*a*	*ạ*	*a*	*ă*	*ă*
◌ֳ		*ḥāṭēp̄ qā́meṣ*	∅/*ŏ*	*o*	*ǫ*	*o*	*ŏ*	*ǫ̆*

Vowels are added in three ways, one using single dots, two with an individual sign for each vowel. A dot above or below a word or suffix distinguishes homographs. The principle is that the dot above marks a fuller vowel — usually *a/ā* — while the dot below indicates a closer vowel — *i*, *u*, or vowellessness; some words have more than one. This system has to some extent been "lexicalized" so that the pointing used for weak verbs (with vowels different from those of corresponding strong verbs) reflects the strong pattern rather than the actual vowels, and a final *-h* with point above represents a

i. As for Hebrew, the Syriac vowel signs are not differentiated by length; a more accurate transliteration of the signs would be *i ẹ ę a å o u* (the western system, reflecting the dialect, does not notate two qualities of *e* nor an *o* distinct from *u*). Parentheses indicate the eastern names.

Table 7[i]

Jacobite (western)	Nestorian (eastern)	name	transliteration
◌ܺ	◌ܼ	*ḥḇāṣā*	*i*
◌ܶ	◌ܹ	(*r. karyā, zlāmā qašyā*)	*ē*
	◌ܸ	*rḇāṣā* (*r. arrīḵā, z. pšīqā*)	*e*
◌ܰ	◌ܲ	*pṯāḥā*	*a*
◌ܳ	◌ܵ	*zqāpā*	*ā*
	ܘܿ	(*ᶜṣāṣā rwīḥā*)	*o*
◌ܽ	ܘܼ	*ᶜṣāṣā* (*ᶜ. allīṣā*)	*u*

feminine singular suffix, whatever its vowel. The two explicit systems of vowels are shown in Table 7. The ones based on the Greek letters (which may appear indifferently above or below their letters, as there is room) are used with Serto, and the ones developed from the dot system are used with the Nestorian alphabet.

A point above *b d g p t k* indicates non-spirantized; below, spirantized pronunciation. Two dots above some letter of a word (ܪ or ܕ if possible — over ܪ they replace its dot) mark the word as a plural form. A stroke over a letter marks it as silent. Certain suffixes are written with final, etymological, vowel letters, but they are not pronounced: ܘ -, ܝ -, ܝܗܘ -. The enclitic verb forms are written as separate words, even in Modern Aramaic.

Table 8

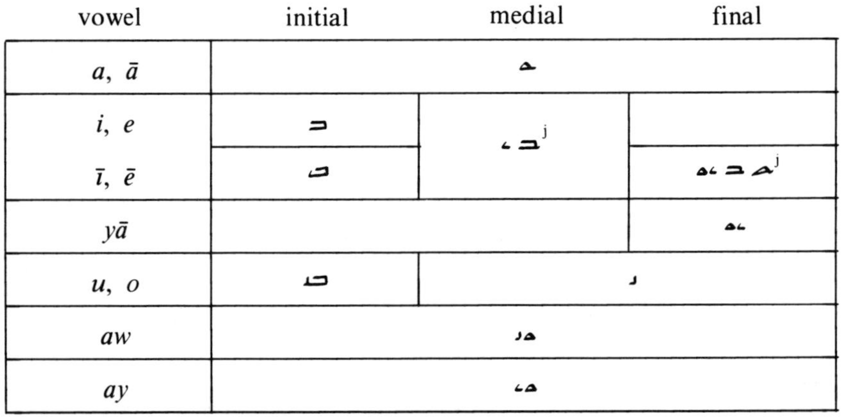
vowel
initial
medial
final
a, ā
i, e
ī, ē
yā
u, o
aw
ay

j. After the letters with v-shaped descenders, and in the word הע 'she.'

§ **B.1.3** Mandaic is unique among Semitic scripts in having developed a full system of vowel-writing using just the consonantal letters (Table 8). The letters with v-shaped descenders enter into ligatures with the ones with vertical spines (Table 9). (It is usual for Mandaic to be transliterated into Hebrew characters for typographical convenience.)

§ **B.1.4** In Arabic there may be as many as four forms of each letter, according as they are joined on both sides, left, right, or neither (Table 10). Note that a number of letters turn into mere spikes in the line, distinguished only by the dots above or below them. Ligatures include *lā* لا, *kā* كا, *kl* كل.

Table 9

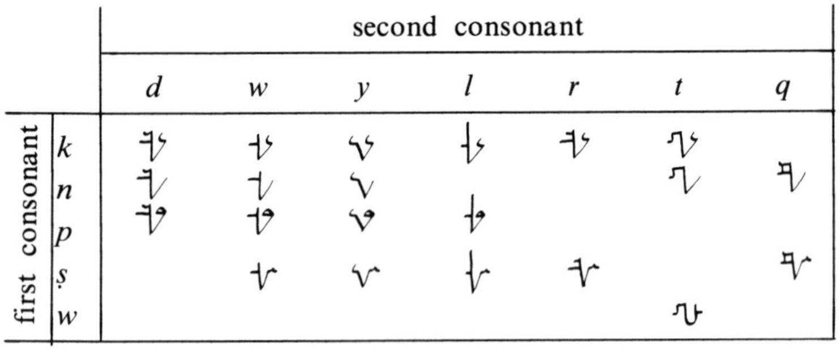
second consonant
d
w
y
l
r
t
q
first consonant
k
n
p
ṣ
w

Table 10

transliteration	final	medial	initial	alone	name	numerical value
ā	ـا			ا	*alif*	1
b	ـب	ـبـ	بـ	ب	*bā*	2
t	ـت	ـتـ	تـ	ت	*tā*	400
θ	ـث	ـثـ	ثـ	ث	*θā*	500
ǰ	ـج	ـجـ	جـ	ج	*ǰīm*	3
ḥ	ـح	ـحـ	حـ	ح	*ḥā*	8
ḫ	ـخ	ـخـ	خـ	خ	*ḫā*	600
d	ـد			د	*dāl*	4
δ	ـذ			ذ	*δāl*	700
r	ـر			ر	*rā*	200
z	ـز			ز	*zāy*	7
s	ـس	ـسـ	سـ	س	*sīn*	60
š	ـش	ـشـ	شـ	ش	*šīn*	300
ṣ	ـص	ـصـ	صـ	ص	*ṣād*	90
ḍ	ـض	ـضـ	ضـ	ض	*ḍād*	800
ṭ	ـط	ـطـ	طـ	ط	*ṭā*	9
θ̣	ـظ	ـظـ	ظـ	ظ	*θ̣ā*	900
ᶜ	ـع	ـعـ	عـ	ع	*ᶜayn*	70
γ	ـغ	ـغـ	غـ	غ	*γayn*	1000
f	ـف	ـفـ	فـ	ف	*fā*	80
q	ـق	ـقـ	قـ	ق	*qāf*	100
k	ـك	ـكـ	كـ	ك	*kāf*	20
l	ـل	ـلـ	لـ	ل	*lām*	30
m	ـم	ـمـ	مـ	م	*mīm*	40
n	ـن	ـنـ	نـ	ن	*nūn*	50
h	ـه	ـهـ	هـ	ه	*hā*	5
w	ـو			و	*wāw*	6
y	ـى	ـيـ	يـ	ى	*yā*	10

١	٢	٣	٤	٥	٦	٧	٨	٩	٠
1	2	3	4	5	6	7	8	9	0

ء ا لـكـد ذ ر ز عـبـنـيـتـثـشـسـحـجـخـغـعـصـضـظـطـفـقـهـو هـمـه كا كل لا غـة

t# γ lā kl kā h# m h w h q f ṭ θ̣ ḍ ṣ ᶜ γ ḫ ǰ ḥ s š θ t y n b ᶜ z r δ d k l ā ᵓ

The glottal stop is not indicated by *alif*, as in Syriac, but by ء *hamza*. This sits on a *y*, *w*, *alif*, or nothing, according to the vowels on either side: a *yā*-seat indicates an ⁽*ī*⁾ on one side or both, a *waw*-seat an ⁽*ū*⁾ but no *i*, etc. Initially it goes above *alif* for ʾ*a* and below it for ʾ*i*. To avoid writing double consonants, a *hamza* beside a long vowel has no seat at all, nor has it one when it ends a word-final cluster.

Vowels are َ *a*, ِ *i*, and ُ *u*;[k] final nunation is indicated by doubling the vowel sign, ً, ٍ, ٌ, and never by adding the letter *n*. -*an*, however, is supported by a final *alif*. Long vowels are marked by vowel letters, except that in a few common words *ā* is not written. In vocalized texts it is then indicated by ٰ. Where two *alif*'s would be adjacent (in the combination ʾ*ā*) they are written آ. A long consonant is marked ّ. A vowelless consonant has ْ.

k. Called *fatḥa*, *kasra*, and *ḍamma* respectively.

Certain morphophonemic (sandhi) phenomena are noted at the beginnings and ends of words. The definite article is written ال even before dentals etc., but its assimilation is indicated by ّ over the following consonant. After the preposition *l*- the *alif* is omitted, as is the -*l*- before initial *l*- of the noun. The initial *alif* of *ibn* 'son' is omitted when the word conjoins name and patronymic. The feminine ending -*a*(*tun*) is written ةٌ, and not تٌ; -*atan* is ةً. The weak ending -*a* (diptote, also < -*aya*) is ى. The plural -*ūna* when it loses its -*na* takes a merely decorative *alif*. A prothetic vowel supporting an initial cluster is written with *alif* without *hamza*; when this vowel is supplanted by the final vowel of the preceding word, its sign is replaced by ٱ on the *alif*.

§ B.1.5 The modern Maltese alphabet comprises the following 29 letters: a, b, ċ (= *č*), d, e, f, ġ (= *ǰ*), g, h (silent except finally [= *ḥ*] and in the digraphs għh and ħh [= *ḥḥ*]), ħ (= *ḥ*), i, j (= *y*), k, l, m, n, għ (silent, representing Cl ʿ; replaced by ' finally after a), o, p, q (= ʾ), r, s, t, u, v, w, x (= *š*), ż (= *z*), z (= *c*).

H and gh̄ lengthen neighboring vowels. Spelling is largely phonemic, with some etymological admixture.

§ B.2 Ethiopic is read from left to right.

The earliest Ethiopic inscriptions do not indicate vowels. From the middle of the reign of Ezana, ca. 350 A.D., the letters were modified to express the seven vowel phonemes of the Ethiopic languages. The syllabary provides each of the 26 consonants with seven shapes, listed in conventional sequence as 1st through 7th orders. The basic sign shape, 1st order, stands for C*a*; the 2nd order appends a stroke on the middle right to represent C*ū*; 3rd order has a similar stroke at bottom right for C*ī*. The 4th order marks C*ā* by lengthening a right-hand leg, or by bending a single leg to the left. The 5th order represents C*ē* by altering C*ī*'s stroke to a circle; likewise the 7th order changes C*ū*'s stroke to a ring for C*ō*, or else lengthens a left leg. The 6th order ambiguously stands for C∅ or C*e*, and has no consistent graphic device. 6th-order signs do often involve a break in a stroke (Table 11).

Furthermore, when the four velars *q ḫ k g* are labialized their forms are modified; there are no signs for the labiovelars + rounded vowels, as these are neutralized. Seven palatalized consonants used in Amharic are marked with a top horizontal bar added to the seven ordinary signs. Many of the 4th order (C*ā*) signs can add a bottom horizontal for a labialized consonant (this modification tends to vary from scribe to scribe and even from typeface to typeface).

The ambiguity of the sixth order of vowels makes for difficulty in determining word structure; consonant length is not indicated. A colon separates words, a double colon is a punctuation mark. The numerals are based on the Greek ones.

Some of the signs are easily confused. Vowel marks that do not represent what the principles suggest they do are ዮ *yō* not *yū*; ው *we* not *wū*; ዎ *wō* not *wā*; ም *me* not *mā*;

Table 11

	Geʿez										additional letters for Amharic								
	a	*ū*	*ī*	*ā*	*ē*	*e*	*ō*	name[1]	°*ā*		*a*	*ū*	*ī*	*ā*	*ē*	*e*	*ō*	ʼ°*ā*	—
h	ሀ	ሁ	ሂ	ሃ	ሄ	ህ	ሆ	*hōi*											
l	ለ	ሉ	ሊ	ላ	ሌ	ል	ሎ	*lawe*	ሏ										
ḥ	ሐ	ሑ	ሒ	ሓ	ሔ	ሕ	ሖ	*ḥaut*											
m	መ	ሙ	ሚ	ማ	ሜ	ም	ሞ	*māi*	ሟ										
š	ሠ	ሡ	ሢ	ሣ	ሤ	ሥ	ሦ	*šaut*											
r	ረ	ሩ	ሪ	ራ	ሬ	ር	ሮ	*reʾes*	ሯ										ፘ *riya*
s	ሰ	ሱ	ሲ	ሳ	ሴ	ስ	ሶ	*sāt*	ሷ	*š*	ሸ	ሹ	ሺ	ሻ	ሼ	ሽ	ሾ	ሿ	
q	ቀ	ቁ	ቂ	ቃ	ቄ	ቅ	ቆ	*qāf*											
q°	ቈ		ቊ	ቋ	ቌ	ቍ													
b	በ	ቡ	ቢ	ባ	ቤ	ብ	ቦ	*bēt*	ቧ										
t	ተ	ቱ	ቲ	ታ	ቴ	ት	ቶ	*tawe*	ቷ	*č*	ቸ	ቹ	ቺ	ቻ	ቼ	ች	ቾ	ቿ	
ḫ	ኀ	ኁ	ኂ	ኃ	ኄ	ኅ	ኆ	*ḫarm*											
ḫ°	ኈ		ኊ	ኋ	ኌ	ኍ													
n	ነ	ኑ	ኒ	ና	ኔ	ን	ኖ	*nahās*	ኗ	*n′*	ኘ	ኙ	ኚ	ኛ	ኜ	ኝ	ኞ	ኟ	
ʾ	አ	ኡ	ኢ	ኣ	ኤ	እ	ኦ	*alf*											ኧ ʾ*ä*
k	ከ	ኩ	ኪ	ካ	ኬ	ክ	ኮ	*kāf*		*ḫ*	ኸ	ኹ	ኺ	ኻ	ኼ	ኽ	ኾ	ዃ	
k°	ኰ		ኲ	ኳ	ኴ	ኵ													
w	ወ	ዉ	ዊ	ዋ	ዌ	ው	ዎ	*wawē*											
ʿ	ዐ	ዑ	ዒ	ዓ	ዔ	ዕ	ዖ	ʿ*ain*											
z	ዘ	ዙ	ዚ	ዛ	ዜ	ዝ	ዞ	*zai*	ዟ	*ž*	ዠ	ዡ	ዢ	ዣ	ዤ	ዥ	ዦ	ዧ	
y	የ	ዩ	ዪ	ያ	ዬ	ይ	ዮ	*yaman*											
d	ደ	ዱ	ዲ	ዳ	ዴ	ድ	ዶ	*dant*	ዷ	*ǰ*	ጀ	ጁ	ጂ	ጃ	ጄ	ጅ	ጆ	ጇ	
g	ገ	ጉ	ጊ	ጋ	ጌ	ግ	ጎ	*gaml*											
g°	ጐ		ጒ	ጓ	ጔ	ጕ													
ṭ	ጠ	ጡ	ጢ	ጣ	ጤ	ጥ	ጦ	*ṭait*	ጧ	*č̣*	ጨ	ጩ	ጪ	ጫ	ጬ	ጭ	ጮ	ጯ	
ṗ	ጰ	ጱ	ጲ	ጳ	ጴ	ጵ	ጶ	*ṗait*											
ṣ	ጸ	ጹ	ጺ	ጻ	ጼ	ጽ	ጾ	*ṣadai*	ጿ										
ḍ	ፀ	ፁ	ፂ	ፃ	ፄ	ፅ	ፆ	*ḍappā*											
f	ፈ	ፉ	ፊ	ፋ	ፌ	ፍ	ፎ	*af*	ፏ										
p	ፐ	ፑ	ፒ	ፓ	ፔ	ፕ	ፖ	*psā*											

Α	Β	Γ	Δ	Ε	ϛ	Ζ	Η	Θ	Ι	Κ	Λ	Μ	Ν	Ξ	Ο	Π	ϙ	Ρ	—
፩	፪	፫	፬	፭	፮	፯	፰	፱	፲	፳	፴	፵	፶	፷	፸	፹	፺	፻	፼
1	2	3	4	5	6	7	8	9	10	20	30	40	50	60	70	80	90	100	10,000

ሀ ህ ክ ከ ሰ ስ ለ አ እ ደ ይ የ ዖ ዓ ዐ ፀ ወ መ ቀ ዋ ዎ ቃ ታ ፓ ፖ ጋ ገ ኀ ኅ ጎ ን ና ኖ ኆ ፋ ፉ
ha he ke ka sa se la ʾa ʾe da ye ya ʿō ʿā ʿa ḍa wa ma qa wā wō qā tā pā pō gā ga ḫa ḫe gō ne nā nō ḫō fā fū

ሥ *še* not *šā*. *r* and *f* do not lend themselves to the overall system, but at least resemble each other in vowel-modification. The °*ī* and °*e* series are especially similar to each other; the horizontal marking °*ī* is broken, and °*e*'s is straight. Besides the signs compared at the end of Table 11, the full series *l s b k*; *ḥ ṭ*; *r g f*; *t p*; ᶜ *ḍ*; *d ṗ ṣ*; and the 4th and 7th orders of each sign should be studied together so the distinctions become clear. On the whole, though, the Ethiopic syllabary is not difficult to learn; many signs are not common, and reading through the texts provided here will familiarize the student with most of what is necessary.

1. These letter names are unknown in Ethiopia, but are usually (and perhaps misleadingly) included in discussions of the Semitic names of the letters. Either they have been lost since the seventeenth century, or perhaps Hiob Ludolf, the first European Ethiopist, "prompted" his Amharic informant with the Hebrew letter names and recorded Geᶜez cognates or substitutes.

§ B.3 The earliest cuneiform documents (ca. 3200 B.C.) bear fairly recognizable, representational pictures. It is not until nearly a thousand years later that Akkadian texts appear; by then the signs had evolved to more abstract shapes. These cuneiform signs are composed of marks that were impressed in wet clay tablets with a square-ended stylus that characteristically produced wedge-shaped indentations (Latin *cuneus* 'wedge'). (The clay hardens upon drying, and may thus survive the millennia to be excavated and read; additionally the tablets might be baked, either in antiquity intentionally or accidentally [in a conflagration], or else in the modern museum workshop, whereupon they become virtually indestructible.) The wedges may be horizontal, vertical, or diagonal. Modern lists of signs include about six hundred, but only a couple of hundred were in everyday use at any one time.

Akkadian is read from left to right.

A cuneiform sign usually stands for a vowel, a consonant plus vowel or vice versa, or a vowel with consonant on each side. But because the writing system was used first for Sumerian and only later for Akkadian, many signs have more than one value, typically reflecting both the Sumerian word(s) represented by the original picture and the Akkadian equivalent. Thus the same sign may be read both a n ('heaven' in Sumerian) or d i n g i r ('god'), and *il* (from *ilu* 'god' in Akkadian). Further polyphony arises in part because typically a sign containing *i* may also be read with *e*, and because the sound system of Akkadian is richer than that of Sumerian: the triplets of voiced, voiceless, and emphatic consonants may indifferently be represented by the same sign. There is also considerable homophony, whereby several different characters may have a common reading. Thus several different signs can be read *šu*. Normally, however, at any one place and epoch only one sign with a particular value was common.

Assyriologists have developed a number of conventions for transliterating cuneiform signs so that the original sequence is immediately recoverable ("transliteration": unambiguous replacement of one set of signs by another, for mere typographic or other convenience; "transcription": interpretation of the original writing into words according to a particular understanding of the grammar, etc.).[m] Akkadian is presented in italics, Sumerian in letterspaced roman. The signs making up a word are joined in Akkadian by hyphens and in Sumerian by periods. Logograms (in Akkadian context, see below) are written with the appropriate Sumerian value in small capitals; determinatives designating proper names and the dual number are superscript: ^{d} = god's name; ^{f} = woman's name; ^{I} = man's name; ^{II} (dual number); ^{ki} = place name; ^{kur} = country name; ^{uru} = city name. Names are written with an initial capital. When it is uncertain which value of a sign is the appropriate one, or when a sign is mentioned qua sign, the name of the sign in the modern lists — usually the most common of its values — is given in small capitals. Homophonous signs are distinguished by numerical subscripts, assigned many years ago in the supposed order of frequency overall in cuneiform documents; except that the most common sign for a particular reading has

m. Even transliteration, though, involves interpretation, choosing from the numerous possible combinations of letters and type styles the one required by the context.

no index, and the subscripts $_2$ and $_3$ are replaced by acute and grave accents respectively. Thus the first five ŠU signs are transliterated *šu*, *šú*, *šù*, *šu*$_4$, *šu*$_5$. In a transcription, ordinarily not included in the publication of a text, features like vowel and consonant length, not always consistently indicated in the original, are added, while full information on the signs in the text is sacrificed.

Akkadian words may be written either phonetically, e.g., *ú-lam-mi-da-an-ni* = *ulammidannī* 'he has reported to me,' or logographically (*λόγος* 'word' + *γράφω* 'write'), in which a single sign is understood to represent the meaning rather than the sound, e.g. É 'house' not é (Sumerian) or *bīt* (Akkadian); GIŠ 'wood' not giš (Sumerian) or *iṣ* (Akkadian); KUR 'mountain' not kur (Sumerian) or *šad* (Akkadian). A common use of logograms is as semantic determinatives, where they precede (or in a few cases follow) a word and mark it as denoting something classified among, e.g., buildings or wooden objects or lands. The two principles may be combined, when a logogram with several readings — both noun and verb, say — is disambiguated by a "phonetic complement" read in Akkadian, e.g., KUR-*u* = *šadû* 'mountain,' KUR-*tim* = *māt*(*āt*)*im* 'land(s)' (genitive), KUR-*ud* = *i*/*akšud* 'he/I conquered,' KUR-*ad* = *i*/*akaššad* 'he/I conquer(s)' (occasionally a phonetic complement is supplied to help with the reading of a rare Akkadian sign, e.g., *ak-šud*^{ud}); or when a grammatical meaning is indicated by a logogram attached to a phonetically-written word. The most common of these is MEŠ marking plurality (of either noun or verb — i.e., the iterative stem); this may also be indicated by repeating the word's logogram. Another sort of grammatical logogram arises when a particular sign is read phonetically but its use is virtually confined to representing a particular morpheme, e.g., -*šú* used for the third person masculine singular possessive suffix or *ù* used

[Note n is on p. 254.]

only for 'and.' Idiosyncratically, the sequence *-a-a-* can stand for *-ayya-*.

Space precludes presenting a complete sign list, even for the texts included here, but the list for the Code of Hammurabi is given. It is organized by the modern standard system, according to the shapes found in the Neo-Assyrian period, and taking the wedges left to right within the sign: those with one or more horizontals followed by those with one or more diagonals, then one or more Winkelhaken (German, 'elbow angle'; made with the corner of the stylus), then one or more verticals (Table 12).

It is customary to present a pen-and-ink copy of the signs on a tablet when publishing a text, and different styles are shown here; formerly cuneiform type could be used, also exemplified in our texts; and now photographs of the tablet may suffice.

Table 12^{n}

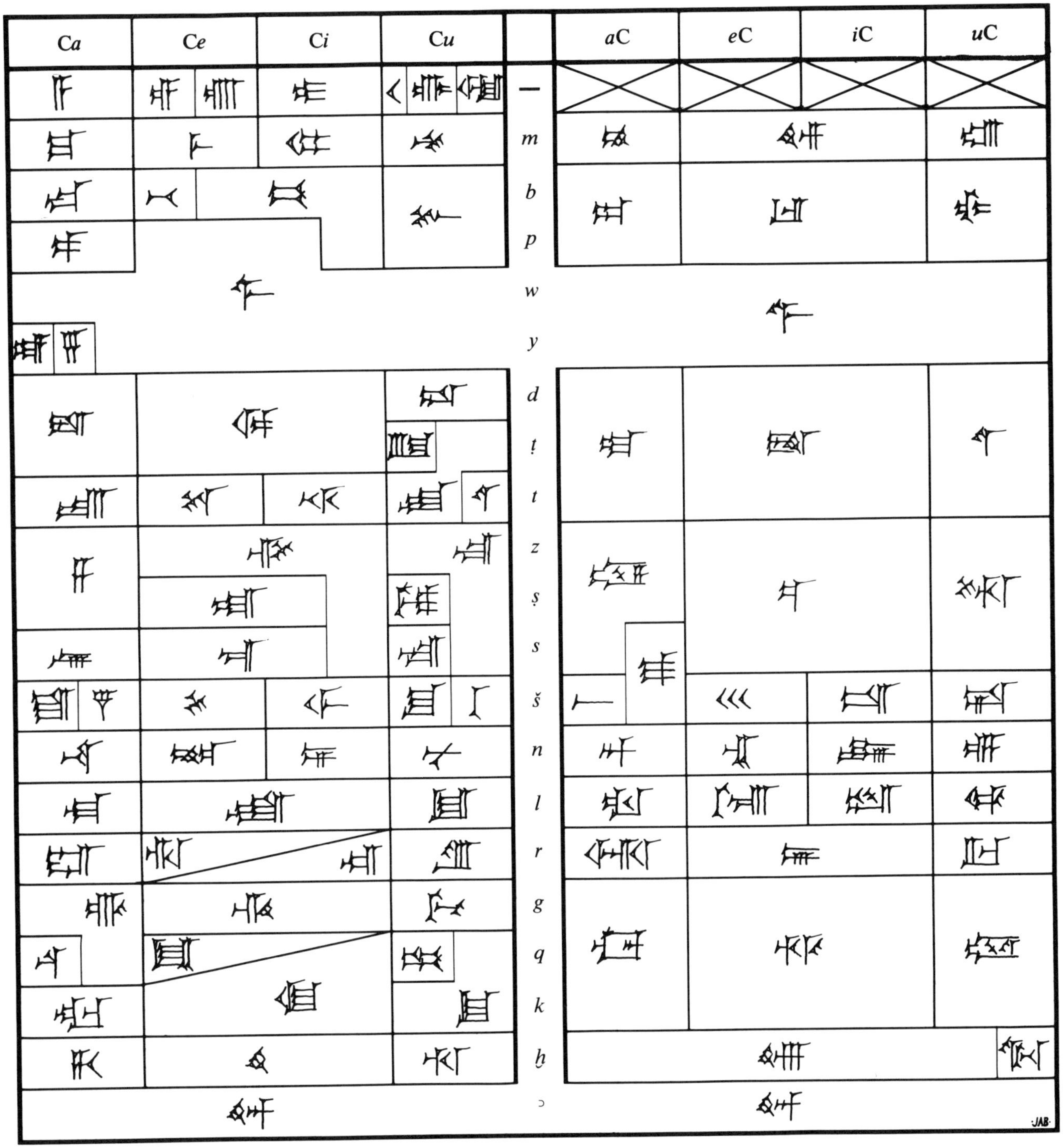

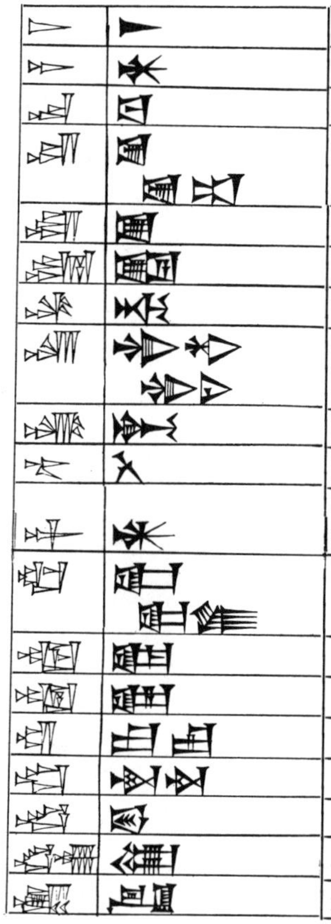

1	*aš dil rum rù*; *ina* 'in'
2	*ḫal*
3	*ba*
4	*zu s/ṣú* ZU.AB = *apsū* 'subterranean waters'
5	*su*; KUŠ* = *mašku* 'skin'
6	*rug šin*; ŠEN.ŠEN = *qablu* 'battle'
7	*b/pal*; BAL = *palū* 'reign'
8	*ád gír* GÍR.NI = *karzillu* 'scalpel'
9	BÚR = *pašāru* 'release'
10	*t/ṭar k/qud ḫaš/z s/šil*
11	*an*; = *šamū* 'heaven'; DINGIR* = *ilu* 'god'
12	*ka*; = *pū* 'mouth' ZÚ.LUM = *suluppū* 'dates'
13	EME = *lišānu* 'tongue'
14	*nag*; = *šatū* 'drink'
15	*rí/é*; URU* = *ālu* 'town'
16	ARAD = *ardu* 'slave'
17	ITI* = *arḫu* 'month'
18	*ša/iḫ* ŠAḪ = *šaḫū* 'pig'
19	EBUR = *ebūru* 'harvest'

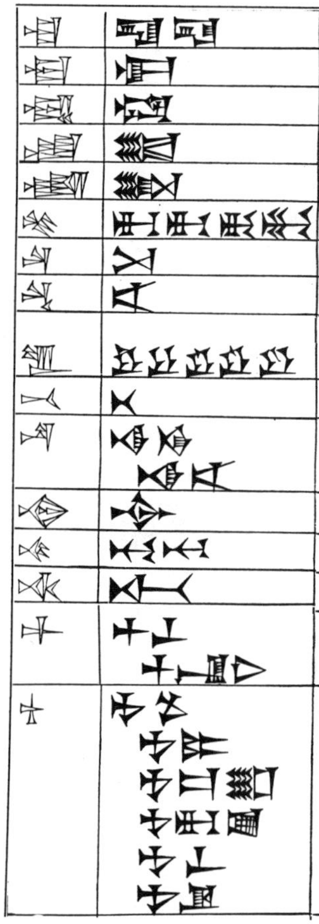

1	*la*
2	(GIŠ.)APIN = *epinnu* 'plow'
3	*maḫ*; = *ṣīru* 'excellent'
4	*tu*; KU$_4$ = *erēbu* 'enter'
5	*li/e*
6	*mu*; = *šattu* 'year,' *šumu* 'name'
7	*qa*; SÌLA = *qū* (a measure of capacity)
8	*kád*
9	*ru šub*; ŠUB = *maqātu* 'fall,' *nadū* 'drop'
10	*be bad mid til ziz*
11	*na* NA.GADA = *nāqidu* 'herdsman'
12	*šir*
13	*k/qul*; NUMUN = *zēru* 'seed'
14	*ti*; = *balāṭu* 'live'
15	*maš bar pár* MAŠ.EN.KAK = *muškēnu* 'commoner'
16	*nu* NU.BÀNDA = *laputtū* 'foreman' NU.GIŠ.SAR = *nukaribbu* 'gardener' NU.MU.SU = *almattu* 'widow' NU.BAR = *kulmašītu* (a holy woman) NU.SÍG = *ekūtu* 'destitute girl'

n. The chart gives the most common monoconsonantal signs. The intersections of vowel columns and consonant rows are sometimes subdivided to include more than one homophonous sign. The "*q* row" thus reads *qa qá qe qé qi qí qu qú aq eq iq uq* (where *qá* is GA, *qé/í* is KI, and *qú* is KU).

The signlist (signs reproduced from Harper, op.cit. § 2 note p pls. 83-98; numerals drawn by J. A. Black) gives in its first column the Neo-Assyrian form of the sign, and in its second column one or more forms of the sign as it appears in the Code of Hammurabi. Subsequent lines within a box contain sign combinations (usually logograms). In the third column, Akkadian syllabic readings are in italics, logograms (i.e., Sumerian readings) in small capitals (separated by semicolons). An asterisk designates signs used as determinatives. Thus the eleventh box reads: "syllabic value *an*; the logogram AN stands for *šamū* 'heaven'; in another Sumerian reading, the logogram DINGIR stands for *ilu* 'god' or is the determinative designating gods." Parentheses enclose signs (usually determinatives) omitted from the drawing but which must be used for the logogram to have the indicated sense.

Signs with final *b d g z* may also be read with their voiceless or emphatic counterparts; C*i*C signs may also be read C*e*C; and CV*š* signs may also be read CV*s*.

Note that only common readings are given in this table, and full details must be sought in the standard signlists □ B.3.

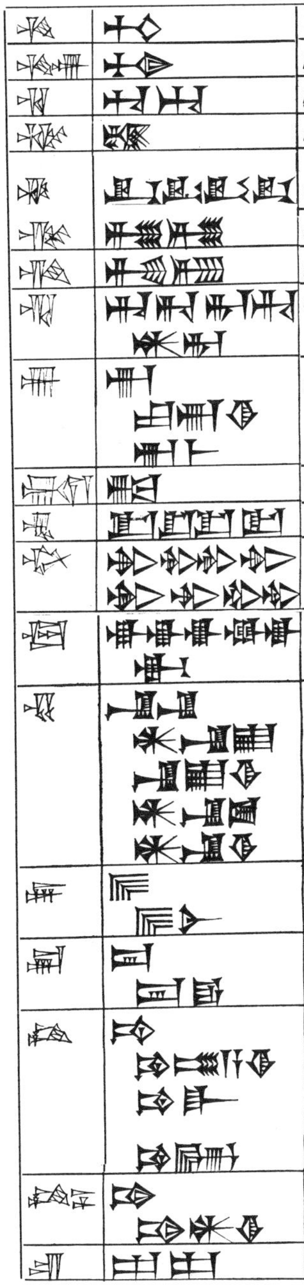

Signs	Values
see image 1	MÁŠ = *urīṣu* 'goat'
	kun; = *zibbatu* 'tail'
	ḫu pag; MUŠEN* = *iṣṣūru* 'bird'
	nam
	i/eg; (GIŠ.)IG = *daltu* 'door'; GÁL = *bašū* 'be'
	zi/e ṣí/é
	gi/e; GI* = *qanū* 'reed'
	ri/e d/tal ᵈMÙŠ = Ishtar (a goddess)
	nun; = *rubū* 'prince' URU.NUN^{ki} = Eridu (a town) NUN.ME = *apkallu* 'expert'
	TÙR = *tarbāṣu* 'cattle pen'
	kab; GÙB = *šumēlu* 'left'
	d/tim
	ag ENGAR = *ikkaru* 'cultivator'
	en; = *bēlu* 'lord' ᵈEN.LÍL = Enlil (a god) EN.LÍL^{ki} = Nippur (a town) ᵈEN.ZU = Sin (a god) ᵈEN.KI = Ea (a god)
	sa SA.SAL = *šašallu* 'back'
	IKU = *ikū* (a measure of area) IKU.E 'per iku'
	tig; GÚ = *kišādu* 'neck' GÚ.DU$_8$.A^{ki} = Cutha (a town) GÚ.GAL = *gugallu* 'canal inspector' GÚ.UN = *biltu* 'load, talent (weight), tribute'
	d/ṭur túr DUR.AN.KI (a name for Nippur)
	g/qur; GUR (a measure of capacity)

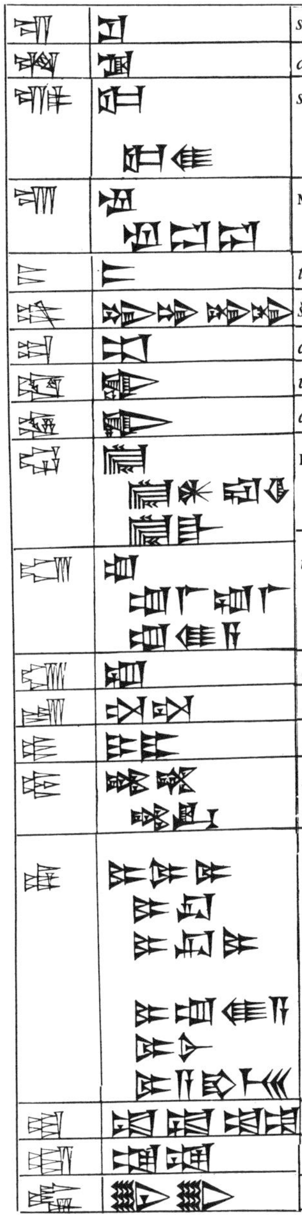

Signs	Values
see image 2	*si/e*; SI = *qarnu* 'horn'
	dar t/ṭár
	s/šag riš; SAG = *rēšu* 'head' SAG.GÍG = *ṣalmāt qaqqadi* 'black-headed'
	MÁ* = *elippu* 'boat' MÁ.LAḪ$_4$ = *malāḫu* 'sailor'
	tab
	šum tag
	ab
	ug
	az
	KÁ = *bābu* 'gate' KÁ.DINGIR.RA^{ki} = Babylon (a town) KÁ.GAL = *abullu* 'town gate'
	um; *šid lag rid mis* KIŠIB.LÁ = *rittu* 'hand'° UM.MI.A = *ummānu* 'artisan'
	d/t/ṭub; DUB = *ṭuppu* 'tablet'
	ta
	i
	g/k/qan ḪÉ.GÁL = *ḫegallu* 'plenty'
	tur; = *ṣiḫru* 'small'; DUMU = *māru* 'son' DUMU.ÚS = *aplu* 'heir' DUMU.ÚS DUMU = *aplum mār* . . . 'heir who is the son of' DUMU UM.MI.A = *mār ummāni* 'man of the artisan class' DUMU.SAL = *martu* 'daughter' DUMU A.GÀR.MEŠ = *mār ugārī* 'peasant'
	ad
	ṣi/e
	in

o. *um* and *šid* . . . KIŠIB are two different signs, virtually indistinguishable in Old Babylonian script.

		LUGAL = *šarru* 'king'
		s/šar; SAR = *mušaru* (a measure of [area, volume)
		sì/è; SUM = *nadānu* 'give'
		raš kas; KASKAL = *ḫarrānu* 'road, [journey'
		g/qab; GABA = *irtu* 'breast'
		am; = *rīmu* 'wild bull'
		UZU* = *šīru* 'flesh'
		ne b/pil bí kúm; IZI = *išātu* 'fire'
		b/píl
		ŠÁM = *šīmu* 'price,' *šāmu* 'buy'
		qu g/k/qum
		UNUG UNUG^{ki} = Uruk (a town)
		SUḪUŠ = *išdu* 'foundations'
		úr
		il
		du; = *alāku* 'go'; GUB = *uzuzzu* ['stand'; TÚM = *abālu* 'bring'
		d/t/ṭum
		ANŠE* = *imēru* 'donkey'
		uš úz nid
		iš mil
		bi pí/é bé kaš; KAŠ = *šikaru* 'beer' (LÚ.)KAŠ.DIN.NA = *sābū* 'inn-[keeper'
		šim rig
		k/qib
		NA$_4$* = *abnu* 'stone'
		gag kak qaq dà; DÙ = *epēšu* 'do'
		ni/é z/ṣal lí ì *ì-lí* (genitive of *ilu* 'god') Ì.BA = *piššatu* 'ration of oil (for [anointing)' Ì.GIŠ = *šamnu* 'oil'
		i/er

		mal MAL.GI$_4$.A = Malgū (a town)
		AMA = *ummu* 'mother'
		KISAL = *kisallu* 'courtyard'
		ÙR = *ūru* 'roof'
		UBUR = *tulū* 'breast'
		pa ḫad PA.PA = *wakil ḫaṭṭi*(?) (an over-[seer)
		SIPA = *rēʾū* 'shepherd'
		i/ez; GIŠ* = *iṣu* 'wood' GIŠ.APIN = *epinnu* 'plow' GIŠ.APIN.TÚK.KIN = *ḫarbu* 'plow' GIŠ.MÁ = *elippu* 'boat' GIŠ.GÁN.ÙR = *maškakātu* 'harrow' GIŠ.PA = *ḫaṭṭu* 'stick, staff' GIŠ.MAR.GÍD.DA = *eriqqu* 'wagon' GIŠ.SAR = *kirū* 'garden, orchard' GIŠ.GU.ZA = *kussū* 'chair' GIŠ.TUKUL = *kakku* 'weapon'
		GUD = *alpu* 'ox' GUD Á.ÙR.RA = *alpu arkū* rear ox' GUD ÁB.MURUB$_4$.SAG = *alpu maḫrū* ['front ox'
		al
		ub ár
		mar
		e
		un; = *nišū* 'people'; KALAM = *mātu* ['land'
		g/k/qid líl
		ú šam; U* = *šammu* 'plant'; KÙŠ = [*ammatu* 'cubit'
		lu/à/ìḫ
		ga qá; GA = *šizbu* 'milk'
		ÍL = *našū* 'raise'
		kal rib la/ib d/tan ^{d}LAMMA = *lamassu* (female spirit)

		bit; É* = *bītu* 'house, temple'
		É.ZU.AB = Eabzu (a temple)
		É.AN.NA = Eanna (a temple)
		É.SAG.ÍL = Esagil (a temple)
		É.ZI.DA = Ezida (a temple)
		É.MAḪ = Emah (a temple)
		É.MES.MES = Emesmes (a temple)
		É.GI$_4$.A = *kallatu* 'bride'
		É.GAL = *ekallu* 'palace'
		É.GAL.MAḪ = Egalmah (a temple)
		É.KUR = Ekur (a temple)
		É.BABBAR = Ebabbar (a temple)
		É.UD.GAL.GAL = Eudgalgal (a temple)
		É.UL.MAŠ = Eulmash (a temple)
		É.KIŠ.NU.GAL = Ekishnugal (a temple)
		É.ME.TE.UR.SAG = Emeteursag (a temple)
		É.SIG$_4$ = *igaru* 'wall'
		É.50 = Eninnu (a temple)
		gi$_4$ ge$_4$; GI$_4$ = *tāru* 'turn'
		ra
		DÙL
		AN.DÙL = *ṣulūlu* 'roof'
		LÚ* = *amēlu* 'man'
		LÚ.DU$_8$.A = (an occupation)
		LÚ.PA = *aklu* 'overseer'
		LÚ.AD.KID = *atkuppu* 'reed worker'
		LÚ.SIMUG = *nappāḫu* 'smith'
		LÚ.(BUR.)GUL = *purkullu* 'stone-cutter'
		LÚ.ḪUN.GÁ = *agru* 'hireling'
		NAGAR = *naggāru* 'carpenter'
		šeš šiš/z; ŠEŠ = *aḫu* 'brother'
		ŠEŠ.UNUG^{ki} = Ur (a town)

		g/kàr qar
		i/ed; Á = *idu* 'arm, side'
		Á.SÀG = *asakku* (a disease demon)
		d/ṭa tá
		da-rí (= *dārû*) 'long-lasting'
		áš/z
		ma
		^{d}*Ma-ma* (a goddess)
		g/qal kál; GAL = *rabû* 'big'
		GAL.UŠUM = *ušumgallu* 'dragon, autocrat'
		g/k/qir b/piš
		AGA = *agû* 'crown'
		UKU.ÚS = *rēdû* 'soldier'
		b/pur
		ša
		šu qat; ŠU = *qātu* 'hand'
		ŠU.I = *gallābu* 'barber'
		ŠU.LUḪ = *šuluḫḫu* (a purification ritual)
		šu-ši (*šūši*) 'sixty'
		ŠU.NIGÍN = *napḫaru* 'total'
		ŠU.ḪA = *bā'iru* 'fisherman, hunter'
		sa$_6$; (GIŠ.)GIŠIMMAR = *gišimmaru* 'date palm'
		ALAM = *lānu* 'form,' *ṣalmu* 'statue'
		kur m/n/š/lad kìn; KUR* = *šadû* 'mountain,' *mātu* 'land'
		še; * = *še'u* 'barley'
		ŠE.BA = *ipru* 'barley ration'
		ŠE.NUMUN = *zēru* 'seed, acreage'
		ŠE.GIŠ.Ì = *šamaššammu* 'sesame'
		ŠE.GUR 'GUR of barley'
		^{d}ŠE.TIR = *ašnan* 'grain'
		b/pu gíd
		uz
		tir
		te ṭe$_4$

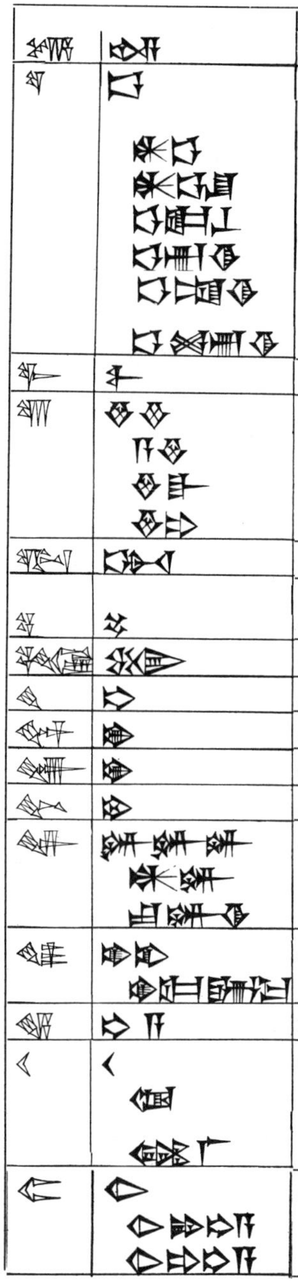

kar; = *kāru* 'mercantile establishment'
ud u$_4$ tam tú pa/ir la/iḫ ḫiš; UD = *ūmu* 'day, storm' ^{d}UTU = *Shamash* (a god) ^{d}UTU-*šu* = *šamšu* 'sun' UD.KA.BAR = *siparru* 'bronze' UD.NUN^{ki} = Adab (a town) UD.UNUG^{ki} = Larsa (a town) UD.KIB.NUN(= ZIMBIR)^{ki} = Sippar (a town)
wa/e/i/u pi/e
šà lìb; ŠÀ = *libbu* 'heart' A.ŠÀ = *eqlu* 'field' ŠÀ.GAL = *ukullû* 'fodder' (LÚ.)ŠÀ.GUD = *kullizu* 'oxherd'
úḫ
z/ṣab; ERÉN = *ṣābu* 'contingent of workers, army'
(KUŠ.)USÀN = *qinnazu* 'whip'
ḫi/e
a/e/i/uʾ ʾa/e/i/u
a/e/i/uḫ
kam g/qám
i/em; IM* = *šāru* 'wind' ^{d}IM = Adad (a god) ^{d}IM^{ki} = Qarqar (a town)
ḫa/ur mur ḪUR.SAG.KALAM.MA = Hursagkalamma (a temple)
ḪÁ* (collective-plural marker)
u (^{d})*Iš$_8$-tár* (a goddess) (LU.)ŠAMÁN.LÁ = *šamallû* 'agent, apprentice'
lid; ÁB = *arḫu*, *littu* 'cattle' ÁB.GUD.ḪÁ = *lātu* 'cattle' ÁB.GUD.ḪÁ = *lātu* 'cattle'

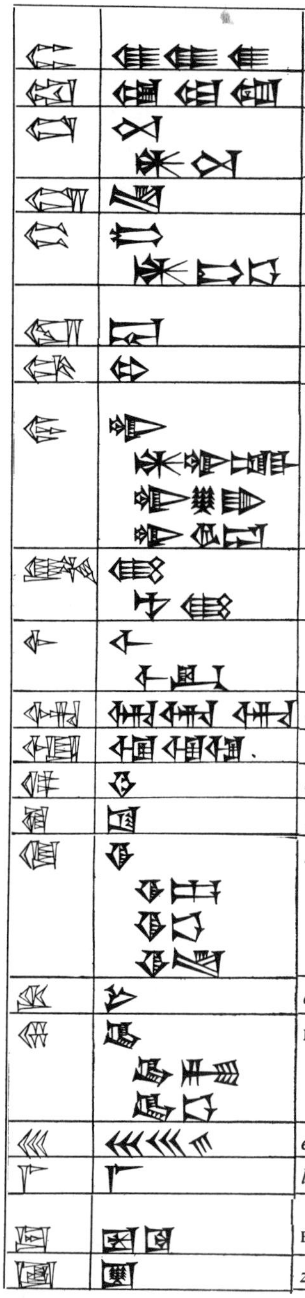

mi/é; GI$_6$ = *mūšu* 'night,' *ṣalmu* 'black'
gul k/qúl sún
ni/um AN-*nim* (genitive of Anu [a god])
lam
z/ṣur; AMAR = *būru* 'bull calf' ^{d}AMAR.UTU = Marduk (a god)
g/k/qim d/ṭím; DÍM = *banû* 'create'; GIM = *kīma* 'like'
ul
k/qiš/s; KIŠ = *kiššatu* 'totality'; GÌR = *šēpu* 'foot' ^{d}NÈ.ERI$_{11}$.GAL = Nergal (a god) GÌR.SÈ.GA = *girsequ* 'attendant' GÌR.PAD.DU = *eṣemtu* 'bone'
qiq; GIG = *marāṣu* 'be ill' NU.GIG = *qadištu* (a holy woman)
ši lim; IGI = *īnu* 'eye' IGI.GÁL = *igigallu* 'wisdom'
ar
ù
d/ṭi/e
DU$_6$ = *tillu* 'hill'
ki/e qí/é; KI* = *erṣetu* 'earth' KI.KAL = *kankallu* 'wasteland' KI.UD = *maškanu* 'threshing floor' KI.LAM = *maḫīru* 'market, price'
d/tin tén
KÙ = *ellu* 'holy, pure' KÙ.GI = *ḫurāṣu* 'gold' KU.BABBAR = *kaspu* 'silver'
eš sin
lal lá
ENGUR = *apsû* (cosmic subterranean waters)
z/ṣar

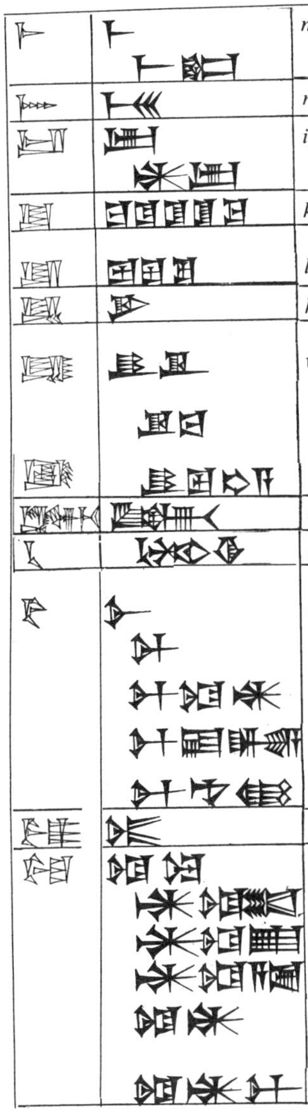

mì/e š/sib; ME.LÁM = *melammu* 'terrifying splendor'
meš; * (plural marker)
i/eb; ^{d}URAŠ = Urash (a god)
ku qú; TÚG* = *ṣubātu* 'clothing'
lu d/t/ṭib dab; UDU* = *immeru* 'sheep'
k/qin qi/e
U$_8$ = *laḫru* 'ewe'; *šík/q*; SÍG* = [*šīpātu* 'wool'][p]
SÍG.BA = *lubūšu* 'clothing allowance'
U$_8$.UDU.ḪÁ = *ṣēnu* 'sheep and goats'
GUR$_7$ = *karū* 'storage pile of barley'
šú
s/šal rag mim; SAL = *sinništu* 'woman'
SAL.ME = *nadītu* (a holy woman)
SAL.ME NIN.DINGIR = *ugbabtu* (a priestess), *ēntu* 'high priestess'[q]
SAL.ME É.GI$_4$.A = *kallatu* 'bride'[q]
SAL.ME NU.GIG = *qadištu* (a holy woman)[q]
z/ṣum súm ṣu
nin; = *bēltu* 'lady,' *aḫātu* 'sister'
^{d}NIN.TU = Nintu (a goddess)
^{d}NIN.LÍL = Ninlil (a goddess)
^{d}NIN.A.ZU = Ninazu (a goddess)
NIN.DINGIR = *ugbabtu* (a priestess), *entu* 'high priestess'
NIN.DINGIR SAL.ME = *ugbabtu* [*nadītu* 'an *u.* or a *n.*']

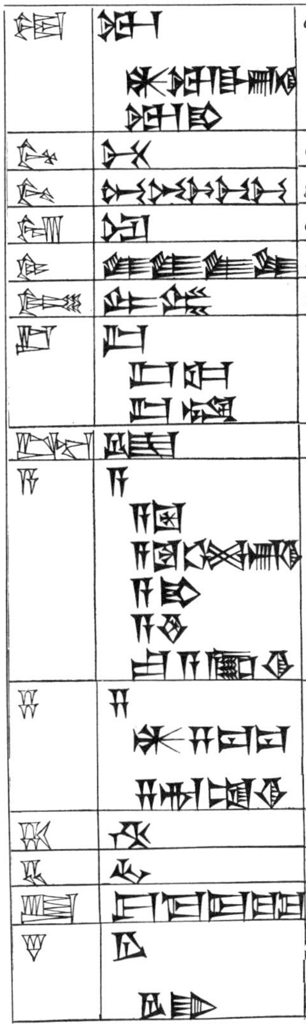

d/ṭam; DAM = *aššatu* 'wife'
^{d}DAM.GAL.NUN.NA = Damgalnunna (a goddess)
DAM.GÀR = *tamkāru* 'merchant'
GEMÉ = *amtu* 'slave girl'
gu
el
l/ḫum
SIG$_4$ = *libittu* 'brick, brickwork'
ur lig d/taš tíš
UR.SAG = *qarrādu* 'warrior'
UR.MAḪ = *nēšu* 'lion'
GIDIM = *eṭemmu* 'ghost'
a; = *mû* 'water,' *aplu* 'son'
ÍD* = *nāru* 'river'
ÍD.UD.KIB.NUN^{ki} = *Purattu* 'Euphrates'
A.GÀR = *ugaru* 'arable land'
A.ŠÀ = *eqlu* 'field'
URU.A.ŠUR$_4$^{ki} = Assur (a town)
z/ṣa
^{d}ZA.BA.BA = Zababa (a god)
ZA.MÙŠ.UNUG^{ki} = Zabalam (a town)
ḫa; KU$_6$* = *nūnu* 'fish'
s/šig/k/q
ṭu; GÍN = *šiqlu* 'shekel'
šá nig gar; NINDA* = *akalu* 'bread'
NÍG.GA = *makkūru* 'property, valuables'

p. U$_8$ and SÍG are two different signs.

q. The SAL.ME is wrong and should be ignored.

§ B.3 Cuneiform *Akkadian*

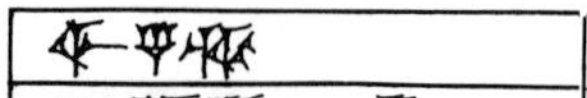	1/4(IGI.4.GÁL)
	1/3(IGI.3.GÁL)[r]
	1/2
	1
	2
	3
	4
	5
	6
	7
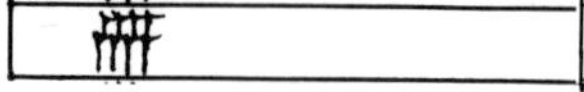	8

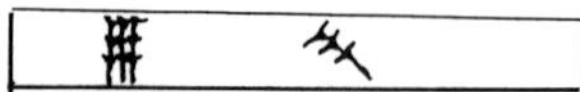	9[r]
	10
	11
	25
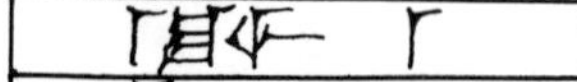	60 (1 *šu-si*)[r]
	70
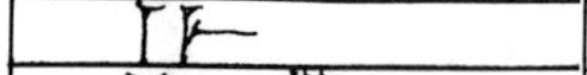	100 (1 ME)
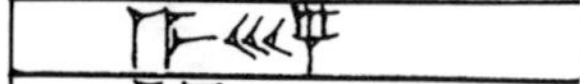	134
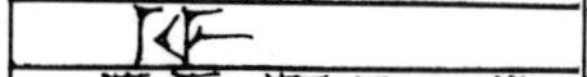	1000 (1 LIM[10+ME])
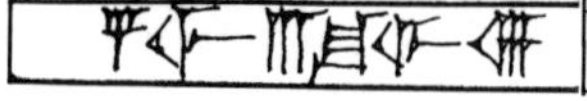	4196

r. Two alternate forms of the numeral.

Principal Periodicals and Collections

Besides the abbreviations used in the bibliography, this list includes the other major sources for articles and monographs in Semitic linguistics. Places and dates of publication are given where possible as an indication of the contributions likely to be included. A few interesting changes of name or place are marked with < "earlier called" > "later called" or "merged into" (or "moved to"). Sources for text publications and philological, rather than grammatical, studies have not been listed; these are well covered in □1:15.

AAL *Afroasiatic Linguistics* (Los Angeles, 1974-).

AbN *Abr-Nahrain* (Melbourne, 1961-).

AcOr *Acta Orientalia* ediderunt societates orientales danica, fennica, norvegica, suecica (Copenhagen, 1923-).

AfO *Archiv für Orientforschung* (Graz > Vienna, 1923-) < *Archiv für Keilschriftforschung.*

AION Instituto Orientale di Napoli: *Annali* (1929-38, NS 1940-).

AIONL ibid.: *Annali, Sezione linguistica* (1959-).

AJSL *American Journal of Semitic Languages and Literatures* (Chicago, 1895-1941) < *Hebraica* (1884-1895), > JNES.

AKM Deutsche Morgenländische Gesellschaft: Abhandlungen für die Kunde des Morgenlandes (1859-).

ANLM Accademia Nazionale dei Lincei, Atti, Classe di Scienze morale, storiche e filologiche: Memorie (Rome, 1877-).

ANLR ibid.: *Rendiconti* (Rome, 1892-).

AnOr Pontifical Biblical Institute: Analecta Orientalia (Rome, 1931-).

AOAT Alter Orient und Altes Testament: Veröffentlichungen zur Kultur und Geschichte des Alten Orients (Neukirchen-Vluyn, 1969-).

AOS American Oriental Society: American Oriental Series (New Haven, 1925-).

ArOr *Archiv Orientální* (Prague, 1929-).

AS University of Chicago, Oriental Institute: Assyriological Studies (1931-).

BA *Beiträge zur Assyriologie und vergleichenden semitischen Sprachwissenschaft* (Leipzig, 1890-1913) (East Berlin: Zentral-Antiquariat, 1968).

BANE G. Ernest Wright, ed. *The Bible and the Ancient Near East* (Garden City: Doubleday, 1961) (Winona Lake: Eisenbrauns, 1979).

BASOR American Schools of Oriental Research: *Bulletin* (Jerusalem > Ann Arbor, 1919-).

BiOr *Bibliotheca Orientalis* (Leiden, 1943-).

BibOr Pontifical Biblical Institute: Biblica et Orientalia (Rome, 1928-).

Brockelmann Mem. Vol. *Studia Orientalia in memoriam Caroli Brockelmann* (Wissenschaftliche Zeitschrift der Martin-Luther-Universität Halle-Wittenberg, Gesellschafts- und Sprachwissenschaftliche Reihe 17/2-3, 1968).

BSAW (Königliche) Sächsischen Gesellschaft/Akademie der Wissenschaften zu Leipzig, philologisch-historische Klasse: *Berichte über die Verhandlungen* (1849-).

BSLP Société de Linguistique de Paris: *Bulletin* (1869-).

BSOAS London, School of Oriental and African Studies: *Bulletin* (1917-).

CBQ *Catholic Biblical Quarterly* (Washington, 1939-).

CIS Académe des Inscriptions et Belles Lettres: *Corpus Inscriptionum Semiticarum* (Paris, 1881-): 1. Phoeneciae, 2. Aramaicae, 3. Hebraicae, 4. Ḥimyariticae et sabaeae, 5. Saracenicas.

CLS Clavis Linguarum Semiticarum (Munich: Beck).

CTL Thomas A. Sebeok, ed. *Current Trends in Linguistics,* 14 v. (The Hague: Mouton, 1963-76).

DLZ *Deutsche Literaturzeitung für Kritik der internationalen Wissenschaft* (East Berlin, 1880-).

EI *Eretz-Israel* (Jerusalem, 1951-).

Florence Pelio Fronzaroli, ed. *Atti del secondo congresso internazionale di linguistica camito-semitica, Firenze, 16-19 aprile 1974* (QS 5, 1978).

GGA *Göttinger/Göttingische gelehrte Anzeigen* (1887-).

GLECS Groupe Linguistique d'Études Chamito-Sémitiques: *Comptes rendues* (Paris, 1931-).

HAR *Hebrew Annual Review* (Columbus, 1977-).

HSS Harvard Semitic Series (Cambridge, Mass., 1924-).

HUCA *Hebrew Union College Annual* (Cincinnati, 1924-).

ICO International Congress of Orientalists: *Proceedings* (1873-1973).

IEJ *Israel Exploration Journal* (Jerusalem, 1950-).

Islam *Der Islam*: Zeitschrift für Geschichte und Kultur des islamischen Orients (Strassbourg, 1910-).

Islamica *Islamica*: Zeitschrift für die Erforschung der Sprachen und der Kulturen der islamischen Völker (Leipzig, 1924-35).

IOS *Israel Oriental Studies* (Tel Aviv, 1971-).

JA *Journal Asiatique* (Paris, 1822-).

JANES Ancient Near East Society of Columbia University: *Journal* (New York, 1968-).

JAOS American Oriental Society: *Journal* (New Haven, 1849-).

JBL *Journal of Biblical Literature* (1881-).

JCS *Journal of Cuneiform Studies* (New Haven > Philadelphia, 1947-).

Jerusalem *Proceedings of the International Conference on Semitic Studies held in Jerusalem, 19-23 July 1965* (Jerusalem, 1969).

JLm Janua Linguarum: studia memoriae Nicolai van Wijk dedicata, series minor (1956-).

JLp ibid., series practica (1963-).

JNES *Journal of Near Eastern Studies* (Chicago, 1942-) < AJSL.

JNWSL *Journal of Northwest Semitic Languages* (Stellenbosch, 1971-).

JQR *Jewish Quarterly Review* (London > Philadelphia, 1888-1908, NS 1910-).

JRAS London, Royal Asiatic Society: *Journal* (1834-).

JSS *Journal of Semitic Studies* (Manchester, 1956-).

Leshonenu *Lĕšonénu*: A Journal for the Study of the Hebrew Language and Cognate Subjects (Jerusalem, 1928-).

Lg. *Language*: Journal of the Linguistic Society of America (Washington, 1924-).

London James and Theodora Bynon, eds. *Hamito-Semitica: Proceedings of a Colloquium Held by the Historical Section of the Linguistics Association (Great Britain) at the School of Oriental and African Studies, University of London, on the 18th, 19th and 20th of March, 1970* (JLp 200, 1975).

LSS Leipziger Semitischen Studien (1903-17, NS 1931-32) (Leipzig: Zentralantiquariat, 1968).

Maarav *Maarav*: A Journal for the Study of the Northwest Semitic Languages (Santa Monica, 1978-).

MAD Gelb, I. J., ed. Materials for the Assyrian Dictionary (Chicago: Oriental Institute, 1952-).

MANE *Monographs on the Ancient Near East* (Malibu, 1974-).

MDOG Deutsche Orient-Gesellschaft: Mitteilungen (1899-).

MO *Le Monde oriental*: Revue des études orientales (Uppsala, 1906-41) >AcOr.

MSOS Berlin, Friedrich-Wilhelms-Universität, Seminar für Orientalische Sprachen: *Mitteilungen* (*Ostasiatische, Westasiatische, Afrikanische Studien*) (1898-1939).

Muséon *Le Muséon*: Revue d'études orientales (Louvain, 1882-).

MUSJ Université de Saint-Joseph: *Mélanges* (Beirut, 1908-).

MVAG Vorderasiatisch-Aegyptische Gesellschaft: Mitteilungen (Berlin, 1896-1944).

Near Eastern Studies Albright Goedicke, Hans, ed. *Near Eastern Studies in Honor of William Foxwell Albright* (Baltimore: Johns Hopkins, 1971).

NGWG Gesellschaft/Akademie der Wissenschaften zu Göttingen, philologisch-historische Klasse: *Nachrichten* (1845-).

NS New Series, Nova Series, Neue Folge

OIP University of Chicago, Oriental Institute: Publications (1924-).

OLZ *Orientalistische Literaturzeitung* (East Berlin, 1898-).

Or. Pontifical Biblical Institute: *Orientalia* (Rome, 55 v., 1920-30; NS, 1932-).

OrAn Istituto per l'Oriente, Centro per le Antichità e la Storia dell'Arte del Vicino Oriente: *Oriens Antiquus* (Rome, 1962-).

OrSu *Orientalia Suecana* (Uppsala, 1952-).

Palestinskij Sbornik *Palestinskij sbornik* (Moscow, 1954-).

Paris André Cacquot & David Cohen, eds. *Actes du premier congrès international de linguistique sémitique et chamito-sémitique, Paris 16-19 juillet 1969* (JLp 159, 1974).

PIASH Israel Academy of Sciences and Humanities: Proceedings (Jerusalem, 1967-).

PLO Porta Linguarum Orientalium (Berlin: Reuther & Reichard, NS Wiesbaden: Harrassowitz).

Prace Językoznawcze Polska Akademia Nauk, Komitet Językoznawczy: Prace Językoznawcze (1954-).

PSSM Istituto Orientale di Napoli, Seminario di Semitistica: Memorie (1970-).

PSSR ibid.: Ricerche (1966-).

QS Università di Firenze, Istituto di Linguistica e di Lingue Orientali: Quaderni di semitistica (1971-).

RA *Revue d'assyriologie et d'archéologie orientale* (Paris, 1886-).

RB *Revue biblique* (Paris, 1892-).

RÉtS *Revue des études sémitiques* (Paris, 1934-45).

RO *Rocznik Orientalistyczny* (Warsaw, 1914-).
RSem *Revue sémitique d'épigraphie et d'histoire ancienne* (Paris, 1893-1914).
RSO *Rivista degli studi orientali* (Rome, 1907-).
Semitica *Semitica*: Cahiers publiés par l'Institut d'Études Sémitiques de l'Université de Paris (1948-).
SMS *Syro-Mesopotamian Studies* (Malibu, 1977-).
SS Università di Roma, Istituto di Studi del Vicino Oriente: Studi semitici (1958-).
SSS Semitic Study Series (Leiden, NS 1952-).
SSU Språkvetenskapliga sällskapets i Uppsala (= Societas Linguisticae Upsaliensis) förhandlingar (in UUÅ) (1886-1960) > acta (NS, 1962-).
StOr Societas Orientalis Fennica: *Studia Orientalia* (Helsinki, 1925-).
Studies Driver D. Winton Thomas & W. D. McHardy, eds. *Hebrew and Semitic Studies Presented to Godfrey Rolles Driver*. . . (Oxford: Clarendon, 1963).
Supp. Supplement
Supp. Dict. Bible Supplément au dictionnaire de la Bible (Paris, 1928-).
SWAW Wiener/Österreichische Akademie der Wissenschaften, philosophisch-historische Klasse: Sitzungsberichte (1848-).
SY *Semitskie yazyki* (Moscow, 1963-).
Syria Institut Français d'Archéologie du Proche Orient: *Syria*, Revue d'art oriental et d'archéologie (Paris, 1920-).
UCPSP University of California Publications: Semitic Philology (Berkeley and Los Angeles, 1905-).
UF *Ugarit-Forschungen*: Internationales Jahrbuch für die Altertumskunde Syrien-Palästinas (Neukirchen-Vluyn, 1969-).
UUÅ Uppsala Universitets Årsskrift (1861-1960) (> Acta Universitatis Upsaliensis).
ViOr *Vicino Oriente*: Annuario dell'Istituto di Studi del V.O. dell'Università di Roma (1978-).
VT *Vetus Testamentum*: Quarterly Published by the International Organization for the Study of the Old Testament (Leiden, 1951-).
WHJP *World History of the Jewish People* (New Brunswick: Rutgers, 1961-).
Word *Word*: Journal of the Linguistic Circle of New York > International Linguistic Association (1945-).
WZKM *Wiener Zeitschrift für die Kunde des Morgenlandes* (Vienna, 1887-).
ZA *Zeitschrift für Assyriologie und vorderasiatische Archäologie* (1886-) < *Zeitschrift für Keilschrift-forschung und verwandte Gebiete.*
ZAW *Zeitschrift für die alttestamentliche Wissenschaft* (1881-).
ZDMG Deutsche Morgenländische Gesellschaft: *Zeitschrift* (1847-).
ZKM *Zeitschrift für die Kunde des Morgenlandes* (Göttingen, 1837-50).
ZP *Zeitschrift für Phonetik und allgemeine Sprachwissenschaft* (East Berlin, 1945-).
ZS *Zeitschrift für Semitistik und verwandte Gebiete* (Leipzig, 1922-35).

Bibliography

The language/dialect subdivisions of the bibliography follow those of the chapters; further subdivisions are indicated with slash plus numeral or with lowercase letters: these are chronological or geographical. The order of the lists is firstly that of the (decimal) outline system, so that in particular all the grammars, of whatever period or area, and likewise all the dictionaries are kept together. Secondly, each section is then organized by the subdivisions. Within each subdivision the order is that of publication of the original edition of the book. Reprints are mentioned when known. The list includes only the most basic references and those mentioned in the notes, excludes textbooks except in a few significant cases, and of course reflects the current interests of the compiler. Entries themselves rich in bibliography are preceded by the solid box ■.

Classification

□ **0:1** von Soden, Wolfram. "Zur Einteilung der semitischen Sprachen." WZKM 56 (1960) 177-91.

□ **0:2** Rabin, Chaim. "The Origins of the Subdivisions of Semitic." Studies Driver (1963) 104-15.

□ **0:3** Rabin, Chaim. "Lexicostatistics and the Internal Divisions of Semitic." London (1975) 85-99.

□ **0.3:1** Goetze, Albrecht. "Is Ugaritic a Canaanite Dialect?" Lg. 17 (1941) 127-38.

□ **0.3:2** Friedrich, Johannes. "Kanaanäisch und Westsemitisch." *Scientia* 84 (1949) 220-3.

□ **0.3:3** Segert, Stanislas. "Ugaritisch und Aramäisch." *Studia semitica philologica necnon philosophica Ioanni Bakoš dicata* (Bratislava, 1965) 215-25.

□ **0.4:1** Friedrich, Johannes. "Zur Stellung des Jaudischen in der nordwestsemitischen Sprachen." AS 16 (1965) 425-9.

□ **0.5:1** Hetzron, Robert. *Ethiopian Semitic: Studies in Classification* (JSS Monograph 2, 1972).

□ **0.6:1** Hetzron, Robert. "Les Divisons des langues sémitiques." Paris (1974) 180-94.

Proto-Semitic

□ **1:1** Wright, William. *Lectures on the Comparative Grammar of the Semitic Languages* (Cambridge: Cambridge University, 1890).

□ **1:2** Zimmern, Heinrich. *Vergleichende Grammatik der semitischen Sprachen* (PLO 17, 1898).

■ **1:3** Brockelmann, Carl. *Grundriss der vergleichenden Grammatik der semitischen Sprachen*, 2 v. (Berlin: Reuther & Reichard, 1908-1913) (Hildesheim: Olms, 1961).

□ **1:4** Brockelmann, Carl. *Kurzgefasste vergleichende Grammatik der semitischen Sprachen* (PLO 21, 1908).

□ **1:5** Nöldeke, Theodor. "Semitic Languages." *Encyclopaedia Britannica* 24:617-30 (1911^{11}) (= *Die Semitische Sprachen: Eine Skizze*).

□ **1:6** Bergsträsser, Gotthelf. *Einführung in die semitischen Sprachen* (Munich: Hueber, 1928). **R1** E. Braunlich, *Islamica* 3 (1927) 493-6. **R2** C. Brockelmann, DLZ 44 (1928) 2153-6. **R3** V. Christian, WZKM 36 (1929) 203-19. **R4** H. S. Nyberg, GGA 1932/3:104-15. **R5** J. Pedersen, OLZ 1928:1084-7. **R6** A. Schaade, Islam 18 (1929) 167-70.

■ **1:7** Fleisch, Henri. *Introduction a l'étude des langues sémitiques* (Paris: Maisonneuve, 1947).

□ **1:8** Spuler, Bertold, ed. *Semitistik*. Handbuch der Orientalistik 3 (Leiden: Brill, 1953-4).

□ **1:9** Polostky, H. J. "Semitic." WHJP 1 (1961) 99-111.

■ **1:10** Levi della Vida, Giorgio, ed. *Linguistica Semitica: Presente e Futuro* (SS 4, 1961).

□ **1:11** Moscati, Sabatino, et al. *Introduction to the Comparative Grammar of the Semitic Languages* (PLO NS 6, 1964).

□ **1:12** Diakonoff, Igor. *Semito-Hamitic Languages* (Moscow: NAUKA, 1965).

□ **1:13** Garbini, Giovanni. *Le lingue semitiche* (PSSR 9, 1972).

□ **1:14** Grand'e, B. M. *Vvedenie v sravitel'noe izucenie semitskix jazykov* (Moscow: NAUKA, 1972).

■ **1:15** Hospers, J. H., ed. *A Basic Bibliography for the Study of the Semitic Languages*, 2 v. (Leiden: Brill, 1973).

Phonology

□ **1.1.1:1** Cantineau, Jean. "Le Consonantisme du sémitique." *Semitica* 4 (1952) 78-94.

□ **1.1.1:2** Martinet, André. "Remarques sur le consonantisme sémitique." BSLP 49 (1953) 67-78.

□ **1.1.1:3** Moscati, Sabatino. *Il sistema consonantico delle lingue semitiche* (Rome: Pontifical Biblical Institute, 1954).

□ **1.1.1.2:1** Aro, Jussi. "Pronunciation of the 'Emphatic' Consonants in Semitic Languages." StOr 47 (1977) 5-18.

□ **1.1.1.3:1** Vilencik, Y. "Welchen Lautwert hatte ḍ im Ursemitischen?" OLZ 1930: 89-98.

□ **1.1.1.3:2** Fischer, W. "Die Position von ض im Phonemsystem des Gemeinsemitischen." Brockelmann Mem. Vol. (1968) 55-63.

■ **1.1.1.3:3** Steiner, Richard C. *The Case for Fricative-Laterals in Proto-Semitic* (AOS 59, 1977).

□ **1.1.1.4:1** Růžička, R. "La Question de l'existence du ġ dans les langues sémitiques en général et dans la langue ugaritienne en particulier." ArOr 22 (1954) 176-237.

□ **1.1.1.6:1** Stehle, D. "Sibilants and Emphatics in South Arabic." JAOS 60 (1940) 507-43.

□ **1.1.1.6:2** LaSor, W. S. "The Sibilants in Old South Arabic." JQR 48 (1957) 161-73.

□ **1.1.3:1** Sarauw, Christian. *Über Akzent und Silbenbildung in den älteren semitischen Sprachen* (Danske videnskabernes selskab. Hist.-fil. med. 26/8, 1939).

□ **1.1.3:2** Brockelmann, Carl. "Neuere Theorien zur Geschichte des Akzents und des Vokalismus im Hebräischen und Aramäischen." ZDMG 94 (1940) 332-71.

Morphology

■ **1.2:1** Petráček, Karel. "Die innere Flexion in den semitischen Sprachen." ArOr 28 (1960) 547-606, 29 (1961) 513-45, 30 (1962) 361-408, 31 (1963) 577-624, 32 (1964) 185-222.

□ **1.2:2** Gelb, I. J. *Sequential Reconstruction of Proto-Akkadian* (AS 18, 1969).

□ **1.2.0:1** Landsberger, Benno. "Die Gestalt der semitischen Wurzel." ICO 19 (Rome, 1935 [1938]) 450-2.

□ **1.2.0:2** Greenberg, Joseph. "The Patterning of Root Morphemes in Semitic." *Word* 6 (1950) 162-81.

□ **1.2.1:1** Barth, Jakob. *Die Pronominalbildung in den semitischen Sprachen* (Leipzig: Hinrichs, 1913) (Hildesheim: Olms, 1967).

□ **1.2.1.2:1** Pennacchietti, F. A. *Studi sui pronomi determinativi semitici* (PSSR 4, 1968).

□ **1.2.2:1** Cohen, Marcel. *Le Système verbal sémitique et l'expression du temps* (Paris: Imprimerie nationale, 1924).

□ **1.2.2:2** Speiser, E. A. "The Pitfalls of Polarity." Lg. 14 (1938) 187-202.

□ **1.2.2:3** Kuryłowicz, Jerzy. "Le système verbal du sémitique." BSLP 45 (1949) 47-56; "Esquisse d'une théorie de l'apophonie en sémitique." BSLP 53 (1958) 1-38; *L'Apophonie en sémitique* (Prace Językoznawcze 24, 1961); *Studies in Semitic Grammar and Metrics* (Prace Językoznawcze 67, 1973).

□ **1.2.2:4** Rundgren, Frithiof. *Intensiv und Aspektkorrelation* (UUÅ 1959/5); "Das altsyrische Verbalsystem: vom Aspekt zum Tempus." SSU Förhandlingar 1958-60:49-75; "Der aspektuelle Charakter des altsemitischen Injunktivs." OrSu 9 (1960) 75-101; *Das althebräische Verbum: Abriss der Aspektlehre* (Stockholm: Almqvist & Wiksell, 1961); *Erneuerung* *des Verbalaspekts im Semitischen* (SSU Acta NS 1/3, 1963).

□ **1.2.2.1.1:1** Haupt, Paul. "The Oldest Semitic Verb." JRAS NS 10 (1878) 244-51.

□ **1.2.2.1.1:2** Driver, S. R. *The Use of the Tenses in Hebrew* (Oxford: Clarendon, 1892[3]).

□ **1.2.2.1.1:3** Bauer, Hans. *Die Tempora im Semitischen.* BA 8/1 (1910).

□ **1.2.2.1.1:4** Sarauw, Christian. "Das altsemitische Tempussystem." *Festschrift Vilhelm Thomsen* (Leipzig: Harrassowitz, 1912) 59-69.

□ **1.2.2.1.1:5** Christian, Viktor. "Das Wesen der semitischen Tempora." ZDMG 81 (1927) 232-58.

□ **1.2.2.1.1:6** Driver, G. R. *Problems of the Hebrew Verbal System* (Edinburgh: Clark, 1936).

□ **1.2.2.1.1:7** Fleisch, Henri. "Sur le système verbal de sémitique commun et son évolution dans les langues sémitiques anciennes." MUSJ 27/3 (1947-8).

□ **1.2.2.1.1:8** Brockelmann, Carl. "Die 'Tempora' des Semitischen." ZP 5 (1951) 133-54.

□ **1.2.2.1.1:9** Hetzron, Robert. "The Evidence for Perfect **y'aqtul* and Jussive **yaqt'ul* in Proto-Semitic." JSS 14 (1969) 1-21.

□ **1.2.2.1.2:1** Kienast, Burkhart. "Das Punktualthema **japrus* und seine Modi." Or. NS 29 (1960) 151-67.

□ **1.2.2.4.1:1** Poebel, Arno. "Notes on the Pi^{c}el and Šaf^{c}el-Pi^{c}el." (AS 9, 1939) ch. 2.

□ **1.2.2.4.1:2** Goetze, Albrecht. "The So-Called Intensive of the Semitic Languages." JAOS 62 (1942) 1-8.

□ **1.2.2.4.2:1** Praetorius, Franz. "Zur Kausativbildung im Semitischen." ZS 5 (1927) 39-42.

□ **1.2.2.4.2:2** Bravmann, M. M. "The Semitic Causative-Prefix *s/ša*." Museon 82 (1961) 517-22 (= idem, *Studies in Semitic Philology* [Leiden: Brill, 1977] 200-5).

□ **1.2.2.4.3:1** Goetze, Albrecht. "The Akkadian Passive." JCS 1 (1947) 50-9.

□ **1.2.2.4.4:1** Fleisch, Henri. *Les Verbes à allongement vocalique interne en sémitique* (Paris: Institut d'ethnologie, 1944).

□ **1.2.2.6.2:1** Solá-Solé, J. M. *L'Infinitif sémitique* (Paris: Champion, 1961).

□ **1.2.3:1** de Lagarde, Paul (= Böttscher). *Übersicht über die im Aramäischen, Arabischen und Hebräischen übliche Bildung der Nomina* (Göttingen: Dieterich, 1889).

□ **1.2.3:2** Barth, Jakob. *Die Nominalbildung in den semitischen Sprachen* (Leipzig: Hinrichs, 1894[2]) (Hildesheim: Olms, 1967).

□ **1.2.3:3** Christian, Viktor. "Die Entstehung der semitischen Casusendungen." ZS 3 (1924) 17-26.

□ **1.2.3:4** Brockelmann, Carl. "Deminutiv und Augmentativ im Semitischen." ZS 6 (1928) 109-34.

□ **1.2.3:5** Cantineau, Jean. "Racines et schèmes." *Mélanges offerts à William Marçais* (Paris: Maisonneuve, 1950) 119-24; "La Notion de schème et son alteration dans diverses langues sémitiques." *Semitica* 3 (1950) 73-83.

□ **1.2.3:6** Cohen, David. "Remarques sur la dérivation nominale par affixes dans quelques langues sémitiques." *Semitica* 14 (1964) 73-93.

□ **1.2.3:7** Fontinoy, Charles. *Le Duel dans les langues sémitiques* (Paris: Belles lettres, 1969).

□ **1.2.3:7** Rabin, Chaim. "The Structure of the Semitic System of Case Endings." Jerusalem (1969) 190-204.

Vocabulary

□ **1.4:1** Fronzaroli, Pelio. "Studi sul lessico comune semitico." ANLR 8/19 (1964) 155-72, 243-80, 20 (1965) 135-50, 246-69, 23 (1968) 267-303, 24 (1969) 285-320, 26 (1971) 603-43.

□ **1.4:2** Cohen, David. *Dictionnaire des racines sémitiques ou attestées dans les langues sémitiques* (The Hague: Mouton, 1970-).

■ **1.4:3** Fronzaroli, Pelio, ed. *Studies on Semitic Lexicography* (QS 2, 1973).

West Semitic

■ **1/2:1** Lidzbarski, Mark. *Handbuch der nordsemitischen Epigraphik*, 2 v. (Weimar: Felber, 1898)

(Hildesheim: Olms, 1962).
☐ **1/2:2** Garbini, Giovanni. *Il Semitico di Nord-Ovest* (QS 1, 1960).
☐ **1/2.2.2.1.2:1** Gelb, I. J. "The Origin of the West Semitic *qatala* Morpheme." *Symbolae linguisticae in honorem Georgii Kuryłowicz* (Wrocław: Polska Akademia Nauk, 1965) 72-80.
☐ **1/2.2.2.1.2:2** Fleisch, Henri. "*yaqtula* cananéen et subjonctif arabe." Brockelmann Mem. Vol. (1968) 65-76.
☐ **1/2.2.2.4.1:1** Ryder, Stuart A. *The D-Stem in Western Semitic* (JLp 131, 1974).
☐ **1/2.2.4:1** Ullendorff, Edward. "The Form of the Definite Article in Arabic and Other Semitic Languages." *Arabic and Islamic Studies in Honor of H. A. R. Gibb* (Cambridge, Mass.: Harvard, 1965) 631-7 (= idem. *Is Biblical Hebrew a Language?* [Wiesbaden: Harrassowitz, 1977] 165-71).
☐ **1/2.2.4:2** Lambdin, Thomas O. "The Junctural Origin of the West Semitic Definite Article." Near Eastern Studies Albright (1971) 315-33.
☐ **1/2.4:1** Jean, Ch.-F., & J. Hoftijzer. *Dictionnaire des inscriptions sémitiques de l'ouest* (Leiden: Brill, 1965).

Akkadian

(chronologically), Eblite, Amorite

☐ **2/1:1** Delitzsch, Friedrich. *Assyrische Grammatik* (PLO 10, 1906[2]).
☐ **2/1:2** Ungnad, Arthur, & Lubor Matouš. *Grammatik des Akkadischen* (CLS 2, 1964[4]).
☐ **2/1:3** Ylvisaker, Sigurd. *Zur babylonischen und assyrischen Grammatik* (LSS 5/6, 1912).
☐ **2/1:4** von Soden, Wolfram. *Grundriss der akkadischen Grammatik* (AnOr 33/47, 1969[2]).
☐ **2/1:5** Reiner, Erica. *A Linguistic Analysis of Akkadian* (JLp 21, 1966).
■ **2/1:6** Reiner, Erica. "Akkadian." CTL 6 (1970) 274-303.
☐ **2/1a:1** Gelb, I. J. *Old Akkadian Writing and Grammar* (MAD 2, 1961[2]).
☐ **2/1b:1** Hecker, Karl. *Grammatik der Kültepe-Texte* (AnOr 44, 1968).
☐ **2/1c:1** Aro, Jussi. *Studien zur mittelbabylonischen Grammatik* (StOr 20, 1955).
☐ **2/1d:1** Labat, René. *L'Accadien de Boghaz-Köi* (Bordeaux: Delmas, 1932).
☐ **2/1d:2** Finet, André. *L'Accadien des lettres de Mari* (Brussels: Académie Royale, 1956).
☐ **2/1d:3** De Meyer, Léon. *L'Accadien des contrats de Suse* (Leiden: Brill, 1962).
☐ **2/2:1** Gelb, I. J. "Thoughts about Ibla." SMS 1/1 (1977).
☐ **2/2:2** Cagni, Luigi, ed. *La Lingua di Ebla* (Naples: Instituto Universitario Orientale, 1981).
☐ **2/3:1** Gelb, I. J. "La Lingua degli amoriti." ANLR 8/13 (1958) 143-64.
☐ **2/1.0:1** Landsberger, Benno. "Die Eigenbegrifflichkeit der babylonischen Welt." *Islamica* 2 (1926) 355-72, tr. T. Jacobsen et al. *The Conceptual Autonomy of the Babylonian World.* MANE 1/4 (1976).
☐ **2/1.0:2** Edzard, D. O. "Der gegenwärtige Stand der Akkadistik (1975) und ihre Aufgabe." ZDMG Supp. 3/1 (1977) 47-54.
☐ **2/1d.1:1** Jucquois, Guy. *Phonétique comparée des dialects moyen-babyloniens du nord et de l'ouest* (Louvain: Institut Orientaliste, 1966).
☐ **2/1.2.2.4.3:1** Whiting, R. M. "The R-Stem(s) in Akkadian." Or. NS 50 (1981) 1-39.
■ **2/1.4:1** *The Assyrian Dictionary of the Oriental Institute of the University of Chicago* (Locust Valley: Augustin, 1956-).
☐ **2/1.4:2** von Soden, Wolfram. *Akkadisches Handwörterbuch* (Wiesbaden: Harrassowitz, 1959-81).
☐ **2/1a.4:1** Gelb, I. J. *A Glossary of Old Akkadian* (MAD 3, 1957).
☐ **2/2.4:1** Gelb, I. J. *Computer-Aided Analysis of Amorite* (AS 21, 1979).

Canaanite

Ugaritic, Hebrew (chronologically), Moabite, Phoenician

□ **3:1** Harris, Zellig S. *The Development of the Canaanite Dialects* (AOS 16, 1939).

■ **3:2** Moran, William L. "The Hebrew Language in Its Northwest Semitic Background." BANE (1961) 54-72.

□ **3:3** Ginsberg, H. L. "The Northwest Semitic Languages." WHJP 2/1 (1970) 102-24.

■ **3:4** Rabin, Chaim. "Hebrew." CTL 6 (1970) 304-46.

□ **3:5** Kutscher, E. Y. *A History of the Hebrew Language*, ed. R. Kutscher (Jerusalem: Magnes, 1982).

□ **3a:1** Böhl, F. M. Th. deL. *Die Sprache der Amarnabriefe mit besonderer Berücksichtigung der Kanaanismen* (LSS 5/2, 1909).

□ **3a:2** Aistleitner, J. *Untersuchungen zur Grammatik des Ugaritischen* (BSAW 100/6, 1954).

□ **3a:3** Gordon, Cyrus L. *Ugaritic Textbook* (AnOr 38, 1967[2]).

□ **3b:1** Ewald, Heinrich. *Ausführliches Lehrbuch der hebräischen Sprache des Alten Bundes* (Göttingen: Dieterich, 1870[8]).

■ **3b:2** König, E. *Historisch-kritisches Lehrgebäude der hebräischen Sprache*, 2 v. in 3 (Leipzig: Hinrichs, 1881-97).

□ **3b:3** Steuernagel, Carl. *Hebräische Grammatik* (PLO 1, 1926[7]).

□ **3b:4** Kautzsch, Emil. *Hebräische Grammatik* (Leipzig: Vogel, 1909[28]) (Hildesheim: Olms, 1962), tr. A. E. Cowley. *Gesenius's Hebrew Grammar* (Oxford: Clarendon, 1910[2]).

□ **3b:5** Strack, H. L. *Hebräische Grammatik* (CLS 1, 1911[11]).

■ **3b:6** Bergsträsser, Gotthelf. *Hebräische Grammatik*, 2 v. (Leipzig: Vogel, 1918-29[29]) (Hildesheim: Olms, 1962).

□ **3b:7** Bauer, Hans, & Pontus Leander. *Historische Grammatik der hebräischen Sprache des alten Testaments* (Halle: Niemeyer, 1918-22) (Hildesheim: Olms, 1962).

□ **3b:8** Lambert, Meyer. *Traité de grammaire hebraïque* (Paris: Leroux, 1931-38).

□ **3b:9** Joüon, Paul. *Grammaire de l'hébreu biblique* (Rome: Pontifical Biblical Institute, 1947[2]).

□ **3b:10** Meyer, Rudolf. *Hebräische Grammatik*. 4 v. (Berlin: de Gruyter, 1962-72[3]), tr. Peter T. Daniels (Winona Lake: Eisenbrauns, in preparation).

□ **3b:11** Lambdin, Thomas O. *Introduction to Biblical Hebrew* (New York: Scribner's, 1971).

□ **3b:12** Blau, Joshua. *A Grammar of Biblical Hebrew* (PLO NS 12, 1974).

□ **3c:1** Albrecht, K. *Neuhebräische Grammatik auf Grund der Mišna* (CLS 5, 1913).

□ **3c:2** Segal, M. H. *A Grammar of Mishnaic Hebrew* (Oxford: Clarendon, 1926).

□ **3c:3** Kutscher, E. Y. *The Language and Linguistic Background of the Isaiah Scroll (1 Q Isa[a])*, tr. anon. (H. Rosén?) (Leiden: Brill, 1974). **R1** J. Barr, JSS 21 (1976) 186-93. **R2** E. Qimron. *Indices and Corrections* (Leiden: Brill, 1979).

□ **3d:1** Rosén, Haiim B. *A Textbook of Israeli Hebrew* (Chicago: University of Chicago, 1962).

□ **3f:1** Schröder, P. *Die phönizische Sprache* (Halle: Waisenhaus, 1869).

□ **3f:2** Harris, Zellig S. *Grammar of the Phoenician Language* (AOS 8, 1936).

□ **3f:3** Friedrich, Johannes, & Wolfgang Röllig. *Phönizisch-Punische Grammatik* (AnOr 46, 1970[2]).

□ **3f:4** Segert, Stanislas. *A Grammar of Phoenician and Punic* (Munich: Beck, 1976).

□ **3b.2.0:1** Koskinen, K. "Kompatibilität in den dreikonsonantigen hebräischen Wurzeln." ZDMG 114 (1964) 16-58.

■ **3b.2.2:1** McFall, Leslie, *The Enigma of the Hebrew Verbal System* (Sheffield: Almond, 1982).

□ **3b.2.2.4:1** Williams, R. J. "The Passive *Qal* Theme in Hebrew," in J. W. Wevers & D. B. Redford, eds. *Essays on the Ancient Semitic World* (Toronto: University of Toronto, 1970) 43-50.

□ **3b.3:1** Brockelmann, Carl. *Hebräische Syntax* (Neukirchen, 1956).

□ **3e.3:1** Andersen, F. I. "Moabite Syntax." Or. NS 35 (1966) 81-120.

Vocabulary

□ **3a.4:1** Aistleitner, J. *Wörterbuch der Ugaritischen Sprache* (BSAW 106/3, 1967^{3}).

■ **3b.4:1** Brown, Francis, S. R. Driver, & C. A. Briggs. *A Hebrew and English Lexicon of the Old Testament* (Oxford: Clarendon, 1906).

□ **3b.4:2** Buhl, Frants. *Wilhelm Gesenius' Handwörterbuch über das Alte Testament* (Leipzig: Vogel, 1921^{17}) (Berlin: Springer, 1949).

□ **3b.4:3** Köhler, Ludwig, & W. Baumgartner. *Lexicon in Veteris Testamenti Libros* (Leiden: Brill, 1958; 1967^{3} in part).

□ **3c.4:1** Levy, J. *Neuhebräisches und chaldäisches Wörterbuch über die Talmudim und Midraschim*, 4 v. (Leipzig: Brockhaus, 1876-89).

□ **3c.4:2** Jastrow, Marcus. *A Dictionary of the Targumim, the Talmud Babli and Yerushalmi, and the Midrashic Literature*, 2 v. (New York: Putnam, 1903).

□ **3c.4:3** Dalman, Gustav. *Aramäisch-neuhebräisches Handwörterbuch zum Targum, Talmud und Midrasch* (Göttingen: Pfeiffer, 1938^{3}) (Hildesheim: Olms, 1967).

□ **3d.4:1** ben-Yehudah, Eliezer, et al. *Thesaurus totius hebraitatis et veteris et recentioris*, 15 v. (Jerusalem, 1911-59).

□ **3d.4:2** Alcalay, R. *The Complete Hebrew-English Dictionary*, 4 v. (Tel Aviv: Massadah, 1964-65).

Aramaic

(chronologically)

■ **4:1** Rosenthal, Franz. *Die aramäistische Forschungen seit Th. Nöldeke's Veröffentlichungen* (Leiden: Brill, 1939). **R1** H. L. Ginsberg. "Aramaic Studies Today." JAOS 62 (1942) 229-38. **R2** F. Rosenthal. "Aramaic Studies during the Past Thirty Years." JNES 37 (1978) 81-91.

□ **4:2** Rosenthal, Franz, ed. *An Aramaic Handbook*, 4 v. (PLO NS 10, 1967).

■ **4:3** Kutscher, E. Y. "Aramaic." CTL 6:347-412 (1970).

□ **4:4** Kutscher, E. Y. "Aramaic." *Encyclopaedia Judaica* 2:259-88 (1971).

□ **4:5** Greenfield, Jonas C. "Aramaic." *Interpreter's Dictionary of the Bible Supplementary Volume* (Nashville: Abingdon, 1976) 39-44.

□ **4/1a:1** Kautzsch, Emil. *Grammatik des biblisch-Aramäischen* (Leipzig: Vogel, 1884).

□ **4/1a:2** Marti, Karl. *Kurzgefasste Grammatik der biblisch-aramäischen Sprache* (PLO 18, 1925^{3}).

□ **4/1a:3** Strack, Hermann L. *Grammatik des Biblisch-Aramäischen* (CLS 4, 1921^{6}).

□ **4/1a:4** Bauer, Hans, & Pontus Leander. *Grammatik des biblisch-Aramäischen* (Halle: Niemeyer, 1927) (Hildesheim: Olms, 1962).

□ **4/1a:5** Leander, Pontus. *Laut- und Formenlehre des ägyptisch-Aramäischen* (Göteborg: Elanders, 1928) (Hildesheim: Olms, 1966).

■ **4/1a:6** Rosenthal, Franz. *A Grammar of Biblical Aramaic* (PLO NS 5, 1963^{2}).

□ **4/1a:7** Degen, Rainer. *Altaramäische Grammatik* (AKM 38/3, 1969).

■ **4/1a:8** Kaufman, Stephen A. *The Akkadian Influences on Aramaic* (AS 19, 1974).

□ **4/1a:9** Segert, Stanislas. *Altaramäische Grammatik* (Leipzig: VEB, 1975).

□ **4/1b:1** Cantineau, Jean. *Grammaire du Palmyrénien épigraphique* (Cairo: Institut français d'archéologie orientale, 1935).

□ **4/1b:2** Rosenthal, Franz. *Die Sprache der palmyrenischen Inschriften und ihre Stellung innerhalb des Aramäischen* (MVAG 46/1, 1936).

□ **4/1c:1** Cantineau, Jean. *Le Nabatéen*, 2 v. (Paris: Leroux, 1930-2).

□ **4/1d:1** Dalman, Gustav. *Grammatik des Jüdisch-*

Palästinisch Aramäisch (Leipzig: Hinrichs, 1905[2]) (Darmstadt: Wissenschaftliche, 1960).

☐ **4/1d:2** Stevenson, W. *Grammar of Palestinian Jewish Aramaic* (Oxford: Clarendon, 1962[2]).

☐ **4/1d:3** Odeberg, Hugo. *Short Grammar of Galilæan Aramaic* (Lunds Universitets Årsskrift NS Avd. 1: 36/4, 1936).

☐ **4/1d:4** Kutscher, E. Y. *Studies in Galilean Aramaic*, tr. M. Sokoloff (Ramat-Gan: Bar-Ilan, 1976).

☐ **4/1e:1** Petermann, J. H. *Brevis linguae samaritanae grammatica* (PLO 3, 1873).

☐ **4/1e:2** Vil'sker, L. X. *Samaritjanskij jazyk* (Moscow: NAUKA, 1974).

☐ **4/1e:3** Macuch, Rudolf. *Grammatik des samaritanischen Aramäisch* (Berlin: de Gruyter, 1982).

☐ **4/1f:1** Schulthess, F. *Grammatik des christlich-palästinischen Aramäisch* (Tübingen: Mohr, 1924) (Hildesheim: Olms, 1965).

☐ **4/1g:1** Petermann, J. H. *Brevis linguae chaldaicae grammatica* (PLO 2, 1872[2]).

☐ **4/1g:2** Levias, C. *A Grammar of the Aramaic Idiom Contained in the Babylonian Talmud* (Cincinnati: Bloch, 1900).

☐ **4/1g:3** Margolis, H. L. *Lehrbuch der aramäischen Sprache des Babylonischen Talmuds* (CLS 3, 1910).

☐ **4/1h:1** Nöldeke, Theodor. *Mandäische Grammatik* (Halle: Waisenhaus, 1875) (Darmstadt: Wissenschaftliche, 1964).

☐ **4/1h:2** Macuch, Rudolf. *Handbook of Classical and Modern Mandaic* (Berlin: de Gruyter, 1965).

☐ **4/1i:1** Duval, Rubens. *Traité de grammaire syriaque* (Paris: Vieweg, 1881).

☐ **4/1i:2** Nöldeke, Theodor. *Kurzgefasste Syrische Grammatik* (Leipzig: Weigel, 1898[2]) (Darmstadt: Wissenschaftliche, 1966), tr. J. Crichton. *Compendious Syriac Grammar* (London: Williams & Norgate, 1904).

■ **4/1i:3** Brockelmann, Carl. *Syrische Grammatik* (PLO 5, 1968[11]).

☐ **4/1i:4** Ungnad, Arthur. *Syrische Grammatik* (CLS 7, 1913).

Modern Aramaic

☐ **4/2/1:1** Spitaler, Anton. *Grammatik des neuaramäischen Dialekts von Maᶜlūla (Antilibanon)* (AKM 23/1, 1938).

☐ **4/2/2:1** Stoddard, D. T. *Grammar of the Modern Syriac Language, as Spoken in Oroomiah, Persia and Koordistan.* JAOS 5 (1855).

☐ **4/2/2:2** Nöldeke, Theodor. *Grammatik der neusyrischen Sprache am Urmia-See und in Kurdistan* (Leipzig: Weigel, 1868) (Hildesheim: Olms, 1974).

☐ **4/2/2:3** Duval, Rubens. *Les dialectes néo-arameens de Salamas* (Paris: Vieweg, 1883).

☐ **4/2/2:4** MacLean, A. J. *Grammar of the Dialect of Vernacular Syriac as Spoken by the Eastern Syrians of Kurdistan, North-West Persia and the Plain of Mosul* (Cambridge, 1895).

☐ **4/2/2:5** Siegel, A. *Laut- und Formenlehre des neuaramäischen Dialekts des Ṭūr-ᶜAbdīn* (Hannover: Lafaire, 1923) (Hildesheim: Olms, 1968).

☐ **4/2/2:6** Polotsky, H. J. "Studies in Modern Syriac." JSS 6 (1961) 1-32.

■ **4/2/2:7** Tsereteli, Konstantin. *Sovremennyj assirijskij jazyk* (Moscow: NAUKA, 1964), tr. D. Locchi. *Grammatica di Assiro Moderno* (Naples: PSSM 1, 1970), tr. P. Nagel. *Grammatik der modernen assyrischen Sprache* (Leipzig: VEB, 1978), tr. B. A. Zhebelev. *The Modern Assyrian Language* (Moscow: NAUKA, 1978).

☐ **4/2/2:8** Garbell, Irene. *The Jewish Neo-Aramaic Dialect of Persian Azerbaijan* (JLp 3, 1965).

☐ **4/2/2:9** Jacobi, Heidi. *Grammatik des thumischen Neuaramäisch (Nordostsyrien)* (AKM 40/3, 1973).

☐ **4/2/2:10** Sara, Solomon I. *A Description of Modern Chaldean* (JLp 213, 1974).

■ **4/2/2:11** Macuch, Rudolf, & Estiphan Panoussi. *Neusyrische Chrestomathie* (PLO NS 13, 1974).

Grammar, Vocabulary

☐ **4/1.2.2:1** Rosén, H. B. "On the Use of the Tenses in the Aramaic of Daniel." JSS 6 (1961) 183-203.

☐ **4/1.2.2:2** Kutscher, E. Y. "Two 'Passive' Constructions in Aramaic in the Light of Persian." Jerusalem (1969) 132-51.

☐ **4/1g.3:1** Schlesinger, Michael. *Satzlehre der aramäischen Sprache des babylonischen Talmuds* (Leipzig: Asia Major, 1928).

☐ **4/2/1.3:1** Correll, Christoph. *Untersuchungen zur Syntax der neuwestaramäischen Dialekte des Antilibanon (Maᶜlūla, Baḫᶜa, Ǧubb ᶜAdīn) mit besonderer Berücksichtigung der Auswirkungen arabischen Adstrateinflusses nebst zwei Anhängen zum neuaramäischen Dialekt von Ǧubb ᶜAdīn* (AKM 44/4, 1978).

☐ **4/1a.4:2** Vogt, Ernestus. *Lexicon linguae aramaicae veteris testamenti documentis antiquis illustratum* (Rome: Pontifical Biblical Institute, 1971).

■ **4/1a.4:1** Vinnikov, I. N. *Slovar' arameiskix nadpisei. Palestinskij Sbornik* 3, 66 (1958) 171-216; 4, 67 (1959) 196-240; 7, 70 (1962) 192-237; 9, 72 (1962) 140-58; 11, 74 (1963) 189-232; 13, 76 (1965) 217-62.

☐ **4/1f.4:1** Schulthess, F. *Lexicon syropalaestinum* (Berlin: Reimer, 1903).

☐ **4/1g.4:1** Levy, J. *Chaldäisches Wörterbuch über die Targumim und einen grossen Theil des rabbinischen Schrifttums* (Leipzig: Baumgärtner, 1867-68).

☐ **4/1h.4:1** Drower, E. S., & Rudolf Macuch. *A Mandaic Dictionary*. (Oxford, 1963).

☐ **4/1i.4:1** Payne Smith, R. *Thesaurus Syriacus*, 2 v. (Oxford: Clarendon, 1879-1901); P. Margoliouth. *Supplement to the Thesaurus Syriacus of R. Payne Smith* (Oxford: Clarendon, 1927).

☐ **4/1i.4:2** Payne Smith, J. *A Compendious Syriac Dictionary* (Oxford: Clarendon, 1903).

☐ **4/1i.4:3** Brockelmann, Carl. *Lexicon syriacum* (Halle: Niemeyer, 1928²) (Hildesheim: Olms, 1965).

☞ **4/1.4** See also 3.4.

☐ **4/2/1.4:1** Bergsträsser, Gotthelf. *Glossar des neuaramäischen Dialekts von Maᶜlūla* (AKM 15/4, 1921).

☐ **4/2/2.4:1** Maclean, A. J. *A Dictionary of the Dialects of Vernacular Syriac* (Oxford: Clarendon, 1901).

☐ **4/2/2.4:2** Oraham, A. J. *Dictionary of the Stabilized and Enriched Assyrian Language and English* (Chicago: Consolidated, 1943).

☐ **4/2/2.4:3** Ritter, Hellmut. *Ṭūrōyo: Die Volkssprache der syrischen Christen des Ṭūr ᶜAbdîn. B. Wörterbuch* (Beirut: Orient-Institut der Deutschen Morgenländischen Gesellschaft, 1979).

South Arabic—Ethiopic

Geᶜez, North, South Ethiopic (alphabetically)

☐ **5:1** Conti Rossini, Carlo. *Etiopia e genti d'Etiopia* (Florence: Bemporad, 1937).

■ **5:2** Leslau, Wolf. *An Annotated Bibliography of the Semitic Languages of Ethiopia* (The Hague: Mouton, 1965).

■ **5:3** Leslau, Wolf. "Ethiopic and South Arabian." CTL 6 (1970) 467-527.

■ **5:4** Bender, M. L., ed. *Language in Ethiopia* (London: Oxford, 1976).

☐ **5/1:1** Dillman, August. *Grammatik der äthiopischen Sprache*, ed. C. Bezold (Leipzig: Tauchitz, 1899²), tr. J. Crichton. *Ethiopic Grammar* (London: Williams & Norgate, 1907).

☐ **5/1:2** Praetorius, F. *Äthiopische Grammatik* (PLO 7, 1886) (New York: Ungar, 1955).

☐ **5/1:3** Chaîne, M. *Grammaire éthiopienne* (Beirut: Imprimerie Catholique, 1907).

☐ **5/1:4** Conti Rossini, Carlo. *Grammatica elementare della lingua etiopica* (Rome: Instituto per l'Oriente, 1941).

☐ **5/1:5** Lambdin, Thomas O. *Introduction to Classical Ethiopic (Geᶜez)* (HSS 24, 1978).

☐ **5/2/1a:1** Leslau, Wolf. "The Verb in Tigre." JAOS 65 (1945) 1-26; "Grammatical Sketches in Tigre." JAOS 65 (1945) 164-203; "Supplementary Observations on Tigre Grammar." JAOS 68 (1948) 127-39.

☐ **5/2/1b:1** Praetorius, F. *Grammatik der Tigriña-Sprache in Abessinien, hauptsächlich in der Gegend von Aksum und Adoa* (Halle: Waisenhaus, 1871).

South Arabic—Ethiopic

☐ **5/2/1b:2** Leslau, Wolf. *Documents tigrigna (éthiopien septentrional)* (Paris: Klincksieck, 1941).

☐ **5/2/2:1** Cohen, Marcel. *Études d'éthiopien méridional* (Paris: Geuthner, 1931).

☐ **5/2/2a:1** Praetorius, F. *Die amharische Sprache* (Halle: Waisenhaus, 1879).

☐ **5/2/2a:2** Cohen, Marcel. *Traité de langue amharique* (Paris: Institut d'Ethnologie, 1936); *Nouvelles études d'éthiopien méridional* (Paris: Champion, 1939).

☐ **5/2/2a:3** Leslau, Wolf. *Amharic Textbook* (Wiesbaden: Harrassowitz, 1967).

☐ **5/2/2a:4** Hartmann, Josef. *Amharische Grammatik* (Wiesbaden: Steiner, 1980).

☐ **5/2/2b:1** Leslau, Wolf. *Étude déscriptive et comparative du gafat* (Paris: Klincksieck, 1956).

☐ **5/2/2c:1** Hetzron, Robert. *The Gunnän-Gurage Languages* (PSSR 12, 1977).

☐ **5/2/2d:1** Cerulli, E. *Studi etiopici. I. La lingua e la storia di Harar* (Rome: Instituto per l'Oriente, 1936).

South Arabic (alphabetically)

☐ **5/3a:1** Höfner, Maria. *Altsüdarabische Grammatik* (PLO 24, 1943).

☐ **5/3a:2** Beeston, A. F. L. *A Descriptive Grammar of Epigraphic South Arabian* (London: Luzac, 1962).

☐ **5/3b:1** Jahn, A. *Grammatik der Mehri-Sprache in Südarabien* (SWAW 150/6, 1905).

☐ **5/3b:2** Bittner, M. *Studien zur Laut- und Formenlehre der Mehri-Sprache in Südarabien*, 4 v. (SWAW 162/5, 168/2, 172/5, 174/4, 1909-14).

☐ **5/3b:3** Johnstone, T. M. "The Modern South Arabian Languages." AAL 1/5 (1975).

☐ **5/3c:1** Bittner, M. *Studien zur Šḫauri-Sprache in den Bergen von Dofâr am Persischen Meerbusen*, 3 v. (SWAW 179/2, 179/4, 183/5, 1916-17).

Grammar, Vocabulary

☐ **5.1:1** Ullendorff, Edward. *The Semitic Languages of Ethiopia: A Comparative Phonology* (London: Taylor, 1955).

☐ **5/1.1:1** Littmann, Enno. "Ge^{c}ez-Studien." NKGG 1917:627-702, 1918:318-39.

☐ **5/1.1:2** Cohen, Marcel. "La Prononciation traditionnelle du guèze (éthiopien classique)." JA 1921:217-69.

☐ **5/1.1:3** Mittwoch, E. "Die traditionelle Aussprache des Äthiopischen." MSOS 28/2 (1925) 126-248.

☐ **5.2.2.1:1** Leslau, Wolf. "The Imperfect in South-East Semitic." JAOS 73 (1953) 164-6.

☐ **5/2/2d.2.2:2** Leslau, Wolf. *The Verb in Harari* (UCPSP 21, 1958).

☐ **5/1.4:1** Dillmann, August. *Lexicon linguae Aethiopicae* (Leipzig: Weigel, 1865) (Osnabrück: Zeller, 1969); S. Grébaut. *Supplément. . .* (Paris: Imprimerie Nationale, 1952).

☐ **5/2/1a.4:1** Littmann, Enno, & Maria Höfner. *Wörterbuch der Tigrē-Sprache* (Wiesbaden: Harrassowitz, 1962).

☐ **5/2/1b.4:1** de Bassano, Francesco. *Vocabolario tigray-italiano e repertorio italiano-tigray* (Rome: de Luigi, 1918).

☐ **5/2/2a.4:1** Leslau, Wolf. *Concise Amharic Dictionary* (Wiesbaden: Harrassowitz, 1976).

☐ **5/2/2c.4:1** Leslau, Wolf. *Gurage Etymological Dictionary*, 3 v. (Wiesbaden: Harrassowitz, 1981).

☐ **5/2/2d.4:1** Leslau, Wolf. *Etymological Dictionary of Harari* (Berkeley and Los Angeles: University of California, 1963).

☐ **5/3a.4:1** Conti Rossini, Carlo. *Chrestomathia arabica meridionalis epigraphica* (Rome: Instituto per l'Oriente, 1931) 99-261.

☐ **5/3a.4:2** Beeston, A. F. L., et al. *Sabaic Dictionary (English-French-Arabic)* (Louvain: Peeters, 1982).

☐ **5/3b.4:1** Johnstone, T. M. *Ḥarsūsi Lexicon and English Ḥarsūsi Word-List* (London: Oxford, 1977).

☐ **5/3d.4:1** Leslau, Wolf. *Lexique soqoṭri (sudarabique moderne)* (Paris: Klincksieck, 1938).

Arabic

(geographically, east to west)

☐ **6:1** Rabin, Chaim. *Ancient Westarabian* (London: Taylor, 1951).

☐ **6:2** Bateson, Mary Catherine. *Arabic Language Handbook* (Washington: Center for Applied Linguistics, 1967).

■ **6:3** Killean, Carolyn G. "Classical Arabic." CTL 6 (1970) 413-38.

■ **6:4** Fischer, Wolfdietrich, ed. *Grundriss der arabischen Philologie*. I. *Sprachwissenschaft* (Wiesbaden: Reichert, 1982).

☐ **6/1:1** Wright, W. *A Grammar of the Arabic Language* (Cambridge, 1896-98).

☐ **6/1:2** Brockelmann, Carl. *Arabische Grammatik* (PLO 4, 1960[14]).

■ **6/1:3** Fleisch, Henri. *Traité de philologie arabe*, 2 v. (Beirut: Institut de lettres orientales, Recherches 16 & NS A 11, 1961-79).

☐ **6/1:4** Fleisch, Henri. *L'Arabe classique: Esquisse d'une structure linguistique* (Beirut: Institut de lettres orientales, Recherches 5, 1968[2]).

☐ **6/1:5** Beeston, A. F. L. *The Arabic Language Today* (London: Hutchinson, 1970).

■ **6/1:6** Fischer, Wolfdietrich. *Grammatik des klassischen Arabisch* (PLO NS 11, 1972).

■ **6/2:1** Abboud, Peter F. "Spoken Arabic." CTL 6 (1970) 439-66.

■ **6/2:2** Fischer, W., & O. Jastrow. *Handbuch der arabischen Dialekte* (PLO NS 16, 1980).

☐ **6/2a:1** Johnstone, T. M. *Eastern Arabic Dialect Studies* (London: Oxford, 1967).

☐ **6/2a:2** Diem, W. *Skizzen jemenitischer Dialekte* (Beirut: Steiner, 1973).

☐ **6/2b:1** Erwin, Wallace M. *A Short Reference Grammar of Iraqi Arabic* (Washington: Georgetown, 1963).

☐ **6/2c:1** Cowell, M. W. *A Reference Grammar of Syrian Arabic* (Washington: Georgetown, 1964).

☐ **6/2d:1** Mitchell, T. F. *Teach Yourself Colloquial Arabic* (London: English Universities, 1962).

☐ **6/2e:1** Harrell, Richard S. *A Short Reference Grammar of Moroccan Arabic* (Washington: Georgetown, 1962).

☐ **6/2f:1** Aquilina, Joseph. *Teach Yourself Maltese* (London: English Universities, 1965).

☐ **6/1.2.1:1** Fischer, August. "Die Quantität des Vokals des arabischen Pronominal suffixes *hu* (*hi*)." *Oriental Studies Published in Commemoration of the Fortieth Anniversary (1883-1923) of Paul Haupt as Director of the Oriental Seminary of the Johns Hopkins University* (Baltimore, 1926) 390-402.

☐ **6/1.3:1** Reckendorf, H. *Arabische Syntax* (Heidelberg: Winter, 1921) (Amsterdam: A.P.A., 1973).

☐ **6/1.4:1** Lane, E. W. *Arabic-English Lexicon*, 8 v. (London: Williams & Norgate, 1863-93).

☐ **6/1.4:1** Wehr, Hans. *Arabisches Wörterbuch für die Schriftsprache der Gegenwart* (Leipzig: Harrassowitz, 1958[3]), tr. J M. Cowan. *A Dictionary of Modern Written Arabic* (Wiesbaden: Harrassowitz, 1979[4]).

■ **6/1.4:3** *Wörterbuch der klassischen arabischen Sprache* (Wiesbaden: Harrassowitz, 1957-).

Scripts

☐ **B:1** Jensen, Hans. *Die Schrift in Vergangenheit und Gegenwart* (Berlin: Wissenschaften, 1969[3]), tr. G. Unwin. *Sign, Symbol and Script* (London: Allen & Unwin, 1970).

☐ **B:2** Diringer, David. *The Alphabet*, 2 v. (London: Hutchinson, 1968[3]).

☐ **B:3** Driver, G. R. *Semitic Writing* (London: Oxford, 1976[3]).

■ **B:4** Février, James-G. *Historie de l'écriture* (Paris: Payot, 1959[2]).

☐ **B:5** Gelb, I. J. *A Study of Writing* (Chicago: University of Chicago, 1963[2]).

Scripts

■ **B:6** Cohen, Marcel. *La Grande invention de l'écriture et son évolution*, 3 v. (Paris: Klincksieck, 1958).

□ **B.0:1** Pirenne, Jacqueline. *Paléographie des inscriptions sud-arabes* (Brussels: Koninklijke Vlaamse Acad. Kl. der Letteren, Verh. 26, 1956).

■ **B.0:2** Cross, Frank M. "The Development of the Jewish Scripts." BANE (1961) 133-202.

□ **B.0:3** Peckham, J. Brian. *The Development of the Late Phoenician Scripts* (HSS 20, 1968).

□ **B.0:4** Albright, W. F. *The Proto-Sinaitic Inscriptions and Their Decipherment* (Cambridge, Mass.: Harvard, 1969).

□ **B.0:5** Naveh, Joseph. *The Development of the Aramaic Script* (PIASH 5/1, 1970).

■ **B.0:6** Garbini, Giovanni. *Storia e problemi dell'epigrafia semitica* (AION Supp. 19, 1979).

■ **B.0:7** Naveh, Joseph. *Early History of the Alphabet* (Jerusalem: Magnes, 1982).

□ **B.1:1** Morag, Shelomo. *The Vocalization Systems of Arabic, Hebrew, and Aramaic* (JLm 13, 1961).

□ **B.1.1:1** Cross, F. M. & D. N. Freedman. *Early Hebrew Orthography* (AOS 36, 1952).

□ **B.1.1:2** Birnbaum, S. R. *The Hebrew Scripts*, 2 v. (Leiden: Brill, 1954-71).

□ **B.1.1:3** Zevit, Ziony. *Matres Lectionis in Ancient Hebrew Epigraphs* (ASOR Monograph 2, 1980).

□ **B.1.2:1** Segal, J. B. *The Diacritical Point and the Accents in Syriac* (London: Oxford, 1953).

□ **B.1.3:1** Abbott, Nabia. *The Rise of the North Arabic Script and Its Ḳur^{c}ānic Development* (OIP 50, 1939).

□ **B.3:1** Labat, René. *Manuel d'épigraphie akkadienne* (Paris: Geuthner, 1976^{5}).

□ **B.3:2** von Soden, Wolfram, & W. Röllig. *Akkadisches Syllabar* (AnOr 42, 1976^{3}).

□ **B.3:3** Reiner, Erica. "How We Read Cuneiform Texts." JCS 25 (1973) 3-58.

■ **B.3:4** Edzard, D. O. "Keilschrift." *Reallexikon der Assyriologie* 5:544-67 (1980).

■ **B.3:5** Borger, Rykle. *Assyrisch-Babylonische Zeichenliste* (AOAT 33/33A, 1981^{2}).

Index of Authors

Each author's works are listed in the order of its number in the bibliography; in addition, references are given to the pages of the text on which each author is mentioned.

Macuch, R. 4/1e:3, 4/1h:2, 4/2/2:11, 4/1h.4:1, p. 77
Margoliouth, P. 4/1i.4:1
Margolis, H. 4/1g:3
Marti, K. 4/1a:2
Martinet, A. 1.1.1:2
Matouš, L. 2/1:2
McFall, L. 3b.2.2:1
Meek, T. p. 36
Meyer, R. 3b:10
Miles, J. p. 36
Mitchell, T. 6/2d:1
Mittwoch, E. 5/1.1:3, pp. xx, 128, 135, 140
Morag, S. B.1:1
Moran, W. 3:2
Moscati, S. 1:11, 1.1.1:3, p. xv
Naveh, J. B.0:5, B.0:7
Nöldeke, T. 1:5, 4/1h:1, 4/1i:2, 4/2/2:2, p. xix
Nyberg, H. 1:6, pp. 59, 85, 87, 88, 92, 97, 116, 119
Odeberg, H. 4/1d:3
Oppenheim, A. L. pp. 44, 48
Oraham, A. 4/2/2.4:2
Pardee, D. p. xvi
Payne Smith, J. 4/1i.4:2
Payne Smith, R. 4/1i.4:1
Peckham, J. B.0:3
Pedersen, J. 1:6
Pennacchietti, F 1.2.1.2:1
Petermann, J. 4/1e:1, 4/1g:1
Petráček, K. 1.2:1
Pirenne, J. B.0:1
Poebel, A. 1.2.2.4.1:1
Polostsky, H. 1:9, 4/2/2:6, p. 113
Praetorius, F. 1.2.2.4.2:1, 5/1:2, 5/2/1b:1, 5/2/2a:1
Qimron, E. 3c:3
Rabin, C. 0:2, 0:3, 1.2.3:7, 3:4, 6:1, p. 1
Rawlinson, H. p. 44
Reckendorf, H. 6/1.3:1
Reiner, E. 2/1:5, 2/1:6, B.3:3, pp. xvi, 48
Ritter, H. 4/2/2.4:3, p. v
Röllig, W. 3f:3, B.3:2
Rosén, H. 3d:1, 4/1.2.2:1
Rosenthal, F. 4:1, 4:2, 4/1a:6, 4/1b:2
Rundgren, F. 1.2.2:4, p. 22
Růžička, R. 1.1.1.4:1
Ryder, S. 1/2.2.2.4.1:1
Samuel, H. p. 74
Sara, S. 4/2/2:10
Sarauw, C. 1.1.3:1, 1.2.2.1.1:4
Schaade, A. 1:6, pp. 156, 159
Schahbaz, D. p. 115
Schlesinger, M. 4/1g.3:1
Schröder, P. 3f:1
Schulthess, F. 4/1f:1, 4/1f.4:1
Segal, J. B.1.2:1
Segal, M. 3c:2
Segert, S. 0.3:3, 3f:4, 4/1a:9
Shileiko, V. p. 42
Siegel, A. 4/2/2:5
von Soden, W. 0:1, 2/1:4, 2/1.4:2, B.3:2
Solá-Solé, J. 1.2.2.6.2:1
Speiser, E. 1.2.2:2
Spitaler, A. 4/2/1:1, pp. xvi, 108
Spuler, B. 1:8
Stehle, D. 1.1.1.6:1
Steiner, R. 1.1.1.3:3, pp. 4, 153
Steuernagel, C. 3b:3
Stevenson, W. 4/1d:2
Stoddard, D. 4/2/2:1
Strack, H. 3b:5, 4/1a:3, p. 93
Stumme, H. pp. xx, 206
Tsereteli, K. 4/2/2:7
Ullendorff, E. 1/2.2.4:1, 5.1:1
Ungnad, A. 2/1:2, 4/1i:4, p. 43
Vilencik, Y. 1.1.1.3:1
Vil'sker, L. 4/1e:2
Vinnikov, I. 4/1a.4:1
Vogt, E. 4/1a.4:2
Waterman, L. p. 48
Wehr, H. 6/1.4:1
Whiting, R. 2/1.2.2.4.3:1
Williams, R. 3b.2.2.4:1
Wright, W. 1:1, 6/1:1
ben Yehudah, E. 3d.4:1
Ylvisaker, S. 2/1:3
Zevit, Z. B.1.1:3
Zimmern, H. 1:1

Colophon

Designed by the translator.

Set in Times Roman and Frank Ruehl Hebrew on a Varityper 4560 multi-language phototypesetter by Cyndy Miller, with paradigms set on a Varityper 5900 phototypesetter by Ray LaBorde, Eisenbrauns; and in Estrangelo by Gary Horn, J. J. Augustin Inc., Locust Valley, N.Y. and Glückstadt, West Germany; Nestorian, by Mr. G. S. Benjamin, Chicago; Ethiopic, by Helmut Schroeder, J. J. Augustin; and Arabic, by Mohammed Rabatah, Communica International, LaGrange Park, Ill.

Akkadian calligraphy by Jeremy Black; Mandaic (after Bibliothèque Nationale sabaeus seu mandaiticus 1) and other calligraphy by the translator.

Layout by K.D.Z.; production supervised by Rick Clark and Jim Eisenbraun; text specimen photography by Warsona Printing, Winona Lake, Ind.

Printed on 60 lb. EB Bookwhite and bound in Roxite B vellum finish (cloth) or Kivar (paper) by Edwards Brothers, Ann Arbor, Mich.